THE WORLOCK ARCHIVE

The
Worlock
ARCHIVE

Clifford Longley

GEOFFREY
CHAPMAN
London and New York

Geoffrey Chapman
A Cassell imprint
Wellington House
125 Strand
London WC2R 0BB

370 Lexington Avenue
New York
NY 10017–6550

First published 2000

British Library Cataloguing-in-Publication Data
A catalogue record for this book is available from the British Library.

ISBN   0–225–66857–2 (hardback)

Designed and typeset by Kenneth Burnley, Wirral, Cheshire.
Printed and bound in Great Britain by TJ International Ltd, Padstow, Cornwall

Contents

This book is dedicated to my five grandchildren –

Francesca Muccio, Natasha Longley, Christina Muccio, Michael Longley and Jessica Muccio

– without whom this book might have been written by someone else (for why, see Introduction);

and to my wife, Elizabeth, who is part of everything I am and do.

Introduction

The whole of a man's life reduced to cardboard boxes. And in those boxes, secrets. My task was to reverse that process, to reveal his secrets and thus to bring the man back to life. But Derek Worlock was not just a private man: he was a key player for half a century in the affairs of his Church and his nation. Those secrets also reveal other people as we may not have known them before. And the institution, the Roman Catholic Church, had its secrets too; and some of them were in those boxes. It is an organization surrounded by a more-than-average aura of mystery. It dearly liked to present a united front to the outside world. Here was part of its private as well as its public history, why things really happened the way they did and not just the official version published at the time (cleaned up of contention and controversy).

The process of bringing all this material to life has had to involve a long and complicated detective investigation. All these thousands of papers in all these hundreds of boxes were not designed to be read by strangers. As in all internal communications within a long-established institution, they use shorthand and code. A random letter or report of a meeting taken from the files of the Worlock Archive may indeed contain some new information of sensational significance, but it won't be signposted. One glance may not give the game away. Two glances, however, may begin to reveal a hidden drama. Suddenly it becomes clear that somebody is accusing somebody of double-crossing somebody – who, what, why, when, where? The answers are somewhere in those other boxes.

It showed an extraordinary degree of confidence in Derek Worlock on the part of his two literary executors, Canon Nicholas France of Portsmouth diocese and Bishop Vincent Nichols of Westminster, that they decided to give a third party complete and total access to these files not much more than a year after Derek Worlock died. I was, in a way, bound to conduct an inquest into Derek Worlock's life: I could not avoid sitting in judgement on him. And to do that, while many of his closest friends were eager to protect his memory from misrepresentation. Neither Bishop Nichols nor Canon France sought, nor were they given, any control over the contents of this book. We discussed some of the difficult bits, but that is all. I will not know what they think of it until it is published.

In 1996 the Archive had been removed from Archbishop's House in Mossley Hill, Liverpool, and lodged in a large, light and airy chamber at St Joseph's College, Upholland, a listed building and former Catholic seminary now partly empty, partly used as church offices. Virtually no one had been allowed access to it, not to sort it, not to remove embarrassing papers, not even just to see what was there. There is a private-private set of files, mainly personal information about priests, which is not part of the Archive and which has been handed over to Worlock's successor, Archbishop Patrick Kelly. The rest is subject to the normal rule where official Catholic archive material is concerned, of being withheld from public access for 30 years. I was the one exception, and my special status was confirmed by a legal document drawn up by my agent and signed by Canon France, Bishop Nichols and myself.

Meanwhile Dr Meg Whittle was appointed by the Archdiocese to take care of the Worlock collection and any other collections of Catholic documents that might come her way. One of her duties was to assist me in my research, which, considering I lived 250 miles away, was more than necessary if the work was to be done inside a decade, and essential if it was to be done properly on any time scale. She has become an invaluable partner in this project, an assiduous hunter-down of obscure references and every inch the literary detective a good archivist ought to be.

The only limitation on my use of material was one I accepted voluntarily, indeed proposed myself, whenever I wished to make use of official documents of the Bishops' Conference of England and Wales. In a sense, Derek Worlock only had them on loan himself. I have defined 'official documents' narrowly – excluding, for instance, letters which mentioned Conference business. In fact the only important documents of this kind I have used referred to the *Humanae Vitae* crisis in 1968, which were in any case outside the 30-year rule. Several documents never before published are included in Appendix I. They throw new light on that critical period. What was really happening was not quite what people thought was happening at the time, nor why. I suspect my findings may revive some of that controversy, as well as revising our understanding of it. In Appendix II, readers will find some light refreshment, supplied by Derek Worlock himself.

By far the most interesting documentation in the Archive refers to the Second Vatican Council, which met in Rome from 1962 to 1965. It takes the form of the 'secret diary' which Derek Worlock kept throughout that period – a sometimes scandalous, sometimes gossipy, sometimes racy, often irreverent record of the Catholic Church going through one of the most significant episodes in its entire 2,000-year history. Because of that vast time scale, I also had to widen my horizons. I had to read what the Council of Trent had said in the sixteenth century, and work out why it had said it, because the Second Vatican Council was the start of a new chapter, the first of its kind since Trent. It gave a fresh definition of what Catholicism was (and indeed what Christianity was), to replace the version received from the Reformation and Counter Reformation. I also had to form a clear picture of the impact the Counter Reformation had had on English church life, Catholic and otherwise, in order to establish a benchmark for the enormous changes that were to follow from Vatican II.

The more I tried to put these documents into their context, the broader the context grew. Sometimes the real reason why a Catholic Church leader said or did something seemed not to lie in the present at all, but long ago, as far back as the sixteenth century, possibly further.

Especially when he was dealing with other Catholic leaders, he was working within a common culture of shared assumptions that did not need to be spelt out but which were taken for granted by both sides as the way things are. Sometimes it meant that nobody had examined the underlying basis of the argument, which had become as invisible to them as the concrete in the foundations of a great building.

This becomes the central issue when the story to be told is about changes to long-established, long-taken-for-granted ways of doing things. The Roman Catholic Church went through such a revolution in the years starting with the reign of Pope John XXIII, who was elected in 1958. Some of those who were caught up in that revolution seemed to have little idea what was going on. Among them, at least for a while, was Derek Worlock himself. John XXIII called the Second Vatican Council shortly after his election; Worlock was by then Private Secretary to the Archbishop of Westminster, Cardinal William Godfrey, having previously been Secretary to Cardinal Griffin.

It would not be unfair to say they were both bemused by the beginning of the Second Vatican Council. Godfrey died in 1963, never having grasped the plot. With Worlock the penny eventually dropped, but only so far. It is right to give notice that this examination and explanation of the Worlock Archive will sometimes be respectfully critical of its primary subject, the man who collected it, and of its other primary subject, the Catholic Church. To some extent my research has changed my view of both of them. I am a Catholic myself, but I am now a Catholic in a slightly different way. I knew Derek Worlock well and admired him a great deal: and I see him differently too, and admire him differently. It is easier to like someone when you are allowed to admit that he had his faults. One of his faults was that he did not like to admit he had any. Yet he was also humble. He had carried other people's bags too often to get high and mighty about carrying his own.

Most of the papers in the Archive are of little or no historical interest: letters about matters long since resolved, minutes of meetings of the smallest moment. A small proportion of the Archive constitutes the pieces of a larger jigsaw, which might be assembled to give a wider picture. Those I have tried to assemble. But one or two items were like jigsaws already completed. They were Worlock's own personal recollections and reflections, often spanning considerable periods and commenting (sometimes with brutal candour, but sometimes also with considerable distortion) on other public figures. Even so there was always a bigger jigsaw still, into which these completed pieces also had to fit. Sometimes, the way he had assembled the jigsaw did not seem quite right, and I had to make my own version.

Worlock was a good writer. In those passages included here, where I have decided there was no point in trying to improve on his style I have left the narrative in his own words, though minimally edited with my own interruptions and footnotes to make the meaning clear. To that extent this book is at least in part autobiographical – or to put it another way, it is partly co-authored by Derek Worlock himself. It is slightly autobiographical in another way – here and there I have a walk-on part myself. I was a journalist involved in covering many of the events the material deals with. If journalism, as somebody said, is the first draft of history, then this is my second. I now know how much I got wrong.

Would he have minded all this attention? I think not, in principle; though he would not necessarily have accepted my general analysis. It is not certain whether he ever expected anyone to look through his files and notebooks after his death, though we do know he did not leave instructions for it all to be burnt, and we also know that before his final illness in 1995, he had been warning his friends that he was going to be out of circulation for a while because he was planning to sort through his papers. The best evidence that he hoped some of it would see the light of day is the material itself. It is not written purely for his own purposes, because it explains much more than it would need to explain if that was all it was for. He is conscious of literary style: it is designed to be read by someone else. To adapt one of the arguments for the existence of God: if there is a clock, is there not somewhere a clock maker? If there is a writer, is there not somewhere an intended reader? He left these documents to the archdiocese. He said to two of his best friends, Bishop Vincent Nichols and Canon Nicholas France, that they would know what to do with them when the time came.

Nichols and France, in the role of literary executors, looked round for someone to undertake research into the material and possibly write a book about it. They found me. (It wasn't difficult – I have five grandchildren, three of whom were baptized by Bishop Nichols, two by Canon France. In other words we were already firm friends.) Meanwhile Derek Worlock's own former Secretary, Monsignor John Furnival, teamed up with the well-known Catholic journalist Anne Knowles to write a more conventional kind of biography. I hope they will not mind if I recommend it to the interested reader. They relieved me of any requirement to fill in the cradle-to-grave details of his life, and freed me to concentrate on the politics and history behind the events in which he had played a part. To that extent this book is not so much a biography, more a social history. Nor is it strictly chronological, though enough so, I hope, to be understandable. Some of the issues are pursued thematically, which means the imaginary calendar in the reader's mind will jump about a bit.

From 1944, when Worlock became Cardinal Griffin's new young Secretary, until 1996 when he died of lung cancer, Worlock had been the one continuous thread in the post-war story of the English Catholic Church. For much of that time he was a central figure – indeed, arguably *the* central figure. The institutional mechanisms for running the Catholic Church needed a fundamental reshaping, and he took that work in hand. Very little happened that he did not know about; indeed very little happened that he had not personally approved.

But the argument of this book takes a broader sweep even than that. Where possible with Worlock's help, even with Worlock's own words, I have tried to reconstruct the key events in the life of the institution he served so diligently and watchfully. But I have had to step back from him sometimes, to place him in his historical and social context. He was the product of a way of being Catholic, and of being a Catholic priest, that went right back to the sixteenth century – that is to say he was a product of the Counter Reformation. Yet the Counter Reformation was launched as a spiritual war against Protestants, and one of the many things Derek Worlock is remembered for is his strong relationship with Protestants, above all with Bishop (now Lord) David Sheppard, his Church of England opposite number in Liverpool. Given Liverpool's history of sectarian tension, and given the violence a few short miles away across the Irish Sea when these two first came together on Merseyside, their partnership is widely held to have saved the community peace where it was most sorely threatened.

I am not quite sure that is true, as I am not quite sure the threat was ever as big as some suggested. I once asked a parish priest why there seemed to be so little pro-IRA graffiti on the walls of mainly Catholic working-class residential districts in Liverpool. He didn't say it was the achievement of Worlock and Sheppard. He said most of the Irish people who passed through Liverpool in the middle of the nineteenth century knew who they were and where they wanted to go – London, America, wherever. Those who stayed in Liverpool were the most desperate, most deprived, who didn't know who they were or where they were going. Many of them didn't even know which part of Ireland they had come from. So they had little sense of identity with Ireland, little taste for its partisan politics.

Worlock is also remembered as a social prophet, denouncer of injustices, untiring advocate of the interests of Liverpool and its people. But it is not possible here, as elsewhere, to look at his contribution without asking certain questions about it. How nearly right was he?

On the national stage, Worlock gave the Catholic Church in England and Wales its internal structures of secretaries and boards, committees and commissions. He held together forces that were tending to pull it apart: the dissatisfaction of many laity with certain aspects of Catholic teaching such as over birth control, the impatience of younger priests to get a move on, to aim for more ambitious targets, to take reform further and faster, and so on. Was all this reconciling a good thing? Would a little more abrasion with the Left have been helpful?

Worlock was less good at keeping conservatives on his side, perhaps surprisingly as he had been one himself for the greater part of his life. Thus there were those who regarded him as symbolizing more or less everything that had gone wrong in the Catholic Church since the 1960s. I am sure they are wrong, but I am also sure that he was far from perfect. He was, to paraphrase a comment I make towards the end, too much in love with the Church, not enough in love with God. How had the Church produced a man of whom that could be said? We are back into history again, looking for the remotest causes and explanations of things we see all around us. But if we do not do that, we shall never solve the jigsaw. If we do not learn from history we shall be its prisoner. I hope my book will be found interesting, but also gently liberating.

FURTHER INSIDE INFORMATION

"A YOUNG PRIEST, ANXIOUS FOR PASTORAL WORK, IS APPOINTED ASSISTANT SECRETARY TO THE BISHOP. HIS LEARNING IS CONFINED TO THE DULL TASK OF ADDRESSING ENVELOPES TO THE CLERGY AND THANKING NUNS IN THE NAME OF HIS LORDSHIP FOR SENDING IN THEIR COLLECTIONS FOR GOOD SHEPHERD SUNDAY."
— "THE PEOPLE'S PRIEST" (ON UNCONGENIAL WORK).

Further Inside Information by Derek Worlock. Courtesy of Liverpool Roman Catholic Archdiocesan Archive at St Joseph's, Upholland, Lancashire. This and other cartoons were drawn by Derek Worlock as home-made Christmas cards to be sent to other bishops' secretaries when he was secretary to Cardinals Griffin and Godfrey.

1

Faith of our Fathers[1]

This book is about Derek John Harford Worlock, the Roman Catholic Archbishop of Liverpool who died of lung cancer on the day – 8 February 1996 – he was due to receive the Companion of Honour from Her Majesty the Queen at Buckingham Palace. He was the only leader of a British church of any denomination to have been awarded this royal Companionship.[2] This book is also an attempt to throw light on a richly varied phenomenon: English Catholicism. Worlock can help us understand it; it can help us understand him. His successes and failures as one of its most important leaders ran according to its fault-lines. Worlock never became what for half his life had seemed to be his destiny – Cardinal Derek Worlock, Archbishop of Westminster. A full explanation of that will take us a long way back in time, to historical sources and influences that are still not fully played out and will continue to shape the future for many years to come. He never saw a providential pattern or purpose to those events, but it is there to be found if we dig deep enough. It lies in the character and history of English Catholicism itself.

From 1944 onwards, Worlock was a central player in that history. That year he became Private Secretary to Cardinal Bernard Griffin, Archbishop of Westminster. Almost immediately, he started writing Griffin's sermons and speeches, dealing with his correspondence, developing a network of official Whitehall and Westminster contacts in the Cardinal's name, and acting as the Catholic Church's chief press officer. He served Griffin's successor Cardinal William Godfrey in the same capacity, and for a while, his successor Cardinal John Heenan. Gradually he became *de facto* and eventually *de jure* Secretary to all the Catholic bishops of England and Wales, especially during the period of the Second Vatican Council from 1959 (when the Council's preparatory commissions started work) to the end of 1965. On becoming the first post-Vatican II English bishop in December 1965 he moved to prominence on the national stage as Episcopal Secretary of the Bishops' Conference of England and Wales and President of the Conference's Laity Commission. He was crucial in defusing the conflict in the English Catholic community following the papal encyclical on birth control in 1968. As Archbishop of Liverpool he was Vice President of the Bishops' Conference under the Presidency of Cardinal Basil Hume, a very equal, fruitful but never easy relationship.

Worlock was an ecumenical pioneer both on the national stage and in his extraordinarily close personal relationship with the Church of England Bishop of Liverpool, the Right Revd David (later Lord) Sheppard, and his wife, Grace (later also their daughter Jenny, who became a Catholic). From 1944 until 1995, when he retired on reaching the age of 75, very little moved in the undergrowth of English Catholic life that Worlock did not know about, and quite probably, caused. He was the manipulator and fixer, the spin doctor, the man with contacts, the backstairs negotiator and late-night phone-caller, the precise minute-taker, the ingenious resolution drafter, the committee chairman who could quote standing orders backwards (because he wrote them). As they say in politics, he knew where the bodies were buried. From 1944 onwards, the story of the Catholic Church in England and Wales and the story of Derek Worlock are utterly entwined; indeed they are the same story.

The roughly ten per cent of the population who regard themselves as belonging to the Roman Catholic Church (they call themselves 'Catholic' or 'RC') make up the largest single group in English society that deviates, in various significant respects, from the majority. It is a genuine sub-culture, containing sub-sub-cultures of its own. All sorts of assumptions about the English do not entirely apply to the English Catholic mindset. Such everyday labels as 'conservative' and 'liberal', 'right-wing' and 'left-wing', can take on a subtly different meaning in this context. English Catholics tend to Left-leaning in their attitudes to social justice, Right-inclined in their approaches to personal and sexual morality – at least according to the conventional Left-Right divisions of the rest of British social attitudes.

Yet they have a characteristically English way of being different. If at times they have seemed more Catholic than the Pope, at other times they have seemed more English than the English. If Catholics are said to be over-represented in the population of British prisons, they are also said to be over-represented among winners of the Victoria Cross in the British army. The word 'ethnic' does not exactly describe them, nor are they a racial minority (though they have a large component which is at least partly of Irish origin, and there are parishes in London and elsewhere where some 50 different foreign languages can be counted). They have every social class and racial group in their ranks. They constitute a good microcosm of English society, containing their fair share of most of the problems with which wider society is burdened. An analysis of the social–economic class structure of the English Catholic community has shown it to be within one or two percentage points of the overall national figures, in every section. In that respect it is more typical of the English nation even than the Church of England, which has a lower level of representation among the working class (as indeed do the major Nonconformist denominations).

But this is not the same as saying it is a better representative of 'Middle England'. True, in the seven largest conurbations of England, especially London, by the middle of the twentieth century the religiously observant Catholic presence was larger than any other, Anglican included.[3] But in the rural areas and ancient county towns of England (with one or two exceptions in parts of Yorkshire and Lancashire) it was decidedly under-represented. In this respect a map of Catholic density was virtually a photographic negative of a map of Anglican density. Where there are unexpected pockets of Catholic concentration in the rural areas, this is almost invariably associated with the presence in the neighbourhood of a Catholic landowner of ancient lineage. Only in the suburbs (the grey area on that negative, where town meets country) is the presence of these two largest English 'faith communities' about equal. And it is not in the large cities that one would go in search of 'Middle England', however one might choose to define it.

An explanation of the whys and wherefores of English Catholicism has to be an incomplete one. There is far too much that can never be known, because most of its life since the sixteenth century has been deliberately hidden from public view. Yet this community has a peculiar and intimate relationship with English history and English national identity that belongs to no other. It has been at times intensely controversial, at times a threat to the very State itself. Large slices of English history have been about questions concerning the Catholic Church. The relationship between Catholicism and Protestantism in Northern Ireland is still by no means fully resolved: relations between the two States either side of the Irish Sea have been dominated by religious issues since long ago.

The English public is still very aware of the effect this history has had on the institutions of the State, including the Monarchy, Parliament, and the Established Church. It is still commonly stated in the mass media that the Church of England was 'started' by Henry VIII in the sixteenth century, when he broke with Rome over his divorce. Issues of divorce, the Royal Family and the Church are still newsworthy, not least because the British Monarch bears the title Defender of the Faith which was first awarded to Henry by the Pope, then withdrawn, then re-awarded by Henry to himself.

This version of the origins of the Church of England in the matrimonial problems of a Tudor king is still commonly assumed to be true, though academics will disagree how close these simplicities come to reality.[4] But the clear implication is that before this breach, the national religion of the English was, routinely, naturally and comfortably, something else – it was Roman Catholic.

This is too easily dismissed as a popular misconception, or a label the twentieth century pins on something that would not recognize itself in that description. Ground-breaking research by Dr Eamon Duffy, the Cambridge historian,[5] has shown how 'Roman Catholic' in flavour popular English religion actually was in the century or so before the Reformation. It was a vibrant religion of saints and statues, Masses and Mary, processions and purgatory, relics and shrines, at a time of great piety and religious passion. It was pious and sentimental – and superstitious, as the English have always been – and it roused strong feelings of loyalty in ordinary people (not least against the clergy, if they got in the way). Nor, as past generations of tendentious anti-Catholic historians have depicted it before Duffy went out to look for the facts, was it especially decadent and corrupt (though it was rather too relaxed and earthy for later Puritan tastes).

Thus Duffy[6] argues:

> Late medieval Catholicism exerted an enormously strong, diverse and vigorous hold over the imagination and loyalty of the people right up to the very moment of Reformation. Traditional religion had about it no particular marks of exhaustion and decay; indeed in a whole host of ways, from the multiplication of vernacular religious books to adaptations within the national and regional cult of saints, it was showing itself well able to meet new needs and new conditions . . . When all is said and done, the Reformation was a violent disruption, not the natural fulfilment, of what was vigorous in late medieval piety and religious practice.

Every English person who had ancestors in England 500 years or more ago had English Catholic ancestors who would have been entirely at home in the world Duffy describes. It is they, after all, who built the thousands of medieval parish churches which now dot the English countryside. Inspected with a careful eye, their interiors still betray evidence of the violent disruptions of religion that occurred in the sixteenth century – an altar stone still used as a flagstone on the porch floor[7] here, the broken bracket of a holy water stoup,[8] or niche for a statue of Our Lady, there.

The English Catholic community has always claimed a shared identity with followers of that Old Religion. Those who died resisting its demise are the Catholic heroes of today – Thomas More, John Fisher, the Forty Martyrs, names that crop up repeatedly in every English town as the names of parish churches or Roman Catholic schools. That continuity with the persecuted Catholic Church of the sixteenth, seventeenth and eighteenth centuries implies continuity with what went before. At one point, it is reported, Queen Elizabeth I sacked many magistrates in England because she doubted their loyalty to the religion she was introducing, and their zeal in imposing fines and other penalties on Catholics who refused to attend the compulsory services of the new religion. A screening operation carried out by the bishops in 1564 revealed that of 850 JPs examined, more than half were suspected of being recusants. Given that magistrates were usually appointed from among the ranks of local squires – gentry landowners – this figure suggests that the population at large, at least among that class, was split approximately 50–50. In fact the bloody persecution of Protestants that had taken place under Mary's reign owed a lot to the religious zealotry of Justices of the Peace than to the activities of Church officials as such. Magistrates were subsequently required to swear an oath – under the notorious 'Test Acts' – denying Catholic doctrines.

Being English, the Catholic community wears its history proudly. English Catholics will unblinkingly assert that the England of John of Gaunt's great oration in Richard II – 'This royal throne of kings, this sceptred isle, This earth of majesty, this seat of Mars, This other Eden, demi-Paradise' – was none other than Catholic England. He was of course a Catholic himself, and all the people he knew were Catholics too. (It is a curious twist that Shakespeare set the scene for this speech in the Bishop of Ely's London palace, whose medieval chapel is now St Etheldreda's Catholic Church, Ely Place, just by Holborn in the City of London. Some of the flagstones of the old palace are still visible, viewable by arrangement with the parish priest.)

The breach with Rome under Henry was followed by a brief period of reconciliation under Mary Tudor, his daughter, whose attempts to suppress the Protestant religion were conducted with such extreme savagery that it is still a part of English folk memory. Even with the arrival of Elizabeth on the throne in 1558 and the restoration of Protestantism, the future of the large population still secretly or openly loyal to Rome was uncertain. Or at least the future of their religion was, as battle commenced to persuade them into the Church of England and away from their previous adherence. But things were happening on the Catholic side which were designed to frustrate that process but which in fact accelerated it. Those events gradually conspired to give Catholicism the branded image of England's enemies, especially Spain. Catholicism became associated with disloyalty. Even today, English Catholic historians look back on the reign of 'Good Queen Bess' as anything but good; from their point of view 'Bess' was bloodier than her half-sister who bore that epithet. In the formation of English identity, the breach with Rome and the more or less continuous but undeclared naval war with Spain laid the foundations of the English nation state; and in the New World, the beginnings of Empire. English Catholic identity had little share in that formative process. For centuries afterwards Catholics felt excluded from English history altogether.

Nothing sharpened that process of separation more than the excommunication of Elizabeth I by the Pope in 1570, perhaps one of the greatest examples in all history of a policy having the opposite effect to the one intended.[9] The bull of excommunication purported to depose her and released Elizabeth's subjects from their duty of loyalty to her. Thereafter, loyalty to Catholicism (and acceptance of the bull) was *prima facie* proof of disloyalty to the English Crown, that is to say of treason. The job of sustaining a Catholic presence in England suddenly became immensely more difficult and dangerous (though it was difficult enough previously, which is why the bull was drawn up in the first place). It meant that those who were the visible presence of the Catholic Church in England – its priests – were, almost by definition, traitors.

Two years earlier, a missionary college had been founded at Douai, then in The Netherlands. It was an attempt, only ten years after the failure of Mary's revival of Catholicism, to provide a home for Catholic clerics and academics who had had to flee Oxford and Cambridge, and to provide somewhere where they could resume or continue the training of priests for the Catholic priesthood, English style. The hope was that it would be a brief spell in exile. As the 1570 bull showed, Catholic policy at that time was based on a vastly unrealistic expectation of quick results.

But the Catholic Church was changing; and English Christianity was changing too. Historical trends and events were pulling them apart. Through the 39 Articles of Religion, England saw the national Church embrace Protestantism in its worship and doctrine (though often in a form which allowed a more Catholic interpretation so as not to drive more people back into the arms of Rome). The Church of England began to acquire a *raison d'être* through the work of the Caroline Divines building on foundations laid by such as Richard Hooker[10] (1554–1600); and a distinct spirituality based on its Prayer Book[11] and the version of the Bible authorized by King James I, not to mention the work of the metaphysical poets such as John Donne and George Herbert.

English Church history still had a lot to do with Catholicism, not least during the convulsion of the Civil War and then in the revolution against the last Catholic King, James II, which split the Established Church over the issue of loyalty to the throne. But it was now largely felt as an outside force, a potential disturbance to the English *status quo*. Recusant landowners were significant not only as a political threat of their own, manifested above all in the Gunpowder Plot, but in numerous other plots and conspiracies, real or imagined, some of the latter even got up by government agents. Their greater significance was as harbourers of a well-trained and bold Counter Reformation priesthood, both from the Society of Jesus[12] and from the English seminaries abroad. While the Catholic aristocracy pursued a policy of trying to replace a Protestant royal dynasty with a Catholic one by court intrigue or force – an essentially medieval, even feudal approach – the strategy of the mission priests was to win the English back to the Catholic faith primarily by the superiority of their arguments and example. This led to bitter disagreements about tactics and strategy between the Catholic gentry and the priests,[13] disagreements which have not entirely subsided even today.

The Catholic Church meanwhile began the long period in its history and culture known as the Counter Reformation. The word Counter is appropriate both in the sense of countering, or moving to block, the actual Reformation so called; but also in the sense of a rival or alternative Reformation (reform of the Church) to the one started by the Protestants. Some scholars prefer to talk of a Catholic Reformation as well as the Counter – (the Protestant) – Reformation. Some of the abuses it attempted to put right had been identified before they were denounced by Martin Luther and John Calvin, and were corrected not necessarily to meet the Protestant case but for the good of the Church. Aside from the Protestants, there had long been pressure for reform of the Catholic Church from dissatisfied, but doctrinally loyal, Catholics such as Erasmus. The policies adopted by the Church at that time were thus not entirely reactive nor entirely reactionary. Catholicism drew a renewal of vitality from these policies, as well as the energy to embark on a global mission to the New World and the Far East in the centuries to come.

The Council of Trent in northern Italy, which ended in 1563, attempted to address many of the grievances and distortions that had provoked the Protestant Reformation, with special emphasis on the reform of the priesthood. It simplified and reformed the liturgy, giving the Catholic world one uniform rite of Mass (the Tridentine Rite[14]). It attempted to resolve the dispute with the Reformers over salvation by faith alone and the role of good works, in which each side had accused the other of the Pelagian heresy – that salvation could be 'earned' by one's merits. (The Counter Reformers claimed that the Reformers had turned faith into a 'great work'; the Reformers that the Catholic Church's stress on indulgences[15] being earned by meritorious acts was a form of 'salvation by good works'.)

Above all the Council ruthlessly reformed clerical training and discipline. Chapter XVIII, on the training of the clergy, began by declaring:

> Whereas the age of youth, unless it be rightly trained, is prone to follow after the pleasures of the world; and unless it be formed, from its tender years, unto piety and religion, before habits of vice have taken possession of the whole man, it never will perfectly, and without the greatest, and well-nigh special, help of Almighty God, persevere in ecclesiastical discipline; the holy Synod ordains, that all cathedral, metropolitan, and other churches greater than these, shall be bound, each according to its means and the extent of the diocese, to maintain, to educate religiously, and to train in ecclesiastical discipline, a certain number of youths of their city and diocese.

Such seminaries were introduced – in theory, in every diocese – as educational and semi-monastic communities apart, where priests could be rigorously and intensively trained and 'formed' into the sort of young men who could stand up to Protestantism, preach effectively against it, and if necessary brave the hazards of working in hostile territory. These were not negligible. The penalty for being a Jesuit or seminary priest in England was death. The training had to be tough, the formation thorough. In case they missed the point, priests training at the Venerable English College in Rome (established in 1579, at the site of a medieval hostel for English pilgrims) could see large paintings of their predecessors in the college chapel, undergoing various stages of the grisly execution by hanging, drawing and quartering that awaited them if they were caught.

As a result, what most clearly distinguished the Church of the Counter Reformation from what had gone before was the quality of the clergy. In the Middle Ages and Renaissance periods, it was notorious that clergy discipline had become lax, and many priests were ill-educated and ill-equipped to offer their people spiritual leadership or guidance. This was more true of the 'secular' clergy than others (the term 'secular' has in this context a specifically Catholic usage, meaning attached to a diocese and not a member of a religious order). But even some religious orders were not noted for the learning, or indeed the holiness, of their members. The same was occasionally true of senior clergy, even of bishops and Popes. The medieval Church went through several cycles of loosening and tightening up. It would be a mistake to categorize it as uniformly or continuously decadent, or as exceptionally so just prior to the Reformation, though the late fifteenth- and early sixteenth-century papacy had become a disgrace, notorious throughout Europe. Nevertheless, corrupt though it may have been in many places, it worked. The Catholic Church provided the financial and spiritual inspiration for the extraordinary flowering of European culture known as the Renaissance.

Because the medieval clergy were sometimes no more holy nor better educated than the literate laity, there was not a vast gap between the two classes. Both found their appropriate levels within the structures of feudalism. The reforms instituted at the end of the Council of Trent in 1563 produced a new kind of 'secular' priest, the seminary priest, and put the emphasis on a new kind of religious order, the Jesuits, founded in 1534 and just emerging by the end of Trent as a kind of spiritual SAS of the Counter Reformation. (Many more new religious orders were to be founded in the subsequent centuries, while long-established monastic orders such as the Benedictines and Franciscans tended to sit out the Counter Reformation, being not altogether in sympathy with its tone. The Dominicans, on the other hand, went to the task with zeal). But as a result of the post-Tridentine emphasis on priestly 'formation', a gap began to open between clergy and laity which became characteristic of the Counter Reformation period and one of its more enduring features. The clergy had, in modern terms, been professionalized. The laity remained the amateurs (a state of affairs which eventually gave the very word 'layman' its modern meaning of 'not an expert').

With the professionalization of the clergy went a strong sense that the laity were likely to depart from the straight and narrow in matters both of doctrine and morals unless they had the clergy's close attention. Sheep tended to stray: it was the job of the shepherd to prevent them from doing so, and to bring back any that did. This sheep–shepherd metaphor for the relationship between the people and their priests seemed to be well founded on the Bible, confirmed in such New Testament parables as the Good Shepherd. Trent also emphasized private confession and private penance, and the medieval practice of public penance died out. Priests became experts at making nice moral distinctions in the confessional, skills which required considerable training to use properly. This inevitably disempowered the laity, who did not have equal access to this training and body of learning. It became a sophisticated system, not without its own penetrating insights into human behaviour. Ideally it represented the gentleness and shrewdness of Christ Himself in dealing mercifully with the penitent sinner. But is also served to enhance still more the status of the clergy against the laity, who were increasingly both ill-informed and ill-formed by comparison with the products of the rigorous education provided by new seminary system.

In many instances, the total devotion of priests to their flocks went all the way to public martyrdom. The ideal held out to priests was one of absolute and intensive commitment, emphasized by the Church's insistence on celibacy and chastity. In essence, the Catholic Church's answer to the question 'What had gone wrong?' in the early sixteenth century and before was simply 'The clergy had gone wrong.' It would not make that mistake again.

This tendency to over-correct for the abuses of the medieval period and the criticisms of the Protestant reformers became a mark of the Counter Reformation. In response to the window-smashing iconoclasm of the more extreme Reformers, the Catholic Church emphasized the beauty of art and music in the service of God. There was a distinctive Counter Reformation style, the Baroque, whose direct purposes was to beautify Catholic architecture and worship. The Reformers denied Transubstantiation; the Counter Reformation gloried in it, making the Blessed Sacrament the centre of devotional life and artistic display. The Reformers denounced papal supremacy: devotion to the successors of St Peter became a touchstone of Catholic piety. The Reformers attacked the cult of saints, above all the special place of Mary. She became the Counter Reformation ideal of the perfect woman, the Queen of Heaven. The Reformers wanted reform, indeed reform without end. The Counter Reformation emphasized the permanence of what had been wrought at Trent (and at Bologna, where the Council transferred to), and hence the irreformability of the Catholic faith henceforth.[16] While Trent did not exactly sanction holy war against the enemies of the Church, many Catholic princes, the Habsburgs in particular, took their cue from it and did just that. The Inquisition, which away from Spain may not have been as terrible an institution as Protestant historians would have had us believe, was nevertheless becoming a sharp and systematic instrument for the rooting out of heresy.

All this meant that the Catholic priest was becoming a different creature both from the priesthood of the Old Religion and from the clergy of the Church of England, who continued to be trained in ways current prior to the Council of Trent. (It is still part of the character of the Church of England that it is pre-Tridentine,[17] for instance its attitude to clergy discipline and clergy training are conspicuously more relaxed. Unlike the Counter Reformation emphasis on the ascendancy of the clergy, however, Anglicanism brought them under State – and therefore ultimately lay – control.) Douai[18] was one of the first seminaries to apply the Council of

Trent's policy. Henceforth the battle for English Catholicism was to be part of the story of the Counter Reformation. The Catholic religion English Catholics wished to see installed in their land was no longer the Old Religion, but the post-Tridentine kind.

Or at least up to a point. One historian of English Catholicism has written:

> during this period the religious practice of English Catholics underwent the same kind of sea-change as that of the great majority of Englishmen who had accepted the Reformation: how much one may attribute this to influences from the English environment, how much one should treat it as a normal effect of the Counter Reformation, is a delicate question . . . We cannot simply regard post-Reformation English Catholicism, in practice, as a continuation of medieval English Christianity; on the other hand we evidently cannot regard it as something totally different.[19]

Such pockets of Catholicism as did survive in the populace between 1558 (the death of Mary) and 1778 (the beginning of Catholic emancipation) had done so largely under the protection of rich Catholic landowners, who had sought their own accommodation with the powers-that-be on a basis that eventually fell well short of the restorationist hopes of ardent sixteenth-century Catholic missionary priests. They were slow to adjust to Rome's new ways. Arguably, without the Counter Reformation, English Catholicism might have stood a better chance of survival, especially as it would have been attractive to religiously conservative people instead of seeming just as 'modern', after Trent, as Anglicanism. The Old Religion would have been powerfully attractive, against the grimmer outlook of Genevan Protestantism. But apart from backwaters which were out of the main religious current in the sixteenth century, such as the Franciscan, Benedictine and Cistercian orders whose houses in England Henry VIII had suppressed, the familiar Old Religion had been superseded by the novelties both of the Reformation and the Counter Reformation.

From the Catholic point of view, the influence in England of Calvinism, a strongly anti-Catholic school of theology, was one of several self-inflicted wounds resulting from the extreme persecution of Protestants under Mary. Many Protestant scholars fled abroad (just as Catholic scholars were to flee in the reign of Elizabeth shortly afterwards). Some of the more important went to Geneva and came under the influence of John Calvin. His radical brand of Christian faith, which became known slightly tautologically as Reformed Protestantism, 'was to become the lode-star of the Edwardian Reformation and its early Elizabethan successor'.[20]

The experience of lay Catholics as time went on was of a constant tug-of-war between the influence of their priests and the pull of conformity. During the most intense persecution of Catholics, under Elizabeth and James I, harbouring a priest was a capital offence. Even as this became gradually relaxed,[21] fines were regularly levied for non-attendance at Sunday services of the Established Church. By a law passed in 1700, rightful Catholic heirs to an estate had to give way to a Protestant claimant from the same family. Many families went through regular changes of religion with each change of generation, from Catholic to Anglican and back again. It was common for the head of the family to outwardly conform (as a 'church papist'[22]), but to allow his wife to stay overtly Catholic (including working for the support of clandestine priests). The law sought endless devices to make the game not worth the candle, such as (in 1754) making the celebration of Catholic marriages a crime. For safety's sake after that, Catholics tended to be married out of doors, and to rely on a pre-Tridentine custom of regarding as valid any marriage that met the usual conditions, whether a priest was present or not. In the North of England, some Catholic nobility crept over the Scottish border to marry. Similarly, access to country churchyards was denied to Catholics, and it was not uncommon for burials to take place secretly at night or at dawn, when parish clergy and sacristan were safely in bed.[23] One side-effect of the difficulty of educating well-to-do Catholic children in England was the superior education many Catholic girls received on the Continent, usually in convents, often returning fluent in French and accomplished at music and similar useful skills.[24] Their Protestant neighbours' girls were often thought dull by comparison.

Priests could not function without these Catholic landowners. As time went by and the Catholic community was gradually relieved of these penalties, the gentry founded and paid for new chapels and eventually Catholic schools and seminaries on English soil. Through a system of pew rents they provided the clergy with a regular income, replacing the earlier system of 'domestic chaplains' in the great Catholic manor houses (who were sometimes employed as manservants to disguise their real function). Because a manor house could keep and if necessary hide a priest who could say Mass and administer the Sacraments, the local community thereabouts would tend to have a higher proportion of Catholics than the general population. It was they who eventually provided the congregations for the new chapels, once they were allowed. In cities such as London, foreign residents, especially ambassadors, were allowed to keep Catholic chaplains, and they would also unofficially service the local Catholic community.

The spirituality of these surviving Catholics would be shaped by the most popular devotional work of its time, the *Garden of the Soul* published by Bishop Challoner, the most famous of the English vicars-apostolic,[25] in 1740. Given the shortage of priests, it could be used as a do-it-yourself manual of personal spiritual growth, listing the prayers to be said and the times of day they were to be said at, including private devotions to be undertaken while attending Mass. (Mass became known among English Catholics as 'prayers', partly because that was the congregation's chief role in the service, partly because it was a convenient euphemism or code to conceal from non-Catholics that what was being spoken of was a highly illegal activity.) The *Garden of the Soul* was an invaluable spiritual guide to a Catholic family which might not see a priest for months on end.[26]

Broadly, the phase of European history defined as the conflict between the Reformation and the Counter Reformation is usually limited to the sixteenth and seventeenth centuries, or at least not much into the eighteenth. The spiritual renewal of the Catholic faith that dated from the Council of Trent continued beyond that, indeed continues to this day. But gradually new factors began to predominate, less theological, more practical and political. In the case of countries where Catholicism was persecuted, Great Britain especially, but also Ireland, however, the aggressive and defensive spirit of the Counter Reformation did not decline as it did elsewhere, as the need for it had not been exhausted. Those bulwarks against Protestantism that Trent had erected – devotion to Mary, loyalty to the papacy, the status of the priesthood – were still necessary, indeed more than ever. So when European cultural and political history moved on – to the age of the Enlightenment, the age of Revolution, the rise of industrial capitalism and so on – the Catholic religion in mainly Protestant countries such as those of the British Isles remained largely unaffected, still reflecting the priorities and crises of the sixteenth and seventeenth centuries.

In the sixteenth century, English-speaking Catholicism had been intellectually vigorous; in the nineteenth and twentieth centuries, it found its articulate voice again. But in between, survival took priority over speculation, innovation and creative achievement. Catholicism was not subjected to intellectual examination, at least not by Catholics (and only for controversial purposes, by anyone else). So the particular form it took was not placed in its historical and cultural context. It was regarded as existing outside time. The way it was, came to be seen as the way it had to be.

This was also part of Counter Reformation faith. The Council of Trent concluded in 1563 with the publication of a bull in the name of Pius IV which, among other things, prohibited all interpretations of the Council of Trent or commentaries on it. This was a fencing off of these Church documents from critical scrutiny and analysis more strict than anything applied to Scripture itself. It declared:

We, by apostolic authority, forbid all men, as well ecclesiastics, of whatsoever order, condition, and rank they may be, as also laymen, with whatsoever honour and power invested; prelates, to wit, under pain of being interdicted from entering the church, and all others whomsoever they be, under pain of excommunication incurred by the fact, to presume, without our authority to publish, in any form, any commentaries, glosses, annotations, scholia, or any kind of interpretation whatsoever of the decrees of the said Council; or to settle anything in regard thereof, under any plea whatsoever, even under pretext of greater corroboration of the decrees, or the more perfect execution thereof, or under any other colour whatsoever.

In that intellectual climate it would not be entirely unfair to liken English Catholics of the post-Reformation period to followers of the Melanesian cargo cults: whatever was brought ashore from Catholic lands abroad (especially that most Catholic land of all, Rome) was sacred, a gift from God, necessary for salvation.[27] The actual became the norm; the norm, the perfect. Even to imagine that the Catholic Church might one day need to change was disloyal.

Over the years the sense of Catholicism as a threat to established order greatly declined: Jacobite sentiment (in favour of the deposed Stuarts) had never been very strong among the English gentry or clergy. They wanted acceptance, and the right to enjoy their property in peace. The clergy themselves taught obedience to the lawful authority of the State as a principle of Catholic doctrine, except in those matters, namely religion, where the State had exceeded its authority. Gradually Catholicism took its place alongside other forms of Dissent as a variety of English religion outside the orbit of establishment approval. Needless to say, the long period of persecution had worn down the Catholic population, both in numbers and in energy, to the point where it was marginal to English society, and even less visible than its numbers would have warranted.

This did not stop alarmists occasionally raising the most extreme fears in the non-Catholic populace, leading for instance to the Gordon Riots in London in 1780 to which Dickens gives vivid testimony in *Barnaby Rudge*. In protest at the introduction of a Bill in Parliament which would have relieved Catholics of some of the penalties for following their religion – penalties no longer entirely enforced – large numbers of houses occupied by Catholics in London, and every place of Catholic worship save one, were ransacked and burnt by the Protestant mob. Although written 60 years after the events it purports to describe, Dickens' account of the feelings of the Catholics of London as the riots began has evidential value – if not of what was exactly the case in 1780, then at least what it was reasonable to suppose was the case looking back from the safety of 1840. Two Catholic chapels had already been burnt.

> By midnight. the streets were clear and quiet, and, save that there stood in two parts of the town a heap of nodding walls and piles of rubbish, where there had been at sunset a rich and handsome building, everything wore its usual aspect. Even the Catholic gentry and tradesmen, of whom there were many resident in different parts of the City and its suburbs, had no fear for their lives or property, and but little indignation for the wrong they had already sustained in the plunder and destruction of their temples of worship. An honest confidence in the government under whose protection they had lived for many years, and a well-founded reliance on the good feeling and right thinking of the great mass of the community, with whom, notwithstanding their religious differences, they were every day in habits of confidential, affectionate and friendly intercourse, reassured them, even under the excesses that had been committed; and convinced them that they who were Protestants in anything but the name were no more to be considered as abettors of these disgraceful occurrences, than they themselves were chargeable with the uses of the block, the rack, the gibbet and the stake in cruel Mary's reign.

After much further destruction and violence the mob was bloodily suppressed by troops, the ring-leaders in due course hanged, and the Catholic victims of the disorders compensated. Not long after, violent revolution in France caused hundreds of French noblemen and Catholic priests to seek refuge in England, and the native Protestant (and of course Catholic) populace received them with considerable kindness and sympathy. Many later returned, though some French priests joined the ranks of the English clergy. It is significant that throughout *Barnaby Rudge*, as elsewhere, Dickens is gently (and occasionally scathingly) mocking of No-Popery sentiment: if he has not much time for Catholics, he has even less for their enemies.

But the smoke of those London fires cast a long shadow over the Catholic community in later decades. The fears the Gordon Riots evoked were revived 70 years later, when there was considerable public unrest in England provoked by the so-called Restoration of the English Hierarchy in 1850.

It was this event which began the present phase of Catholic existence in England. The Church reconstituted that year was the Church Derek Worlock was born into in 1920, little changed in its prejudices and principles. That Church inherited all the loose ends and contradictions that history had put together over the previous 400 years, contradictions reaching into its very identity. An incident arising directly from that event still speaks eloquently of a degree of uncertainty on the part of the Church, and on England's part too, as to its exact nature. The uncertainty is still present today, even if now disguised as simply the way things are. The essential question is raised even by the title of that event, Restoration. Did 1850 constitute a more profound continuation, a renewal, or an entirely fresh beginning?

Upon the Restoration, Archbishop Nicholas Wiseman, the first Archbishop of Westminster, issued from Rome an excited letter addressed to the Catholic community in England. Entitled 'From Out the Flaminian Gate', he declared:

> The great work, then, is completed; what you have long desired and prayed for is granted. Your beloved country has received a place among the fair churches, which, normally constituted, form the splendid aggregate of Catholic Communion. England has been restored to its orbit in the ecclesiastical firmament, from which its light had long vanished, and begins anew its course of regularly adjusted action round the centre of unity, the source of jurisdiction, of light, and of vigour.

Not the least of the resonances these words would have had among Catholics was with that old and long-shelved hope that England could eventually be restored to the Old Religion. Not long after,[28] John Henry Newman preached his celebrated Second Spring sermon before Cardinal Wiseman (who wept openly with emotion) and the bishops of the new Catholic dioceses of England on the text: '*Surge, propera, amica mea, columba mea, formosa mea, et veni. Jam enim hems transiit, imber abiit et recessit. Flores apparuerunt in terra nostra*: Cant., ch. ii. vv. 10–12.'[29]

> But what is it, my Fathers, my Brothers, what is it that has happened in England just at this time? Something strange is passing over this land, by the very surprise, by the very commotion, which it excites. Were we not near enough the scene of action to be able to say what is going on, were we the inhabitants of some sister planet possessed of a more perfect mechanism than this earth has discovered for surveying the transaction of another globe, and did we turn our eyes thence towards England just at this season, we should be arrested by a political phenomenon as wonderful as any which the astronomer notes down from his physical field of view. It would be the occurrence of a national commotion, almost without parallel, more violent than has happened here for centuries, at least in the judgements and intentions of men, if not in act and deed. We should note it down, that soon after St Michael's day, 1850,

a storm arose in the moral world, so furious as to demand some great explanation, and to rouse in us an intense desire to gain it. We should observe it increasing from day to day, and spreading from place to place, without remission, almost without lull, up to this very hour, when perhaps it threatens worse still, or at least gives no sure prospect of alleviation.

Every party in the body politic undergoes its influence, from the Queen upon her throne, down to the little ones in the infant or day school. The ten thousands of the constituency, the sum-total of Protestant sects, the aggregate of religious societies and associations, the great body of established clergy in town and country, the bar, even the medical profession, nay, even literary and scientific circles, every class, every interest, every fireside, gives tokens of this ubiquitous storm This would be our report of it, seeing it from the distance, and we should speculate on the cause. What is it all about? Against what is it directed? What wonder has happened upon earth? What prodigious, what preternatural event is adequate to the burden of so vast an effect?

The answer, of course, was the Restoration of the Catholic Hierarchy. It was the revival of the old claim to continuity in its legal, moral and metaphysical essence between the Church suppressed by Henry, revived by Mary and doubly suppressed by Elizabeth, and the Church now reconstituted under the newly appointed Catholic Bishops in their brand new Catholic dioceses.[30]

Wiseman's Flaminian Gate letter set off other less happy resonances. It received extraordinary attention from non-Catholics, who above all were affronted by Wiseman's statement of his new jurisdiction. 'Till such time as the Holy See shall think fit otherwise to provide, we govern, and shall continue to govern, the counties of Middlesex, Hertford and Essex as ordinary therefore', he asserted, and more in the same vein.

The Cabinet met in alarm. *The Times* thundered at 'one of the grossest acts of folly and impertinence which the Court of Rome has ventured to commit since the Crown and people of England threw off its yoke'. The Prime Minister, Lord John Russell, and the Queen, Supreme Governor of the Church of England, were outraged. In 1850 it led to an outpouring of establishment anger: emergency meetings of the Cabinet, an Act of Parliament, some 7,000 riotous protest meetings, and so on. Often these meetings had a semi-official character, being chaired by the Lord Lieutenant of the county, and addressed by the local MPs and JPs. They would usually end with the singing of 'God Save the Queen', (all verses, including the plea that the Queen be rescued from the Pope's 'knavish tricks') and the passing of a Loyal Address to Her Majesty; when the dignitaries went off to eat a Civic Dinner, the more high spirited of the assembly would take it upon themselves to break a few Catholic windows in the vicinity, as an extra demonstration of their loyalty.

Partly this whipping up of public rage was mischief-making by Russell, who had privately been kept informed of the Vatican's intentions and had failed to object when given the chance to do so. Partly it was a calculated reminder by Rome that the Catholic Church's claims and the Church of England's claims could not both be true. Parliament took the point, and hastily passed the Ecclesiastical Titles Act, prohibiting among other things the naming of new Catholic dioceses after the medieval (now Anglican) ones.

For Rome laid claim to a 'Restoration' in the plainest sense – the most common use of the word referred to the restoration of the monarchy after Cromwell. So, Rome implied, the One Holy Catholic and Apostolic Church had at last been formally re-established in England. The event, as presented, gave not the slightest significance to the Church of England. It was not surprising that *The Times* headed its blistering outburst 'Papal Aggression'.

An argument frequently heard among English opponents of the Restoration was that the Pope claimed jurisdiction over all Christians, not just members of the Roman Catholic Church. Hence the erection of new Catholic bishoprics looked like a claim to supplant or replace existing Anglican bishoprics. There was some basis for this complaint. Canon VIII of the Council of Trent's Decree on the Sacraments, under Baptism, asserts: 'If any one saith, that the baptised are freed from all the precepts, whether written or transmitted, of holy Church, in such wise that they are not bound to observe them, unless they have chosen of their own accord to submit themselves thereunto; let him be anathema.'

So alarmed were the Catholic authorities by this widespread public reaction that they started to back-pedal furiously. Wiseman, not least under pressure from the Catholic gentry,[31] tactfully restated his position and his purposes. But it was much more than a climb-down. He produced, in answer to his angry critics, what is surely one of the most moving Church documents of the nineteenth century.

In his pamphlet called 'Appeal to the Reason and Good Feeling of the English People' Wiseman denied that it was his intention or the Pope's to interfere in any way with the existing legal privileges of the Church of England. If Catholics looked elsewhere for spiritual authority than to the Bishops of the Established Church, he said, that was no different from the view taken by the Church of Scotland or the Nonconformist Churches.

Then he explained and defended his use of the name of Westminster – the seat of Parliament, after all – in his new title.

Close under the Abbey of Westminster there lie concealed labyrinths of lanes and courts, and alleys and slums, nests of ignorance, vice, depravity, and crime as well as of squalor, wretchedness and disease, whose atmosphere is typhus, whose ventilation is cholera, in which swarms a huge and almost countless population, in great measure, nominally at least, Catholic; haunts of filth, which no sewage committee can reach – dark corners which no lighting-board can brighten. This is the part of Westminster which alone I covet.

Wiseman's enemies gradually fell silent, cowed as much by such vivid eloquence as by its obvious Christian compassion (and by the growing public perception that the government had been consulted about Rome's plans four years earlier, and had raised no objection. Lord John Russell seemed guilty of bad faith). But by now Wiseman had given to the new Catholic Hierarchy which he headed not one but two foundation documents, his Flaminian Gate letter and his Appeal to the English People. And it is clear at this distance of time that the controversy that he had had to rescue himself from was not entirely due to a misunderstanding. There had indeed been a note of triumphalism, even of Catholic imperialism, in Wiseman's first words. Even disregarding the claim that Rome sought jurisdiction over all Christians, Catholic or not, these two title-deeds of the Catholic community in England are not quite compatible.

They gave rise to two different and in many ways contradictory strategies. The first made it the primary business of the Roman Catholic Church in England to work for the conversion of the nation to (or, as Catholics would have said, back to) the One True Church. That strategy is visible in the great edifice of Westminster Cathedral, which was quite deliberately designed on the instructions of Cardinal Vaughan (Wiseman's successor but one) to be as imposing as, if different from, Westminster Abbey at the other end of Victoria Street in London.

In this conception, the Church of England was certainly not regarded as a sister Church. On the contrary it was, in the words of John Henry Newman, 'the veriest of nonentities'. In his essay on the Anglican Church which appeared as an appendix to his *Apologia* he gave it no weight whatever in the scheme of salvation, except what was due to it as 'a mere national institution'.

Did he have the heart, or the want of charity, to wish to see it overthrown, he asked himself.

I have no such wish while it is what it is, and while we are so small a body. Not for its own sake but for the sake of the many congregations to which it ministers, I will do nothing against it. While Catholics are so weak in England, it is doing our work; and though it does us harm in a measure, at present the balance is in our favour. What our duty would be at another time and in other circumstances, supposing for instance that the Establishment lost its dogmatic faith, or at least did not preach it, is another matter altogether . . . Doubtless the National Church has been a serviceable breakwater against doctrinal errors more fundamental than its own. How long this will last in the years now before us is impossible to say, for the Nation drags down its church to its own level.

Newman's words sketched a provisional strategy for peaceful coexistence with the Anglican Church for the sake of true religion and of the people it served. In many respects, this was the strategy the Catholic Church actually did follow in the generations after 1850, and shorn of its more blunt and unsympathetic language, still follows today. It is on such pragmatic grounds, for instance, that it has become common to find Catholic spokesmen declining to take exception to the legal establishment of the Church of England: it could be useful.

Indeed, it was possible to speak very well of it, as Newman did, so that only one who was watching out for what was not being said would notice the presence of any disapproval at all. 'I recognize in the Anglican Church a time-honoured institution, of noble historical memories, a monument of ancient wisdom, a momentous arm of political strength, a great national organ, a source of vast popular advantage, and, to a certain point, a witness and teacher of religious truth', Newman had written.

Newman's tentative attitude, the attitude of many Roman Catholics of his time and since, has, since the Second Vatican Council, been supplemented by the greater warmth of the ecumenical movement. As a consequence, it is no longer regarded as appropriate for the Catholic Church to approach Anglicanism as a competitor or rival. Instead, they were to maximize the potential for co-operation and convergence. The prospect of eventual full and visible union between the Anglican and Catholic Churches removed the necessity for a strategy for the conversion of England. Reunion offered an alternative strategy: England would become Catholic again by the Church of England returning to Communion with Rome, rather than by converting the English people to Roman Catholicism one by one.

Nevertheless the predominant priority of the Catholic Church in England since 1850 has not been any of the available strategies for fulfilling the ultimate ambition expressed by Wiseman in *From Out the Flaminian Gate* – not the competitive one, not coexistence and tacit acceptance, and not the newer strategy of ecumenism. The predominant priorities have been those of his *Appeal to the English People*.

They were, first, to attend to relief of suffering and misery of the urban poor. These were, as it happened, almost exclusively Irish,[32] and were living in the rookeries of Westminster and elsewhere largely because survival had become impossible in Ireland following the failure of the potato harvest in three successive years. Then, after the emergency provision of relief, the strategy was to provide institutions for the physical and spiritual welfare of the Catholic poor: schools, hospitals, orphanages, chaplaincies, churches and a sacramental and pastoral ministry ranging from baptism through marriage to funerals. The fulfilment of this strategy was only possible with the dedicated assistance of countless members of religious orders, the great majority of whom came from Ireland.

It was a cradle-to-grave system, designed, it may now be seen, on the assumption that the ordinary secular (or rather, Protestant) world was too hostile to Catholicism to be trusted. Hence wherever a fearful clergy thought spiritual damage might be done to Catholics by the use of non-Catholic facilities, Catholic facilities had to be made available instead. For instance 'Rescue Societies' developed residential care for children to rescue them not only from situations of extreme poverty and destitution, but also to provide an alternative to workhouses and other non-Catholic establishments where Catholic children had no chance of being educated in the Catholic faith. They were being 'rescued', in this sense, from Protestantism.

English mid-Victorian society was increasingly prepared to accept this. For instance the Reformatory Schools Act of 1854 allowed Catholic and other voluntary bodies to run schools for delinquent children who would otherwise have gone to prison. The Poor Law Board forbade the instruction of Catholic children in any other religion and required workhouses to keep a 'creed register'. Catholic children in the workhouse could be transferred to Catholic institutions which could claim their maintenance costs from the Board of Guardians. Just as Catholics were concerned to keep their poor out of Protestant hands, so some Protestant children's societies were unwilling to let go of an opportunity to convert Catholic children. Eventually extracts from the relevant Acts of Parliament were included in the *Catholic Directory* to enable priests to quote chapter and verse in their dealings with unhelpful local Boards.

What all this effort amounted to was the creation of an Alternative Society, a protected particle of Catholic England (or Catholic Ireland-in-England) walled off from the rest of the nation. Those whom Wiseman 'coveted' and their descendants have greatly benefited by it. Wiseman's Appeal had already made the point that the poor of Westminster whom he wished to serve were 'in great measure, nominally at least', Catholic. He had no designs, therefore, on those who were not already of his own persuasion (and most of those that were would not even have been English).

This was, however, a Catholic-centred strategy. Non-Catholics were not intended to share in the facilities offered, though a few may have done so. The strategy sought to protect the faithful from contamination, and did virtually nothing to evangelize or convert the rest of the population. Indeed, in many respects this Catholic-centred approach put further obstacles in the way of that evangelization. It represented the fulfilment of the second of those two title-deeds bequeathed to the Catholic community by Wiseman. It left the first, the Flaminian Gate call for the conversion of England, far behind. The Second Spring was indefinitely postponed.[33]

The Restoration of the Hierarchy also represented the final triumph of the clerical caste over the laity. All those chapels and schools that had hitherto been owned and administered by committees of Catholic laymen (gentry and tradespeople), and all those yet to be built, came under the jurisdiction, and also ultimately the ownership, of the official Church. Such tendencies as there had been towards 'congregationalism' – government of the Church by autonomous and self-financing local groups of churchgoers – were nipped in the bud. This was a tendency if anything emphasized by the gradual but growing influence of Irish Catholicism in England. Irish Catholic laity did not have the experience of the English Catholic laity at running their own show; Irish Catholic priests who began working in England after 1850 in ever-increasing numbers had less experience of handling a self-confident and prosperous Catholic laity with strong aristocratic connections.

The lifting of legal restrictions on Catholicism happened gradually over many years, and it was a process often led by an English desire to mollify the Irish. Indeed, the presence of a large block of Irish Catholic MPs in the House of Commons from about the middle of the nineteenth century onwards had far more impact on the condition of English Catholics than anything they had been able to do for themselves. It would be wrong, therefore, to regard the English–Irish Catholic relationship as one between superiors and inferiors. In terms of political power and influence, the balance was the other way round.

In one respect – the effect of popular prejudice against Catholics – the association of Catholicism with Irishness was a set-back, as it now presented two reasons for bigotry and discrimination: a racial or ethnic one on top of the well-established religious one. In addition, one of the ways the English political class chose to react to Irish nationalism was by splitting the old alliance between Presbyterians and Catholics against the (Anglican) Church of Ireland. While the Church of Ireland was the established

Church, wealthy and still adding to its wealth by tithes and taxes, the other two had a common enemy. At the close of the eighteenth century the first Catholic chapels in Belfast had been paid for by Presbyterian businessmen, an act of solidarity between one group of disgruntled non-Anglicans and another. The United Irishmen uprising led by Wolfe Tone (himself from the Protestant side) in 1798 had seen an alliance of Catholics and Protestants against English power, including the English Church. But as the nineteenth century wore on, the English fed into Ireland the toxic *bacillus* of No-Popery, designed to drive Presbyterians and Anglicans together as Unionists, so that Catholic nationalism became their common foe.

The phenomenon of No-Popery forms a constant backdrop to the Catholicism of this period, indeed almost until the present day. Antonia Fraser[34] relates how Guy Fawkes Day, the anniversary of the assassination attempt on James I on 5 November 1605, became and remained each year the focal point of anti-Catholic feeling in England. Opponents of the Restoration of the Hierarchy made the November of 1850 especially memorable in this respect, lighting additional bonfires to burn effigies of the Pope and Wiseman. The ritual searching of the cellars below the House of Lords in the Palace of Westminster immediately before the State Opening of Parliament continues to this day, though the prayer of thanksgiving for the deliverance of the monarch in 1605 – appointed to be said every Guy Fawkes Day – was deleted from the Anglican Book of Common Prayer in 1859. The prayer left no doubt that the discovery of the plot in time to save the king and his retinue, thus preserving the kingdom from Popery, was a direct act of Divine Intervention.

'Predictably enough,' Antonia Fraser writes, 'celebrations waxed or waned according to the waves of anti-Catholicism which periodically shook England. Any apparent support given to that dangerous foreign-based religion, any renewed threat from its supporters, was enough to make the annual bonfires burn brighter.' The event changed its meaning according to the politics of the day: it was a celebration of the deliverance of the monarchy when the monarch was popular, but in periods such as Cromwell's Commonwealth – which had after all succeeded in killing a king for itself – the celebration was directed more at the vanquishing of the Pope and his fellow conspirators.[35]

Since Catholic emancipation, the Catholic community in England has served as a river into which various tributaries flowed on its way to the sea, and the greatest of these by far was the Irish one. The main source of the river is the original Catholic community which survived from the Reformation; and the other important tributary has been the flow of converts, mainly but not exclusively from the Church of England. But there have been various lesser additions too, such as the French émigrés fleeing from the Terror in Paris in the 1790s, and the large remnant of Polish armed forces marooned in Britain after the Second World War.

The Irish influx into Britain was so overwhelming, especially after the great potato famine of 1846–48, that it looked set to impart to English Catholicism a very Irish, and hence un-English, flavour. That is not how it worked out in the long run, however, for an English spirit gradually prevailed. Above all, this may well have been because the English bishops did not look to the Irish Hierarchy for any sort of lead, but tended to regard themselves, if anything, as the senior partners. This did not stop Bishop William Cotter, Bishop of Portsmouth before the Second World War, insisting that he would only employ Irish-born priests in his diocese; which was the reason, Derek Worlock himself was later to claim, why he had to seek priestly training and ordination in the Archdiocese of Westminster.

It is a matter still requiring an adequate explanation why the large Irish population which moved to England, Scotland and Wales in the mid-nineteenth century had by the close of the twentieth century all but lost its Irish identity, whereas similar communities abroad, especially in the United States of America and in Australia, have retained both an enduring sense of their Irishness and their Republican antagonism to Great Britain. One possibility is that the destinations chosen by the three major groups of Irish immigrants reflected their feelings towards the mother country: those who did not dislike England and the English saw no reason to move on elsewhere. That favourable attitude towards England probably meant that that group was likely to integrate well, being prepared, at least to some degree, to take on the values of the host country. Confirmation of that positive attitude may be indicated by the enthusiasm with which volunteers for the British army came forward from various Irish communities in Britain in 1915 and 1916, forming 'pals' battalions' in Kitchener's 'new' army such as the Tyneside Irish Brigade and the London and Liverpool Irish; and the determination with which they fought against the king's enemies. This could also explain why people of Irish origin in Britain, particularly in Liverpool, never displayed much sympathy for the Republican campaign in Northern Ireland after 'the Troubles' resumed in 1969.

Nevertheless, according to Professor David Gwynn of Cork University,[36] the first Irish who settled in Britain after the famine and the Restoration of the Hierarchy were by and large hostile to England. 'The Fenian movement had wide support in England, in spite of the constant denunciations of secret societies by Manning and the bishops,' he wrote. Cardinal Manning's own solidarity with the plight of the poor, and his intervention on the side of striking dock workers in London in 1889, gradually helped to create a more favourable attitude. An alliance was forged between the Catholic (Irish) working classes and the English (or partly English) leaders of their Church. 'There had been a gradual but always increasing assimilation to English life and ways,' Gwynn goes on, 'and the continual intermarriage between English and the Irish men and women was breaking down the old sense of separation . . . In time the strongly Irish tradition, which had still been intensely active in Manning's days, lost most of its force.' He points out that two subsequent Cardinal Archbishops of Westminster, Bourne and Hinsley, both had Irish Catholic mothers. Bourne's father was an English convert, Hinsley's, a Yorkshire recusant.

Nicholas Wiseman (Archbishop of Westminster 1850–65) and Henry Manning (1865–92) had been great Victorians by any measure; but their successors, Herbert Vaughan (1893–1903) and Francis Bourne (1903–35) were not in the same class. Only with the appointment of Arthur Hinsley (1935–43) did English Catholics again have a leader of outstanding national status. John Heenan, in an appreciation written soon after Hinsley's untimely death,[37] remarked: 'Not since Manning has Britain had a Cardinal who so closely identified himself with the lives of the common people. . . .' The *Daily Mail*,[38] in an editorial on his death, said he was 'probably the best loved Cardinal England has ever had'. Not the least of Hinsley's achievements was his eloquent and unswerving advocacy of England's case in the Second World War, which won him firm friends in the Foreign Office and high esteem with the general public. He was one of the first to denounce Nazi atrocities against the Jews in the summer of 1942. He firmly countered Axis propaganda to the effect that because Britain and America were mainly Protestant countries, their alliance was hostile to Catholic interests. He also launched a movement for social reform and international justice, called the Sword of the Spirit; and initiated a remarkable thaw in relations with Anglican and other Church leaders, especially Bishop George Bell of Chichester.

But it is an indication of the continuing outsiderness of the English Catholic community – and an indication that this was not always its own fault – that one of his first disappointments as Archbishop of Westminster was the refusal of the Home Office to allow him to send a loyal address to King George V on his Jubilee. The address, on behalf of the Catholic community of England and Wales, was returned unreceived.

So he wrote directly to Buckingham Palace.[39] 'May it please Your Majesty,' he declared.

> I and my brother Archbishops and Bishops are much concerned lest You should think that they and their people are not truly loyal to Your Majesty as their

King, for the reason that You did not receive an Address from them when You celebrated Your Jubilee. We beg to say that we sent a Loyal Address to Your Majesty on that occasion, but we understand that for some technical reasons the Home Office would not allow this Address to be presented to You. May Your Majesty be pleased to accept our most sincere feelings of loyalty and devotion, and an assurance of our fervent prayers at all times.

This met the same fate, accompanied by a brusque note signed by another Home Office junior official. It led the Home Office to investigate the legal position more fully, and a memorandum of that time offers two reasons why it would have been incorrect for the King to receive a communication from the Catholic Bishops. The first was that they insisted on calling themselves 'Catholics' and not 'Roman Catholics', which the Home Office lawyers advised was their only lawful description; second was their adoption of the names of dioceses which had not been recognized by Act of Parliament (indeed could not be, because of the Ecclesiastical Titles Acts of 1851 and 1871).[40]

Part of the reason for Hinsley's popularity was undoubtedly his human and approachable style. Part was his unflinching and outspoken support for British war aims.[41] He had trained at the English College and been its Rector (though he also had a BA from London University); and therefore must be accounted a product of the Counter Reformation spirit. This merely shows that that spirit did not have to be authoritarian and remote, but at its best shone forth in a life of charity and holiness apparent for all to see. In Hinsley's time the prevailing model for priest–lay relationships was still parent–child: as in the designation 'Father' which gradually spread in the nineteenth century until it was universal by the end of it; as in the treatment of the Church, local and universal, as a family with the priest (or Pope – the 'Holy Father') at the head of it; and as in the common formal opening of sermons and clerical addresses, when the priest would greet the congregation as 'My dear children in Jesus Christ'. Partly this was a deliberate, and partly an unconscious, infantilization of lay people. Models of obedience and disobedience within the Church also had this parent–child aspect, as in the tendency to treat awkward lay people as 'bad Catholics' by which they really meant 'naughty children'. But good fathers could be dearly loved; and it was into that category that Cardinal Hinsley certainly fell.

By the mid-nineteenth century, the practices and attitudes of the Counter Reformation had become so ingrained that they were no longer recognizable as a development that was historically conditioned, but were deemed normal and permanent, the means by which the Catholic Church had conformed itself exactly to the Will of God. This was especially the spirit in English Catholicism, which had suffered too much for the Faith to treat it as anything other than worth dying for. This immutability was reinforced, first, by the sixteenth-century papal ruling that the Tridentine Mass was the final version, never to be altered again; and second, by the convening of the First Vatican Council in 1870 and its decision that the Pope ruled the Church with immediate and universal jurisdiction. That seemed to place the internal structures of Catholicism as beyond debate; or at least any attempt to debate them became an act of extreme disloyalty aggravated by heresy. (There are circles within the Church today where this is still the view.)

Because no Councils were held between the end of Trent in 1563 and the start of Vatican I in 1870, Catholicism remained essentially unchanged throughout that period.[42] It was in fact little changed by Vatican I itself, which in its further centralization of Church power merely took the logic of the Counter Reformation a stage further in the same direction. It was the Council of Pius IX, the formidable 'Pio Nono', who reigned from 1846 to 1878 and who in 1864 had issued his notorious *Syllabus of Errors*. This scathingly condemned liberalism, science, democracy and tolerance, as well as civil marriage, secular education, and religious indifferentism. The Syllabus seemed to be part of the retreat of Roman Catholicism from the changing 'modern' mid-Victorian world, while reasserting the unchanging nature of the One True Church. It was, above all, a refusal to countenance any accommodation of the Catholic Church with the Enlightenment, which had been transforming the basis of intellectual thought in the Western world from the late eighteenth century onwards.

Thus the Catholic Church would have appeared to its members by the mid-1950s as an institution which had survived every sort of challenge of the previous 400 years while remaining fundamentally unchanged by these experiences. It had seen off the Reformation and the Enlightenment, Darwinism and Capitalism, Communism and Nationalism. In England it had survived unpleasant and at times extremely cruel persecution by the State, and hostility from the great majority of the public.

In a private note in his own handwriting, Derek Worlock described what were the standard attitudes of a typical English Catholic in the 1930s, which would have been little different, except for external circumstances, from those of the 1630s or 1730s. 'The need to resist any requirement to conform to the beliefs and practices of the established church was an important if apparently negative element in the faith of English Catholics,' he wrote.

It was part of our inherited pride in the sacrifices of our martyrs from previous centuries. Inevitably this attitude emphasised what divided us from our fellow Christians rather than what we shared. I was brought up not to enter a Protestant building,[43] let alone to take an active part in what took place there. Even to be present at the funeral or wedding of a non-Catholic relation required ecclesiastical permission and due care not to give the impression of taking part in the recitation of Protestant prayers or in hymn singing. Fish on Fridays was as important as not falling into the trap of adding 'for thine is the Kingdom' etc, to the 'Our Father' and 'who', not 'which',[44] was a public protestation of faith.

But it was not all obscuranticism and obduracy. It was a vibrant self-contained and self-assured culture; and it was distinctly interested in making the world a better place. Thus Derek Worlock, not alone of his kind, had a liking for organizations which practised the virtues of disciplined Christian manliness. One of the first with which he worked was the Young Christian Workers. It was no doubt directly on the instructions of Cardinal Griffin that he took up this task: Griffin's encouragement of the YCW was one of the routes through which Worlock was later to claim he acquired his interest in social justice.

In his pastoral letter for Lent 1947, in the drafting of which there is no doubt Worlock would have had a major hand, Griffin stated:

> One of the most promising movements of the present day is that of the Young Christian Workers. The members, the young workers of both sexes, have determined to win the workers of this country back to Christ by their prayers and by their action. The methods they employ are admirably suited to the needs of our time. They study present-day conditions of work, of family life, of civic and national life. They then compare these with the principles of the Gospels and with the Church's teaching given in the encyclicals. They decide how best to remedy the defects, and having thoroughly acquainted themselves both with facts and principles, they decide on action. Their influence is already being felt and their work has already borne fruit. We want to see this movement spread in the diocese. We know of the existence of many similar Catholic organisations working along similar lines which are doing magnificent work. We hope that these movements will prosper and extend their activities.

Worlock was to spearhead that expansion, not least through the élite group of politically active lay people he collected round him, which he called The Team. Griffin (that is to say Worlock, who occasionally referred in various diaries and letters to the need to work on the preparation of papers for the Cardinal[45]) went on to urge Catholics to be active in secular associations.

We have our duties as citizens and we have our duties to our nation. We are anxious that our people should take a greater share in the responsibilities of civic and national life. We are anxious that they should play their part in political groups and parties, subject of course to those not being in conflict with the teaching of the Church.

This was a regular theme. Two years earlier, on a pastoral letter for Advent 1945 (only months after the end of the war) Griffin had declared:

Let everyone who hears this message put the question to himself – 'Am I using to the full all my powers as a Catholic?' There is a wide field of social action. Many organisations in the Church are ready to extend their work if only more apostles offer themselves for duty. We cannot afford to waste one man, woman or child who has the zeal and energy to engage in the work of the apostolate. It is out duty to take some share in this work.

This winter of 1945–46 was a time of extreme hardship across war-damaged Europe, when the British government had to face the painful decision whether to make further cuts in the British food ration, already meagre, in order to prevent the starvation of millions of Germans. Griffin's sentiments are exemplary. 'It is becoming increasingly difficult to preach and practise a living Christianity,' wrote Griffin.

Too many are afraid of expressing Christian sentiments for fear of being accused of softness towards the enemy we have crushed. It is obviously the duty of the Allied Governments to see that German militarism will never again have the opportunity of destroying the peace of Europe and the world. But this worthy end is not to be achieved through a policy of hatred and revenge. We are bound to cherish all those who share with us a common nature made in the image of God. We are told by those who know[46] that millions in Europe, and especially in Germany, are threatened with death by starvation during this winter. Clearly it is the duty of food producing countries to save Europe. But if others fail in this duty this does not provide an excuse for us to cry with Cain that we are not our brother's keeper. Cain was a murderer. We are the brethren of Christ.[47]

Vatican II did introduce many far-reaching and fundamental changes, including changes in the hitherto 'immutable' Latin Tridentine Mass, changes to the doctrine that 'error had no rights' to a doctrine of freedom of conscience (almost its exact opposite), changes in its attitude to other Churches from outright hostility to co-operation and convergence –

including shared worship; changes in its attitude to the Jews and other world religions, to human rights, to democracy, even to Communism. In particular its commitment to ecumenism meant the formal conclusion of the Counter Reformation era, for the Counter Reformation had set out to bury the Protestant Churches, not to embrace them. Vatican II was in many ways an alternative response to Protestantism from the Council of Trent's response. No less radical was the adoption into Catholic social teaching of political theories the Church had once opposed, such as human rights and democracy. The principle of freedom of conscience was the most radical of them all. It was a frank admission that anybody punished or persecuted by the Catholic Church down the centuries for not being Catholic (or not Catholic enough) should not have been, and that the Catholic Church had been guilty of a grave violation of the moral order by such actions. It also seemed to have profound, if unexplored, consequences for the Church's own members and the way they approached the content of their own faith.

By demonstrating that even something as conservative as the Catholic Church was capable of a sudden sharp alteration of course towards liberalization and modernization, the Council undoubtedly contributed to the 1960s *zeitgeist* which shook social structures and attitudes throughout the Western world. So sharp a divide in Catholic history did the Council become, indeed, that there has been ever since a considerable degree of reluctance to submit the Church of the preceding eras to objective historical analysis, or to give it credit for anything. The continuities in the Church before and after the Council have tended to be down-played, even though in one obvious respect, the Church's senior personnel, there was very little change at all. If real change was to happen, it would be a personal change.

Through the eyes of the social historian, Catholicism emerges from the last half-millennium as a product of history, shaped by the politics of its time, a human artefact which pretended to stay the same while being regularly reinvented. But such a historian will not see the deeper reality. The eye of faith, on the other hand, sees the story of the Catholic Church as a momentous but mysterious dialogue between God and mankind, which may be likened to the ever-turbulent relationship between the Lord of Israel and its ancient people, as related in the books of the Hebrew Bible. It is a love-relationship but an unequal one, for while God is always faithful, His people are sometimes not. The Counter Reformation was a faith-filled response to God's call for renewal in the Church. By its very zeal, however, it introduced new avenues by which infidelity could enter in, not least by inaugurating an era of inter-religious wars in Europe which brought devastating social and political consequences, the legacy of which still survives in places today. England did not entirely escape those conflicts, though it experienced them in its own way.[48] If with the eye of faith, all was for the best – it did not always seem so at the time.

Though the era of the Counter Reformation came to an end in those years of the Council, 1962–65, those who had to implement the changes had still been steeped – 'formed', to use the official expression – in its ways. As in the case of the sixteenth-century Reformation itself, there was a fair degree of official ambiguity as to whether the changes were to be regarded as a natural development from what had gone before, or as a radical departure. It is not surprising that the first test of the new dispensation, the crisis in the Catholic Church over birth control in 1968, caught the authorities reacting at first as they would have reacted ten years earlier, with sanction and censure. Only when they were confronted with the radical failure of that strategy – indeed it seemed to be making the crisis rapidly worse – did they draw from the new insights of the Second Vatican Council alternative ways to deal with these serious challenges to Church authority which Cardinal Heenan called 'the greatest shock the Catholic Church has suffered since the Reformation'. But if Heenan was part of the problem, Worlock was part of the solution.

Notes

1 Title of a rousing Catholic hymn by F. W. Faber (1814–63), now rarely sung, which starts: 'Faith of our fathers, living still/In spite of dungeon, fire and sword;/oh, how our hearts/beat with joy/when e'er we hear that glorious word!/ Faith of our fathers, Holy Faith!/ We will be true to thee till death,/We will be true to thee till death.'

2 Cardinal Basil Hume was made a member of the even more illustrious Order of Merit shortly before his death in 1999.

3 By the end of the century Catholicism had lost ground in the inner city to religions from the Indian subcontinent, partly because of Asian immigration, partly as Catholics bettered themselves educationally and economically and moved out.

4 Dr Graham Leonard, then the Church of England Bishop of London and later a Roman Catholic priest, wrote in October 1992: 'No one, as far as I know, has challenged or refuted the famous opening sentence of Professor Powicke's book on the English Reformation. The one definite thing which can be said about the Reformation in England is that it was an act of State.'

5 Eamon Duffy, *The Stripping of the Altars, Traditional Religion in England 1400–1580*, Yale, 1992.

6 *Ibid.*, p. 4.

7 This was so that the people attending Sunday services would have to walk across the once sacred altar stone, defiling it with their feet (those not attending would be fined).

8 Medieval English *stope*.

9 The disastrous consequences of excommunicating Elizabeth I were cited in the Catholic Church in the early 1940s as a reason for not excommunicating Hitler.

10 Hooker's *Of the Lawes of Ecclesiastical Politie* worked out a basis for Anglicanism which claimed to reconcile Scripture, Tradition and Reason, thus offering an attractive alternative to the Geneva Protestantism that had prevailed.

11 (Or Books, as a succession of them were to be published before the 1662 version stabilized the liturgy until the twentieth century.)

12 The Jesuits, run from Rome, and the seminary priests, administered under the system of so-called vicars-apostolic (missionary bishops), were often at odds over strategy and tactics.

13 See *The Gunpowder Plot* by Antonia Fraser, Weidenfeld and Nicolson, 1996.

14 The Tridentine Rite replaced various other Catholic rites in use previously, including the Latin Sarum Rite used in England, while retaining many of their features. Cranmer's Rite for Holy Communion, later modified into the 1662 Book of Common Prayer rite, was also a modified (and translated) form of the Sarum Rite, which is why the Tridentine and Cranmerian rites still had a lot in common.

15 An indulgence is technically a release from the punishment due for sins already confessed and absolved: it shortens the time the soul has to spend in purgatory before being admitted to the presence of God in heaven. What so inflamed Martin Luther was the granting of indulgences in return for a donation to the church, and the claim that indulgences thus paid for could be put to the benefit of those already deceased. The Council of Trent introduced reforms which tacitly acknowledged the force of many of his criticisms.

16 Fortunately the quality of the work done at Trent was high, and many of its doctrinal formulations were intellectual masterpieces that have stood the test of time.

17 Tridentine is the adjective derived from Trent.

18 One of its first projects was an English translation of the Bible, which in many passages foreshadows the language of the later King James' version.

19 John Bossy, *The English Catholic Community, 1570–1850*, DLT, 1975, p. 147.

20 *The Panther and the Hind* by Aidan Nichols OP, T&T Clark, 1993, p. 30.

21 Trying to relax it too sharply was one of the reasons James II lost his Crown.

22 The existence of 'church papists' preoccupied the Protestant establishment in the seventeenth century as they were thought to be the 'enemy within', secret agents of a foreign power. In fact they were usually lukewarm Catholics who were prepared to conform outwardly. Recusants, who refused to conform and paid the price, had not much more time for them than the Protestants did.

23 Bossy, *ibid.*, p. 140.

24 Mark Bence-Jones, *The Catholic Families*, Constable, 1992.

25 A bishop appointed to rule a missionary district.

26 Bossy (p. 365) says of it: 'In its fusion of the meditative and the instructional with the sacramental and liturgical it was a normal product of the Counter Reformation; its most obvious debt was to St Francis de Sales. What also made it characteristically of the Counter Reformation was that it was not primarily world-escaping but activist in its orientation.'

27 From the middle of the nineteenth century onwards this was even more noticeable among some Church of England clergy of the Tractarian (Anglo–Catholic) party, who, to the dismay of worthies of the Low Church, slavishly adopted such Roman fashions as the title 'Father', the biretta, and the Roman collar (which even Protestants eventually succumbed to).

28 July 1852.

29 'Arise, make haste, my love, my dove, my beautiful one, and come. For the winter is now past, the rain is over and gone. The flowers have appeared in our land.'

30 Newman was in no sense a product of the Counter Reformation, his special interest being patristic studies, and before he contacted the Italian Passionist Father Dominic Barberi and requested to be received into the Catholic Church, he claimed never to have met a Catholic priest.

31 The present Duke of Norfolk, premier member of the English peerage not of royal blood and senior Catholic aristocrat, says his ancestors 'went on strike' for four years, in protest at the Restoration (conversation with author).

32 As thousands fled from the potato famine, John Bossy, in *The English Catholic Community 1570–1850*, DLT, 1975, estimates the proportion of Irish to English in the Catholic community at two to one, but the Irish Catholic population was among the poorest of all while English Catholics included, as Dickens had noted, many gentry and tradesman.

33 David Edwards, in *Christian England Volume 3*, Collins, 1984, said the Second Spring sermon simply showed how out of touch Newman was with the realities. 'It suited Newman's religion, both supernatural and nostalgic, to consider the centuries since the Reformation as a long decline fit to be compared with autumn and winter, so that the bishops could be welcomed as daffodils, appearing by a miracle to herald the return of the Middle Ages . . . In reality, however, the task confronting the bishops in the 1850s was to build churches and schools where the priests could teach the Irish and any others willing to be taught.'

34 *The Gunpowder Plot*, Weidenfeld and Nicolson, 1996. She is generally sympathetic to the plotters, 'whose motives, if not their actions, were noble and idealistic'.

35 There is no evidence, of course, that the Pope knew of the plot; had he done so, he would surely have taken the side of the Catholic clergy in England, who profoundly disapproved of armed insurrection.

36 'The Irish Immigration' by Denis Gwynn of University College, Cork, a chapter in *The English Catholics 1850–1950*, Burns Oates, 1950, a collection edited by Bishop George Beck.

37 *Cardinal Hinsley* by J. C. Heenan, Burns Oates, 1944.

38 18 March 1943.

39 Text given by Heenan.

40 *Westminster, Whitehall and the Vatican* by Thomas Moloney, Burns and Oates, 1985.

41 In 1942 he was one of the very first public figures anywhere in the world to draw attention to the growing evidence of the Nazi holocaust against the Jews, first-hand reports of which he had received from sources close to the Polish Underground and the Polish government-in-exile in London. Unlike the Home Office in 1935, the Foreign Office regarded his help as invaluable. Moloney, *ibid.*, p. 174; also see *Britain and the Vatican During the Second World War* by Owen Chadwick, Cambridge University Press, 1986.

42 The impossibility of shifting the official Catholic position was underlined by the bull *Apostolicae Curae* of 1896 of Leo XIII, which not only pronounced Anglican Holy Orders 'absolutely null and utterly void' but added for good measure that this judgement was irreversible, for ever and ever. The bull came after heavy lobbying from the Archbishop of Westminster, Cardinal Vaughan, who thought recognition of Anglican Orders would undermine his own position and discourage Anglican conversions. In other respects, however, Leo XIII's reign was the beginning of a somewhat spasmodic

ecumenical thaw in relations between the Catholic Church and other Churches.

43 This taboo may have dated from the time when entering a Church of England church could have meant walking across a desecrated altar stone.

44 The Catholic version of the otherwise identical Lord's Prayer in English began 'Our Father *who* art in heaven' and ended with 'deliver us from evil.'.

45 In an unpublished essay he wrote in 1981 he said: 'For most of the 19 years when I was Private Secretary at Westminster I was letter-writer-in-chief and script writer of speeches, articles, forewords galore . . . As the servant of two Cardinals I had even to develop different styles, reflecting two very different men. The speeches of Cardinal Griffin, because of speech difficulty following his stroke, had to be written almost entirely in monosyllabic words; and one could let oneself go in articles, pastoral letters, etc.'

46 The Minister for German Reconstruction in the Attlee Government was Frank Pakenham, later Lord Longford, a devout Catholic and friend of Worlock.

47 The British bread ration was indeed cut again, to a lower level than at any time in actual wartime. In the light of such bold and transparently Christian pronouncements as this, it is not possible to sustain Adrian Hastings' scathing judgement that 'Griffin was the least important Archbishop of Westminster of the century, a nice hard-working nonentity.' (*The History of English Christianity 1920–90*, SCM, 1991, p. 478. Unless, of course, this is all pure Worlock.

48 In some respects the Troubles in Ireland constitute a late continuation of the religious conflicts of the Reformation and Counter Reformation.

2

Worlock's
Secret Vatican II Diary

Derek Worlock let slip from time to time the fact that he had kept a full daily diary throughout the Second Vatican Council, adding that its content was such that it could not be published during his lifetime. He kept each volume padlocked. It is indeed a comprehensively revealing – and in the process, self-revealing – record of those times. It is rich with plots and intrigues, rows and rumours. But it is surprisingly short in the analysis of ideas. Those who prefer to regard the Second Vatican Council as a high-minded Great Debate, an argument between two positions that was thrashed out in a fair intellectual fight, will find the role of personalities irrelevant, and conflict between them boring or scandalous. The latter view will appeal particularly to those who think it is a matter of faith to regard the outcome as the Will of God. The Fathers of the Council prayed; and after a sufficient amount of prayer, the decrees of the Council got written.

That is not how Worlock sees it: in most matters he is as astringently unsentimental and sceptical as the journalist that he might have become (and indeed, as the author of this daily record, was). The Will of God requires a helping human hand or two. If Worlock has anything to do with it, one of those hands will be his. The outcome of deliberations such as these was ultimately bound to be the product of quasi-political processes: deals, alliances, compromises, squeezes, even betrayals and pressure some-times akin to blackmail. To win a political battle, you have to organize. Worlock organized. His only slight problem was that it was never quite clear what he was trying to achieve.

Protestants and Anglicans may not entirely agree that the Second Vatican Council was the single most important thing to happen to the Christian faith in the twentieth century.[1] But they would see the point of such a proposition. The Roman Catholic Church was larger than any other Church by a factor of ten. Perhaps because of its dogmatic and absolutist character and its longer history, its influence on world affairs would have been greater than theirs by a factor larger than that. The issues being addressed were of intense interest in the internal life of the other branches of Christianity, not least the issue of Christian unity. Nor did the thinking that emerged from the Council stop at the boundaries of other Churches. It pervaded them too. Indeed, the most likely grounds for reducing this estimate of the importance of the Council would be the fact that separate Churches were – and above all regarded themselves as – very self-contained at that time. They did not 'need' Rome; they were therefore indifferent (they would have said) to what happened inside it. Yet it was the Second Vatican Council that signalled the end of that self-containment.

Furthermore, some of the ideas that had most effect in the course of the Council were recognizably of Protestant or Anglican origin. Cardinal John Henry Newman, for instance, has been described by some, including Pope John Paul II, as the 'father' of the Second Vatican Council, notwithstanding the fact that he died 72 years before it started. Because Newman in his Catholic years was regarded by the English public above all as a notorious controversialist who had betrayed the Church of England for Rome, they neglected to notice how Anglican he still was in his manners and attitudes. It was this that shaped his theological outlook; it was that outlook that in turn helped shape the Second Vatican Council.[2] But the channel through which his ideas flowed was that of contemporary Northern European – that is to say not English, nor even English-speaking – theology. With one or two exceptions such as Abbot Christopher Butler (present at the Council not as a bishop but as President of the English Benedictines) and to some extent Archbishop (later Cardinal) John Carmel Heenan, the English-speaking presence at the Council exerted its influence in the opposite direction to that associated with the name and thought of Newman. He was above all a hero to the so-called progressives. It was his theory of the 'development of doctrine' that enabled people to move beyond the rigid doctrinal certainties of the Counter Reformation, and to understand that the Catholic religion can and should move on, express itself differently, even find fresh things to say. Newman showed how this could happen in an organized and controlled way, and so did not necessarily lead to the disintegration of the faith that had seemed to be threatened by the Reformation in the sixteenth century. It was as a patristic scholar, during his years as an Anglican academic at Oxford – some said the most brilliant of his day – that Newman had developed his own doctrine of the development of doctrine.

The English-speakers were overwhelmingly on the conservative side. None more so than Monsignor Derek Worlock, Secretary to Cardinal William Godfrey[3] of Westminster – and as the Council progressed, Secretary in effect also to the whole English group of bishops stationed in Rome.

It becomes increasingly clear that Worlock did not like Heenan, a sentiment fully reciprocated. Nor was this entirely to be explained by their theological differences, or even Worlock's desire to prevent Cardinal Godfrey from being overshadowed by a younger, fitter and more able man. The dislike was visceral.

Derek Worlock's father had been a journalist before becoming a political agent for the Conservative Party in Winchester, and he once admitted that he envied his father's writing skills. The son never quite lost the idea that he was made in his father's mould in this respect. He sometimes claimed that writing was his hobby as well as his 'necessary occupation'. But most of his life up to then did not lend itself to the unfolding of a sustained journalistic narrative. He made frequent attempts to keep a diary with precisely this intent. They always petered out. He would blame himself for this, but it could be that the nature of his work was too fragmentary, too detailed, to allow the drawing of general conclusions or provide a setting for trenchant observations about his life and times. The Second Vatican Council was just such a project, however, and in the opening passage of his Vatican II diary he explains why he decided to keep it. 'I am writing this personal record because it seems right that, in spite of all the usual bonds of secrecy, I should leave such an account available to those who in future days may not be bound by those same bonds,' he had stated. So it is his contribution to historical research.

How does it merit as history? The answer has to be that it stands up very well. Some views of the Second Vatican Council may have to be adjusted in the light of it. The first passages reproduced below, for instance, relate to the preparatory period, when a vast amount of work was done in anticipation of the first meeting of the Council itself. Cardinal Godfrey was a member of the Central Commission, which was instructed by Pope John XXIII to oversee the preparations; Worlock was by his elbow every day, though not in the actual commission meetings.

Here we see the unfolding of the human drama that lay beneath the dry ecclesiastical politics of the time. Cardinal Godfrey refusing to share a car with Cardinal Heard; Cardinal Godfrey discussing the Orpington by-election with Cardinal Döpfner (without realizing that was what they were talking about); Cardinal Ciriaci trying to defuse the tension in the Central Commission by the use of humour. Personality clashes, and his own likes and dislikes, are laid bare; so are the plots and schemes that Vatican officials were using to try to turn the forthcoming Council into an event that did not threaten their interests.

Above all, Worlock highlights, as no other eyewitness or analyst has done, how quickly and fiercely battle was joined between the two major armies that were colliding in Rome at that time. The commanding general on one side was Cardinal Ottaviani, head of the Holy Office of the Inquisition. He was not content with defence, but wished to use the Council to further his own reactionary agenda. If he had his way, its result was likely to be an updated *Syllabus of Errors* along the lines of that issued by Pope Pius IX in 1864. The leader on the other side was Cardinal Bea, a Jesuit of German extraction, who had been promoted by Pope John XXIII to head the new Secretariat for Christian Unity. Worlock accuses him of trying to Protestantize the Catholic Church.

The definitive academic work on this period is Volume I of the *History of Vatican II*,[4] which states categorically:

> Even in the Central Commission some personalities who only twelve months later would play dominant roles in the development of the Council – Alfrink, Suenens, Léger, Koenig, Liénart, not to mention Montini – for a long time acted timidly and awkwardly; perhaps Bea is the only exception here. An explicit clash of different positions only began in the spring of 1962.[5]

Worlock's diary contradicts that, and talks of 'the fat falling into the fire' and the 'balloon going up' as early as November 1961. Cardinal Bea led the attack, supported by Cardinals Koenig of Vienna and Alfrink, leader of the Dutch bishops, and others. Some of the language they used was very outspoken.

This collision was at the heart of the Second Vatican Council. For all the antagonism which Worlock describes, the preparatory phase was a preliminary skirmish. Very few of the documents they laboured so mightily to produce had any great effect – 90 per cent of these drafts were never considered when the Council actually met in the autumn of 1962.[6] This is because the progressives were by and large worsted in the preliminary phase, and chose to wait for their revenge until the rest of the residential bishops arrived from dioceses all over the world. Then they ambushed the conservatives, who were comprehensively defeated, at least in their grand strategy of using the Council to stage a rearguard action against the perils and errors of the modern world.[7]

Those early clashes defined the battlefield which was later to prove the decisive one.

*　　　　　*　　　　　*

The Second Vatican Council: A Personal Record[8]

June 1962[9]*:* I am writing this in Rome at what looks to be the end of a chapter in the preparations for the Second Vatican Council, which is due to start here in October next. I am writing this personal record because it seems right that, in spite of all the usual bonds of secrecy, I should leave such an account available to those who in future days may not be bound by those same bonds. I know from bitter experience and from the many half-completed diaries and records in my possession,[10] that to write such an account by hand each day is beyond my resources. In many ways I have a memory which is too retentive and in setting down an account I am apt to write at such great length that the passage of time overtakes me. My only hope is to be able to put down on tape at regular intervals an account of what has seemed important to me. Probably when the full history of these events comes to be written, the error of my views and even of my reporting of facts will be obvious. Nevertheless a contemporary account has interest in that it shows the developments which may lead to a result which, stated baldly, may seem dry as dust.

I suppose that in many ways I should have started to write this account some considerable time ago. At the same time I then had no knowledge of the way things were shaping and in any case, whilst one can give a blow by blow description of what happens at the Council itself, (or at least what I can find out about it) such a treatment of the preliminaries would have been tedious.

For me the Council opened on 25 January 1959. During the previous few months we had been in Rome three times. In the late autumn we came out for the funeral of Pius XII, then had to nip off home whilst the Cardinals assembled for the conclave lest the Archbishop of Westminster (without a red hat[11]) might have seemed to have been canvassing or suffering from sour grapes. We were back again in November 1958 for the Coronation of Pope John XXIII and three days after our return the said Archbishop of Westminster received notification that he was to be raised to the Sacred College. This performance kept us in Rome for most of December and Cardinal Godfrey returned with the red hat for a solemn Reception on New Year's Eve.

January 1959 was therefore a time when one was endeavouring to catch up upon back correspondence and postponed engagements. It was an exciting time in that it was the beginning of the new Pope's reign and John XXIII had got off to a good start so far as the British Press were concerned. On 25 January I had been out at the Grail[12] at Pinner, lecturing to some group of lay apostles and I recall driving back that evening arriving at the front door of Archbishop's House at about 7 pm. As I pulled up, Bishop Cashman[13] came down the front steps and, laughing, said 'You had better hurry up and pack your bag: you are off to Rome again.' This remark took me completely by surprise and my first reaction was that the Pope must be dead. The bishop however added: 'John XXIII has really done it this time. He's called an Ecumenical Council.'

As the bishop drove away, I found myself racking my brains, trying to think what exactly an Ecumenical Council was and all I could remember was that the Vatican Council in the last century had lasted so long that it had never been completed and we had been told in the Seminary that it was unlikely that we should ever see another called in our time.[14] Once again such advice proved wrong. As I went in the front door of Archbishop's House, the telephone rang. It was the Press asking when we would be leaving. I had to play for time and just put them off with the assurance that when the time of departure was fixed we would let the Press know. Then I went upstairs to try to find out what really had happened. Since that time the Pope has made known how he decided to call a Council after talking with his Secretary of State, Cardinal Tardini. But there is no doubt that he took everyone else by surprise. That day, the feast of the Conversion of Saint Paul, the Pope had visited the Basilica of Saint Paul and had delivered an address to a small gathering of Curial Cardinals. He said that he had been considering how to help his diocese of Rome and had decided that it would be best to consult the priests: therefore he would call a Synod of Rome. Then his gaze had wandered further and he had considered how he could help the Church as a whole. It would be best, in his opinion, to consult the Bishops and therefore he proposed to hold an Ecumenical Council. Put like that it all sounded very simple and one wonders very much whether either the Pope or Cardinal Tardini realised the immense task which they had undertaken so early in the new reign.

At first nothing much seemed to happen. The 'experts' said that the Holy Father had bitten off more than he could chew and that it would not prove practical to hold an Ecumenical Council under modern conditions with something like 3,000 bishops involved. The proof that something was happening was when an announcement was made that Cardinal Tardini had been put in charge of a pre-Preparatory Commission and in June 1959 all the Bishops received from Cardinal Tardini a letter inviting them to send to him by the end of August a list of all the points which they felt could rightly come under consideration at a General Council of the Church. The reaction of most Bishops was one of horror at having to prepare such a letter at such a busy time of the year when so much was at stake. Could they really mean by the end of August? Cardinal Godfrey set to work whilst he was at Hare Street[15] in order to draw up a number of points about which he felt strongly, particularly with regard to the discipline of the clergy. No sooner had this document been prepared, put into Latin, polished up and finally typed than a further request came that the Hierarchy should jointly express its views from its next Meeting or Conference. At that Meeting it became pretty clear that very few of the Bishops had yet done their homework. One or two aired their views and there seemed general agreement that one of the things to be tackled was the autonomy of Religious[16] and the problems of the Local Ordinary when required to dispense enclosure, etc. In the end the Cardinal was asked to send from the Hierarchy the views which he had expressed at the Meeting and these inevitably reflected what he had already prepared as his own list of points. So far as I can recall and without reference to correspondence, all this was dispatched to Rome by the end of November 1959 and there one might have expected the matter to rest.

But in March 1960, when we were out in Rome for the Consistory at which Cardinal Rugambwa received the Red Hat, Cardinal Tardini took Cardinal Godfrey on one side and remarked that there were some eight or nine bishops who had not sent their replies and would he kindly chase them up as the reply was wanted from each individual bishop.[17] The Cardinal asked for a list and when the list arrived, it included of course some of the bishops from Scotland so we had tactfully to return these via the Apostolic Delegation. To follow this point right through, one might add that when we were in Rome again in July, en route to Malta for the Pauline celebrations, Cardinal Tardini once more told the Cardinal that there were still two or three bishops, including his own auxiliaries, who had not sent their views and it was to be understood that the views of every bishop were needed. So far as I can tell, this eventually did the trick.

Now let us go back to the beginning of 1960 when, through the Apostolic Delegation, the Cardinal was asked to put forward the names of certain experts who might serve on the various Preparatory Commissions it was proposed to establish. Theologians, Canon Lawyers, Liturgical experts and persons well-experienced in dealing with non-Catholics were required. The Delegate made one or two suggestions; the Cardinal made others and, from what eventually happened, one can only imagine that others were consulted and still further so-called experts were put forward.

The know-alls who had said that the Council could never happen took their first big knock at Pentecost in 1960 when the Pope published a *Motu Proprio*[18] setting up the Preparatory Commissions. Over each a Cardinal would preside (customarily the Cardinal at the head of the Congregation normally concerned with that particular subject) and each Commission would have a Secretary resident in Rome. The Commissions were varied in size. Customarily each Preparatory Commission would have about 30 members, mostly Bishops but otherwise experts in the particular subject and perhaps as many consultors whose views could be sought either outside or at the actual Sessions of the Commissions but who would not normally be involved in the discussions or in voting for or against a resolution.

The Commissions were as follows:

1. The Theological Commission, to which I regret no Englishman was appointed either as a member or as a consultor.
2. The Commission for bishops and the government of dioceses, on which Bishop Dwyer of Leeds served as a member (this was an important Commission in that inevitably it dealt with the relations between the Local Ordinary and Religious Houses in his territory).
3. The Commission for the Discipline of the Clergy and the Faithful upon which Monsignor Lawrence McReavy, the Professor of Canon Law at Ushaw,[19] served as a consultor. Quite late on in the proceedings Monsignor Whitty, formerly Vice-Rector of the Beda, got himself appointed to this when he left Rome, having failed to be nominated for the Rectorship. The wags said that the Americans with whom he was very friendly, needed him back to make a four at bridge!
4. The Commission for Religious – no representative from England and Wales.
5. The Commission for the discipline of the Sacraments – again no English representative.
6. The Commission for the Sacred Liturgy, where Canon J. B. O'Connell of Menevia turned up as a full member.

(One may add a small diversion here because of some rather delicious stories told by the Bishop of Ghent who was on this Commission and who alleged that many of its members were those who had made their name through writing about liturgical eccentricities. He claimed that one had proposed that there should be a different formula used by the priest in absolving from mortal sin: a nice decision for any Confessor to make. He also alleged that a Confessor should impose hands on the absolved penitent before making the sign of the cross in absolution: one fears there might have been a little difficulty in confessionals where there is a grill. And he had an even more outrageous story regarding proposals for the anointing of the sick, which should not be limited to the senses but should include those parts of the body which had been troublesome in life![20]

But perhaps the nicest story of all concerned the final Session of this rather self-conscious Commission. The Pope had been attending one Session of each Commission and finally turned up for the last Session of the Liturgical Commission. There the experts and pundits were gathered, expecting some particularly profound liturgical homily. However, John XXIII decided that the whole business was being taken too seriously and so he trotted out the old chestnut about the shipwreck where each passenger was told that he must throw some possession overboard to save the ship from sinking. According to the Pope the Captain threw his wife and the Chaplain threw his breviary. Altogether a nice finish for a Liturgical Commission!)

7. The Commission for Studies and Seminaries: no representative.

8. The Commission for the Oriental Churches, of which Bishop Sipovic was a member. As his normal base is London, I suppose he can be included as one of 'ours'.

9. The Commission for the Missions to which Archbishop David Mathew, Ordinary[21] to the Catholics in Her Majesty's Forces, was appointed Secretary. This meant that the Archbishop had to reside in Rome and the Chaplains saw him for a fleeting visit of a few weeks each summer: a state of affairs which aroused considerable comment both from the Chaplains and from the Catholics in the Forces.

10. The Commission for the Lay Apostolate, under of all people Cardinal Cento. I know that quite a lot of people were unhappy about the fact that there were no English representatives amongst the members or consultors and this was a strange tribute to a country which, since the first World Congress of the Lay Apostolate ten years ago, has played a leading part in the development of the relationship between the lay apostolic organisations. I don't suppose it mattered much in the end because, as we shall see later, its findings had to pass through the hands of the Central Commission where our Cardinal could give his views but, as a side issue, it could have been helpful to the Hierarchy if some English priest or bishop had been appointed, as it would have enabled us to stave off the charge that the English Hierarchy is behind the times, whereas in fact its relationship with the laity is the envy of many other countries.[22]

Subsequently a Ceremonial Commission was added to these Preparatory Commissions: it was very small, consisting of the leading members of the Papal Household and the Papal Masters of Ceremonies. Quite what their task was has not, as yet, become apparent. It may just have been an easy way of letting the boys[23] inside.

The Pope also established three Secretariats, whose task was to be mainly administrative, though in practice this was not always strictly the case. The first of these was the Secretariat for the Press, Radio etc. On this we had Bishop Beck of Salford as a member (his father was a journalist!) and Father Agnellus Andrew as a consultor. (I recall now receiving his solemn oaths of secrecy during a lunch hour break from the BBC when we nipped out and sat in a bench in a corner of the Church of St Charles in Ogle Street.[24] I wonder how many people who saw two priests apparently chattering in a corner realised what was going on.)

Then there was an Administrative Secretariat concerned with such matters as finance, and thirdly, a Secretariat for the Promotion of Christian Unity, as it came to be called: and this was the heart of the trouble so far as we in England have been concerned. We should remember first of all what was the Pope's stated object. He said in his *Motu Proprio* 'To show more fully our love and benevolence towards those who are decorated with the Christian name but who are separated from the Apostolic See and so that they may follow the work of the Council and may come more easily to that unity for which Jesus Christ prayed to His heavenly Father, a special office or secretariat should be set up which would have one of the Cardinals as its Moderator and would operate in the same manner as the Preparatory Commissions.' So far so good. It was understood that it should be a channel of communication but in next to no time it was understood in England to be an Organisation which was working for Christian Unity. To this Secretariat Archbishop Heenan of Liverpool was appointed, together with Father Corr of the Servites, a simple priest who had next to no knowledge of official relations with other denominations. Later Bishop Holland, the Coadjutor of Portsmouth, was also appointed to the Secretariat as a member, and from the first Father Bevenot SJ, was appointed as a consultor, as also was Monsignor Davis of Birmingham.

The Archbishop of Liverpool then let it be known in England that he had been appointed in order to lead the work for Christian Unity in the country. Indeed so far as the Press was concerned, they never really got over the idea which was given at that time that the Archbishop of Liverpool was representing the Hierarchy at the Ecumenical Council. Time after time I had to try to deal with this problem with the Press and one could only have killed the story by dealing the Archbishop a very severe blow and this, with the Cardinal's agreement, I steadfastly refused to deliver. But it was very difficult.

When Dr Geoffrey Fisher, the Archbishop of Canterbury, made his famous visit to the Pope,[25] the Archbishop of Liverpool more or less suggested to the Press that it had been done with his connivance. It was certainly done with his knowledge, knowledge which he did not pass on to Westminster and landed us in great difficulties with the Press. The irony of the situation was that the archbishop who had to attend a certain number of meetings in Rome in connection with his work for the Secretariat and made so many public pronouncements about these visits that he was thought by the Press to be the only bishop going to Rome at all, came to regard the meetings as being utterly futile and a hopeless waste of time.

At the same time when the Pope announced the establishment of the various Preparatory Commissions and Secretariats, he also announced the Central Preparatory Commission. This, under the chairmanship of the Dean of the Sacred College, Cardinal Tisserant, was again made up of members and consultors and originally was about 50 strong so far as members were concerned, with about 30 consultors, the heads of the principal Religious Orders and the Secretaries of the various Congregations and Preparatory Commissions. There is no doubt that this Central Preparatory Commission was originally written off in the estimation of Romans and knowledgeable clerics outside as a 'Committee of honour' to which were appointed a number of people who, in the estimation of the experts, were to be given this honorary or consolation prize. Generally speaking it was regarded as a sieve through which the findings of the individual Commissions and Secretariats would pass on their way to the Pope. That's how it all started and the fact that it emerged as what came to be called 'the little Council', vastly outweighing in importance any of the other Preparatory Commissions, was undoubtedly something which was never anticipated.

I don't want to jump the gun too far at this stage but one should add that there were originally about 60 or 70 members of this Central Commission, about 50 of them Cardinals and about half of this number Curial Cardinals. The other members were perhaps the principal member of each individual Hierarchy if he was not already a Cardinal, and the heads of the principal Religious Orders. There were also a number of consultors who included the Secretaries of the different Preparatory Commissions and a certain number of outstanding experts in different fields. As the work of the Central Commission progressed, and its importance increased, it came to be a matter almost of prestige value to be appointed a member and indeed a Cardinal who was not a member began to look as though he had something against him. Therefore the number increased. With regard to the Americans, for whom such great distances were involved, there was by the beginning of 1962 a fairly widespread representation so that the American Cardinals could take it in turn to come to the meetings in order to make sure that their viewpoint was expressed. In the end I suppose there were about 70 or 80 members and a great number of consultors, though inevitably attendance was not always 100 per cent. That it was as high as it was is in itself remarkable.

Having dealt at such great length with the set-up and the preparations, I should say one word about someone whom I regard as a man of genius, namely the Secretary of the Central Commission and indeed of the whole Council, Archbishop Felici. At the time of his appointment his name was unknown outside Rome and indeed when the first announcement was made, one had a terrible fear that perhaps the photographer[26] had got himself appointed. But the work undertaken by Monsignor Felici's office has been remarkable and from what I have seen of it has shown a degree of efficiency and understanding which, quite frankly, one could not have anticipated. This may become apparent from what I shall write later but one should add that through it all Monsignor Felici, adding remarkably to his weight as well as to his stature as the months have gone by, has smiled his way, never appearing flustered and showing an astonishing degree of anticipation with regard to the provision of what has been needed. Normally one thinks of the Romans as being great improvisers. Monsignor Felici has gone beyond this: he has shown that he is able to anticipate requirements and have everything ready when needed. Altogether a remarkable achievement.

The announcement of all these bodies was made, as I have said, at Pentecost in 1960. Not all the members of the Commissions were announced at once but by the autumn their membership was known and a letter arrived from Cardinal Tardini inviting all members of all Commissions to come to Rome at the beginning of November for a solemn ceremony to mark the commencement of this preparatory work. There was a note at the bottom of the letter to the effect that if attendance conflicted with important pastoral duties, the individual concerned would of course be dispensed and Cardinal Godfrey, who I don't think at that stage realised precisely what the work of a Central Commission was going to be, rapidly claimed a prior engagement. In fact I think he was anxious to avoid Rome at that time as there were all sorts of difficulties at the English College which rendered his presence a source of unnecessary embarrassment to him. It was particularly painful as he was suspected of opposition to the Rector and Vice-Rector, whereas in fact time has shown that he saved their bacon – not that even now they appreciate this fact. This opening of the preparatory work coincided with or followed by a few days the official opening of the new Beda College[27] and here again the Cardinal was strangely reluctant to attend this function, even though it was rumoured, and at the last minute announced, that the Holy Father would be present for the opening. In the end the Bishop of Brentwood went out for the opening and was more or less the only member of the Hierarchy present. It really was not the other bishops' fault because it was not until the last minute that Monsignor Duchemin sent them invitations, probably because he could not get a definite answer as to whether the Pope was going or not. At all events when the solemn opening ceremony for the preparatory work took place in Rome, unless perhaps Archbishop Mathew was there as by this time he had taken up residence in Rome, England was fairly gloriously unrepresented but not many weeks passed before the work of some of the Commissions and Secretariats got under way.

We began to hear word of immense volumes of printed material being given to all the different members of the Commissions but their contents were alleged to be so highly secret that it was impossible to find out exactly what these volumes contained. It was at this stage that Archbishop Fisher made his famous *démarche* to Rome and more and more the impression was given that the Council was concerned only with the question of Christian Unity and that the Secretariat for the Promotion of such, under the Jesuit Cardinal Bea, was the organising committee for the Council.[28] Inevitably therefore the impression was given – and I have never seen it denied by the individual concerned – that the Archbishop of Liverpool was the man who was handling Council affairs for the English Hierarchy. Indeed he wrote himself that he had been selected for this work by the Pope and there is no doubt that a number of priests in England felt that in this matter he had been brought forward over Cardinal Godfrey's head.

By the beginning of 1961 I felt that the time had come to take some positive action which would make it clear that Cardinal Godfrey also had a part to play in this Council. Week by week we read of the visits being paid to Rome for the work of the Preparatory Commissions and Secretariats and it seemed to me that the only thing to do was to tell the Cardinal to go down to Rome and we could use the occasion at least to remind the Catholic public that he was a member of the Central Preparatory Commission, even though at that stage we were not particularly clear as to what it meant. Luckily the situation was solved by the fact that we had a number of business matters to see to in Rome – it was also important that the Cardinal should take a look at what was happening at the College and have a word with the Rector before the Low Week Meeting of 1961 – and I remember that when the time came for us to leave for Rome, I made a count of the jobs to be done and they mounted to 48: which is quite a lot to get through in a period of ten days.

Therefore in March 1961 we flew down to Rome and I suggested to the Cardinal that one of his earliest calls should be at the office of the Secretariat so that he could meet Monsignor Felici and find out a little bit more about these bound and secret volumes. The Cardinal had a great welcome when he arrived and we were told that the volumes were being placed in the car whilst we were in the office. This indicated some fairly smart piece of backstairs organisation and by the time we got down we discovered the Vatican autista sweating like a pig, having loaded about a dozen enormous volumes into the boot of the car. This I may add was only the first consignment and in the course of the next few months we paid a great deal of excess baggage, bringing supplementary volumes back to London by air.

But what was in these now famous red bound books? Herein lay the eagerly sought replies from all the bishops and other ecclesiastical beaks whose views on matters suitable for discussion at the Council had been sought by Cardinal Tardini. Volumes and volumes of them. Arranged for the most part on a national basis but there were also sections giving the replies of Rectors of Catholic Universities and so on . . .

One doubts very much whether many of the Bishops in sending their replies to Cardinal Tardini did so with a view to the publication of their letters. Although the contents must at the present time be regarded as secret, it seems inevitable that these volumes will in due time become part of ecclesiastical history. How embarrassing therefore for the American bishop who started off his letter: 'Your Eminence, I am very sorry that due to the fact that I have been absent from my diocese for one reason or another during the past few weeks I have not found time to reply to your earlier letter.' That is the sort of way in which so many of these official replies started and relatively few were couched in the formal Latin which I am glad to say the Archbishop of Westminster phrased his own reply.

They made immense reading and I suppose that there must be a great many of these volumes whose pages are still uncut. Certainly I saw a whole stack of unbound volumes lying in the corner of a room of the Secretariat for the Promotion of Christian Unity when I was in there recently and there are alarming reports that a complete set of the volumes was handed by the Secretariat to the Archbishop of Canterbury. If so, it is alarming to realise that the Anglicans in England now know what the Catholic bishops think about them. Perhaps it will do no harm but they would not expect to be solemnly presented by the Holy See with such indirect abuse. Nor does one imagine that Cardinal Bea realised what he was doing.

*   *   *

If anyone in the Church of England ever did read those preliminary papers it would have been Canon Bernard Pawley, first Anglican liaison officer in Rome and an official ecumenical observer at the Council. He mentions having to 'study the preparations' for the Council before it began. If he saw anything that offended him he did not make a point of it. In fact relations between the two Churches were such that a certain tone of disparagement, or at least of condescension, would have been regarded as normal on either side. Worlock shared that attitude, and this no doubt partly explains his disapproval of the pioneering ecumenical activities of Archbishop Heenan of Liverpool.

However, Pawley confirms Worlock's complaint that the Press thought the Vatican Council was mainly going to be about Christian unity. In 1974[29] he wrote: 'the world Press lost itself for once in enthusiasm for the possibilities thus opened up', so much so that the Pope felt he had to damp them down again. Yet there was 'undoubtedly a charismatic quality about Pope John's conception of the Council which quickly broke through barriers of prejudice and faithfulness and set it firmly in the centre of ecclesiastical interest all over the world'. But signals from the Vatican were very mixed; one day a generous gesture, another, a move backwards. Pawley saw the whole project as being in danger.

While Worlock was at this stage of the proceedings firmly in the arch-conservative camp, being a loyal disciple of Cardinal Godfrey, Pawley was picking up the disappointments of those who wanted a more progressive future. Many of the appointments to the preparatory commissions had gone to conservatives (he may even have had Godfrey and some other English bishops in mind when he wrote this).

Against this, however,

> One feature of the preparations had enough promise in it to counterbalance the gloom produced by all the rest, which was the formation in 1960 of the new Secretariat of State for the promotion of Unity among Christians, and the appointment as its president Father (later Cardinal) Augustin Bea, the Jesuit head of the Biblical Institute, and of Father Jan Willebrands as Secretary.

His account of the circumstances of the visit of the Archbishop of Canterbury, Dr Geoffrey Fisher, to Rome in 1960 does not bear out Worlock's testy assertion that Heenan had had a hand in bringing it about (yet hadn't bothered to keep the Cardinal Archbishop of Westminster informed).

Fisher had called on the Pope on his way back from a visit to the Orthodox Patriarchs of Constantinople and Jerusalem, 'no doubt' as Pawley remarks 'to assure any suspicious Anglicans that he had not lost his sense of priorities' – that is to say, the Orthodox were thought to be a more comfortable prospect for dialogue than Rome, as there was much less of a difficult historical legacy. Fisher himself, says Pawley, was 'not himself among the first rank of zealots for resuming relations with Rome'.

The coolness was mutual. The Vatican curia tried to lay down ungenerous conditions for this visit, such as no Press statements afterwards, no photographs, and not even Cardinal Bea himself would be in attendance. The Pope himself overruled these demeaning arrangements, and of course Cardinal Bea was there. Despite these obstacles, the visit was a success.

Heenan himself more or less categorically refutes Worlock's insinuation that he helped to bring about the Fisher visit when he writes about it in his autobiography.[30]

> The initiative for this meeting of Canterbury and Rome came about from Geoffrey Fisher. Two years later, he told me how it came about. 'Like everyone else,' he said, 'I was impressed by the change of outlook in the Roman Church since John became Pope. It struck me quite suddenly one day that if I was going to Jerusalem to see the orthodox Patriarch and to Istanbul to meet the Ecumenical Patriarch why shouldn't I visit the Head of the Church of Rome.' It was a much more delicate business than in these days,

Heenan adds. If Fisher was explaining it to Heenan two years later, it seems unlikely they were secretly collaborating at the time. Unless, of course, this was a smokescreen.

But Worlock's jealous complaint that Heenan was scene-stealing had some basis. It was to Heenan rather than to Godfrey that the Press turned for a comment on the archbishop's visit to the Pope, and it was he who obliged them. 'Courtesy translated in the language of religion means charity,' he had said. 'The Primate's visit to the Pope is significant because it shows the differences of theology need not prevent mutual respect and love.'

Because of the Curia's restrictions on media coverage of the event, no television camera was allowed to follow Archbishop Fisher into the papal apartment. 'Defrauded of a sight of the protagonists in conversation', Heenan wrote later,

> BBC television mounted a minor summit in the person of the other Anglican primate, Dr Ramsey, Archbishop of York, and myself . . . It was a pleasant occasion. There was no need for Michael Ramsey and me to perform. We knew each other well enough to have a conversation without attempting to outwit each other. The archbishop came to lunch a few days before we were due to go down to the television studios in London . . . The television programme, like the meeting of the Pope and Archbishop, was significant simply because it took place.

It was almost as widely remarked upon in the Press, to the obvious chagrin of the Godfrey camp. In the days that followed, the Press, seeking follow-ups, turned some attention upon Liverpool itself, the one city in England where Catholic and Protestant factions were notorious for mutual antagonism. Violence was still not far below the surface, including a near riot when Heenan visited a Catholic resident in a Protestant neighbourhood. But he always reacted with soothing words and conciliatory gestures.

Heenan and his Anglican opposite number, Dr Clifford Martin, had already established good personal relations. When a newspaper article had attacked Protestant and Anglican clergy as useless, Heenan had written to defend them in the most glowing terms. In 1961, when Michael Ramsey succeeded Geoffrey Fisher as Archbishop of Canterbury, Heenan had hosted an unprecedented lunch party at Archbishop's House, Liverpool, for Ramsey and Martin and their wives to wish the archbishop good luck. 'It was one of the happiest luncheon parties I have ever known', wrote Heenan afterwards.

A journalist wrote of him at this time that though he came to his archdiocese only four years previously 'he has already made a great impact, not only on the people of his own faith but on those of what were once rival faiths who perceive the truth and wisdom that lie behind his maxim – "We must love one another until we come to see the same truth . . . we must stand to our principles and yet we must go on loving".'

These sentiments were very far from the secret thoughts Worlock was recording in his Vatican II diary at around this time. As the Council progressed, the dislike of Worlock for Heenan did not appear to lessen, even though Worlock's views came a lot closer to Heenan's over time. Whether the ill-feeling was always mutual cannot be established for certain – Heenan gives us no equivalent access to his private thoughts – but it seems likely.

There are grounds for thinking, for instance, that Heenan sabotaged Worlock's chances of succeeding him as Archbishop of Westminster in 1975. (The actual appointment was made in 1976, after Heenan's death.) No less significantly, Worlock offers evidence in his Vatican II diary that Heenan sabotaged Cardinal Godfrey's chances of election to one of the commissions which were set up in 1962 at the start of the Council to undertake the detailed work and prepare new drafts of documents for formal debate. Needless to say, Worlock, ever Godfrey's devoted servant, was working tirelessly to bring about that election. Heenan thwarted him.

Heenan's own version is as follows:[31]

The bishops were handed books containing names of those who during the preceding two years had been members of the preparatory commissions. Cardinal Liénart, Bishop of Lille, rose to make a speech of protest. It would be absurd to vote immediately for members of commissions, he said, because as yet the fathers were unacquainted with each other. It would be much wiser and fairer to allow time for bishops to exchange information and discuss the merits of the proposed candidates . . . The cardinal proposed that the various hierarchies should first consider what talent they could offer and then pass on to other hierarchies the names of their strongest candidates . . . The reaction of the bishops was unmistakable, and the first General Congregation of the Second Vatican Council was suspended after exactly 15 minutes.

For the next three days hierarchies met and sent each other lists of names regarded as most suitable for election to the commission. There was a generous exchange of views through envoys who went round the national colleges where the various hierarchy meetings were being held. When all the available information had been collected each hierarchy was able to produce a comprehensive list . . . Before the voting took place bishops had sufficient knowledge of candidates to vote intelligently. They knew, at least second hand, who were best qualified to serve on a commission. The bishops from the north acted in concert from the beginning and were in frequent touch with their English brethren.[32]

All consultations had to take place between Saturday's abortive meeting and the following Tuesday when the Council was due to resume. The intervening days were perhaps the most strenuous of the whole council. It was useless to put forward the name of a candidate without letting groups of bishops know something of his background and worth. Even using every spare moment it was impossible to learn enough about sixteen people for each commission.

Historians of the Second Vatican Council have regarded the rejection of the Curia's lists of nominations for the commissions as one of the key turning points. International preparatory commissions – Cardinal Godfrey had been a member of the main commission – had already been working for two years preparing documents for consideration by the full Council. But they had been selected by the Curia, and had been working under the auspices of the Curia to agendas set by the Curia. The Curia by and large did not want the Council. They certainly did not want anything much to come of it. Those who wanted to free the Council from the Curia's control in the name of far-reaching reform had therefore to achieve two things.

At the outset they had to ensure that the membership of the actual commissions was different from the preparatory commissions. If the membership was the same or similar, the chances were the results would be similar. And having secured a different membership, they then had to secure the rejection of the original draft documents. This they managed, in varying degrees, sometimes dramatically. In effect, therefore, each of the new commissions with new membership had to start again on the work that the preparatory commissions thought they had more or less finished.

As Heenan indicates and Worlock confirms in his diary, this revolt against the Curia was largely the work of Northern European prelates. There is no sign that any English bishop apart from Heenan was engaged in the more intense and conspiratorial back-stairs negotiations, though Worlock – not then a bishop himself – was also lobbying hard, albeit with opposite intentions. While Heenan was being courted and encouraged by such progressive firebrands as Bishop de Smedt of Bruges,[33] a key figure, Worlock and Godfrey were being drawn into the camp of Archbishop Marcel Lefebrve, the arch-conservative.[34] What made Worlock's job all the harder was the fact that Heenan had stolen his list, deliberately to prevent the election of Cardinal Godfrey. But there is only the merest hint of all this factionalism in Heenan's own writings. 'The Cardinal is still suffering the effects of an operation last year and it is hard to put a point which he can grasp quickly or clearly.'[35] One can only guess how much exasperation this concealed, during some of the most stressful days of the whole Council.

*　　　*　　　*

Not long after this, Derek Worlock acknowledged – with some relish, it seems – the all-too-human side of some of the senior church dignitaries present in Rome for the preparatory meetings. Cardinal William Heard, a noted canon lawyer, was a member of the Vatican civil service who had been elevated to the Sacred College in 1959. Though a Scot, he lived in the English College in Rome where Godfrey also liked to stay. Why he disliked Cardinal Godfrey (and why the ill-feeling was so wholeheartedly reciprocated) is not recorded.

This particular session was unique in that it brought about the first, though so far as I was concerned inevitable, clash with Cardinal Heard. He had informed the Rector of the College before we arrived that he supposed he would have to share a car with Cardinal Godfrey and that as two Cardinals were travelling together it was unnecessary for them to be accompanied. Cardinal Godfrey accepted the situation but I stood by waiting for the bang which was not long in coming. Michael Tuck, a Westminster student at the College, one of whose duties was to serve as a valet to Cardinal Heard, used to bring the latter down to the Cortile in time to get the car at 9.10 am.

The first morning I got Cardinal Godfrey down in good time and when Cardinal Heard arrived he barked that we were early. The next morning he fairly galloped down the stairs ahead of us and was waiting at the bottom to say to Cardinal Godfrey that he was late. What went on at the other end is no one's business but I gather that Cardinal Heard would gallop down the steps to the car whilst Cardinal Godfrey might delay talking to some other Cardinal and then there was a frightful row when they both got into the back seat.

It all sounds very childish but . . . with those particular Eminences it was almost inevitable. One must say that this was the first and last time that such an arrangement was attempted and I breathed a sigh of relief when, on the following occasion, the Cardinal agreed that I should insist upon a separate vehicle.

Divisions of a more fundamental character were also appearing in the ranks of the prelates in Rome preparing for the Council.

To state it briefly, one must say that this November session was the most important of all Sessions, not because the matters discussed were necessarily of greater moment than those considered at other Sessions, rather it was the first sign of positions being adopted, groupings formed and, most important of all, a clear indication given to the Curia and the members of the other Commissions that those outside Rome also had a viewpoint. From the very first meeting it was clear that members of the Central Commission did not propose to serve merely as a sieve. When one comes to think of it, if you place about 40 cardinals round a table and ask them to discuss the views of others without giving their own views on the same subject, it was hoping too much to imagine that the Central Commission could merely be a rubber stamp. Every matter which came to the table had to be churned over and it was, at length. As the months went by one noticed that the first days of any Session usually saw little progress. It seemed impossible that the material due for discussion could be covered. But with the passage of time, members of the Commission became exhausted and were more prepared to let matters through – or at least have them hustled through – than they would be at the beginning of the session.

It was also at this November Session that battle was joined between the two parties. These parties had a number of names and at one stage it was thought that it was the Curia versus the rest. However, it soon became clear that there were a number of cardinals in Rome who did not adhere to the traditional viewpoints expressed by leading members of the Curia. Sometimes these groups were called the Conservatives and the Liberals, sometimes the Traditionalists and the Progressives, sometimes just plain Left and Right.

At this stage I may be allowed to insert another reminiscence which is strictly anachronistic for, if I remember rightly, the incident occurred in June 1962, at a time when things were going remarkably badly for the Macmillan Government in England. After one of the very long Sessions of the Central Commission, I found myself in the lift, descending into the Cortile S. Damaso, together with Cardinal Godfrey and Cardinal Döpfner of Berlin, who was certainly to be included among the Progressives. It would seem that there had been a long battle during that morning's Session between the Traditionalists or Conservatives (and Progressives or Liberals, according to your own point of view).

Cardinal Döpfner was evidently trying to make conversation and he must have seen an English newspaper of the time. In his guttural but precise English, he said to Cardinal Godfrey: 'The Conservatives seem to be having a tough fight at this time.' Cardinal Godfrey looked as though he had been slapped across the face and said: 'You think so?' The situation was rendered no easier by Cardinal Döpfner (who, by the way, had been transferred recently to Munich from Berlin: my earlier designation was therefore incorrect)[36] who went on to say: 'These Liberals, they are having some success, yes?' I think it was the fact that the German Cardinal had apparently described himself as a

Liberal rather than as a Progressive, which made me realise that he was talking about the by-elections in England and not about the battles within the Central Commission. Luckily he went on to ask if Macmillan was worried but only then did Cardinal Godfrey realise what had happened.[37]

I have mentioned the formation of various groupings and although these became even more apparent as the various sessions took place, they were evident from the earliest days. Certainly their leaders showed their hands from the earliest days. Doubtless they will become even more clearly defined in the Council itself, but one cannot believe that they will differ much in their position from that which they adopted during those important days in November 1961.

Although, as I have said, there were a certain number of Roman cardinals who were not as Right as others, generally speaking the members of the Curia could be counted upon to rally to the cause of tradition. The undoubted leader of this group within the Curia was Cardinal Ottaviani, especially after the death of Cardinal Tardini in the summer of 1961. Here was the true and traditional voice of the Holy Office[38] – and I must say that, for my insignificant opinion, my money was with him.[39] There have been times in the past when I have felt quite honestly critical of the Holy Office, at the time of the ban upon our membership of the Council of Christians and Jews, which I always felt was worthy of being banned but not for the reasons given by the Holy Office.[40] However in the early battles of the Central Commission there can be no doubt that Cardinal Ottaviani was one of the outstanding figures.

*   *   *

There can be no doubt that the leader of the opposition to Cardinal Ottaviani was Cardinal Bea, a Jesuit and a German and a Biblical scholar into the bargain. He attacked from the word go and to his side flocked those who came to be known as the Progressives or Liberals. They were also called the Teutons, because their most prominent members were Cardinal Koenig of Vienna, Cardinal Döpfner of Munich, Cardinal Alfrink of Holland and then such people as Bishop Suhr of Copenhagen and one or two German bishops in missionary territories. One cannot quite be sure at the moment but one imagines that they could carry Cardinal Montini of Milan[41] with them. Cardinal Montini has had his critics in Rome since the days of Pius XII but one imagines that his backing next October[42] will be heavily German. The most prominent Italian Cardinal outside Rome has so far undoubtedly been Cardinal Siri of Genoa. When the newspapers describe him as Right of Right, such reports are probably an understatement of his rightness.

The position of the French is rather more difficult to determine. Regarding themselves as the eldest daughter of the Church, they do not seem to know whether they should slap their mother's face or just be beastly to the Germans.

Then there is undoubtedly an English-speaking group. The Americans and Canadians, together with the Australians, Irish and Scots have found in Cardinal Godfrey their principal spokesman. I must confess that this has surprised me: it certainly surprised the Cardinal, the more so as he has never to my knowledge ever consulted any of them concerning their views. One reason for the prominent position he has achieved is undoubtedly his masterly use of simple Latin: the Americans are not good in this respect and are flattered into support when they can understand what is being said. Another reason is that, because of his long experience in Rome, he is known to the Roman cardinals who are delighted to give their support to someone who gives expression to their views but who is not a member of the Curia. On the other hand because he is a residential bishop,[43] he has the support of many residential bishops who find in his plain statements of the kind of difficulties and experiences which we have in Westminster an easy expression of their own experiences and difficulties.

This is not an attempt to belittle what has undoubtedly been a very great achievement. Westminster, which has always been so proud of the role of Cardinal Manning in the First Vatican Council,[44] undoubtedly already has the name of its seventh archbishop in the history of the church so far as the Second Vatican Council is concerned. Word about this seems to have trickled out of Rome and we hope that it will have been good for humility in the North of England to realise that in the opinion of others the achievement outweighs the importance of being a member of the Secretariat for Christian Unity![45]

*　　　　*　　　　*

It will not be out of place for me to pay tribute here to the laborious way in which the Cardinal set about his task. I am quite sure that whatever pre-eminence he achieved during the Sessions of the Central Commission, it was due in large measure to the trouble which he had taken prior to the meetings to formulate his thoughts. His views may not have been original but they were clearly set out and I am quite convinced that one of the reasons why so many people gave their vote '*ad mentem Cardinalis Godfrey*'[46] was because he presented a common sense point of view in language easily understood. There is no doubt that the Cardinal enjoyed this part of his work considerably. I do not mean the preparation but I do mean the delivery of his *vota*.[47] My only regret was that the typing of them always seemed to be at the last minute. No matter how long in advance the booklets[48] reached us in England – and the Cardinal would work his way through them all perhaps twice before we left for Rome –

it was only the rarest occasions that before leaving for Rome, I was handed a sheet of paper and told that this would do to get on with. It usually meant that I had half as much typing to do on the actual night of arrival in Rome. After that we were back to the usual drudgery.

*　　　　　*　　　　　*

What caused the fat to fall into the fire during those famous meetings of November 1961? I see that the first item on the Agenda was entitled (my translation) 'Concerning non-Catholics to be invited to the Second Vatican Ecumenical Council'. After this item is the magic name of Cardinal Bea. There is no doubt that there was a fairly sharp division of opinion on this issue. It seemed that Cardinal Bea wanted as much of the Council as possible to take place fully in the open and that non-Catholic religious leaders should be present all the way. You can imagine how a man like Cardinal Godfrey reacted to this. He is always shocked if two fifth-rate curates disagree about anything in front of a layman, so you can imagine what his reaction was at the suggestion that Archbishop Ramsey should be present to hear the Bishop of Leeds or some other character like that disagree with another member of our Hierarchy.

I must say that I sympathise with him though my views are not important in this, but it would seem that for this first meeting the Traditionalists were fairly polite to Cardinal Bea. Polite but firm. I think that other members of the Curia had not realised that they might be nursing an asp in the bosom of Mother Church and in any case thought they would all be able to settle it quite peacefully afterwards when the other members of the Commission were out of the way. From what has been announced subsequently I would think that Cardinal Bea had some success at this session. More likely he was merely acquainting the members of the Central Commission regarding a policy which he may already have been given by the Holy Father. At least the Traditionalists won in that non-Catholics were to be invited only as observers and then only at certain sessions.

There seem to have been a great many *iuxta modums*[49] on this one and indeed one got the impression that views were expressed but no solid vote was taken.

The balloon went up concerning the second item of Agenda entitled *Formula nova professionis fidei* for which item Cardinal Ottaviani was responsible. I seem to remember that as we drove to the Vatican that day the Cardinal remarked that this booklet must have its origins in the views of the Holy Office and so that there would not be much discussion. Perhaps he was echoing in his own way what Cardinal Heard said viz: 'These men in Rome, who are the experts, have got all this together, so what's the point in arguing? You can't improve on them.' And here was the big bang. As far as I can remember discussion went on for at least two or three days and at the end of it no formal decision was taken because of an obvious division of opinion. Cardinal Ottaviani undertook to withdraw the booklet and to consider whether any revision was desirable in the light of what he had heard. He must have known that put to a vote it would have been rejected.

Not that there was very much to which we in England would have taken any objection. It was just that here was the occasion when the opposition rose up and said that they would not be dictated to by the Holy Office. They knew what was best for their dioceses and there was no point in the Holy Office insisting that all these things must be served up in the same precise form to all groups of the faithful in all parts of the world. Here was the first clash on the authority of the Holy Office which some have taken to be a clash on the authority of the Holy See. Even now it is probably too early to say which is the correct assessment. But battle was certainly joined.

I have said that this second item of the Agenda occupied two or three days of discussion. The third item was *De Fontibus Revelationis* also to be dealt with by Cardinal Ottaviani. I gather on this he had a little more success but again I do not think it was put to the vote. The opposition seems to have come from Cardinal Bea who was all for cutting out anything which was not strictly necessary, and who gave the impression of falling over backwards in order not to offend non-Catholics. His attitude was regarded by others as implying that Catholics must continually be beating their breasts in an unwarranted manner in order to avoid giving offence to Protestants. This was very much the position which he adopted throughout the meetings of the Central Commission and I can recall that on one occasion Cardinal Godfrey was positively shocked by the manner of the attack on the Holy Office.

The rather wider attack on the Curia as such was led off by Cardinal Alfrink who, in a rather exaggerated manner according to my informants claimed that the Curia was 'bureaucracy run riot' and that all the Monsignori would be much better employed out in the parishes which were short of priests. I suppose that most people felt that there is always a danger of bureaucracy in any form of central government but few would have been willing to attack that central government in this way. At first it was all thought to be rather a joke until it became clear that the Germans, Cardinal Koenig and a number of others, were prepared to back Cardinal Alfrink to the hilt. This took everyone by surprise and Rome was full of rumour.

Officially the matters under discussion were absolutely confidential but it would seem that the Italians have different ideas about confidence from our own. A press release of some character, usually giving the historical background to the point under discussion that day was released by the Vatican to the Press and used to appear in the evening after the discussion had taken place (even though issued before) in the *Osservatore*.[50] On the other hand a fairly detailed account of the actual discussions appeared at this stage in the *Messagero*[51] who not only knew what had been said in the meetings of the Central Commission but also who had said them. Either the *Messagero* got tired of this or else the General Secretariat discovered the source of the leak and clamped down. So far as I remember no similar reports appeared at other Sessions. With regard to the rather curious procedure of issuing this historical background or *status quaestionis* before the meeting took place it must be said that this method was adopted by Monsignor Felici so as to ensure that in what was issued to the Press there could be no reference, direct or indirect, to the actual discussion which took place.

There was always a certain amount of dissatisfaction regarding these Press releases. Some thought them too full and likely to give rise to comment and others that they were not full enough. From my knowledge of the Press I would say that the Press Office would have been advised to issue either less or more. If you give the Press more than the minimum and indicate lines of thought, then it is inevitable that they will make conjecture regarding further developments. Given such a situation it is probably better to issue more and rule out unreliable conjecture. I am usually on the side of the Press but I think that in this case the General Secretariat might have been wiser to say less. Sometimes by their mere mention of a subject under discussion, they would lead newspapers in other countries to make altogether false conclusions.

Let us give an example. On one occasion the Central Commission was discussing the Sacraments and they announced one day that the Cardinals were discussing the Sacrament of Confirmation, the age at which it was to be administered, the person by whom it was to be administered and so on. Given this information the journalist has to draw some conclusion and so it was widely reported that members of the Commission were considering recommending that the age at which at which Confirmation was to be received should be raised. They could hardly have suggested that it should be lowered! Press relations are always difficult and it remains to be seen how they will cope with the great influx of journalists likely to be in Rome next October.

Where the *Messagero* got its information is still unknown to me but it was enough to fan the rumours which already existed. On the other hand some of the members of the Commission and the consultors would give pretty broad hints that all was not well. After the first week of meetings, I heard Bishop Suhr of Copenhagen telling a notoriously garrulous Servite that he hoped in the course of the second week the Commission would gets it first *Placet*.[52] If this sort of thing was being said generally, and I rather imagine that, here was food for the rumour-mongers.

The situation seems to have been eased by the introduction of humour.

When the second week of meetings began it seemed quite hopeless that all the remaining points on the Agenda could be covered. But this was reckoning without the next Cardinal Relator, Cardinal Ciriaci, who had to introduce a series of booklets on the discipline of the clergy.

Looking more than ever like the French comic Fernandel, Cardinal Ciriaci proved himself for all time the master of the Latin language and joked his way through the most complicated material. I gather that he was absolutely fluent and easy to understand. Amongst the members and consultors on this Commission were a number who had been his students when he had lectured at Propaganda.[53] They knew him of old and were ready with the laughs which encouraged him still more. Under this benign influence the heats and tensions of the previous week gradually reduced and, generally speaking, the matters under discussion, though important, were not such as to cause the battles which had taken place earlier. In so far as these matters dealt with the discipline of the clergy, there were often subjects about which the Cardinal wished to speak.

I recall that amongst these was the question of the use of the cassock and whether we should be allowed to wear grey suits instead. This was typical of the sort of item where there was a ready made division between the Progressives[54] and the Liberals. The former said that the cassock should be retained as it was a safeguard to the priests and the very sign of their Priesthood: the latter said that, off the altar, there was little point in making a priest too different in appearance from those amongst whom he must work and certainly he should not be impeded by having to wear a cassock. One might imagine from what was said that a priest spent all his day upon a bicycle.

Thus this last week passed on the discussion of the ways of clerical life, the obligations to provide and if necessary to divide parishes; and all the things about which bishops have views but about which there was a general measure of agreement. The whole speed of procedure increased and the final meeting took place on the morning of the Friday and we were able to fly back to London the following day, 24 hours earlier than anticipated.

I have dealt with this Session at considerable length because I consider that what took place in Rome during those two weeks will be of the greatest consequence in the future of the Church. It was the time when the Curia learned that there were opinions outside Rome and that those outside Rome were not prepared to accept the ruling of the Curia as the last word and without discussion. If it was a shock to the Curia it was also a shock to such members of the Sacred College as Cardinal Heard and I think that I can truthfully say that one of the reasons why things went more easily during the second week was that the Curial gentry had decided that time and place were on their side and the thing to do was to get these meetings over as quickly as possible. They surely imagined that once the residential Bishops had returned to their Sees, then those left behind in Rome could get on with the job. When it was made clear that the residential bishops attached the greatest importance to these meetings and even suggested that a Central Commission should be preserved after the Council as a cabinet of advisers for the Pope, the Romans decided that the only thing to do was to shake off the outsiders by arranging for further meetings to be held sufficiently frequently that those outside Rome simply would be unable to make the journey.

In the light of what happened this may seem a puerile point of view but I have little doubt in my own mind that this was the attitude in the Curia after that November Session. At the end of the Session it was announced that the next Session would take place in the middle of January. It was still believed at that stage that the Council would not start for perhaps another two or three years and there was quite an outcry amongst the bishops who were furthest afield that having to come back so soon would be exceedingly difficult for them. However, they received little sympathy from the Romans who saw in this difficulty precisely the opportunity for which they were hoping to get on with the work themselves.

But it did not work out like. When we got back I was repeatedly asked when the Council would take place and I must say that I had fallen for the idea that it was unlikely to commence before the autumn of 1963. All the members of the Central Commission, after their November experience, were claiming that they needed more time to examine these booklets which were being presented for their approval. The Germans were saying: 'It is more important that the Council should take place well than that it should take place.' However it seemed that the Holy Father thought otherwise and one does not yet know whether he pressed for its opening in 1962 because he feared that the Council might outlive his pontificate.

At all events he announced before Christmas that the Council would definitely open before the end of 1962. No precise date was given at this stage and it may be that he was awaiting further reports before committing himself. But it was only a matter of weeks before he announced the date for the opening, 11th October and we all knew then that the pressure was on. Indeed the members of the Central Commission knew that the pressure was on almost immediately after Christmas when they received the dates, not just of the Third Session in January but of all the Sessions right up to the end of June. There had already been two Sessions of the Central Commission; there would have to be a further five within the first six months of 1962.

It appeared formidable and so it has proved. Each Session was of at least ten days' duration and this meant that we should have to spend roughly ten days of every month out of the diocese and out of the country. What it really meant was that one had to compress into three weeks one's normal month's work and then go out and do ten days' hard work on top of that. It has been a wearying experience and needless to say one has come to know very well the appearance of the Alps from 30,000 feet. In this connection one may be allowed to say how much our labours have been eased by the kindness of the people at London Airport who have been particularly friendly and have given every possible facility, cutting down all tiresome waits and questionings.

I must confess that when I saw the dates set for the five Sessions in the first six months of 1962, I was confirmed in my opinion that here was evidence that the Curia was endeavouring to shake off the influence of the Cardinals from outside Rome. The Pope had said that the council must take priority over all other commitments but could it reasonably be hoped that Cardinals would go backwards and forwards to Rome every month? I have little doubt that the Curia entertained no such hope and, with full guile,[55] deliberately plotted a programme which would enable them to get on with the preparation of the material for the Council without outside interference. They were mistaken.

If attendance at the November meeting had been 90 per cent, attendance at the January meeting was certainly not less than 80 per cent. It was a remarkable effort but two months had passed since the previous session and one wondered how many would turn up in February. Suffice it to say that throughout the sessions of the Central Commission numbers never fell, some bishops went backwards and forwards over an incredible distance: the little bishop from Vietnam turned up time and again; and I am proud to say that we never missed. But the journey from London was nothing compared with, say, that of Cardinal McIntyre flying across from Los Angeles.

Notes

1 The late Peter Nichols, London *Times* correspondent in Rome during this period, was not persuaded. In *The Pope's Divisions*, Faber and Faber, 1981, he wrote: 'Like many people, I mistook it for the greatest religious event of the century. Something worthy of that name has yet to come.' He felt the dramatic reforms of the Council itself had subsequently been undermined by the machinations of the Vatican Curia. It is difficult to suggest any religious event since 1965 that has eclipsed it in importance, however.

2 For more on this theme see *From Newman to Congar* by Aidan Nichols OP, T&T Clark, 1990.

3 Adrian Hastings says of Godfrey that 'no-one was more sure of his mind or had less to offer that was unexpected' (*A History of English Christianity 1920–1990*, SCM, 1991, p. 478. As Rector of the English College in the 1930s he was said to have put up a notice forbidding the possession of Protestant Bibles (p. 274).

4 By Giuseppe Alberigo and Joseph A. Komonchak, Orbis/Peters, 1995.

5 *Ibid.*, p. 504.

6   *Ibid.*, p. 501.

7   *Ibid.*, p. 508. Alberigo says that many of the ideas in these preparatory papers, so igno-
    miniously abandoned, 'would surreptitiously find their way back into the various
    constitutions and decrees'. That may be why Peter Nichols was eventually to be disap-
    pointed.

8   This is Worlock's own title for it.

9   There has to be some doubt about the significance of this date, as the first page of the
    Vatican II diary (as far as 'New Year's Eve') shows every sign of having been written
    some while after subsequent pages. No manuscript is available: Worlock's own file copy
    is in a different typeface and even a different literary style from the rest; and later pages
    have an immediacy (and lack of hindsight) that suggests a contemporaneous record. It
    is more likely this first page was revised from an earlier draft in June 1962, to add a jus-
    tification for his decision to keep a diary despite having taken an oath of secrecy.

10 There are indeed many unfinished diaries, some barely started, some kept for months,
    in the earlier Worlock papers. Often they open with a firm declaration that 'this time',
    the diary will be kept up, only to fade away after a few dozen pages. This may explain
    the myth, widely believed by many who dealt with him, that he had kept a complete
    daily journal throughout his lifetime. The only diaries he kept continuously were desk
    diaries, used for appointments, messages and notes.

11 Catholic code for not yet having been made a cardinal. Worlock is being characteristi-
    cally sardonic, as in his reference to 'this performance'.

12 A study centre used for conferences, run by an association of lay Catholics called The
    Grail.

13 Auxiliary Bishop of Westminster.

14 Worlock gives an alternative version in his Introduction to his *Give Me Your Hand*, St
    Paul Publications, 1977: 'Eighteen years have passed,' he wrote there, 'since on 25th
    January 1959 a newspaperman telephoned me to say 'Pope John's done it again. He's
    called an ecumenical Council. Your comments, please.' All I could remember from my
    theological training was my professor's opinion that with the coming of the dogma of
    infallibility there would never need to be another council.'

15 A London residence used by Archbishops of Westminster when they wanted to get
    away from the office.

16 Members of religious orders. 'Dispensing enclosure' means giving permission for a
    member of an enclosed religious order, usually female, to leave a religious house or
    convent.

17 Canon Bernard Pawley, one of the Anglican observers at the Council, reported with a
    shudder in his *Rome and Canterbury Through Four Centuries*, Mowbrays, 1974, that one
    English bishop had written in his diocesan newsletter 'It is an open secret that bishops
    are assembling with great hopes of new definitions to supplement the dogmas of the
    Catholic Faith already revealed. It is my own personal hope that the Holy Father will
    see fit to crown our love of our glorious and Blessed Mother, Queen of Heaven and Ever
    Virgin, with the definition of the dogmas of *Maria Mediatrix* and *Maria fons gratiae*,
    which have ever been in the prayers and devotions of the faithful.'

18 A form of canon law directive.

19 One of the northern seminaries.

20 The nearest Worlock ever gets to a blue joke!

21 The bishop in charge of Catholic military and naval chaplains.

22 What he probably means is that it would have been nice if they had appointed himself.

23 'the boys' as in 'jobs for . . .'

24 London W1.

25 3 December 1960, the first visit of an Archbishop of Canterbury to the Vatican since the Reformation.

26 The official Vatican photographer had the same surname.

27 The Rome seminary for mature English-speaking student priests.

28 One reason for the confusion was the fact that the forthcoming Council was officially described as an 'Ecumenical Council'. This may have been technically correct, to distinguish it from a local or regional council ('ecumenical' means world-wide). But the word 'ecumenical' was already in use among Anglicans and Protestants to describe the process of building Church unity, mainly through the World Council of Churches (which even sometimes described itself as 'the ecumenical movement'). It has yet another use in the Eastern Orthodox context.

29 *Rome and Canterbury Through Four Centuries*, Mowbrays, 1974.

30 *A Crown of Thorns*, Hodder and Stoughton, 1974.

31 *Ibid.*, p. 343.

32 Or, to be exact, with Heenan.

33 He writes (*ibid.*): 'The Bishop of Bruges was rather reluctant to meet any other bishops as his communication was highly confidential, but I persuaded him that GPD [George Patrick Dwyer, later Archbishop of Birmingham] was safe . . .'

34 After the Council he started a schismatic movement and was later excommunicated for ordaining bishops without papal approval and for rejecting some of the key doctrines of Vatican II such as religious liberty.

35 From Heenan's unpublished Vatican II diary.

36 This correction 'on the hoof', as it were, arises because Worlock was dictating this into his recording machine.

37 This was the time of the famous Orpington by-election which was won, to the surprise and dismay of the Conservative Government, by the Liberal Party candidate Eric Lubbock.

38 Full title the Holy Office of the Inquisition, which later became the Sacred Congregation for the Doctrine of the Faith. This senior department of the Curia was responsible for clergy discipline and for ensuring orthodoxy, and eliminating heresy, from among the faithful. The Roman Inquisition was never as terrible as the Spanish Inquisition, though in its own way it was still to be feared.

39 Here is the first time Derek Worlock places himself firmly in the conservative camp.

40 Later in his career he was to give a far more sympathetic account of his attitude to the banning of the Council of Christians and Jews.

41 Soon to become Pope Paul VI.

42 When the Council opens.

43 That is, he resides in his home diocese.

44 He was one of the main architects of the decree defining papal infallibility in 1870, and a leading proponent of the 'ultramontane', highly centralized view of the Catholic Church (which the Second Vatican Council greatly modified).

45 In fact the verdict of history has been the exact opposite. Archbishop Heenan of Liverpool (later Godfrey's successor as Cardinal Archbishop of Westminster) became an important voice in the Council and afterwards; Godfrey's own role is virtually forgotten.

46 In favour of Cardinal Godfrey's position.

47 His reasoned position for or against a proposal.
48 This is Worlock's expression for the draft documents etc. that were sent out before each meeting.
49 Qualified agreement.
50 *Osservatore Romano*, the Vatican daily newspaper.
51 A secular Rome daily paper.
52 A yes vote.
53 Propaganda Fidei, the department of the Curia concerned with foreign missions.
54 This is surely a mistake: Worlock must mean the Conservatives.
55 Underlining is Worlock's own in his typescript.

3

The Battle of the Lists

The recording and subsequent revelation of the private foolishness of great men is one of the chief pleasures of the diarist's art, except that in this case Worlock is among his own victims. His loyalty to Cardinal Godfrey, and his tendency to make a personal enemy out of anyone who did not accord Godfrey the deference Worlock thought he deserved – for instance Cardinal Heard, or Archbishop Heenan – occasionally led him to the heights of absurd pomposity. Similarly, throughout the various meetings of the Central Preparatory Commission, Worlock portrays Godfrey as a key player when the verdict of history has been pretty unanimous that he was not much more than a minor one.

There was a character trait in Derek Worlock that meant whatever he was involved in had to be special, out of the ordinary, at the centre of the stage. Often it was so in fact. Sometimes his saying so made it become so: these things can be self-fulfilling. But sometimes he said it was when it really wasn't. There was nothing meek and mild in Worlock's approach, as in the childish wrangling he describes (and takes part in) over the celebrations of the 600th anniversary of the English College in Rome and the trivial quarrel he provoked over precedence between the two Cardinals involved, Heard and Godfrey. Worlock became remarkably worked up about it. Given its triviality, and how ungracious it made him look, it is surprising that he chose to record it at such length and with such vehemence. He seemed at this period to lack all insight into his own attitudes and conduct. He was self-righteous: sometimes he was a bully. He was beginning to develop, however, a shrewd judgement about the likely progress of the Second Vatican Council. He was among the first (at least among the English) to recognize the extent of the upheaval that was about to overtake the Catholic Church. And in sniffing the way the wind was blowing, he was preparing to move with it. Nor was this a cynical calculation. He was a loyal servant of his master the Cardinal because he was above all a loyal servant of his mistress the Church. Her wish was his command.

Worlock's personal faith was elusive; but, paradoxically, wide open. It was elusive in that it is rare to find in his writings any statement of a personal conviction. What he really thought and felt about his faith is hard to excavate. On the other hand it was wide open. He would be the first to insist that he believed what the Church believed; and that what the Church believed was plain for all to see. If it changed – or to use a characteristic Catholic expression, 'developed' – then his faith changed (or 'developed') likewise. This is very much a Catholic thing, even rather shocking to members of other Churches. It invests the Church with a decisive role in the authoritative interpretation of the content of Christian belief. This made sense to Catholics like Worlock because the Church for them was not merely a natural body but also a supernatural one, charged, so to speak, with divine energy and authority.

When Worlock routinely said the Nicene Creed, he would mean the words 'We believe in One Holy Catholic and Apostolic Church' to be a continuation of 'We believe in one God, the Father, the Almighty . . . We believe in one Lord, Jesus Christ . . . We believe in the Holy Spirit'; in each case the words 'We believe' being a similar declaration of faith. And the One Holy Catholic and Apostolic Church that would have been present in his mind as the object of this fourth declaration of faith would be the Roman Catholic Church itself, not some formless wraith comprising all baptized Christians. This religious devotion towards the Catholic Church strikes some Protestants as verging on idolatry. For them, the fourth 'We believe' of the Nicene Creed is not like the previous three. It certainly does not elevate the Catholic Church, or any other, to the status of being an object of Christian faith like the Three Persons of the Trinity. But to understand Worlock's personal religious development during the years of the Second Vatican Council, it is necessary to see the Catholic Church through his eyes. Whatever it did, was right. More or less.

*　　　*　　　*

It is not the purpose of this document to give a complete record of all the views expressed by Cardinal Godfrey at the various Sessions of the Central Commission. His written *vota* are in our files and one imagines that future historians will also have access to the records preserved at the Vatican. It will however have been seen from what has been written that the Cardinal had a great deal to say at this particular session on a number of practical issues with which he has personally been concerned. Once again one had the impression that he was emerging as a key figure in the Commission. Cardinal Alfrink has written that in some ways the work of the Commission was more important than the Council itself: that remains to be seen but there can be no doubt about the part played by the Cardinal and the role he was achieving through being acceptable to the Romans as one of themselves and to the residential bishops on account of his experience in Liverpool and London.

It was at an audience at the end of this Session that the Holy Father made reference to this when speaking to the Cardinal, who of course was delighted. Indeed he had every reason to be so. The Pope told him that he had heard from many quarters that the views expressed by the English Cardinal were – and I use the translation which the Cardinal used himself when telling me of the incident – 'something special'. The Pope thanked him and congratulated him and I have never seen the Cardinal happier than when he emerged from that audience. I gather that the Pope went further and told him about the small Committee of Amendment. This was made up of four or five Cardinals whose task was to batter the *schemata* into shape in the light of the discussions which had taken place at the Central Commission. It seems that they had been meeting in the evening. They comprised a couple of Romans and Cardinal Siri and Cardinal Léger. Possibly because of the pressure of work the Pope was wondering whether they would be able to complete their task and he warned the Cardinal that it might be necessary to bring him on to this small Committee. However the Pope insisted that nothing was settled yet.

I do not know whether the Cardinal really wanted to serve on this committee or not. It would have been a great honour but it would have been a great burden and we spent the next few weeks wondering whether and when we might be called back to Rome. As things turned out, they seem to have brought Cardinal Browne in and the work went ahead without having to trouble Cardinal Godfrey. At all events it is nice to think that he was in such a strong position that he should be considered for such a task, though it would have wrought havoc with our work in England and I doubt whether the Cardinal's health would have stood up to the evening meetings after the long morning Sessions of the Central Commission. It certainly would have limited him in the time he had to give to the preparation of his *vota* for the final Session in June. Even the possibility of his inclusion in this Committee remained absolutely secret.

I think that the Cardinal told Bishop Cashman but apart from that I was the only one who knew. Word of it never reached the Press nor other members of the Hierarchy but word did start at this stage to get back to England about the strength of the Cardinal's position. The Delegate[1] heard from various American friends, including Monsignor Brennan, the Dean of the Rota, and I suspect and hope that similar reports reached Liverpool.[2] Wherever one has been in

England these last few weeks one has been conscious of the fact that people have known the heavy demands which the Council has made upon the Cardinal's energy and time, but more of this would seem to lie in the future.

*   *   *

The holding of this Session in the middle of June provided another complication. The previous year the Rector had asked the Cardinal about the observance of the sixth centenary of the foundation of the English Hospice.[3] He had wanted to hold it at Trinity[4] as this was the titular feast of the chapel and the Cardinal had explained that with Trinity ordinations, few if any of the bishops could be there. Personally I think that John Tickle[5] welcomed this in order to give the new Cardinal Protector, Cardinal Heard, a free run.

When it was realised that the Cardinal would be in Rome for the celebrations at Trinity an awkward situation arose. As soon as we arrived at the College we were informed by the students that the Pope was going to receive the College authorities and students in audience on the Friday morning and that Cardinal Heard was going to pontificate[6] in the chapel on the Sunday morning. There would be a reception at the College on the Thursday afternoon. Jock said nothing about all this to the Cardinal but it soon became clear to me that he hoped that the Cardinal would stay out of the way. After a few days this was suggested to me quite openly and I was asked outright whether the Cardinal would expect to be at the audience on the Friday morning. I pointed out that it was not for the Cardinal to suggest anything at all. If the Pope summoned him with the other members of the College he would of course be there but he would have no wish to gatecrash if Cardinal Heard felt it was his sole preserve. I hastened to add, however, that I thought that all concerned might have considerable difficulty in explaining to people in England and possibly even in Rome why Cardinal Godfrey, one of the most distinguished Rectors of the College and actually present in Rome at the time, had not been included in the audience. It became quite clear that the opposition really came from Cardinal Heard.

It was all very sickening and a difficult situation arose when the students began to ask Cardinal Godfrey if he would be with them. Even on the Thursday night nothing was settled and I spoke to Jock in the morning in a way in which I was quite sure he would have to pass on to Cardinal Heard. I pointed to the embarrassing position in which we had been placed, the dangers of misunderstanding and at the same time our unwillingness to take any step without the concurrence of Cardinal Heard as Cardinal Protector of the College.

On the Thursday afternoon there was a reception at the College for clerics and laity. It was quite a big affair and the Cardinal purposely did not go down into the garden where the reception was being held until half an hour after it had started. As soon as he appeared he was surrounded by friends and he remained there until the bitter end talking most patiently to anyone who approached him. Cardinal Heard on the other hand put in a fleeting appearance announcing that he wished to go to another reception given by Prince Colonna and generally showing himself completely out of tune with the spirit of the reception. The effect on Nobby Clark and others was immediate and overpowering. For the first time they suddenly realised in what a false position they had placed themselves. By the end of the Reception Jock having had a hurried word with Cardinal Heard who had returned from the Colonna reception came to me to ask me to plead with Cardinal Godfrey to attend the audience the following morning. Cardinal Heard would be most distressed if Cardinal Godfrey felt unable to attend. It was just that he did not think that people in the Vatican would be expecting a second Cardinal, etc. etc. We told him that we had little doubt that the Vatican would be expecting a second Cardinal and His Eminence would answer the implied command of the Pope that he be present. Scarcely had we sorted this one out when Nobby Clark came to Cardinal Godfrey to thank him for all his kindness to the guests of the reception who had been almost affronted by the in-and-out tactics of Cardinal Heard.

The audience took place the following morning at 8.30. Cardinal Godfrey and I drove there separately from the other official party and moved in to the Consistorial Hall just as soon as the students had gathered. A second chair was provided for him, and Cardinal Heard came in and sat next to him and talked to him as if there had been no incident at all. How fickle prima donnas can be. The Pope delivered a delightful talk to the students who were a little disappointed when it was considered necessary that it should be interpreted to them.[7] As soon as the interpretation was over the Pope lent forward and said that he would now like to talk to them in his own words and proceeded to chat away in a most easy fashion. When he had finished he went and spoke to the two Cardinals and crossed the line in the front. It was my big moment. When he reached me – and I was on my knees – the Rector began to try to explain to the Pope who I was and to my unending pride the Pope gave me a big grin, looked across to the Cardinal, pulled me up off my knees and told the Rector that he knew who I was. It was a great moment.

All this sounds rather petty in retrospect but they were difficult days. When Cardinal Heard sang the Mass on the morning of Trinity Sunday Cardinal Godfrey and I kept out of the way until the Mass had started and then went up into the gallery to watch. I was awfully sorry for Cardinal Godfrey, though obviously he could not take his place in the sanctuary. Worse was to follow at lunch which was a splendid affair with very many guests, ambassadorial, clerical and lay, not to mention Cardinal Amleto Cicognani, the Secretary of State. Cardinal Heard, as Cardinal Protector, presided. At the end of the meal the Rector made a very good and very amusing speech in which he skated on thin ice with his customary evasive skill. One never quite knows how polished this performance is but it is most effective and causes a great deal of amusement.

When Cardinal Heard rose to reply it was worse than I would have thought possible. He quite deliberately proceeded to attack the Hierarchy claiming that they did nothing to help the College, the full burden of which fell on the shoulders of the Rector. He referred to the outstanding building works which the Rector was carrying out and made absolutely no mention of the fact that the latter was only carrying out these works on the instructions of the bishops and after Cardinal Godfrey had secured for him from the bishops a grant of £10,000. In his endeavours to praise the Rector he went on to say that the poor Rector spent all his day trying to look after pilgrims[8] and even worked late into the night typing letters. The boys thought this most amusing because they knew how seldom the Rector ever put pen to paper. And when Cardinal Heard said that he frequently heard the Rector's typewriter tapping out across the cortile, there was some considerable amusement because the only typewriter which was heard in those days was my own, hammering away *vota* for Cardinal Godfrey to turn into the Central Commission. Even the Rector was embarrassed by this.

I must confess that when we went upstairs after lunch to have coffee and liqueurs with the students I was flaming angry with the Cardinal Protector and had the greatest difficulty in restraining myself from saying anything. I suppose that the boys thought it was a bit of a joke that Cardinal Heard should have been indiscreet: young men are apt to be amused by such a situation but there is no doubt that Cardinal Godfrey personally was very hurt indeed.

More or less as a sop the Rector then invited the Cardinal to give Benediction at 4.30 and the Cardinal graciously agreed. I was quite determined that he should have every possible honour for the occasion and even though my presence would add little to this I was determined to go on as his Master of Ceremonies[9] in order to show that a Cardinal Archbishop of Westminster should not be outdone. When the College MC came to me and more or less hinted that I should keep off the square[10] I let him commit himself and then gently and firmly told him that England's Cardinal had been sufficiently insulted that day and that although the students regarded it as a great day for themselves they must also remember that it was a great day for the Cardinal who had given so many years of service to the College.[11] Accordingly I for one was not prepared to deny him any right to which he was entitled and as his rights included that of having his own personal Master of Ceremonies I should be there. The boy was a little taken aback but saw the point and later came to me and apologised. I do not often ride the high horse like this but it was a lesson the young man had to learn. In the event when I reached the sanctuary I knelt to one side and told the boy to carry on. Honour was thereby served on all sides.

The climax came that evening at the end of supper at which the Cardinal Protector was not present. The Rector rose to say that no College function could ever be complete without Cardinal Godfrey and they wanted to propose a drink to his health. The Cardinal then rose and spoke off the cuff what was quite the best speech I have ever heard him give in his life. He spoke of the glory of the College, its traditions, its martyrs, and its role in preparing priests for the English Mission.[12] He went on to talk about the priesthood and although he is always at his best when talking to priests and students he really excelled himself that night. The ovation he received at the end was unprecedented and I do not think that anyone present will ever forget. Certainly Dr William Purdy who was present wrote to this effect in the *Tablet* the following week and I know from the students how much this particular talk meant to them. Thereby an end came to what was a most difficult situation, certainly not of our making, and there is no doubt that both the Rector and the Vice-Rector learned a very real lesson. So, I suspect, did the Cardinal Protector.

*   *   *

The Seventh Session then commenced on the Tuesday of Whit week, 12th June, and with a very heavy Agenda . . . Cardinal Masella, for the Sacraments, had two booklets: the first was on the preparation for Marriage (when Cardinal Godfrey had a great deal to say about the work of the Catholic Marriage Advisory Council and of the shift of emphasis from patching up marriages to preparing people for marriage); and the second – unhappy company – dealt with fallen priests.[13] Here Cardinal Godfrey again made one of his impassioned appeals that if this matter had to be discussed, no word of it should appear in any printed document subsequently. It was not a question of refusing to face up to facts but if mercy was to be shown to fallen priests one should have mercy also upon the faithful who could be scandalised by the mention of such matters just as they were scandalised by the fall of a priest. I gather that he commanded very great support for what he said and only one member of the Council openly said that the matter should be freely and fairly discussed.

And now at last, at this final and seventh Session, we got a look at the booklets on the Commission for the Lay Apostolate. On the whole they do not appear to be particularly inspired and were pretty straightforward with no really revolutionary ideas. Rather to my surprise Cardinal Godfrey was most insistent that he should make known at this Session the work carried out by the members of my 'Team', emphasising the necessity of training before laymen are loosed upon missionary territory. He also made my pet points about the type of training the lay apostle should receive: sacramental, doctrinal, social and professional. The third consideration, and one upon which I am very keen, is that it is a mistaken belief to encourage priests to become experts in secular affairs in order to be able to guide the laity. It is the layman who must become an expert in union matters and other industrial subjects which are of such a great concern to the laymen today. The layman should then bring those problems to a priest for advice and guidance from the social principles which have been laid down by the Church. Whilst a priest must know about the conditions in which his people are living and working, it is totally unnecessary for him to become an expert in these industrial and secular matters: indeed in some ways it is better for him to steer clear of them but remain at hand to advise the layman in their treatment of the problem.

*   *   *

That morning the Pope had attended the first part of the meeting and delivered his final address of gratitude to the Central Commission. They have been stirring days and I think that in one matter at least I agree with Cardinal Alfrink, who appears to have stated that in some ways the work of the Central Commission may prove of greater importance than the Council itself. It will be interesting to see the outcome and whether some form of Central Commission will be preserved in the future, to serve as the Holy Father's international cabinet.

It has taken me many hours and many pages to reach this far but I think it has been worth while recording this background because it would seem to me that, anyhow in the early Sessions, a bloodless revolution took place in the Church when the Curia, already internationalised at a lower level, suddenly found themselves confronted with the Latin voice of the Universal Church.

*   *   *

Worlock liked to make snide remarks at the expense of Archbishop Heenan who was quickly emerging as a popular progressive; Godfrey as a conspicuous conservative (as therefore was Worlock). Progressives put much emphasis on the significance of the coming Council in fostering the reunification of a divided Christianity. Conservatives had centuries of habit on their side in regarding 'non-Catholics' (as they invariably called Christians of other denominations) as deluded rebels or ignoramuses. Even his humorous observations about the behaviour of non-Catholic observers at the opening of the Second Vatican Council enabled him to parade this distaste. Ironically, he saw no connection between this and the issue that was to preoccupy him on and off for the next few months – managing Godfrey's increasingly serious illness while keeping Church and public in ignorance of it. But the battle was ultimately in vain and Godfrey's untimely death cleared the way for Heenan to succeed him, and thus become Worlock's immediate boss. And so Worlock, too, became a progressive.

The alternative, probably, was resignation. That would have meant giving up his considerable handle on power, which had made him virtually indispensable to the efficient running of the operation. In any event, self-interest and loyalty to his master apart, the tide in the Church was running the progressives' way. Many participants in the Council were swept along with this at least as much as he was. It was a sincere conversion. But it wasn't one he liked to talk about. Nor was it a conversion to Heenan, personally. This was a clash which was to have the profoundest consequences for the Catholic Church in England and Wales, not least because Heenan later undermined Worlock's chances of succeeding him as Cardinal Archbishop of Westminster and thus paved the way for the Abbot of Ampleforth, Basil Hume.

*   *   *

It is interesting that during these past few weeks whilst making powerful progressive utterances at one moment, the Archbishop of Liverpool has seemed to be pulling back a little on the question of Unity. Maybe he is beginning to fear the recriminations at which we[14] have hinted so often as being likely to follow disappointment on the part of non-Catholics who have undoubtedly been encouraged by many of the things the Archbishop has said to expect far more than can possibly come from this Council in the Cause of Unity.

However, at the time of writing there is another thought which is uppermost in my mind. When I returned from holiday at the end of August I learned that the surgeon, Desmond Mulvany, had told the Cardinal that there must be yet one more operation of a kind rather similar to that which he underwent last Easter, only this time it has been for the removal of the glands from the other groin. I got the Cardinal into hospital secretly on 9th September and the following morning he underwent this further operation which proved rather more difficult than the ones before. On this occasion there was already infection there and, although we were able to move him back to Archbishop's House five days later, the wound then became infected and we had a very anxious week. Only on Friday last, 28th September, were we able to move him back to Hare Street and he is there at this time with David Norris,[15] resting and trying to regain strength. It has meant cancelling all the engagements arranged for the second part of September but so far we have got away with it – or at least we had done until two days ago when Bishop Cashman unfortunately said in a sermon at Clapton that the Cardinal was not well and must refrain from outdoor engagements if he was to take part in the Council.

There was a mild flurry in the Press at the weekend and we seem to have got off lightly. As things stand, it seems that there is reasonable hope that I shall be able to fly with him to Rome on 8th October. Even at that time the wound will still be open and one of the doctors will be in Rome for the first three weeks in order to carry out the daily dressing. Poor Cardinal, it would indeed be almost a death-blow to him if his great hopes of being able to take an important part in the Council were dashed to the ground through illness at this stage. What the future holds none can be sure and I must say that the prospect of being the only dog's body at the English College endeavouring to serve a sick Cardinal and about eighteen members of the Hierarchy is a sombre thought. Just how it will all work out we must hope that these pages will show.

*   *   *

9 October: By the grace of God and the favour of the Apostolic See[16] we flew to Rome yesterday, Monday 8th October. So many have been the hazards during the past few weeks that there have been times when I have wondered whether the Cardinal would make it. Although the surgeons claim that the operation was a success, the wound has taken a long time to heal and it was not until we were able to get him away to Hare Street that he began to recover strength. He really was not fit enough to come back to Archbishops House until Friday last by which time I had completed the many memoranda for the Hierarchy meeting. One wonders whether anyone in the future will ever take note of what goes into this informal diary but one point to remember is that the Hierarchy meeting in Rome in something to be avoided, as it is utterly dependent on consultation with official documents and papers and the idea of having to make a selection from all one's files of papers which might possibly be required is as terrifying as the selection is, in fact.

The weather in England yesterday was splendid, with a fine blue sky, and it was hard to believe as we drove out to London airport, that we should not be returning to London until shortly before Christmas; or at least that is the hope at the present time.

In next to no time we were through the customs and the journey to the College was without event . . . We got the Cardinal's bags unpacked and after he had a cup of tea he retired to bed where he slept until 6.30, when Dr Noel Moynihan came in to examine him. Noel Moynihan had a holiday owing to him and kindly agreed to spend three weeks of it here in Rome to coincide with the first part of the Cardinal's stay here. He reported that the Cardinal had made the journey well, the wound was no worse and I dispatched Michael Ashdowne to buy an electric stove and saucepan so that I could sterilise the instruments. It all takes one back to days of not so long ago.

Supper at the College was at 8.30, which I think the bishops found a little late but apparently it suited the nuns[17] best, though it looks as though it will make it increasingly difficult for as to have much contact with the students themselves. The idea is that they should eat three quarters of an hour before the bishops and be out of the way.

I got the Cardinal to bed shortly before eleven and having settled him for the night, retired to my room to try to get my own cases straight. I had not been there long before first Father Ashdowne and then Monsignor Clark[18] and finally the Rector himself all arrived in order to talk over plans. It is a delicate situation in that the Rector naturally regards himself as host but clearly it is beyond his resources to make all the arrangements which will be required for the easy conduct of a visit of eighteen bishops in the College. It was nearly midnight when I shooed them out but by then I had made up my mind that some definite plan and move would have to be made today before things ran too far out of control.

It was a 6.15 am rise this morning and I called the Cardinal at quarter to seven and saw that he was all right. In fact he had slept very well and I got him some hot coffee. I said Mass at 7.30 and the Cardinal followed at 8.00.

After breakfast my anxieties of last evening became more acute and one bishop after another came to me for direction and for answers to enquiries and there was really fear lest there should be some clash with the College authorities. I spoke with Archbishop Grimshaw and Archbishop Murphy[19] who agreed that the next move should be made and I suggested to the Cardinal that a meeting of the bishops be held in the new Council chamber at 6.30 in the evening to get things sorted out.

*   *   *

Between sixteen and twenty bishops (depending who you count) made up the English contingent at the Second Vatican Council. They arrived in Rome with little idea of what they were into. The English and Welsh bishops, with one or two exceptions, saw no great need for a Council of the Church. In this they were entirely in step with the other two Hierarchies of the British Isles, the Scots and the Irish. They took little heed of theological trends on the Continent (hence the row which quickly flared up – provoked by Heenan, Worlock indignantly records – about whether there were any real theologians among them).

Alberigo and Komonchak,[20] after exhaustive study of the replies of individual bishops to the pre-Council questionnaires the Vatican had circulated, found a distinct pattern of expectations among Catholic prelates who operated in mainly English-speaking Protestant countries. (They included Ireland, which of course was Catholic by a large majority but which still saw its Catholicism as under threat, for historical reasons.) These local Churches 'retained a very strong Ultramontane outlook that caused them to emphasize what characterized their Catholic identity in order to distinguish themselves more clearly from the Protestant world that surrounded them'. They had 'undeniable reservations' about Christian unity. A 'legalistic mentality and a concern to stick firmly to classical positions' had produced a 'scrupulous or timid conformism', for instance in liturgical matters.[21]

Simply by being present together and sharing responsibility for their input to the Council, the bishops of England and Wales were exposing themselves to the winds of change. It was a tangible expression of 'collegiality', a key concept of Vatican II that had scarcely, at that point, found its name. But being present in one place does not make them organized. What they needed was an administrative genius, and one was on hand in the person of Derek Worlock. There is no need whatever to doubt the centrality of the role he described himself as taking on. Thus it was in those early days that the structures of the post-conciliar Church began to take shape, not just internationally in the Vatican and worldwide but also in that tiny community of English-Catholicism-in-temporary-exile, the bishops who clustered at the English College in the autumn of 1962. And Worlock was at the centre of it, as he remained for the next 30 years or more.

I was anxious to ensure that we got some mandate from the bishops to take over the arrangement of their affairs.

On the whole the meeting this evening was a success, the bishops asked me to form a secretariat to liaise with the College authorities and to be responsible for all their arrangements, secretarial, transport, Mass times[22] and even small finance. This small secretariat will be made up of Monsignor Monaghan of Lancaster, Father Bill O'Brien of Birmingham, Michael Ashdowne, Monsignor Clarke and Father Basil Loftus who has been left here for a few months by the Bishop of Leeds in order to be of some help to the College. This evening I was able to parcel out various jobs and responsibilities and I think the thing should move fairly smoothly once one has convinced the members that someone has to take control and make arrangements and not wait to be told.

During the day we have had a flood of journalists here, most of them English or American and coming to one whom they cheerfully call 'the angel of Fleet Street' to provide them with answers to questions for which they can obtain no answers at the official Press secretariat. This is due to the fact that the Italians will never answer questions and think it adequate to pass over set hand-outs which no journalist worth his salt will touch because he knows that everyone else has got it.

On the whole journalists at this stage are merely in search of background information and it is relatively easy to keep them away from the difficult sub-jects by feeding them with background chatter, e.g. on the bishops taking part, this ancient College and so on. My last visitor this evening was Father Agnel-lus who came to arrange for me to do a broadcast for the BBC next Sunday, though to be recorded here on Friday afternoon. It will be a bit of a push as it is meant to deal with the ceremony on Thursday and therefore cannot be written before that.

*   *   *

With a houseful of bishops there are always remarks which figure in one's mind but today has produced three rich comments worth recording. At supper tonight I heard the Bishop of Northampton saying that he would like to abolish the cassock, that he was all in favour of short jackets. He appeared to mean what he said. Meantime the Bishop of Leeds, whose flow scarcely stopped throughout the whole of supper, talked at some length about the prospect of long-winded bishops who would address the Council for more than a quarter of an hour at a time. His final comment was rich: 'If it goes on for long, I shall shake the assembly by crossing the floor and going to sit with the observers.'

However the best remark of the day undoubtedly came from the Arch-bishop of Cardiff at breakfast. He was talking about the cats and their scrimmaging in the cortile last night. 'You could hear them' he said 'working their way laboriously through every stage of the pre-nuptial enquiry.'[23] To which Monsignor McReavy, universally known as Bomb, added the final shot: 'And from where I was sleeping, you could tell precisely which stage they had reached!'

*   *   *

13th October: The Feast of St Edward and one of the first occasions for many years when I have failed to visit the tomb of the principal patron of our city of Westminster.

As may be seen from the date of this entry, the opening days of the Council have been so busy that it has not been possible to make any entry on the day itself. For the last three nights I have not been to bed before midnight and one is scarcely in a condition to make the comprehensible entry at that time.

Last Wednesday, 10th October, 'V–C Day' minus one, brought matters suddenly and fully to the boil. But first let us have the follow through on Archbishop Murphy's saga of the cats in the cortile. At breakfast that morning the Archbishop claimed that there was only one cat to be heard during the night. 'It must have been a mixed marriage' the Archbishop said. 'And the dispensation had been refused.'

We had a first meeting of our own little secretariat at 10am that morning when we were able to allocate various responsibilities to the different members. It seemed to work very well and Alan Clarke was particularly pleased with the sharing out of the burdens. The only thing we shall have to watch is the over enthusiasm of Ashdowne and Loftus, both of whom seem eager to assume responsibility for every aspect with the resultant clash of two strong personalities!

After the meeting was over I went round to the Grail[24] to dictate some letters but not before I had arranged for Cardinal Godfrey to pay a visit to Cardinal Heard. It was on this occasion that we got our first inkling of the lobbying which was on the verge of breaking out all over Rome. Cardinal Heard gave to Cardinal Godfrey a list of French bishops, whom he had been advised by Cardinal Julliens, his predecessor as Dean of the Rota, might be regarded as suitable candidates for the elections due to take place to the ten commissions. These ten commissions have the same subject matter as the preparatory commissions and are to consist of 24 members each, eight to be elected by the Holy Father and sixteen to be elected by the Fathers of the Council. Cardinal Heard also suggested that the English bishops might like to put down a few names from amongst their number and we were able to tell him that we had already arranged a meeting of the bishops of England and Wales, residential and auxiliary, for the Friday morning and for this very purpose. Before the evening was out I had been deputed by our Hierarchy to make contact with the Scots Hierarchy and with the Irish Hierarchy to see if they had any names for consideration, and during the afternoon a bishop of Bruges called on Archbishop Heenan whom he knew from earlier meetings.

The Bishop of Bruges[25] claimed to be acting for a combined group of Belgian, Dutch and German bishops. They would be glad to hear of anyone whom our Hierarchy wished to back and similarly they would be willing to let us have their list in due time. And so the thing snowballed. By the evening I had further lists received by Cardinal Heard from the Rota and prepared for him by members of the Rota from different countries after the latter had consulted the hierarchies of the countries from which they had come originally. Through this machine we received an American list and an Italian list but the difficulty was to determine how far these lists reflected the views of the local hierarchy, and how far they were merely a list of bishops from any one country known by the local man on the Rota to be safe men so far as Rome was concerned . . .

Late that evening there were lots of final preparations to get the bishops away safely the following morning[26] and I clambered rather tired into bed soon after midnight, conscious of the fact that I had to get up at 5.15 the following morning.

When the great day, 11th October, dawned and we were up by then, the rain was still pelting down and everyone was recalling the tremendous thunderstorm which had accompanied the declaration of Papal Infallibility at the close of the First Vatican Council.[27]

The Cardinal rather reluctantly agreed not to say Mass until 6.30 that evening and we had him on parade with all his robes in time to leave the College by car at 7.30 am. It was quite an operation to get all the bishops moving that morning but we had a fleet of six cars with Father Loftus acting as beach-master . . .

There was very little delay and we succeeded in reaching the cortile San Damaso soon after 7.45 am. I took the Cardinal up to the room where all the cardinals were robing . . . Standing around in the room adjoining the cardinals' vesting room, one began to meet a number of old friends.

It is said no two witnesses ever remember the same event identically. The reference to 'old friends' must have been to a student at the English College by the name of Tony Dodd, a young man with an eye to the main chance. He was looking for a way into the Council to observe the opening, but had no ticket. Dodd spotted an African bishop he knew, looking very lost. If they were challenged, Dodd told him to say that he was his Secretary. He led him past all the guards in the Vatican until they reached the robing rooms, where they found one less full than all the others (as it turned out it was reserved for cardinals).

'It was at this point that Derek Worlock suddenly appeared', Dodd recalled,[28]

and asked – 'Tony, what on earth are you doing here?' I explained everything much to his amusement and he saw Cardinal Godfrey off on his way in the huge procession. We then started to discuss the prospects for the current MCC tour of Australia which was just beginning and the chances of David Sheppard having a good series after his long lay-off because of his ministry.[29]

We had just come to the conclusion that no Catholic priest in a similar situation would have been allowed a sabbatical to resume his cricketing interests when all of a sudden both he and I got a prod in our ribs – '*Permesso!*' said an Italian voice. We both parted to let the speaker past – only, to our horror, to discover that he was none other than Pope John XXIII himself. He had emerged totally on his own at this stage with no flunkeys as yet and the two of us were in a sense physically preventing him going on his way to open his Council. It was an episode that we would both often wistfully recall whenever we were alone together.

(Dodd became a curate in Chichester, before eventually leaving the priesthood; even after that they remained in touch.)

This is not easy to reconcile with Worlock's own account of the same event in his diary. Was he chatting about England's test match chances under David Sheppard (of all people), or helping Cardinal Godfrey down the stairs, or both?

The cardinals did not to move off in procession until nine and then we went down, each assisting our cardinals to the Pauline chapel, there to await the Pope. His Holiness came through with all his attendants and went into the chapel to make a visit to the Blessed Sacrament. When all was ready for the cardinals and the Pope to come out, the procession of bishops was still in progress and we delayed until nearly 9.25 before eventually the master of ceremonies stopped the bishops in order to get the cardinals and the Pope under way.

The Scala Regia is an ordeal at any time but with an half open wound in his side, it was a great ordeal for Cardinal Godfrey. I hung on as tight as I could to his right arm and at times seemed almost to be carrying him down the staircase. Because I knew that the television cameras were on us it was essential to keep smiling and merely to give the impression that I was chatting to him. I gathered subsequently that all this was seen in England but we appear to have got away with it. Eventually we moved out into the piazza and there were gathered the clergy of Rome and some of the students. I must say that the crowd was not very great but the weather had been so bad that it was not surprising that the piazza itself was only half full. Then we started up to the ramp into St Peter's; as we drew level with the band it burst forth with some triumphant music which I found strangely exhilarating. However our pride comes before the fall and no sooner had we entered St Peter's when I along with all other train bearers was 'chucked'. This always infuriates me because one is forced to attend in this capacity and once you're inside the masters of ceremonies treat one as so much dirt unless one has an actual part to play in the ceremony.

Leaving my Cardinal to make his way up through the great Council chamber, into which St Peter's has been turned, I was pushed off to the right and we were bustled along by an MC, who told us to go up the staircase into one of the tribunes. Just as I got to the top of the stairs another MC came along and said we were all to get out and to go farther up; so we moved again further into the basilica. It was rather like being in an empty hall because the doors and tribunes go right up to the top of the bays of St Peter's and one can see nothing at all if one is behind. It is rather like being shut outside to walk round the outside of a stadium. We were then pushed into a second tribune from which we were evicted and finally driven into a corner where I found myself immediately in front of the diplomatic mission. Mr Lemass the Prime Minister of Ireland, and my old friend Con Cremin, leant over their tribune to shake me by the hand very warmly, only a few seconds before we were chucked once more by yet another MC.

We were moved further down to where there appeared to be a gap almost alongside the throne and I was relieved to see that there was a bench because I had already been standing for well over an hour by this time. Whilst we were standing there Monsignor Willebrands, the man behind the secretariat for Christian Unity, rushed over and shook me warmly by the hand, greeted me most affectionately and then turned to yet another MC and said that 'they cannot stay here'. We were chucked again and to my humiliation I saw our places being taken by the so-called 'observers' of the non-Catholic bodies. Such was my personal price for the cause of Christian unity and eventually I finished up alongside the throne with the Pope's privy chamberlains. It was an excellent position from many points of view except that it meant that by the time I eventually got back into a car I was standing without a break for six hours.

The great basilica of St Peter has been completely transformed into a Council chamber. There are long benches for bishops, eight tiers of them reaching right up on high, and above these, tribunes for *periti* and observers. The cardinals are all in one section of the benches, immediately opposite the famous statue of St Peter, who looked magnificent clad in tiara and cope. When it was all over Cardinal Ciriaci said with a chuckle: 'Peter was all right but we are not all made of bronze.' This was a delightful remark in view of its many implications.[30]

The ceremony was very long but reasonably straightforward. First the hymn to the Holy Ghost, then a Mass of the Holy Ghost sung by the Cardinal Dean, then the obeisance by the cardinals and representative bishops, followed by the profession of faith first by the Pope and then by the secretary of the Council, Archbishop Felici, on behalf of all bishops present. I found the profession of faith by the Pope most moving and it was indeed about the only occasion when one noticed that most of the observers appeared to be strictly observing. Some of them are far more interested in trying to get a good shot with their cameras. The Anglican contingent was reasonably behaved, but the Old Catholic got into great difficulties when his stole became mixed up with the strap of his camera.

When it was all over I managed to regain access to the Cardinal who was in pretty good form in spite of the long ceremony. I got him upstairs where we helped him to undress and then came down into the cortile, where disaster awaited us. This wretched car, which had been lent to the Cardinal by Cardinal Heard who had taken the only Vatican car available, had a faulty battery and I finished the morning in the humiliating position of having to shove the car across the cortile San Damaso in order to try to get it going. It really was the last straw and I was almost exhausted when we got back to the College soon after two o'clock.

Any journalist must sympathize with a colleague who has missed the main story through not seeing the wood for the trees, as in the case of the ballet correspondent of *The Times* who allegedly phoned in a late-night review consisting only of the message: 'As there was no performance tonight I cannot comment on it.' In fact the ceiling had collapsed killing five people, and he hadn't thought it part of his job to say so.

Though he said he was moved by it, Worlock failed to report the contents of Pope John XXIII's opening address, being more concerned with making remarks about the behaviour of the ecumenical observers with their cameras. In fact this speech has come to be regarded as one of the definitive texts of modern Catholicism – possibly the moment the ceiling fell in on the Counter Reformation.[31]

It had four significant points. The first was the Pope's emphatic repudiation of the 'prophets of gloom' – who included, it seems, some of those around him in the Vatican Curia. 'In the daily exercise of our pastoral office,' he said,

we sometimes have to listen, much to our regret, to voices of persons who, though burning with zeal, are not endowed with too much sense of discretion or measure. In these modern times they can see nothing but prevarication and ruin. They say that our era, in comparison with past eras, is getting worse, and they behave as though they had learned nothing from history, which is, none the less, the teacher of life. They behave as though at the time of former Councils everything was a full triumph for the Christian idea and life and for proper religious liberty.

We feel we must disagree with those prophets of gloom, who are always forecasting disaster, as though the end of the world were at hand. In the present order of things, Divine Providence is leading us to a new order of human relations which, by men's own efforts and even beyond their very expectations, are directed toward the fulfilment of God's superior and inscrutable designs. And everything, even human differences, leads to the greater good of the Church.

Secondly, he opened the door to methods of scriptural and theological study which the Catholic Church had frowned on in the past.

From the renewed, serene, and tranquil adherence to all the teaching of the Church in its entirety and preciseness, as it still shines forth in the Acts of the Council of Trent and First Vatican Council, the Christian, Catholic, and apostolic spirit of the whole world expects a step forward toward a doctrinal penetration and a formation of consciousness in faithful and perfect conformity to the authentic doctrine, which, however, should be studied and expounded through the methods of research and through the literary forms of modern thought.

It is a very clever passage, in its simultaneous espousal of the standards of doctrinal orthodoxy dear to the conservatives, namely Trent and Vatican I, while refusing to accept that this ruled out modern approaches. The very use of the word 'modern' would have had resonances with his audience. The anti-Modernist phase of Church policy before the First World War had led to bitter quarrels about the very possibility of modernizing Catholic doctrine.

Then came the single most quoted sentence of his entire pontificate, which suddenly freed the Church from having to stick to expressions of doctrine that had seemed immutable for all time:

The substance of the ancient doctrine of the deposit of faith is one thing, and the way in which it is presented is another. And it is the latter that must be taken into great consideration with patience if necessary, everything being measured in the forms and proportions of a *magisterium* which is predominantly pastoral in character.

It was this principle that was to enable theological conversations to be opened with other Churches to see if, behind differences of language, they were in fact closer together than they thought. This also meant a change of style in the Catholic Church's approach to discipline, and to errors and heresies within the Church, as he then explained.

At the outset of the Second Vatican Council, it is evident, as always, that the truth of the Lord will remain for ever. We see, in fact, as one age succeeds another, that the opinions of men follow one another and exclude each other. And often errors vanish as quickly as they arise, like fog before the sun. The Church has always opposed these errors. Frequently she has condemned them with the greatest severity. Nowadays however, the Spouse of Christ prefers to make use of the medicine of mercy rather than that of severity. She considers that she meets the needs of the present day by demonstrating the validity of her teaching rather than by condemnations.

This refusal to condemn was a deliberate reversal of the Catholic Church's traditional policy towards views it regarded as erroneous. Doctrines such as transubstantiation defined by Trent or infallibility defined by Vatican I had the ancient formula *anathema sit*[32] attached to anyone who said to the contrary. Pope John was making it clear in this passage that he did not intend to allow any such anathemas to be attached to any teaching that the Second Vatican Council might propound. This new attitude had profound implications not only for its internal dissenters but also for the way the Catholic Church treats members of other Churches. 'The Catholic Church, raising the torch of religious truth by means of this Ecumenical Council, desires to show herself to be the loving mother of all, benign, patient, full of mercy and goodness toward the brethren who are separated from her.' He returned warmly to the subject, later in the speech:

The Catholic Church, therefore, considers it her duty to work actively so that there may be fulfilled the great mystery of that unity, which Jesus Christ invoked with fervent prayer from His heavenly Father on the eve of His sacrifice. She rejoices in peace, knowing well that she is intimately associated with that prayer, and then exults greatly at seeing that invocation extend its efficacy with salutary fruit, even among those who are outside her fold.

Indeed, if one considers well this same unity which Christ implored for His Church, it seems to shine, as it were, with a triple ray of beneficent supernal light: namely, the unity of Catholics among themselves, which must always be kept exemplary and most firm; the unity of prayers and ardent desires with which those Christians separated from this Apostolic See aspire to be united with us; and the unity in esteem and respect for the Catholic Church which animates those who follow non-Christian religions.

The Pope concluded with an image that suggests a complete reinterpretation of the history of the Catholic Church over the previous few centuries, an interpretation as unsettling and against the prevailing view in the

Vatican Curia as anything a radical theologian would have dared to offer at that time. He seemed to be suggesting that the Church was at last beginning to emerge from a period of darkness.

'The Council now beginning rises in the Church like daybreak,' the Pope declared, 'a forerunner of most splendid light. It is now only dawn. And already at this first announcement of the rising day, how much sweetness fills our heart.'

The ability of people not to hear pronouncements that they are not expecting to hear, or to dismiss the importance of information presented to them because it does not fit into their prevailing mind-set, appears to have blocked Derek Worlock's ears to the message of the Pope's visionary opening address. For Worlock, the wood was still more important than the trees.

One might have hoped that there would be some respite after such a lone and exhausting ceremony, but no such luck. It was already becoming apparent that some preliminary actions must be taken if we were to have any members of our Hierarchy appointed to the commissions, ten in number and to which voting was due to commence today (Saturday). One had to remember that the Catholics of England and Wales, five million strong, form less than one per cent of the universal Church. There are sixteen members to be elected to each commission and at that rate, on a proportional basis, we might expect to find one of our bishops in the commissions. When one sees the voting power of such countries as Italy and America, there is really no reason why they should not sweep the board and, with our own small Hierarchy, we should have no chance at all.

On Wednesday there had been a first visit from the Bishop of Bruges, acting for the Belgian hierarchy which is in league with Holland, Luxembourg and Germany, who came to see Archbishop Heenan to find out if we had any outstanding candidates. The Archbishop himself, who is not eligible for election to the commissions because he is a member of the Secretariat for unity, consulted no one[33] but seems to have passed on the names of Bishop Dwyer, Bishop Beck and Archbishop Grimshaw.

For our part we managed to get hold of lists which had been supplied to Cardinal Heard through the Rota, the national delegates of which were supplied with names of those regarded as safe in Rome and a certain number of others represented by the hierarchies of the countries from the individual members of the Rota came. I suggested to the Cardinal that we should try to make contact with the Irish and with the Scots to see what they were doing. For the Irish, I was delighted to find that Bishop Conway had been made secretary of their Council committee of which the archbishop of Dublin is chairman. They promised full co-operation, would welcome our list of candidates for the commissions and would let us have their own list the following morning. Similarly the Scots, very anxious to know our list, would pass on theirs when they met on the Friday evening.

*   *   *

At this stage Worlock saw the issue of voting lists simply in terms of national pride – how many Englishmen could they secure on the prestigious Council Commissions? Each Commission was to take over where the various Preparatory Commission had left off, or so he imagined. They were allotted more or less the same list of subjects. It was expected that their task would simply be to amend the draft documents in the light of comments from the floor, and then resubmit the amended draft for approval. He did not know that the work of the preparatory Commissions was about to be overturned, the documents they had prepared more or less torn up, and the work of drafting Council documents begun all over again. But he was becoming aware of canvassing and lobbying in an organized way, and came across both extremes – the ultra-progressive Bishop of Bruges, who was close to Heenan, and the ultra-conservative Archbishop Lefebrve, who wanted Godfrey's support.

The first meeting to have formal discussion about candidates for the commissions was held at ten o'clock yesterday (Friday) morning. The previous evening I had received instructions from the Bishop of Clifton and the Archbishop of Liverpool and the Bishop of Leeds to invite Abbot Butler to attend the meeting since he is one of the Fathers[34] of the Council, ranking as superior general, in that he is president of the English Benedictines. The Cardinal felt that there might be some objection to this move but at the time no one was prepared to express objection so the invitation was conveyed. Further, all the auxiliaries were present and just before the meeting was due to begin, our old friend, Bishop Tony Galvin, former rector of Mill Hill[35] and now a bishop in Sarawak, called to say that the various Mill Hill bishops, now gathered in Rome would be glad to know the recommendations of those they referred to as 'our men'. The Cardinal decided to allow Bishop Galvin to attend the meeting.

This led to a small difficulty a few minutes later when Bishop Hall of Kisumu (Kenya) and Bishop Billington of Uganda, both Mill Hill bishops, called downstairs to ask for information regarding our names. I told them that we had undertaken to keep them informed through Bishop Galvin but did not make known to them that Bishop Galvin was already sitting upstairs in the meeting of our Hierarchy. A lack of liaison somewhere. Just as I was settling these two, Bishop Conway and the Bishop of Dromore arrived, bringing with them the Irish list and promising full support for any of our candidates. Very boldly I gave a reciprocal undertaking and hastened their list upstairs to our bishops.

Yesterday was such a chaotic day that in many ways it is difficult to order precisely the number and manner of the different approaches which we made and which were made to us but perhaps the most important feature was that at the meeting of the bishops the open clash occurred. This came when the bishops, who had agreed to secret ballot for candidates for the various Commissions, came to discuss the appointment of one of their number to the commission for theology. The Archbishop of Liverpool remarked that the only possible selection was that of Abbot Butler as 'We haven't any theologians in the Hierarchy.' I am not too clear about what happened when he threw this bomb-shell but by the time the meeting was over soon after midday, various elements of the Hierarchy were hopping mad. Perhaps it was a good thing that this latent opposition, which has been sniping for some time, at last declared its hand and I am sure that the Cardinal had now more open support from those whom one may call the loyalists than at any time for the last two or three years.

When finally the meeting broke up, some time after midday, it was agreed that further meetings should take place at seven o'clock and that in the mean-time I should make efforts to establish further contacts with the other hierarchies. The lists supplied by Cardinal Heard were also called into question and the Bishop of Leeds[36] said that we should not be fed with names of those acceptable to the Curia but should try to let a little fresh air in on the scene. I suppose that one had anticipated these difficulties but they certainly caused a crisis when they arose. By the evening I had succeeded in getting one or two other groups of names, sometimes from missionary blocs and sometimes from formal hierarchies. We began the labour of preparing these lists which were valiantly duplicated by the Grail and circulated to our bishops, who not infrequently handed them on to others and then came running back for more. There was a constant paper-chase which is still in progress.

At the evening meeting the counter-attack took place. The Bishop of Brentwood[37] stood up to register a formal protest against the allegation that there were no theologians in the Hierarchy and asked that this be recorded. Two other bishops asked that their names be associated with the protest: the matter seems to have come to an end when the Abbot of Downside,[38] who was clearly acutely embarrassed by the whole incident, asked that his name be also associated with this resolution of dissent from the Archbishop of Liverpool's allegation. Late last evening I saw the Archbishop who asked me what I thought about it all. I said that in many ways I felt that the situation might be easier now that quite apparent differences had come to the surface but that none the less I regretted the situation which made it necessary for such disagreements to have to take such formal shape. 'It's all a question of difficulty in communications', he said, which I have heard used before when speaking of the differences between Catholics and non-Catholics.[39]

By last evening the atmosphere still remained tense but I think that on the whole the storm may have helped to clear the air.

*   *   *

Throughout the last day or so Michael Ashdowne has been a great godsend. Our final duty of today was to take copies of our list to the Irish Hierarchy, who are at the Irish College; to the Scots Hierarchy, most of whom are staying at the Anglo-American Hotel, opposite the old Scots College which is now at Marino whilst their new building is being set up; and finally to Cardinal Gilroy for the benefit of the Australian and New Zealand Hierarchies. I found the Cardinal as charming as ever and he gave me his lists which I was able to bring back for duplication and circulation amongst our own men. On the whole it was a satisfactory round, though I must confess that I am usually half out of the seat of the car when Michael Ashdowne is driving. He has all the Italian tricks and on one occasion I had to restrain him while he hung out of the driver's window, saying a few choice words to a rival vehicle and hammering on the driver's door to get someone almost off the bonnet: a trick I used to employ trying to scare the cattle off the roads in the south of Ireland!

This Saturday morning saw the first general session of the Council. It was held in St Peter's at nine o'clock and all the bishops present had to attend in choir dress. It was pouring with rain when we set out a little before half past eight but I managed to get the Cardinal to the Porta Mater just beyond the sacristy entrance: this entrance seems to be reserved for cardinals. Everyone imagined that the session would go on until lunch time and so I got our chauffeur to bring me back to the college and told him to collect me here at eleven o'clock. The other cars, driven either by hired chauffeurs or by members of the College staff had also returned and we had a meeting in my room to plan the arrangements for the next few days. At ten minutes past ten an alarming rumour reached us that Cardinal Heard had been seen in the College and it was generally assumed that he must have collapsed and been taken out. When at last I found him he told me that the meeting was over and there was a frenzied dash for the cars to return to St Peter's. Everyone had been caught on the hop, including the Vatican drivers and there were bishops trying to get into buses and taxis. I must say that our own men were remarkably long suffering about the whole incident but I think they were so excited about what had happened in the Council that they did not appreciate the breakdown in our transport arrangements. I managed to get a lift from the rector and we drove to the Porta Mater where I found the Cardinal, standing with some other cardinals still awaiting their drivers and attended by that dear little man, Bishop Eric Grasar of Shrewsbury who had realised that the Cardinal was on his own and waited with him. Even then I had great difficulty in persuading him to come back us. He was so humble that he was all for trying to get home in a bus by himself.

What in fact had happened was this. First there had been a low Mass celebrated by the Archbishop of Florence with a dialogue Mass, I gather, answered by all those bishops. It must have been a most impressive ceremony. As soon as the Mass was over, from the Table of the Council of Presidents, where the ten cardinals representing the different language groups were seated, there had arisen Cardinal Liénart of Lille. He stated that in his opinion it was premature to proceed to the voting of members to the different Commissions and that more time should be given so that all the bishops gathered in Rome might consult with one another on a private basis and see who would be the best men for the jobs. As soon as he had finished, this de Gaulle of the French Hierarchy was supported by the Adenauer[40] of Germany, Cardinal Frings, who likewise demanded a recess for further consideration. One gathers that Monsignor Felici, the secretary general, was taken quite by surprise. But it was agreed that not later than Monday morning national episcopal conferences, having called private meetings of their own members, should submit to the Secretariat General the names of candidates. The Secretariat would endeavour to compile a composite list, the idea being that with 42 episcopal conferences there would be 42 names put forward for each Commission, and that on Tuesday next the Council should meet again, and from these approximately 420 names, select sixteen for each commission. I have been told that the intervention of Cardinal Liénart and Cardinal Frings was greeted with loud applause from the body of the house and there a varying views as to whether this was a good or a bad thing. All events the early break-up – they left St Peter's before ten o'clock – is being hailed as a triumph for democracy and there is no doubt that the Northern Europeans feel that they have had a triumph over the Curia. There are one or two lovely stories about the Pope looking out of his window and seeing the bishops coming out at ten o'clock and saying: 'Santa fede, they've shut the whole thing down in under an hour and others thought it would last for several years!'

It was perhaps as well that yet another meeting of all our bishops had already been arranged to be held at the College at 7 pm and we had a great task of trying to collect more lists for this meeting. It went on for nearly an hour and a half and the secretary, the Bishop of Clifton, was finally asked to ascertain whether each national hierarchy was to submit to the Secretariat General one candidate or more for each Commission, whether their lists were to be confined to names drawn from their own ranks and, finally, whether all the names submitted would be included in the composite list to be prepared by the Secretariat General or whether this latter body would make selections if the number of names submitted was too large. I felt that there was a bit of a dig in this last question but presumably it had to be asked . . .

The evening has been spent with further dashes to different hierarchies and collection of still further names. I managed to get Bishop Dwyer to go to the Spaniards, whom he seems to have known, and to my delight, by this evening we received the Spanish list which gave the names of two of their own bishops and all the English and Irish bishops. Evidently we are thought of by the Spaniards as being reasonably traditionalist and safe. And so to bed in the early hours of Sunday morning.

Sunday 14th: This morning I had my latest rise since arrival, saying Mass at 7.30. I had a rather frustrating morning trying to collect lists and to disseminate them, with the knowledge that there must be a meeting of the Hierarchy at 5.30 this evening and we had to get out the revised lists from our Hierarchy who had decided to add Cardinal Godfrey's name to its candidates for the commissions. They had decided to put him up for the commission for the Sacraments, on the score that this would give him a foot into the liturgy and the whole question of Holy Orders and celibacy, and into matrimony with the problem of mixed marriages. Yesterday it had been made known at the session of the Council that cardinals could be included in the list so the Grail had to get ready with a lot more duplication this morning. We also had to clear the questions which the bishops wanted answered from last night and Basil Loftus was fortunate enough to catch Monsignor Felici as he came out of his flat, going to say Mass. Monsignor Felici said that each episcopal conference could put up two or three names for each commission if it so wished but that these names must be drawn from its own ranks. He also gave the assurance that every name submitted to the General Secretariat would be printed on the composite lists from which voting would be made on Tuesday next. We managed to get this question and answer business duplicated as well so that none of the bishops this evening should claim that their points had been overlooked. Perhaps the most annoying feature of the day was that the Archbishop of Liverpool, although I had placed new lists from our Hierarchy on his desk, took the old list to the Northern European group and to the Americans. This will inevitably mean that Cardinal Godfrey will not be included in the composite list being drawn up by these blocs. We shall have to hope for the best on Tuesday. One wonders whether this was an accident.[41] During the morning all sorts of other lists came in and there was a festal lunch for the postponed St Edward.

Before lunch I went to the Hotel Columbus to see Archbishop McKeefry of Wellington to ensure that the New Zealand bishops had our new lists. After lunch I set out and went first to the far end of the Via Nomentana to see Cardinal Gracias. To my astonishment I found myself being shown into a meeting of over a hundred Indian bishops who were all most cordial and promised us support. I was a little embarrassed by all this and puzzled by one dusky bishop who kept telling me he was really a cowboy from Texas: I should think his mother must have been a red Indian. As I came out of the hall where the Indian bishops were meeting, it was just my luck to walk into Archbishop Roberts.[42] The latter gave me a dirty look but said nothing. It was interesting to see that he was attending the meeting of the Indian bishops, even though according to official lists supplied by the Secretariat he should really be with the bishops from England.

From the Via Nomentana I went to the Irish College where I saw the Archbishop of Dublin's secretary and explained the reasons for the change in our lists. Then on to the Blue Nuns to see Cardinal Gilroy who was most communicative and told me that the Council presidents are due to have an audience with the Pope tomorrow and they will receive pretty clear instructions. He thought that there might be moves for still further changes next Tuesday, and then he got on to test matches so I had to stay rather longer than I had expected. Luckily I met the Bishop of Argyll and the Isles so I was able to give him new lists for the Scottish Hierarchy. I dispatched further lists to the two groups of bishops from Africa and was able to supply lists for the Spaniards and the Canadians. By this time the Grail was churning out reams of paper and when our bishops went in to meet at 5.30 they had Archbishop Heerey of Onitsha of Nigeria with them. They worked laboriously through all the lists and explained the various steps which I had taken during the day. At the end of the meeting there was a move to see whether we could prepare a list of sixteen names for each commission, the names to be drawn from all the lists and to be supported by the Hierarchy as a whole.

I think that the Cardinal was quite right in claiming that it would be an almost impossible task to secure an agreed composite list, approved by all the members round the table. In his opinion it would have been embarrassing and I learned later that the French bishops had abandoned a similar attempt on their part to draw up a list of 160 names whom all their number would support.

There were over thirty bishops at this meeting and this confirmed me in my view that we could – and will in necessity – easily muster a gathering of bishops from throughout the Commonwealth, though perhaps the French Canadians might be difficult. At a time when at home we are facing the problem of whether or not to enter the common market, we find the Northern European bloc mustered without us, whilst at least in ecclesiastical affairs the countries of the Commonwealth seem to continue to look to England for a lead. Although I am a supporter of European unity, which must be the ultimate goal for the common market, here at least the Commonwealth and Ireland seem to be the basis for approach. Even partition[43] ceases to be a problem . . .

I came down from the Common Room in order to help the Eminence get to bed. There is no doubt that Noel Moynihan, who has been coming in here daily, is not entirely satisfied with the way the wound is healing. One day he is pleased and the next he expresses concern. What concerns me is that, whereas he told me that he would be staying here for three weeks he now tells me that he will have to be back in London by the end of this present week. Yet another problem that will have to be sorted out in the days ahead.

*   *   *

Monday 15th October: And I was right. I lay awake till nearly two o'clock. I seem to remember chuckling at the memory of the greatest triumph Basil Loftus has yet achieved. He took the official list of nomination from our Hierarchy to the General Secretariat at about six o'clock yesterday evening. Needless to say the Secretariat was closed and as I had told Basil that he must not hand over the list to a porter, he solemnly went up to Monsignor Felici's flat on the top floor, rang the bell and the somewhat surprised Monsignor came to the door to be greeted by a charming smile and the English list delivered in person by Basil!

This morning saw the historic first meeting[44] of the Hierarchy of England and Wales held in Rome and to mark the occasion I got a photographer in . . . But whilst all this was going on, more and more lists of various hierarchies were reaching me at the College. The Americans were at it for the greater part of the day and eventually produced a composite list, which presumably indicates how their votes will be cast tomorrow. I was a bit sickened by the fact that Cardinal Godfrey is not on their list but the explanation has already been given.

There is a recurrent suggestion by Worlock that Heenan took advantage of the confusion to circulate lists which he knew, because of a misunderstanding, did not include Cardinal Godfrey's name. Worlock later blamed him for the disappointing outcome. Godfrey's name had been left off because someone – Worlock, Godfrey or another – had mistakenly understood that the Pope was going to supply a separate list of his own, of cardinals who were to serve on the Commissions as his nominees. It was assumed that Godfrey would be one of them, given his membership of the Central Preparatory Commission and the alleged interest the Pope had had in appointing him to the very select and secret Committee of Amendment. As it happened, there was no such intention and he was not elected to anything. This was not surprising: not being on the lists submitted to the large number of North American and Northern European bishops would have been a further handicap. Heenan would have been only too happy to exclude Godfrey from the running in this way. But Worlock lacked proof of the dirty trick he suspected Heenan had played. If his theory was correct, however, he had been thoroughly outwitted. But it may also be that Worlock had seriously overestimated Godfrey's standing and importance. He does not even appear to have been a candidate favoured by the conservatives.

Worlock later goes on to suggest that Heenan had a small group around him, which he called 'the opposition'. Heenan's own recollection of 'the battle of the lists' confirms Worlock's in most particulars, though he was more generous to Godfrey than Godfrey's Secretary had been to him. In his own Vatican II diary,[45] he recorded:

> We are all expected to find out what we can and report back to a meeting to be held this evening. In the event I am better placed than most to make contacts because of my friendships with the bishops on the Secretariat for Christian Unity. In fact I had little to do because during the day the Bishop of Bruges (de Smedt) phoned and said he wanted to see me urgently on behalf of the Belgians, Dutch and Germans. He came round in the early evening. The Bishop of Bruges was rather reluctant to meet any other bishops as his communication was highly confidential, but I persuaded him that GPD[46] was safe and that his knowledge of French would help.
>
> Bruges' news was indeed startling. The cardinals of Brussels, Vienna, Utrecht and Lille[47] were of the opinion that the voting list would be put before us by the conciliar authorities under the guidance of Cardinal Ottaviani (Holy Office), and that little real choice would be given regarding candidates. Since most of the work would be done by the commissions, it is important that the members should be really representative.
>
> Bishops had another meeting in the evening, to piece together rumours and impressions. The Cardinal is still suffering the effects of an operation last year and it is hard to put a point which he can grasp quickly or clearly.

Heenan does not say whether he was told the even more crucial second phase of this plot. Once Ottaviani's candidates had been defeated by the progressives, it was intended to have the draft decrees prepared by the preparatory commissions thrown out in order to enable the preparation of fresh documents, by the new commissions, which would be much more agreeable to the progressives. Worlock, meanwhile, has no scent of any of this:

> The other interesting features about this American list – and one must remember the power of their enormous number of votes – were, first, that outside the United States itself preference appears to have been given to any name which sounds even vaguely Irish in origin; and, secondly the hotly tipped Bishop John Wright of Pittsburgh, held by the progressives to be an essential member of the commission for theology, is not included in the list put forward by his own countrymen . . .
>
> But perhaps the most interesting approach came from the Spaniards shortly before supper time. They admitted quite openly that they were worried by the power of the Italian vote and were considering, after consultation with the Latin American countries, suggesting at the full Council session tomorrow that it was impossible for any individual to select 160 names without more consultation and more information than was generally available. They were wondering whether to propose, that once all lists from the various national hierarchies had been submitted, members of the Council of Presidents should be given the power to select the 160 people for the commissions; alternatively the general body might appoint another selection committee to carry this out; or, finally, a new selection committee be appointed consisting of the heads of the various national episcopal conferences so that they might make the selection.[48]

*　　　　*　　　　*

The second session of the Hierarchy meeting took place this morning; it seems to have been a great success. A number of bishops remarked that the Cardinal was in much better form as a chairman and managed to retain control and apparently to concentrate on the various items put forward . . . But at least it is good news that the Cardinal managed so well and it seemed that the quadripartite forces of the opposition[49] failed to provide more than nuisance value at the conference table. They did however provide some distress to the College authorities. The Cardinal had told the bishops at the meeting this morning that the Vice-Rector had assessed that the cost of hospitality for each bishop each day would be approximately two guineas. This in the opinion of the majority was most reasonable as the terms are inclusive and compare very favourably with what other bishops are having to pay elsewhere. I am told that the Americans at the Flora are moving out, having discovered that their bill for the first week was one hundred dollars per head. It looks as though some of the smaller convents will be in demand before long.

The Cardinal told me that our bishops had accepted the proposed tariff with gratitude, but later in the day the Vice-Rector came to tell me that it had reached his ear that the four[50] members of the opposition were complaining that the price was too high and that it was not right that bishops should have to live above their means. I told him not to worry because I was convinced that no matter what figure had been given, this sort of difficulty would be expressed.

*　　　　　*　　　　　*

We were bidden to lunch today with the British minister[51] to the Holy See, Sir Peter Scarlett. His secretary, Donald Cape, had done a good job in the selection of guests and we found one bishop from most of the Commonwealth countries, including my friends Bishop Delargy from New Zealand and Archbishop Fernandes from Delhi, formerly my opposite number in Bombay. It was a happy reunion. Other guests included the Archbishop of Quebec, Bishop Scanlon of Motherwell and the three members of the Anglican delegation of observers to the Council. We exchanged the usual small talk about mutual acquaintances and one had to be awfully careful not to mention about various persons mentioned 'of course he is a convert'. I gained the impression that the bishop[52] was less at ease than his suave countenance suggested. He asked me if I thought they would be required to take an oath of secrecy. He added that he had been desperately careful not to discuss with anyone anything that he had seen or heard in connection with the council, only to read in the *Messagero* the full account the following morning. I tried to explain the vagaries to him but it is hard for an English mind to comprehend it all. I am trying to make sure he and his colleagues get invited to the College next Sunday, as Ripon is due to go back to England towards the end of next week and it will have been important that he will have been there before his departure. Canon Pawley still preserves a face like a boot and it is hard to understand how frequent reference is made to his great charm. He is the cartoonist's dream for the stage gloomy parson, but I gather that most of his charm comes from his wife. The third member is the Archdeacon of Colombo, and apart from his coffee-coloured features, looks remarkably like a successful Jewish stockbroker. As we are leaving the Legation, after a pleasant lunch, I heard Bishop Scanlon informing the Archdeacon that he had conducted the funeral of the Archdeacon's brother.[53] This sounded dangerous ground and I was glad to get out when I did.

*　　　　　*　　　　　*

When I got upstairs there were messages to say that the American Hierarchy were holding a meeting about the treatise on the Liturgy and 'would we care to send a bishop?' I managed to get hold of the Archbishop of Birmingham and he, together with Bishops Grasar, Foley and Petit[54] duly went off to what turned out to be rather a damp squib. We had hoped that this gathering might give some indication of the way the Americans were likely to move but in fact there were only about thirty Americans there and the whole party was merely treated to a discourse on the various points in the schema, as related to them by a Father McManus, their local liturgical expert. I gathered from Bishop Foley afterwards that one of the American bishops had said that his only hope of suiting all the different national bodies in his diocese was the preservation of the use of Latin. But, as Bishop Foley pointed out, no European could understand this American's pronunciation of Latin.

Also waiting upstairs was a letter from Archbishop Lefebvre, former Archbishop of Dakar and newly appointed Superior General of the Holy Ghost fathers. He was a constant supporter of Cardinal Godfrey at the Central Commission and the staunch defender of Cardinal Ottaviani of the Holy Office. According to Archbishop Lefebvre there were various meetings going on in Rome during the past few days, mostly organised by the French and by the Germans, designed to attack the methods and views of Ottaviani. He claimed that these liberals were intending to try to wrest from the Council a pastoral document to the exclusion of a doctrinal document,[55] which in the opinion of Archbishop Lefebvre, was of far greater importance. He added that he considered the manoeuvre by which the schema on the liturgy had been brought forward for first discussion next Monday, was an attempt to force the pace. Many of the Conciliar Fathers spent their time preparing the first *schema* on Faith and Revelation and they would be at a considerable disadvantage in now having to switch to the liturgy. He also thought this was a move to undermine the forces of Ottaviani who were all lined up in the latter's defence on Faith and Revelation.

Archbishop Lefebvre said he had been approached by bishops from South America, Portugal and Ireland, all of whom wished for Cardinal Godfrey to be their spokesman in defence of Ottaviani and they would be grateful if the Cardinal would make some effort to get the original order of subjects restored, so that the liturgy might take its proper place at a later date.

This is a very interesting move but clearly it was impossible for Cardinal Godfrey to comply completely with their wishes. I think he was perfectly willing to be their spokesman and certainly he is hot in the defence of the Holy Office. But I had to point out to him that the speakers for Monday would already have had to hand in their names by this evening and it would sound like sour grapes and throwing spanners into wheels to try to get the order changed once more. If anything had to be done, it should have been done last Tuesday when the first announcement was made that the liturgy would be taken first on the list. In the Cardinal's presence I rang Bishop Conway to find that the Irish bishops in fact knew very little about this and the Archbishop of Dublin counselled, and indeed I had counselled, that it would be too late to make a formal request for a change in order tomorrow morning. I also managed to get hold of Cardinal Gilroy so that Cardinal Godfrey could talk to him regarding the views of the Council of Presidents. Needless to say Cardinal Gilroy didn't want any change at this date and eventually we managed to persuade him to ask Monsignor Felici tomorrow morning to make some announcement which would do something to satisfy the fears of the South Americans, Portuguese and Archbishop Lefebvre as to why the liturgy was being taken out of order. If no such statement is made, Cardinal Godfrey may make a personal statement expressing concern at what has taken place but not asking for any change to be made now that the decision has been taken.

Putting all this down it all seems very simple but in fact it involved one in long telephone calls.[56]

*   *   *

Saturday, 20th October: This morning we had the first results. So far only seven commissions have been announced and already three of our men have been elected with a very considerable number of votes. Archbishop Grimshaw of Birmingham was sixth on the list of sixteen successful candidates for the Liturgical Commission. Bishop Dwyer was high up on the list for the Rule of Dioceses: it is said that he had votes from about 60 per cent of the Fathers. Bishop Petit was elected to the Commission for the Lay Apostolate . . .

At all events, there we are. Three on and three commissions still to be announced: Religious (where Bishop Beck of Salford stands a good chance), Sacraments (where there is every indication that the Cardinal will be elected) and Seminaries (where it is impossible to assess the chances of Bishop Wall of Brentwood). The unsuccessful men today were, sadly, Archbishop Murphy of Cardiff for the Commission dealing with the Discipline of the Clergy; Archbishop Mathew for the Commission for the Missions – this is a considerable setback for the Archbishop, who was secretary of the Preparatory Commission. One gathers that his manner has alienated many. The third unsuccessful candidate put forward by our Hierarchy was Abbot Butler for the Theological Commission. So much for the manoeuvres of last week! In addition to these three on the Commissions, we have Archbishop Heenan and Bishop Holland on the Secretariat for Christian Unity, which continues in existence and for which there are no elections. No doubt we shall know the other results on Monday.

Today's *Osservatore* has not yet appeared and I have not therefore yet had access to the complete list but this evening's Italian papers are claiming that 'foreigners' have gained a victory over the Italian Hierarchy! The papers seem to know that the Italian Hierarchy put up at least four candidates from their own number to each commission and apparently believed that they would have had 28 successful candidates by this morning. The figure which they gave is that fifteen Italians have been elected. There must be at least 400 or more bishops of Italian nationality here for the Council so perhaps the national pride is a little deflated. But the general feeling is that these commissions will reflect the universal nature of the Church, as indeed the Central Preparatory Commission did in its own way . . .

When I got back to the College I was able to spend a couple of hours dictating letters before returning with Basil Loftus to St Peter's just before midday. No sooner had I taken up my position by the car than the loudspeakers began to call out the names of cardinals who were making their way to the door and thus we found that this first session ended at exactly twelve noon . . .

At the beginning of the session the names of the three other Commissions had been announced, or at least so far as the elected members were concerned. On my way back from St Peter's with the Cardinal, I asked him about the results and he told me that he thought Bishop Beck[57] had been appointed to the Commission for Religious. I had anticipated that this would happen in any case and what I was really interested to know was whether the Cardinal had himself been elected to the Commission for the Sacraments. He told me quite calmly that his name was not among the sixteen announced but he went on to point out that as yet no announcement had been made concerning the eight members to be appointed to each Commission by the Pope. I hope he is right. Certainly he seems quite confident that he will be included in one of the Commissions within this category of Papal appointment and when one recalls his record at the Central Commission there seems no reason to doubt that this will be the case. None the less I have been uneasy lest, because the Cardinal's name was not included in the lists for the Northern European bloc nor in the list prepared by the Americans – all this due to the fact that the wrong lists were taken to those two groups by a member of our Hierarchy[58] – the Cardinal might just have failed to get enough votes to get elected. This evening I have seen the names of those elected to the Commissions and they include no names of cardinals. Therefore one is perhaps justified in thinking that the Cardinal's name was high on the list of those elected to this Commission for the Sacraments, it may well have been pulled out if his name was already on a list selected by the Holy Father.

The only other persons who have expressed any anxiety about what has happened are inevitably Bishop Cashman, who, like I, feared that the Cardinal would have been hurt by not being amongst the elected Fathers; the Bishop of Menevia, who realised, as I did, the double play[59] which took place last weekend with regard to the lists sent to other hierarchies, and strangely the Archbishop of Liverpool who took me on one side in the evening in order to try to see what my reaction to it all had been. I did not disguise my anxiety, though I said that I thought that there was a fair chance that the Cardinal would be amongst the members of the Commissions to be appointed by the Pope. The Archbishop of Birmingham[60] showed one how little he understood the Cardinal when he said that he thought it was good that he had not been appointed and that it would not require too much of his strength merely to deal with the morning Sessions. My own knowledge of the Cardinal suggests that his morale is of greater importance than his health and that he always likes to be in the centre of these things, so that to have no place on any of the Commissions might well cause him distress.

*   *   *

The fourth session of our own Hierarchy meeting took place in the College library at 5.15. It seemed imperative that a move should be got on somehow, and so I spent most of the afternoon with the Cardinal in the College garden, taking him through the various papers and preparing draft resolution for each point. This may seem a very obvious thing to do but there have been occasions in the past when it has not been politic to have such draft resolutions lest certain bishops should claim that the whole matter is being steam-rollered. There were a number of tricky items on the agenda but it seems that they managed to cover this evening almost as many points as they covered in the previous three sessions. Therefore the new method seems to have paid off and the Secretary of the Hierarchy Meeting, the Bishop of Clifton, asked me to make sure that there were always resolutions ready in the future. It is strange how all this business is developing. When I first came to Westminster, I used to see Cardinal Griffin taking in a collection of files to the meeting and from these files he used to wrest papers if and when they were required. Gradually we got the system that I prepared a memorandum, or *status quaestionis* for each item in the agenda, and eventually prepared and implemented the Acta. Now it seems I have to formulate resolutions as well, one wonders how much longer this will go on before the inevitable stage is reached when the Hierarchy, or Board of Bishops, has a permanent Secretariat. Something is needed and it is not right that it should depend on the Archbishop of Westminster's Private Secretary that this work for the Hierarchy should be carried out.

*   *   *

Only this evening I was thinking how strangely out of touch we seem here in Rome with international affairs. The daily papers show us that there is a very real international crisis, with rocket-laden Russian ships heading for Cuba, and the President of the United States having laid a blockade to ensure that these ships will not unload their cargo. With each new day the danger of a show-down seems to draw closer and I have no doubt that were we at home, there would be a very real sense of crisis. It is curious how being far away and looking at newspapers for the most part in a foreign language, it all seems a little unreal. It cannot be regarded as unreal, however, as this evening the Pope has delivered an impassioned appeal to both sides to endeavour to settle their differences without resort to war. Once again it makes one think of the historical accounts of the First Vatican Council which the books all say broke up hurriedly at the approach of the invasion of the Papal States. So often have we been on the brink of war in the course of these last ten years or so that now we have become accustomed to last minute changes by which the danger has been averted. Please God it will be the same this time.

The Perfect Secretary by Derek Worlock. Courtesy of Liverpool Roman Catholic Archdiocesan Archive at St Joseph's, Upholland, Lancashire.

Notes

1 The Apostolic Delegate, the papal representative in Great Britain.

2 Worlock had various ways of making sure word reached Archbishop Heenan.

3 The original purpose of what later became the Venerable English College was as a hostel for English pilgrims to Rome, under royal protection.

4 Trinity Sunday, in early summer, was a traditional day for ordaining new diocesan priests.

5 Gerard Tickle, Rector of the English College, universally known as Jock. (It seems the nickname misled Worlock about his Christian name.).

6 Shorthand for celebrating a Pontifical High Mass.

7 Students at the English College would have prided themselves on a working knowledge of Italian.

8 The College offered accommodation to English visitors.

9 A Master of Ceremonies assists the celebrant during Mass or Benediction, and oversees the role of other participants such as servers and deacons to ensure smooth compliance with the prescribed rituals. Though Worlock refers to him dismissively as a 'boy', the College MC would have been a senior student, probably in his early or mid-20s.

10 Out of the sanctuary and away from the altar. An analogy with cricket pitches.

11 As its former Rector.

12 Throughout the so-called Penal period, the college trained priests who would enter England illegally, knowing that they faced a gruesome death if they were captured by the authorities.

13 This expression was in use at the time to refer to priests who fell into disgrace, often through an affair with a woman.

14 He means Godfrey and himself.

15 A member of the Cardinal's staff.

16 'By the grace of God and favour of the Apostolic See' is an in-joke, it was the official designation used by bishops when they signed pastoral letters, etc.

17 . . . who did the cooking.

18 Alan Clark, later Bishop of East Anglia and co-chairman of the Anglican–Roman Catholic International Commission.

19 Archbishops of Birmingham and Cardiff.

20 *History of Vatican II, Volume I,* p. 117.

21 This passage goes on to note that Godfrey 'no longer had the great influence he had had in the past.'

22 Most Bishops would want to say Mass every day in the College chapel, and though it had several altars some staggering of times would be necessary. Before the Second Vatican Council concelebration, several priests or bishops saying Mass at the same altar together, was not allowed.

23 This was an official process of investigation and instruction that priests conducted with parishioners before they could be married in a Catholic church.

24 Members of this organization had, at the invitation of Worlock, opened a secretarial office near the English College, for his purposes.

25 Émile de Smedt.

26 The formal opening ceremony of the Second Vatican Council.

27 1870.

28 Letter to author.

29 The future Bishop of Liverpool, one-time captain of England and white hope of English cricket, had stood down after his ordination to concentrate on his ministry in the Church of England, but had returned to the national side by 1962 and scored 113 in the Melbourne test (a feat commemorated by a tree planted in his garden in Wirral that was donated by Colin Cowdrey to celebrate their hundred partnership in that game). In fact Sheppard had also played well for England the previous summer.

30 Not least concerning bladder control.

31 Worlock's files do however contain an unfinished account of the opening of the Council, in his own handwriting and apparently written rather later than the diary version, where the significance of this speech is acknowledged. It was possibly intended as a substitute passage for the above.

32 Roughly 'Let them be shunned'.

33 Heenan in fact had consulted Dwyer.

34 I.e. a member.

35 Many English priests had gone out to the Third World from their missionary headquarters at Mill Hill, North London, and some had become bishops.

36 George Patrick Dwyer, later Archbishop of Birmingham, whom Worlock had already referred to as someone Heenan had proposed to the Bishop of Bruges as a candidate worth support from progressives.

37 Bernard Patrick Wall.

38 Dom Basil Christopher Butler, who was himself a theologian of some repute, but not a member of the Hierarchy.

39 Worlock would not have intended this observation as a compliment.

40 It is not clear what personal attributes of General de Gaulle and President Adenauer Worlock thought they corresponded to, except perhaps general awkwardness. Liénart was a friend of Heenan.

41 For what Worlock really suspected, see below.

42 Archbishop Thomas Roberts SJ was a missionary archbishop in Bombay who had retired to make way for an Indian. He was thought by English conservatives to be progressive to the point of scandal.

43 Worlock is referring to the traditional bone of contention between the English and the Irish.

44 That is to say, a formal meeting to deal with the affairs of the Catholic Church in England and Wales as distinct from the regular meetings of all the bishops to deal with Council business.

45 Quoted in *A Crown of Thorns*, Hodder and Stoughton, 1973. He abandoned keeping the diary soon after.

46 Bishop Dwyer of Leeds.

47 Suenens, Koenig, Alfrink and Liénart.

48 Nothing seems to have come of the suggestion.

49 Though Worlock never lists them, the 'awkward squad' appears to comprise Heenan, Dwyer, Beck (of Salford, later Heenan's successor at Liverpool) and Holland (of Portsmouth). Worlock is implying that a split had become established in the ranks of the Hierarchy, between the majority of 'loyalists' who supported Godfrey's line and this 'opposition' led by Heenan.

50 Alberigo and Komonchak (*History of Vatican II, Volume I*) report that in the replies to pre-Council questionnaires, four bishops out of twenty from England – 'not a negligi-

ble figure' – had shown 'a little more openness' than the rest. We do not know whether it was the same four.

51 By a curious diplomatic anomaly dating from the First World War, Britain had a diplomatic mission at the Vatican but there was no reciprocation, the Apostolic Delegation in London having no diplomatic status. (It became a nunciature, equivalent to an embassy – in 1982.)

52 John Moorman, Bishop of Ripon. At the end of the Council in 1965 he wrote 'We outside the communion of the Roman Church have for long been occupied in prayer, in dialogue and in effort for the union of our respective Churches. Now, with the entry of the Roman Catholic Church into this field, we realise that the Ecumenical Movement has taken on a new dimension.' (*The Vatican Observed*, DLT, 1967.)

53 That is to say, a convert to Catholicism.

54 Bishops of Shrewsbury, Lancaster, Menevia (North Wales).

55 A pastoral document would be pragmatic, hence its support among progressives, while a doctrinal document would give the conservatives an opportunity to advance their project of denouncing the errors and evils of the world. A lot of lobbying had gone into giving Faith and Revelation, Ottaviani's draft of a doctrinal document, unstoppable momentum: postponing it would buy time for the progressives to mount a counter-attack.

56 It is not clear that Worlock grasped the crucial significance of all this manoeuvring.

57 Salford.

58 I.e. the perfidious Heenan.

59 Bishop Petit also thought Godfrey had been double-crossed.

60 If this is the same conversation as in the previous sentence. Worlock must mean Liverpool.

4

When Personal Becomes Political

It would misrepresent Derek Worlock entirely to show him as a cold-hearted manipulator or desiccated calculating machine. He liked anecdotes, and sprinkles them throughout his diary. Often they display the human side of events, as he would have intended, but also the human side of himself, about which he was rather more shy. He enjoyed the company of priests, including beginners he could take under his wing.[1] His time at the English College brought him into daily contact with them, and at one point he complains in his diary that his official business prevented him spending the time with them he would have liked. Occasionally he put them before his official duties, as when he skipped an official lunch at the College at which the Apostolic Delegate and a new Bishop of Stockholm were guests of honour.

> Tony O'Sullivan had asked me to lunch with his family, so I had to absent myself from the official festivities. I was glad to be able to go to see his family, the more so as his Mother has made such great sacrifices to see him through to this goal. The lunch was at the Bridgettine Convent in the Piazza Farnese and there were about two dozen of us squashed into a very small room. Nearly all the family and guests were Irish, most of the men folk being employed in London Airport or its surrounds, which probably accounts for the fact that they succeeded in coming out here by air: presumably a certain amount of cheap travel is secured because Tony's family has few pennies with which to bless itself. After the meal I had to propose his health and he replied very nicely, though nervously, with a short speech. I told him afterwards that if he succeeded in maintaining this brevity in the pulpit he was likely to prove a great success. He is a very good lad and the diocese is lucky to have him now as a new priest.

*   *   *

As the progress of the Council began to get bogged down on procedural matters – rules for the debate had omitted to include any provision for a motion of closure and items were dragging on interminably – he also records the start of a brief thaw between himself and Archbishop Heenan, who asked his opinion on one point and later confided in him about a matter that was causing some anxiety. Perhaps Heenan had spotted that Worlock was not as committed to the conservative line as his loyalty to Godfrey may at first have suggested. Heenan was also aware – perhaps more aware than Worlock, even – that Godfrey was seriously, and probably terminally, ill. He must have known he might well succeed him at Westminster – he was close to Cardinal Bea, who was close to Pope John; he was also the most visible of the English bishops by far, to Worlock's chagrin. It was not too soon to work out a *modus vivendi* for dealing with Derek Worlock, who was by then the crucial figure in the machinery of the Catholic Hierarchy in England and Wales.

It is bizarre to note, meanwhile, that the world stood on the brink of a nuclear holocaust; a case of Rome fiddling while the rest of the world was about to burn. Not simply fiddling, in Worlock's case: he was also having a running battle with the Swiss Guard and various other officious Vatican individuals, who did not seem to know quite how to handle this English monsignor with 'attitude'. Unlike the Cuban missile crisis, this conflict even came to blows.

Today was the *Festa del Papa*, the fourth anniversary of the Coronation of the Pope, and this meant being at St Peter's for a solemn function at 9.30. The cardinals and bishops had all to take up their positions in the same stalls as are provided for the Council but first the cardinals had to make their way to the Chapel of St Joseph, there to await the coming of the Pope. Once again train-bearers[2] were ordered for the cardinals and I must confess that I faced the prospect with distaste, knowing that it was unlikely that any provision would be made for us and that, once the Procession was over, we should be tossed about like so much junk until required again. This is precisely what happened. We waited outside the Chapel of St Joseph until the Holy Father had entered and the procession was formed. We had the double row of guards in front of us and were expected to push our way through them in order to get at our cardinals.

We were mauled at this first attempt and there was a fairly disgruntled group of English-speaking secretaries gathered about me when finally we were thrown out of the procession, behind yet another row of Swiss Guards, behind though slightly to the side of St Peter's tomb, over which the Pope was enthroned. We stood there till the ceremony was over shortly before half-past twelve. No benches whatsoever were provided and every so many minutes the guards tried to flatten us against the tribunes holding nuns and other well-placed laity just behind us. The Mass was sung by Cardinal Montini in the Ambrosian rite. It was all very fitting because it was the feast of St Charles but although there were quite a number of differences in this rite which I have not seen before, it was relatively easy to follow. The one strange feature was that the Credo was sung immediately before the Preface. As far as I can make out the minister and servers were brought down from Milan for the occasion and there were some glorious gentry acting as Masters of Ceremonies with long wings flapping out from the arm-pieces of their cottas so that they looked like some form of phantom bat as they flitted about the sanctuary.

After the Last Gospel the Holy Father gave a fairly long address, first in Latin and then in Italian so that he was speaking altogether for about half an hour. From my vantage point I saw the manservant produce from the briefcase a glass which he duly filled from a bottle of Pellegrino and certainly the Pope was in good voice throughout the whole time. It was perhaps a good thing that advertisers of San Pellegrino, who cover so many notice boards in Italy, have not yet decided to show pictures of the Pope as their principal patron.

When the Mass was over we went to join our cardinals and managed to get out as far as the Chapel of St Joseph without too much buffeting. Once we got there we were divided on either side and as soon as the Pope had gone through one of the MCs had the bright idea that we should all be moved over to the same side. We were scarcely told this before the Swiss Guards began pushing us across at the back with their halberds and then some character, known to the boys at the College as 'King Rat', dressed in evening clothes with white tie and with a great silver gong on his breast, gave me a smart blow in the small of the back. I turned round to face him because feeling amongst my brethren was running high and after all these years I am now regarded more or less as their spokesman. As I turned to face him he made to push me in the chest but I caught him by the wrist[3] and I only hope he understood my English when I said to him: 'Although it is clear that you are not a gentleman it is about time that you started to take lessons'.

Looking back on this mauling and buffeting which we now receive, it all seems quite incredible that this can take place in church. One would not stand it anywhere else, yet what can one do? This evening a number of them approached me[4] to see whether we could not make some formal protest. In the old days if you were a cardinal's secretary you always were sure of being able to sit at the feet of your lord and master when all the cardinals were placed alongside one another on their traditional bench. Now they are all up in stalls, no one has yet thought what to do with train-bearers when they are no longer required for a procession. The result is that one is treated in this degrading manner which makes all prayer out of the question and one is apt to finish the ceremony in such a bad temper that clearly this is a situation which cannot continue. Those who spoke to me this evening, including John O'Mara from Toronto and the secretaries from St Louis and Los Angeles, all begged me to try to do something about it. I do not think it is any good appealing to Monsignor Dante[5] but if I have a chance to get a word with Cardinal Marella, the Archpriest of St Peter's, I shall certainly ask whether some provision cannot be made for us to avoid this most unpleasant situation which is now developing.

*   *   *

I found myself in conversation with Archbishop Heenan who asked me for ideas as to how to break the deadlock.[6] I told him that I didn't think that it could be changed radically by a tightening up of procedure, even though some form of guillotine might seem inevitable. But although one can employ such tactics in, say, a TUC conference, if the Council is to be the joint voice of the Fathers no one can easily be deprived of his 'say'. I told him of my belief that common sense and a sense of frustration would triumph and that a speed–up of procedure was inevitable.

I also told the Archbishop that I was under the impression that many of the things that were being said about this first chapter of the schema would prove to be of general application, at least in principle, in the other chapters, and it seemed unlikely that the speakers would wish to repeat themselves. This may turn out to be a vain hope but, after a weekend of thought, it seems likely that there will be some indication tomorrow as to the way in which the wind is blowing.

*   *   *

There have been a series of rumours here all day regarding President Kennedy and Cuba. At first we heard that he had agreed to pull out of Turkey, if Krushchev would remove the bases in Cuba. Then we were told that he had rejected Krushchev's proposals because he could not abandon Turkey. Then we were told once more that he had given the Soviets and the Cubans 48 hours in which to dismantle their missile sites or else he would invade. This story was then reduced to a 24–hour ultimatum but one sincerely hopes that threats of this kind are not tied up with any time-schedule – an anachronism in these days and a threat which seldom can promote an approach to a peaceful solution. The Holy Father is said to have made yet another appeal for peace, but somehow it all seems very remote from here. Let us hope that the Feast of Christ the King will see a solution.

*   *   *

On the way home the Cardinal turned to me and said it looked as though we were going to get our afternoons clear. I did not follow him immediately and I suddenly realised that this meant that he had not been appointed to a Commission. Today the Pope's appointments to the other nine were announced. There is some feeling amongst the English at the proportion of Italians amongst them but to be fair a large number of Spaniards and Latin Curia also figures very strongly in the lists but I suppose that that is only to be expected. In fact to these last nine Commissions announced today only four cardinals have been appointed and it therefore looks as though the original feeling that cardinals were not to be employed in any large extent in the Commissions was accurate. I do not think the Cardinal is anything like as disappointed as he must have been with the result of the elections. Some of our bishops still wish that he had been on the Commission for the Sacraments but on the other hand the last few days have made it clear that speeches in the General Congregations, all of which are passed to the Commission concerned for consideration, are of major importance. On the whole it is better that the Cardinal's voice should be heard there.

Another interesting development today was that Archbishop Heenan received the first copy of my book.[7] He asked me to call in to see him in his room after lunch and I thought it was going to be about the book. But having given it general praise, he then told me of the unhappy position in which he finds himself on the question of unity, which is due to be discussed by the Hierarchy at a special meeting on Tuesday evening. He told me that he felt that he was in a schizophrenic position, because as a member of the Secretariat for Christian Unity he feels bound to advance the views of Cardinal Bea, who he claims represents the views of the Pope, whist he is very conscious that he has also to try to represent the views of the Hierarchy, many of whom do not find themselves in line with the attitude of Cardinal Bea.

Archbishop Heenan let his hair down to me this afternoon in a way which he has not done since the days when I used to talk to him before he was consecrated. He asked me if I thought he should try to explain his difficulty and I recommended that he should do so, at least in order to clear the air. I told him also that I thought he should do so in order to try to explain the apparent inconsistencies of his speeches . . . In one speech he clearly put out the Bea line and in another speech a week or so later he appears to be digging in his heels rather like a right-wing member of our own Hierarchy. He had been working on a statement this evening with Bishop Holland[8] and the impression is that he will probably try to deliver this at the beginning of the meeting in an attempt to disarm the critics. There is no doubt that he will meet with a lot of opposition from Clifton, Southwark and Brentwood[9] and I tried to make the point to him, when we were talking this afternoon, that it would be wrong for him to think that the Cardinal is the most extreme of his critics, even though it clear that the Cardinal does not follow the Bea line.

Archbishop Heenan tried to assure me that Cardinal Bea was doing no more than putting forward the views of the Pope but he gave me little evidence in support of this contention, except the statement that in audience the Pope had told him quite clearly that in the matter of unity Cardinal Bea is his mouthpiece. I would think that this was certainly true a year or two ago but I wonder if it still is, because the Pope speaks with such feeling of Cardinal Ottaviani whose views are diametrically opposed to those of Cardinal Bea. It looks as though the meeting on Tuesday night will be a lively affair. But sufficient for this day.[10]

*   *   *

This evening we had the sixth Session of the Hierarchy meeting, and, after the remaining memoranda had been covered, at last battle was joined on the whole issue of Christian unity. I saw Archbishop Heenan at tea-time and asked him if he had his fighting boots on. He shook his head ruefully and when he came out of the meeting called me on one side and pointed to his feet. He was wearing bedroom slippers! I gather that there was more frank speaking at this meeting than has been known in any meeting of the Hierarchy in recent years. No harm will be done by this.

After the Archbishop had made the distinctions which I anticipated, i.e. between his role as a member of Cardinal Bea's Secretariat and as chairman of the Hierarchy's sub-committee for Christian Unity, there was general sympathy with him but it was made perfectly clear that he did not have to regard himself as our representative on Cardinal Bea's Secretariat because he had been chosen for this by the Pope in his personal capacity and could not be said to be representing our Hierarchy on that Secretariat. The meeting went on two hours, most of the attack on the Archbishop being led by the Bishop of Clifton and the Bishop of Brentwood; apparently the Bishop[11] of Southwark was relatively silent though he is known to be strongly opposed to many of the most recent moves. Bishop Wall made a good point. He said that it was being said all round the Continent by people now accepted as experts[12] but previously regarded as cranks that our bishops were hide-bound and dilatory in ecumenical matters. But what precisely were we expected to do more than was done already?

The Cardinal then took up the point to stress that throughout the years we had faithfully been following out a careful and unbiased interpretation of the teaching of the Church on *communicatio in sacris*. We had been taught that certain things were intrinsically wrong. Why now should they be regarded as intrinsically right? Was it dilatory to be adhering to the teachings of the Church, especially when on many occasions it would have been very much easier not to do so?

Archbishop Heenan's main support came from Bishop Holland, though there were a number who were sympathetic with him and Archbishop Murphy[13] made a good point that it would be most unfortunate if anything were done publicly which might seem to undermine the position of Archbishop Heenan and Bishop Holland. The official minute at the end merely states that after a great deal of discussion, it was agreed to invite Cardinal Bea to discuss the whole question of Christian Unity with our Hierarchy and an invitation is to be extended to him at the end of this week. It is not intended to deal with the remaining point about a new translation of the Bible until after Cardinal Bea has had this opportunity of seeing our bishops. Thus the traditional October Meeting reaches out and on into November. It looks as though in the future it will be known as the Parkinson[14] meeting.

*　　　*　　　*

This meeting was the vital one, the moment when for the majority of English and Welsh bishops present at the Second Vatican Council, the penny began to drop. Heenan's performance at this meeting was obviously strong, and the bishops would have known by then that the tide in the Council was running in his favour – that the progressives, of whom he was identified as the leading English example – were winning the argument. They may well have become aware, also, that he might soon be Cardinal Archbishop of Westminster. Cardinal Godfrey's rather plaintive remark, that it was unfair to criticize them for loyally following what had been the party line, can also be translated as a signal to move on – if the party line changes, those faithful to it must change too. That would also have been Worlock's view.

Heenan does not refer to this crucial Hierarchy meeting in his own notes, nor indeed does it appear to have been recorded anywhere else. Yet it was a momentous turning point in the history of English Catholicism. Without tying it to any particular event, Heenan does, however, record a sharp change of mood among the bishops at almost exactly this time. At the outset of the Council:

a few bishops thought it not only a waste of time but a positive disaster. They were persuaded that in their very different ways Cardinals Bea, Suenens and Alfrink would destroy the unity of the Catholic Church. It is impossible to say how many fathers shared this gloomy view but the number was certainly not large. By the end of the session a very large majority would have been won over and had become enthusiastic about the Council's potential for good. This would not have been true at the beginning or even half way through the session. By the end of those eight intensive weeks, however, almost everyone saw the value of the Council and was confident that with the lessons of the first session learned, the second session would be rewarding.[15]

Alberigo and Komonchak[16] also report this change of mood, which was by no means confined to Great Britain. As already noted, they estimated that at the start of the Council four out of twenty English and Welsh representatives could be identified as open to change, though only moderately so. Meanwhile Cardinal Montini (later Paul VI) had said privately to Cardinal Döpfner that at most 30 out of 344 Italian bishops were of this persuasion. Another estimate said there were only eleven out of 78 Spanish bishops. It is likely similar ratios would apply almost everywhere else. But despite an absence of focused leadership – or even because of it – what these authors called 'the dynamic of the Council' began to exert its effect on almost all those present.

 'Despite all this' they write, 'hardly had the Council taken its first steps when the multitude of the world's bishops began to come to a sense of themselves. The general opinion that took shape and the face that the assembly presented became radically different, to the point where "majority" and "minority" changed their meaning within a very short space of time.' The 'catalyst' responsible for this change was Pope John XXIII. The clearest signal he gave at the first session of the Council was his willingness to withdraw the preparatory documents as soon as they ran into significant resistance. This must have provoked even loyalists like Godfrey and Worlock to think again.

 Heenan, in his published reminiscences, and Alberigo and Komonchak in their exhaustive research into the archives of Vatican II (by no means completed) had the benefit of hindsight. Worlock's diary was written up at the time, devoid of hindsight. He had no idea what would happen next, let alone where it would all lead. Meanwhile he was getting his own back on behalf of the train-bearers, against their tormentors.

*   *   *

We drove on to the Canonica where Monsignor John Mostyn, Canon of St Peter's, was duly waiting for us. The only other guests at lunch were the Bishop of Menevia and Monsignor Curtin from the Beda. In the course of the meal the conversation turned to recent ceremonies in St Peter's. I saw the Cardinal giving me a look and eventually I got my opening. The Cardinal said with some indignation that I had been hit the previous Sunday, and John Mostyn refused to believe it. He asked me what had happened and so I gave him an exposé of the difficulty now facing cardinals' train-bearers, required to report and then, when not particularly in use, discarded like so much refuse. He tried to talk me out of it and said in the end that he had come to the conclusion that 'if you want to get on in Rome you just have to take those things'. I told him that I wasn't interested in 'getting on' but that I did not consider that any priest on any occasion should be treated in this fashion and furthermore that we did not and furthermore that we wouldn't expect it to happen in a tin chapel in a field in Wales.

This was a strange thing to have said with the Bishop of Menevia present but he rallied nobly to my side and I think really spoiled poor John Mostyn's lunch. I should feel penitent about the whole thing but I do not because I have feelings that perhaps John Mostyn will pass on these comments to other members of the Chapter of St Peter's so that in the end something may be done. I feel that I owe it to my fellow secretaries in other parts of the world to try to take a stand on the issue.

*   *   *

This morning as I took the Cardinal to St Peter's, I raised with him a point which I had discussed with Archbishop Heenan last night and again at breakfast. We are a bit concerned about the presence of the Observers at every one of these General Congregations. It has reached a point when Monsignor Davis claims that they are there by right, though the *regolamento*[17] specifically says that on special occasions they may be excluded. We think it would be a good point to establish the principle as soon as possible and exclude them from one morning so that they may get used to the idea and then when it proves necessary to exclude them on a specific issue, for example when mixed marriages are discussed it will not be so obvious to the outside world why they have been excluded.

The particular point which is worrying the Archbishop[18] is the fact that *De Fide* is likely to come under discussion next week. We anticipate that there will be a real set-to between the liberals and the traditionalists. It seems that there are a number of points in the schema which are likely to rile those who have been amongst the people trying to explain away a lot of Scriptural tradition. In this community one can see immediately the figures of Cardinal Bea who used to be at the Biblicum[19] and Cardinal Alfrink who was also a professor of Scripture before he became Archbishop of Utrecht. It seems inevitable that there will be a clash between them and Cardinal Ottaviani as indeed was the case a year ago in the Central Commission. It will not be a good thing for the Observers to witness such a clash. It is one thing to let them see differences of opinion where, say, ecclesiastical discipline is concerned, quite another to hear discussion on matters of faith. I therefore asked the Cardinal whether he did not think it would be a good thing to have a word with the General Secretariat. I therefore left him at the table talking to Archbishop Kroll of Philadelphia, who said he would take note of the Cardinal's point. I fancy that some more action will have to be taken if any real effect is to be registered.

*　　　　　*　　　　　*

When they had gone I had a visit from Bishop Grant[20] in order to talk over with him the decision of the Hierarchy regarding the establishment of the Catholic Fund for Overseas Development. I have had several letters from Canon Rivers all demanding instructions, drafts of news releases and so on. It is very difficult at this distance to try to assess English opinion sufficiently to make a draft of this kind and one can quite easily tread on someone else's toes. Indeed one of the objects of establishing this fund was to make people responsible for the kind of work which we have been trying to play with on the fringe in Archbishop's House for so long. It is of no help at all if all the decisions are to be referred to us. However, eventually Bishop Grant pleaded with me to prepare the document myself, so that was another job to be done this evening.[21]

At this point a number of issues were starting to come together, and the foundations were laid for the way they could later be resolved. The draft decree *De Fide* (Of the Faith), prepared under the auspices of Cardinal Ottaviani, was an attempt to identify and denounce the errors of modernity, a continuation of the battle the Holy See had been conducting since the late nineteenth century against the heresy of Modernism.[22] The draft *De Fontibus Revelationis*, also from the Ottaviani camp, addressed two issues of the same sort.

One was left over from the Reformation, when the Protestant Reformers broke away from Rome over the issue of 'Scripture alone'. The Catholic Church taught that its own Tradition was the authentic guide to the interpretation of the Christian revelation – that the Holy Spirit, which was deemed to guide the Church down the centuries, would not have guided it into erroneous interpretations of doctrine. Scripture was treated as an expression of that Tradition. The Reformers taught Scripture as the supreme guide, and if it conflicted with Tradition, Tradition had to give way. What the progressives wanted was a formula which harmonized these two theories of the sources of doctrine rather than set them at odds. Success at that would have had powerful consequences for relations between the Catholic and Protestant Churches.

The second arose more from the Enlightenment and from the critical study of Biblical texts, which convincingly showed that not all parts of the Bible could be treated as equally reliable as historical records. In the Protestant academic world these studies had been taken to the point where some scholars rejected the reliability of Scripture altogether. Miracles, for instance, were discounted because to believe in them meant preferring uncertain Scriptural evidence against the certainty of scientific fact (i.e., the fact that miracles 'cannot happen'). Crucially, this included the Resurrection itself.

Catholic Biblical research had been more conservative, not least because the Holy Office discouraged theological speculation which might call Catholic dogma into question. But many Catholic scholars, Cardinals Bea and Alfrink among them, were pressing for more freedom for Biblical research and for official recognition that parts of the Bible could best be understood allegorically. The Catholic Church did not teach that the Bible was literally true, as a Protestant fundamentalist would. It was not wedded, for instance, to the 'Creationist' theory that the world was created by God in six days, or that all animal species appeared more or less simultaneously. But there was a strong feeling that a kind of tacit semi-literalism was a useful brake on the more extravagant reinterpretations that progressive Catholic theologians might otherwise pursue. What the progressives had to prove, therefore, was that if the value of critical Biblical scholarship was admitted, this did not mean that henceforth 'anything goes'.

On the one hand, the Council had to realign Scripture and Tradition so that neither was subordinate to the other; on the other hand, it had to make room for the authority of the Church to oversee, and if necessary check, the fruits of Biblical research (as a necessary precaution against extremes, before allowing that research much more freedom). Insofar as Tradition itself represents the exercise of the Church's authority in the past, there is considerable overlap between the 'Scripture versus Tradition' debate and the 'Biblical criticism versus the *Magisterium*' debate. This overlap created possibilities for a satisfactory solution.

The final visitor this morning was Father Lionel Swain who is living at the Beda, and after a successful course at St Edmunds and in Paris, is now down here to do a year at the Biblicum. The reason for his visit was that he was asked yesterday by the authorities at the Biblicum to seek the use of the Cardinal's name in a programme which they are preparing for a thesis to be delivered by some German biblical scholar at the Biblicum in a few days' time. I was a bit canny about this because I know of the row which has been going on between the Biblicum and the Lateran, a row which is likely to be reflected in the course of the next few days in the debate *De Fide*. When I looked at the names of the other cardinals who had given this form of approval and allowed the use of their names, I saw at once that it was all this left-wing crowd with whom the Cardinal is unlikely to find himself in sympathy, though many would claim that the Cardinal is a little too far out to the right on this point.

The whole of this question has been boiling in the College during the day. A certain number of our bishops went yesterday evening to the lecture given by Cardinal Suenens on the subject of the forthcoming schema. There are a large number of bishops who are so dissatisfied with what has been prepared that they want to move its total rejection and they have prepared an alternative document. I managed to see this document this evening and it has the full support of the Hierarchies of Germany, Austria, France, Belgium, and Luxembourg. This is quite a formidable grouping and it seems that they are now moving wider afield in their search for support. Bishop Beck and one or two of the others, who had obtained a copy of the document this evening, are clearly impressed by what they heard.

Even before we left England we heard from Archbishop Heenan that there was dissatisfaction on the Continent with this particular schema.[23] I remember that he wrote that he hoped it would be thrown overboard at once and something more worthwhile and suited to modern conditions would be prepared. My own mind goes back to the meeting of the Central Commission a year ago when Cardinal Ottaviani put forward this schema *De Fide* and *De Fontibus Revelationis*. I think we will find in the earlier pages of this diary my assessment that at that stage, realising that he would never secure a *placet*[24] for his work, the Cardinal Secretary of the Holy Office withdrew the document and said it would be revised in the light of the comment made in the Central Commission and submitted to a later Session. I am also under the impression that it was never re-submitted and these same people who opposed him in the Central Commission a year ago, viz. Cardinal Döpfner and Cardinal Koenig and Cardinal Alfrink, are now the leaders of the opposition as Cardinal Ottaviani tries to present the document once more.

A further irritant has been a notice in *Il Tempo* this morning which claims that during yesterday's debate Cardinal Ruffini took the Fathers to task on the question of applause. So much is undoubtedly true. What he said was that if people wanted to show their approval by applause they must also be prepared to hear disapproval by other vocal means and under these circumstances it would be better for the debate to proceed with silence from the listeners. *Il Tempo* has gone further and said that the Cardinal stated to the Fathers that he deeply regretted the action taken by Cardinal Alfrink in ringing down Cardinal Ottaviani the other day and it was for this reason that Cardinal Ottaviani had attended no further sessions. The fact of the Cardinal's absence is quite true but I don't think it can really be in connection with the attack of Cardinal Alfrink. The next few days will show whether he turns up as the debate moves on to *De Fide*. Presumably he will have to be there then.

This afternoon it was damp but the Cardinal and I managed to get a short walk before five o'clock when Michael Ashdowne drove him to see Cardinal Browne who had asked to discuss certain matters with him. I gather that the conversation with him was in fairly general terms and the Dominican Cardinal certainly knew nothing about the document prepared by Cardinal Suenens and the others. He discounted the reason given by *Il Tempo* for the absence of Cardinal Ottaviani and offered no alternative explanation. He did, however, give it as his opinion that the likely move in the future would be to hand over more of the *schemata* to the Commissions and leave them to get on with it and thus cut down some of the generalisations being produced each morning in St Peter's. It will remain to be seen whether this means that the number of general Congregations will be reduced or whether the Fathers will be sent home. Clearly an announcement regarding the opening date of the Second Session is bound to come shortly as conjecture cannot be left to run at the pace at which it is moving at the present time.

All attention at the moment is focused on the forthcoming *schemata De Fide* and even here in the College this evening a number of the bishops were gathered together taking the document which had been proposed apart. The main criticism of it seems to be that it pays inadequate attention to the developments there have been in Scriptural study in the past few years. Much depends upon the interpretation as to how far Scripture is dependent on tradition and even more the other way round. This brings to the fore those whom I always call the debunkers. My difficulty with them is quite simply 'Where do you stop?' Once you try to explain away traditional beliefs arising from the Scriptures, how much further do you go? There is the danger of course that in the end you treat the whole of Scripture as an unhistorical document and merely as parables from which the truth has to be extracted.

Heenan threw his own light on the issues[25] when he later wrote:

The debate brought to light the extent of confusion regarding ecumenism. Although the debate was ostensibly and immediately about scripture and tradition the point of the underlying disagreement was ecumenical. Some of the fathers were evidently determined that Catholic doctrine must be stated only in terms which were acceptable to Protestants. They did not, of course, put it in this way even to themselves. They took their stand on the Reformers' contention that the Bible is the only authentic source of doctrine. (Scriptural texts are rightly quoted to support all Catholic dogmas but it is taking liberty with language to say that the Immaculate Conception and the Assumption are biblical truths. Some over-enthusiastic ecumenists would jettison all Marian dogma in the quite mistaken belief that this would please Protestants.)

He did not include Cardinal Bea in this latter category.

This is a slightly odd comment, first because jettisoning Marian dogmas such as the Immaculate Conception and the Assumption would indeed please Protestants, secondly because Heenan must have known this was so, and thirdly because it is almost impossible to identify Catholic 'ecumenists' (to use his slightly derogatory term) who actually did desire this. Thus a confidential paper circulated shortly afterwards by the progressive French theologian Yves Congar identified three positions currently being taken in the Catholic Church on the Scripture/Tradition issue, from left to right. None corresponds to the position Heenan exaggeratedly describes above, which therefore may be something of an Aunt Sally.

By the time he wrote this, however, he had regressed to a more conservative position,[26] despairing of the sweeping reforms that were brought in in the name of the Council after it was over. What seemed to betray the English bishops during this period was their ignorance of theology and refusal to take seriously any of the movements that had taken place in the previous 30 years. Most of them, of course, would be unable to follow an argument in French or German. The theologians concerned were no more the 'debunkers' of Worlock's invective than they were the 'cranks', now called 'experts', that the Bishop of Brentwood found so distasteful. Most of the English bishops were content with the thought that the Catholic Church had got it right in the sixteenth century and the Protestants had got it wrong. What is to their credit is their willingness to move once they understood the arguments (or in Worlock's case, once he saw which way the wind was blowing).

Congar's three positions were:[27]

(a) tradition is a source independent of scripture, transmitting truths not contained in scripture (theory of the two sources); (b) tradition is an interpretation and an unfolding of the content of scripture, which is materially sufficient:

everything is in the scripture, everything is in tradition; (c) in regard to essentials, the content of scripture and the content of tradition are identical; tradition goes beyond scripture only in a relative and subordinate way.

The position eventually adopted by the Second Vatican Council is approximately (b).

A strong argument broke out in the Bishops' Common Room this evening quite late on when one of them was saying that if we have to dismiss the traditional interpretation of Scripture, then we were going to run into difficulties regarding infallibility. Conversation became so lively at one stage that I discovered that certain members of our secretariat, notably Monsignor Clark and Father O'Brien had moved out of the room so as not to embarrass the bishops. But by the time I entered . . . the Bishop of Leeds was entertaining the bishops assembled in the Common Room to his personal reminiscences regarding the early work of the Preparatory Commission on 'Bishops and the Rule of Dioceses'. His story was that the basic document upon which they were asked to work gave the following points: 1. That every bishop is entitled to reservation of the Blessed Sacrament in his own house but without indult; 2. That any bishop is entitled to preach in any part of the world provided he has permission of the Local Ordinary.[28] And so, rather perplexed and anxious, to bed!

At this morning's General Congregation Monsignor Felici announced that the Holy Father had decided that the Second Session of the Council will commence on the Fourth Sunday after Easter, 12th May . . . There is not a lot of surprise about that when one learns that the general elections in Italy are due to be held on Sunday 5th May, which is the Third Sunday after Easter. There is no doubt that the Italians have got their way because they regard it as essential that they should be in their dioceses at the time of the elections. When one realises that most presbyteries serve as the election headquarters of local Christian Democrat candidates one can see that a bishop has to be on the spot, even if only to threaten excommunication to those who would otherwise vote Communist.[29]

But the alarming thing is that there is to be no Session in the meantime. I had thought it possible that there would be a Session of six weeks to two months in the first few months of the year and that the third Session would commence in May, for I have always had the idea that the Pope intended the Council should be over within twelve months. Still more alarming is the story that Cardinal Cicognani[30] told some of the English bishops yesterday that the Pope still intended that the whole Council should be over by the Feast of St Peter and St Paul. This can only mean that in the intervening months the Commissions are to go through the *schemata*, slash them to a minimum and prepare a series of decrees which will have to be steam-rollered through the General Council during the six weeks of the summer Session. Whether this can be done seems from this distance highly unlikely but what worries me more is the thought that very many of the bishops will undoubtedly not come back for such a short summer Session. The missionaries and the distant ones even in Latin America are already saying that they will not be back in May. I regard this as grave news because if, for example, the present attendance of 2,100 bishops each day is reduced to 1,500 then with all the Italians present they will be in a strong position to block any decision which they do not like because a two-thirds majority will have to be obtained and they can easily form the nucleus of more than one third. I do not know how many Italian bishops there are but including all those on the missions, if they can get them back they can do more or less what they like.

Of course this is an immediate reaction and experience shows that the Holy Ghost works even through decisions of this kind. Probably in a year's time we shall be blessing the foresight of the Pope in breaking the apparent deadlock[31] but I cannot help feeling that the news will be very badly received outside Rome. One can imagine that in England it will be interpreted as a breakdown in procedure and it will be said that the Council has failed. If it is seriously intended to try to close the Council within six weeks in the summer then all chance of discussion in St Peter's must be ruled out.

*   *   *

At the back of my mind I have also the worry as to whether the Cardinal will remain sufficiently fit to be able to come out and do his work in the spring.[32] The whole matter presents all sorts of problems, not least that of the secretariat in Via dell' Anima.[33] Presumably we shall have to leave some holding force but it would be pointless to keep all of them out here during the intervening months. But there is a month still to run of this Session and no doubt things will become much clearer during that period.

We have a number of sick bishops with heavy colds . . . I have been using Redoxon and every time my cold seems to be coming to the surface I pack myself full of these massive doses of vitamin C and it seems to keep the cold at bay. How long I shall be lucky I do not know . . . This evening I was telling the Archbishop[34] about these and he asked me if he could see them. I brought him out my tube of these big tablets and I was just remarking to him that he should put one into half a glass of water as it was effervescent when he took one out and popped it straight into his mouth saying that he would try it. No sooner had he said that than the wretched thing started to effervesce in his mouth and the last I saw of him was a figure speeding down the corridor, apparently frothing at the mouth, whilst I was shouting at him 'Spit, spit it into a glass of water!' It will be interesting to see how much worse he is in the morning . . .

We got back at half-past three and an hour later I was downstairs welcoming Cardinal Bea who came with Monsignor Willebrands to meet the Hierarchy and to discuss Christian unity and the progress of the Ecumenical Movement in England and Wales. First we all had a cup of tea together and then at five o'clock they moved into the Library for the meeting which finished shortly before quarter to seven. As far as I can make out the meeting was not particularly conclusive. Cardinal Bea treated them to an exhortation of about forty minutes and then various bishops spoke trying to make comments relative to the situation in England. There was praise for the astuteness of the old Cardinal but there was also a feeling that he was not prepared for some of the points which were made. In all events one must hope that the two sides understood each other a little better at the end. Another strange fact, commented on by several bishops this evening was that for once the Bishop of Leeds was silent throughout the entire meeting. Late tonight I discovered why: he is suffering from acute indigestion and has been in poor shape for several days following this wretched cold.

When I got back from the Greg[35] and when the Unity meeting was over, I took the Cardinal out once more to the hospital. The Cardinal says that the doctor is cutting away a little skin each day, presumably trying to ensure that one side of the wound does not overgrow in its healing powers until the other has caught – a strange business. At all events the Cardinal was very tired tonight and retired to bed much earlier than usual. He seems very tired indeed at the moment.

*   *   *

Wednesday, 14th November: Another wet and thundery day but this morning the balloon went up in St Peter's and all the big guns fired. The bishops were buzzing with excitement when they came out at 12.15 and the debate has carried on all day.

It seems that Cardinal Ottaviani went straight into the attack and denounced the circulation of the substitute document by the Northern European bloc.[36] He claimed that the circulation of such substitute schema could not be reconciled with Canon Law as it was for the Pope alone to determine matters to be dealt with in a Council. He seems if anything to have overplayed his hand, stressing that the action taken in the past few days is disrespectful to the Pope, and if the Fathers had emendations to make, they should make them on this schema which is approved by the Pope for discussion. He also attacked the criticism that the schema lacked the pastoral tone. He said that the primary object of the Council was to propound doctrine and the pastoral tone could be added by others later. Of course the real issue is the Scriptural one and on this Ottaviani said that to the charge that the schema was not abreast of the new theology he would reply that fashions in theology come and go and that the function of the Council was to protect and promote the Catholic doctrine, formulate it in exact terms without receding from the sense in which the Church has always interpreted the Divine deposit. One was not looking for new statements but for an increase of doctrine.

The speeches this morning were confined almost entirely to Cardinals and it is generally agreed that the debate was of the highest level achieved so far. This may be due to the fact that cardinals have only to send a note to the Secretariat stating that they wish to speak and they do not have to give the three days' notice. As long as three days notice is required, it is hard to see how there can be any real debate. Cardinal Ottaviani was supported by Cardinal Ruffini, Cardinal Siri and Cardinal Quirog y Palacios. Generally speaking their argument was that on the whole they were prepared to give their *placet* to the schema but if points needed clarifications this should be taken in the course of the discussion with the Fathers and not by substituting another document. The *non placet* came from Cardinals Liénart, Fringe, Léger of Montreal, Koenig, Alfrink, Suenens, Bea and rather surprisingly Ritter of St-Louis. Liénart claimed that the document's whole tenor was inadequate to the matter in question and unrealistic in its frigid and scholastic style. Frings and Léger and Koenig all dealt with this question of Biblical theology claiming that future development would be handicapped by this stultifying document. Cardinal Alfrink claimed that the schema was out of harmony with the allocution of John XXIII, who had said it was not the job of the Fathers to repeat the well-known teachings of theologians. The Pope wanted an expression suited to our times.

From all accounts the best speech came from Cardinal Bea who claimed that the present document does not correspond to the scope set by Pope John who wanted 'the whole and pure truth of God so presented that men would understand it and freely assent to it'. In his opinion the schema was devoid of pastoral character and gave no consideration at all to the question of reunion. It had however much to say about exegetes,[37] speaking of them with a certain suspicion and fear and without any recognition of the problems facing them. It was one thing to condemn collective inspiration which in any case is taught by only one or two but the real question is how the inspired writer was influenced by the collectivity . . .

When the Cardinal came out of St Peter's he was bubbling with excitement. He told me that the Holy Ghost had moved in a big way and had had a great triumph. He said that there had been a motion as to whether or not Cardinal Ottaviani's schema should be withdrawn in favour of the alternative document and that the suggestion had been overwhelmingly defeated by over 2,000 votes to 46. I found this very difficult to understand because it was clear to me that the Northern European bloc would vote pretty well as a whole but if it was true it was a crashing defeat for the leftists and the Biblicum. It turned out however that the Cardinal had been very sleepy during the morning. He had been complaining increasingly of being tired and he must have misunderstood the announcement regarding the votes which was not on the subject of the matter under debate but was a formal vote of approval that the *schemata* on the Liturgy should be returned to the Liturgical Commission with a *placet*, qualified by the understanding that the viewpoints expressed during the last month's debate should, so far as was possible in the opinion of the Commission be written into the document. By lunch time the Cardinal had found out the true state of affairs and he seemed a bit confused about it all, so it turns out that the big battle is still on with no indication as yet as to which way it will blow.

*　　　　　*　　　　　*

I do remember a certain feeling of triumph when everything began to go so much more smoothly for the train-bearers in St. Peter's and I was receiving warm congratulations from Americans, Canadians and others who were all convinced that I had intervened successfully after the shameful performance at the time of the Anniversary of the Pope's Coronation. I cannot say that I have intervened successfully but I have no doubt at all that John Mostyn passed on my complaints and it may be that these did have some effect. Certainly when we moved off with our cardinals, we were not struck, we were not even unduly obstructed, but merely bowed into our places and when we came round by St Peter's tomb, to our utter astonishment we were shown into a bench where we were allowed to sit throughout the ceremony. Such good fortune hasn't fallen to me for a very long time. The biggest triumph of all came at the end of the ceremony when we went across in procession to the chapel where the Holy Father takes leave of the cardinals. It was outside this chapel that I was struck ten days ago and, on this occasion we were duly beckoned to one side and the same man who had struck me, Giovanni Giovanni believe it or not, actually gave us a graceful gesture with his hand and asked us to step to one side 'per favor'. When he used those magic words people were quite astonished. It may be that it was all nothing whatever to do with what happened ten days ago but it was at least a very welcome change and I was fairly wallowing in reflected glory afterwards.

*　　　　　*　　　　　*

All the enthusiasm from last Wednesday seemed to have disappeared and Archbishop Heenan told me that they had spent the entire morning discussing how, if at all, they should proceed. The whole thing is still turning on this question of whether the schema put forward by Cardinal Ottaviani is to be discussed or rejected out of hand and another substituted. Whereas on Wednesday most of the speeches had been made by cardinals, it seemed that on Friday most of them came from bishops. Apparently a very long list of speakers was read out and Archbishop Heenan had given his name but he was not called. They did not reach him. I suspect that he will be against Ottaviani, against whom I have heard him speak with great venom. The number of people who do feel so strongly about him seem to suggest to me that he must at times have hurt a certain number of people by the hardness of his answers. On the other hand there can be little doubt that many of the bishops feel that there is a real danger of heresy in the attitude adopted by the Biblicum or at least in its more extreme exponents and no doubt Ottaviani has felt that, faced with such difficulties, he must act sharply. Monsignor McCreavy has made some sort of summary of the debate on Friday and yesterday (Saturday). I will try to include some points from this later in the diary.

By the time I got back to the College my temperature was well over a hundred and I had to give in and go to bed. I lay in bed with hot water bottles and taking tablets of various kinds at regular intervals . . . Later in the evening there began a procession of bishops into my room all of it meant very kindly but rather exhausting. After the exchange of pleasantries they would begin to discuss the debate which is at present occupying the Council, viz., *de Fontibus.* It is remarkable how they nearly all differ in their accounts of what had taken place to date but although there is a certain amount of criticism for the apparently high-handed attitude of the Holy Office, the views of most of the bishops seem to be moderate with regard to the new methods of interpretation of the Bible as taught at the Biblicum. I think that most of the bishops would like sufficient freedom left for these new methods to be pursued, whilst at the same time providing safeguards until those exercising these new methods are thoroughly mature. On Saturday evening a large number of the bishops went out to the conference organised by the Hierarchy of South Africa at which four or five priests from the Biblicum spoke on the issues involved. On the whole I think the bishops were impressed and they are only just beginning to realise that these methods which they regard as entirely new have in fact been taught in the seminaries by Alec Jones and Hubert Richards[38] and others for ten years or more.

*   *   *

Monsignor McReavy lists as cardinals willing to give their *placet*, with welcome, to the document submitted by the Commission, Cardinal Cerejeira of Lisbon, Cardinal McIntyre of Los Angeles, Cardinal Santos of Manila and Cardinal Rivera of Mexico. All these cardinals feel that there is room for emendation but that on the whole the document is quite satisfactory. A more qualified *placet* has come from Cardinal Camara of Rio, Cardinal Caggiano of Buenos Aires, Cardinal Urbani of Venice and Cardinal Browne. All these claim that the document is satisfactory in substance but that certain amendments are needed and the whole could be given a more pastoral tone.

Non placets have come from Cardinal Lefebvre of Bourges, Cardinal Silva of Chile, very many French and German bishops and the Abbot of Downside who advocated that expert representatives of the two schools of thought should first meet and work out an agreed statement if possible. Otherwise the schema should be rejected.

An interesting speech came from Cardinal Döpfner who moved that the *schema* be rejected and replaced by another prepared by experts of the two schools nominated by the Pope. He claimed that in the preparatory Theological Commission one side had prevailed unduly and that in the Central Commission many objections were raised to the schema but very few changes were made in the final version. Emendations had not been dealt with individually.

It seemed that after Cardinal Döpfner had spoken Cardinal Ottaviani intervened, claiming that Cardinal Döpfner had been misinformed. There were differences of opinion in the Theological Commission but they were separated[39] by debate and vote. The Central Commission did not proceed in summary fashion and all the points had been considered. I think that if we turn back this diary to what I wrote about the Second Session of the Central Commission last November, you will find it recorded that Cardinal Ottaviani withdrew this same document because he knew that he couldn't get it through the Central Commission and undertook to make certain changes and submit it again later. I wonder very much how many changes were made. It may well be this which has led those same opponents of twelve months ago to cry for the blood of Cardinal Ottaviani now.

Certainly Cardinal Ottaviani for whom one must have great sympathy, has not played his cards well. It would seem that yesterday he wielded the big stick again claiming that it would be improper to reject the schema which had been passed by a majority vote in the Central Commission. Earlier he had claimed that to do so was against Canon Law. However on this occasion, one of the Conciliar Fathers passed a note to the President, Cardinal Gilroy, calling the attention of the Fathers to Article 33, paragraph 1, of the *regolamento* which says that any Father can speak about any of the *schemata* put forward '*vel admittendo, vel reiiciendo, vel emendando*'.[40]

This summary provided by Monsignor McReavy gives an interesting report of a speech made by Bishop Charue of Namur, who claims that the *non placet* of Cardinal Suenens is shared by all the bishops of Belgium and others of Belgian origin in the Congo. There must be prudence and serenity in reconciling Christian doctrine with scientific truth but obstacles should not be put in the way of sincere research. The supreme authority of the Church needs to be asserted through the Holy Office but it is not for a General Council to play the part of the Holy Office.

*   *   *

The other item of note today is that the last Session of the Hierarchy Meeting took place at five o'clock. Thus the October Meeting of the Hierarchy has lasted over five weeks and through about seven or eight sessions, each of which has lasted for over two hours . . . It certainly seems to have whetted the appetite of the bishops for meetings and they have now invited one of the Scripture scholars from the Biblicum to come to the College next Sunday to talk to them about these new methods of interpretation of the Bible and to answer questions . . .

This morning's Session of the Council seems to have been fairly inconclusive. Although Archbishop Heenan's name is still on the list of speakers he was not called today. He came to see me this evening and told me that if he does speak he will recommend that the schema should not be rejected but should be changed after careful examination, point by point. He seems to think that this will be the attitude of most of the English bishops. It would seem that the most storming and emotional speech so far delivered came today from the Bishop of Bruges, de Smedt, who claimed that the document was several hundred years out of date; that it was completely out of touch with the whole feeling of the Ecumenical Dialogue and that unless the schema was rejected, a glorious opportunity would be lost for the Church. It seems that it was such an emotional outburst, that when he sat down applause in St Peter's lasted a full two minutes. Even Archbishop Heenan claims that it was a bit much for an Englishman's stomach. To me it seems fairly clear that neither side is likely to get a two-thirds majority, i.e. for the rejection of the schema or for the presentation of it. A great deal will depend upon the manner in which the Council of the Presidency is able to present a proposition for a vote. There are a number amongst the Council Presidents who clearly favour the rejection of this schema but I think they will be outnumbered.

*   *   *

Tuesday 20th November: The bishops did not get back until half-past twelve but it became evident that one of the things that the Cardinal had wanted to be present for is a vote, and a vote had taken place. It would seem that after there had been a number of speeches, Cardinal Ruffini, who was in the Chair, announced that the Council Presidents wished to move a closure of this particular subject and accordingly they wished to take a vote. The whole toss-up was whether the vote would be for the schema as put forward by Cardinal Ottaviani or for its rejection.

The importance of this was that in either case, to be effective, a resolution has to receive a two-thirds majority and it seemed very unlikely that whichever way it was put it would receive such a majority. Accordingly – and I think with some considerable cunning – it was put forward from the Council of the Presidents that the motion was that the *schema* submitted by the Theological Commission should be rejected. This meant that those in favour of its rejection had to put their cross on the square marked *Placet* and those who favoured the schema had got to write *Non Placet*. It was most confusing and it would seem that Monsignor Felici had to go to the pulpit more than once in order to explain what it was all about. Even then it seems pretty clear that some of the bishops voted the wrong way round. I know that for one, the Bishop of Middlesbrough,[41] voted *Placet*, meaning that he was in favour of the rejection of the schema, whereas in fact he thought he was voting in favour of the schema. At all events when the voting was counted, the result was sensational.

I have not got the exact figure but it seems that well over 1,200 bishops voted for the rejection of the schema and only just over 800 were in favour. On the other hand, as there were 2,100 Fathers present, for the resolution to be effective 1,400 votes were required and thus the vote fell short of this. But what a setback for Cardinal Ottaviani! He now knows that the majority of the Fathers have rejected the work of his Commission and he must also realise that in fact it is a personal vote against himself. It is sad to think that this battle of personalities has come so far to the fore but everywhere one goes in Rome it is the same old story: criticism of Ottaviani and to a lesser extent of the Holy Office for its dictatorial tactics and in particular for its recent action in suspending two of the professors at the Biblicum and giving no adequate reason to the Rector of the Biblicum.

I think that the Cardinal was quite prepared himself to hail the result of the vote as a triumph for Ottaviani and it is possible that he might claim that the Holy Ghost had safeguarded the position of the Church by securing that the opposition did not receive a two-thirds majority. On the other hand there can be little doubt that most of the right wing regarded the result of this vote as a defeat and it is said that the look upon the face of Cardinal Ruffini was most revealing. There is a story going around Rome this evening of a shipwreck.

The story takes the form of the well-known riddle: Cardinal Ottaviani, Cardinal Ruffini and Cardinal Siri all went afishing and suddenly the boat sank. Who do you think was saved? And then the horrid answer is: the Church.

*   *   *

Wednesday 21st November: There was to some extent a sense of anti-climax about the gathering in St Peter's. Everyone was watching everyone else and there must have been in the back of their minds a feeling of futility at going on with the discussion of a thesis when it was known that well over 50 per cent of the Fathers rejected it. The interesting fact to me is that, so far as I can find out, the one whom I regard as the real figure in the background and the leader of the whole anti-Ottaviani movement, Cardinal Montini, has not spoken in this debate at all. Yet morning after morning I see him as he enters the side door of St Peter's, approached by all the members of the opposition, notably Cardinal Suenens, Cardinal Alfrink and Cardinal Koenig, and it is strange to say the least that he has not declared himself publicly in this momentous debate.[42] But this morning when I came in all eyes were in another direction as Cardinal Ottaviani was seen making a visit into the Blessed Sacrament chapel. There were a few rather wicked sniggers and diggings in the ribs as people pointed out that the Secretary of the Holy Office was seeking inspiration and consolation. One could not help feeling very sorry for Ottaviani.

After this I went round to the Grail in order to try and make some plans regarding what should happen when this particular Session comes to an end and did not get back to the College until about 10.45 am. I got a great shock then, when I was told that some of the bishops were already back. I had a quick look out of the windows to see if the cars had returned but there was no sign of them and I could not make out what had happened. The Rector told me knowledgeably that the Pope himself had announced that he had thrown out the Ottaviani schema and accordingly some of the bishops had walked out. I went on down to our salon and there I found Archbishop Heenan, who, as far as I could find out, was the only bishop who walked out.

What happened was that right at the beginning of the Session an announcement was made in the name of the Pope to the effect that, after consulting with the Cardinal Secretary of State (and it is believed with Cardinal Tisserant) the Pope had decided that in view of the dissatisfaction of the Fathers with the present schema he would himself set up a small commission to examine the points which had been raised and the points of debate and until that commission had had the opportunity of considering matters further, the whole question of the Theological schema should be set on one side. Clearly he wanted the high feelings to die down but what came as an anti-climax was the suggestion that the rest of the morning should be devoted to the giving of the speeches which would have been made if the schema had not been withdrawn. It is generally thought that this move was decided on because if the Fathers had all come rushing out of St Peter's soon after half-past nine this morning, the Press would have made something much too sensational about it. So the Fathers had to sit there until after twelve o'clock whilst people went through their set speeches.

It will be very interesting indeed to see who the Pope appoints to this small commission. He can scarcely choose the members of either the old Theological Commission or the newly elected Theological Commission and if he brings in some of these to talk to their opponents from the last week or two there will then be nothing more than the protracted difficulty which has absorbed the whole Council for the last ten days. It is thought that he will leave well alone for a little while until feelings cool down and in the meantime apparently an effort is being made to find a subject which will keep the Fathers occupied until the end of this Session without raising too many high spirits. Almost inevitably they have therefore switched to what are commonly called 'Mass-media' and so from the sublime truths of the founts of Revelation, the Fathers have now got to switch to the Press, the cinema, radio and television!

When I went back to St Peter's to collect the Cardinal soon after mid-day I found him standing with Cardinal Browne, almost the last and certainly alone in St Peter's where they were expressing their distress at what had happened. Cardinal Browne described the situation as tragic and there is absolutely no doubt that it was at least historic what has happened in the Council in the last week or so . . .

This evening it has been raining again and we are all getting heartily sick of the weather. Indeed I think most of the bishops are a little depressed, in spite of the excitements in the Council in the past few days, and the manner in which the Press Office has tried to cover up what is going on is really quite laughable. Tonight's *Osservatore* reads as follows: 'Before beginning the work of the Council, the Secretary General by order of the Cardinal Secretary of State, made an announcement relative to the voting yesterday the results of which did not reach the majority required by the regulations. Taking into account that the opinions expressed in the speeches in the past few days gave indication that there would be a laborious and prolonged discussion on the project on the Sources of Revelation, it was thought useful to have it reviewed by a special commission before continuing with its examination. By the wish of the Holy Father, therefore this Commission will be composed of several cardinals and members of the Theological Commission and the Secretariat for the Promotion of Christian Unity. It will be the task of this Commission to reword the project on the Sources of Revelation, making it shorter and placing greater emphasis on the general principles of Catholic doctrine already treated by the Council of Trent and the First Vatican Council. The Commission will submit in due course a new project for the examination and vote of the Fathers.' One wonders who the Vatican Press Office imagines is taken in by a report of this kind and the glorious phrase with regard to the inadequate voting the previous day merely points to a very obvious fault. A week ago when they were announcing the first vote on the Liturgy, they gave the precise figures. Yesterday, faced with the problem of the fact that the figures would reveal an overwhelming defeat for Cardinal Ottaviani, they merely gave the motion . . .

This morning the Cardinal had had an unexpected visit from Archbishop Castelli, the Secretary of the Italian Hierarchy. It would seem that the Old Guard is reforming and he brought to Cardinal Godfrey an invitation to attend a meeting at Domus Marie called by Cardinal Ruffini. The Cardinal was very vague about what the meeting was in aid of . . .

It was still pouring with rain when we took the Cardinal out to Domus Marie which is a long way out and for once Mario missed the turning and it was 6.45 before we got there. In this vast great building, generally thought to have been built with the funds collected for the Pius XII Foundation and now housing, free of charge, the Italian Hierarchy, assembled for the Council, we were led down one corridor after another until a light showed in the distance and there looking very much like a group of plotters were six or seven Cardinals, gathered round Ruffini of Palermo.

Ruffini was anxious to make a last-ditch stand to beat the left wingers and he seems to have prepared some document which he hopes to present to the Pope, signed by a large number of cardinals. The object of this document is respectfully to point out some of the dangers arising from the new theories which have been so strongly condemned by Cardinal Ottaviani.

Cardinal Godfrey was impressed by the tone and the wording of the document and promised his support. There is to be a further meeting on Saturday evening and to my horror, when we came out the Cardinal told me that he had agreed to attend this further meeting at 6 pm on Saturday. He seemed completely to have forgotten about the long-planned meeting of the Commonwealth bishops and thus, as soon as we got back to the College, we had to telephone to Ruffini to say that the Cardinal would be late and to give the reason why. Ruffini's reaction was immediate. Let the Cardinal come late but let him also bring with him as many cardinals from the Commonwealth as he might reasonably expect to find sympathetic with the proposals put forward this evening . . .

*   *   *

The Cardinal had to go off then with Michael Ashdowne for a further meeting convened by Cardinal Ruffini and I stayed behind to help clear up at the Greg. I eventually got back to the College at about a quarter to eight and the Cardinal returned from the meeting of the group whom we now call 'Ruffiniani' about half an hour later. I gather that there were about fifteen cardinals at this second meeting which really does seem to be the re-forming of the Old Guard.

Today there has been the first information regarding the special Commission set up by the pope to examine this problem of the schema on the sources of Revelation. I gather that it is to be under the joint chairmanship of Cardinal Ottaviani and Cardinal Bea and there are a number of other cardinals there, including Ruffini and Browne for the traditionalists and Léger and Lille (Liénart) for the more liberal theories. It is difficult to know just how large this special Commission is but they seem to have put in most of those enjoying episcopal rank who have served on either the Theological Commission or on the Secretariat for Christian Unity. Thus we find that Archbishop Heenan and Bishop Holland are there and they are summoned for a meeting tomorrow night.

*   *   *

We got all the bishops away by car to the Vatican for an audience with the Pope. The Pope has been giving a number of these audiences to hierarchies as bodies, and it is usually said in the *Osservatore* that the Pope first gives a private audience to the cardinal and after that he receives the other members of the Hierarchy with their cardinal. Today it didn't happen like that. We went into the Cortile S. Damaso in a state of great coldness, there was a tremendous wind blowing, and as we went up by the lift who should we see coming along the gallery but Monsignor Nasalli Rocca, the Maestro di Camera. Nasalli Rocca nearly always panics when he sees any more than one person anywhere and tonight's gathering was no exception. I had told the bishops that in my opinion it was most unlikely that anyone other than the members of the Hierarchy would be received. However the Archbishop of Liverpool knew better and insisted that the three English *periti*, McReavy, Davies and O'Connell, should accompany the Bishops together with dogs-bodies like myself. I did not want to appear unduly gloomy but I did warn the others that it seemed to me unlikely that we should get in. What happened was that as soon as Nasalli Rocca saw us, we were pushed off into a very select chamber but an empty chamber in which we had to possess our souls in patience until a quarter to seven. Meantime the Cardinal and bishops were taken through to a *sala di tolnetto*, where there was a small throne for the Pope and a gilt chair for the Cardinal. Even then the Cardinal hoped that he would be taken in to see the

Pope first but as soon as the bishops had got themselves sorted out, out came the Pope and he crossed quickly to his throne and then the Cardinal was told that he could give the salutations of the Hierarchy to the Pope. I gather that he was a little overcome in doing this but in the name of all the Bishops of the Commonwealth, the meeting of which the Cardinal told the Pope, he wished His Holiness a happy birthday and then the Pope went through all the list of names of the bishops which we had supplied. As he called them out so he was able to greet each one in turn.

Most of the Bishops seemed very satisfied with the audience which lasted about forty minutes but they all commented on the fact that the two monsignori in attendance appeared to be like cats on hot bricks, wondering what on earth the Pope was going to say next. He was at his most intimate if not indiscreet and started off by telling them a story of what his father had told the parish priest when he himself was born. I gather that the comment was something like: 'And about time too.' They wished the Pope long life and I gather that Bishop Wall started up the singing of *Multos Annos*. It was a bit much to ask the Hierarchy to provide a choir but they got through somehow and then the old Pope, about whose health there are once more rumours, said – well, he was glad to live for as long as God wanted him to live but that, if ill-health came, he thought it was better for him to move on and not to clutter up the Papacy!

I gathered that he asked the Bishops what they thought about the Council and did not seem unduly worried about the misgivings that were being expressed at the rate of progress. He also asked the Cardinal whether the bishops had any views about the suggestion which is now being canvassed to the effect that the Second Session should not commence until the beginning of next September and then should last three and a half months. I gather that the Americans and the Mexicans are behind this, though it is difficult to know what is the measure of support. I have been told this evening that the Irish are behind it because they are all fishermen and they do not want to miss the mayfly!

I think that the Cardinal said that he personally would be quite happy to come out in May but that he had little idea as to the views of the bishops. Immediately the Archbishop of Liverpool[43] stood up to add his own comment which, needless to say, was in contradiction to what the Cardinal had said. But it seems that the Pope ignored him and the Archbishop was left standing there whilst the Pope went on speaking for several moments. Then the Archbishop of Liverpool announced that in his opinion it would be much better to leave it all over until September in order to allow the different Commissions to get to work. There is quite a lot of laughter about this suggestion that the Commissions are going to need a lot of time to get to work as they seem to make very little progress when they do have the opportunity to meet. If the Archbishop of Liverpool and others are canvassing September, it must really be for other motives, the best of which is surely that it is more economic to come back to Rome for the three and a half months stint than to come for six weeks in the summer.

Notes

1 Despite these manly affections, some of which went deep, there is no trace of overt homosexuality in any of Worlock's writings. Later in his career he would deal sympathetically with homosexual priests under his authority, but without any implications of collusion.

2 It was customary for cardinals to wear a scarlet cloak on formal occasions, and the job of keeping the other end off the floor usually fell to his Private Secretary, who became his train-bearer. The Secretaries of Cardinal Archbishops, unlike those of Curial cardinals, tended to be senior clergy in their own right, usually monsignori, and very conscious of their dignity. Vatican functionaries obviously did not realize who they were pushing around. For the outcome, see below.

3 Worlock had played rugby at school and continued to follow the game.

4 Cardinals' Secretaries would usually move on to higher things: Worlock's contacts with many of them in Rome at this time gave him a ready-made international network he would find useful in later years.

5 A senior Vatican official.

6 The chief talking point had become the repetitive nature of the debates, speaker after speaker saying more or less the same thing.

7 *Take One at Bedtime* by Derek Worlock, 1962.

8 Coadjutor Bishop of Portsmouth and a fellow member of the Secretariat for Christian Unity.

9 Rudderham, Cowderoy and Wall.

10 The Pope later appointed Cardinals Ottaviani and Bea to be joint chairmen of a special revision committee of which Heenan was also a member, and he reported that they got on surprisingly well together. *A Crown of Thorns*, p. 356.

11 In fact, Archbishop.

12 This was an oblique and dismissive way of referring to the corps of progressive theologians, almost all of them Continental Europeans, whose contribution to the Council was immeasurable. They included Hans Küng, Karl Rahner (who collaborated with Joseph Ratzinger), Bernard Häring, Edward Schillebeeckx, Yves Congar, Jean Daniélou, Marie-Dominique Chenou, and Henri de Lubac. Several of them had been investigated by the Holy Office, which may have been enough in the Bishop of Brentwood's eyes to brand them as cranks. The only one well known in England would have been Küng, whose *Council, Reform and Reunion,* Sheed and Ward, published just before the Council, had become a best-seller.

13 Cardiff.

14 The Parkinson's Law principle being that work expands to fill the time available.

15 *A Crown of Thorns*, p. 375.

16 *History of Vatican II, Volume II*, p. 168.

17 Standing orders for the Council.

18 This wasn't Heenan's usual line. Did Worlock perhaps take the initiative in raising it with Heenan, who maybe didn't disagree enough to stop Worlock then telling Godfrey these were Heenan's own opinions? That was one of Worlock's techniques.

19 Jesuit-run Biblical Institute in Rome.

20 Northampton.

21 In later years Worlock was proud to take credit as one of Cafod's founders, rather than describe it, as here, as an attempt to unload some of the administrative burden that had previously fallen on his shoulders.

22 This is the technical term for it, and little to do with artistic or cultural movements for which the secular world attached the same name. Modernism was an attempt to redefine the content of Christian doctrine in the light of modern philosophical and scientific thinking.

23 In these paragraphs Worlock was reporting on a widespread unease in many parts of the Church, albeit still confined to a theologically literate minority, about the preparatory documents. He refers specifically to *De Fide*, and to a critical statement from Continental bishops which had begun to interest the English. In fact dissatisfaction was expressed concerning all the preparatory documents, and there were many statements attacking them in circulation. It is not clear which of these Worlock had got wind of.

24 Majority in favour.

25 A *Crown of Thorns*, 1973, p. 354.

26 Changing places, perhaps, with Worlock, who had by then taken over the progressive mantle from Heenan.

27 *History of Vatican II, Volume II*, p. 386n.

28 The point of the anecdote was that these were ridiculously trivial issues, hence evidence of the dead hand of the Curia.

29 No doubt Worlock was being sarcastic, though this did actually happen on occasion.

30 Vatican Secretary of State.

31 Worlock is being ironic, and indeed, somewhat impious.

32 The diary contains many references to the struggle to keep Godfrey going, including minor operations in a clinic in Rome. He had cancer, and it seemed to be accepted by both Cardinal and his faithful secretary that it was likely to be incurable. He died the following January, and therefore never lived to see the outcome of the bitter conflicts that had swirled around him in the previous two years.

33 The English Hierarchy secretarial team organized by the Grail.

34 Murphy of Cardiff.

35 Gregorian University.

36 It appears to have been drafted by Karl Rahner and Joseph Ratzinger, who was later to become Cardinal Archbishop of Munich and then to occupy Ottaviani's chair when the Holy Office became the Congregation for the Doctrine of the Faith.

37 Interpreters of Biblical texts.

38 Two English Biblical scholars.

39 Sic.

40 In other words they were free to oppose.

41 George Brunner.

42 Alberigo and Komonchak summarize Cardinal Montini's approach at this time as 'an effort to find the middle ground in the face of the prospect of the shipwreck of the preparatory schemas, whose imminence could not escape those who, like Montini, had

an adequate knowledge of what was going on . . . Montini was critical of the prepared schemas mainly because in them, he felt, "there is no organic form to reflect the great purposes which the Holy Father has set for the Council".' This analysis is based on a private letter which Montini wrote to Suenens. Worlock's suggestion that Montini was silently pulling the progressive strings day by day is new, and in view of the fact that he was to become Pope himself within months, an extraordinary one.

43 Obviously the uncharitable feelings Worlock had for Heenan were still there. Heenan was correct about September.

5

New Leaders, New Moods

As the first session of the Second Vatican Council drew to a close at the end of 1962, uncertainty surrounded the leadership of the Catholic Church and the direction it might take. The Council had begun to steer a different course, but these were still early days and the experiment could be abandoned just as rapidly as it had been started. There would be a new Pope sooner rather than later, as Pope John XXIII seemed to have his bags packed and waiting, very serenely. The main question was not so much who his successor would be, but what would be his approach to the divide between conservatives and progressives? Would he belong to either camp? The second question, hardly less important to the English, was about the succession to Cardinal Godfrey. Nobody was relying on his longevity either. Which way would his successor swing?

Before they left Rome after the end of the Session, Worlock found himself discussing such issues with three members of what he had once called the 'opposition' – Heenan, Holland and Dwyer.

There was agreement that the Holy Father was looking far from well this morning and they were all commenting upon the rumours which are now in circulation to the effect that the Pope has cancer of the stomach and has only a few months to go. In that rather cold-blooded way in which clerics discuss other clerics, they were quite clearly writing off Pope John before next September and this inevitably led the conversation to a consideration of possible successors. I think we all agreed that whoever it was, it would be a middle man, probably someone who had said nothing so far during the Council. Almost certainly it would be an Italian and the names mentioned were Marella, Traglia, Antoniutti, all now in the Curia. They could probably be regarded as middle men but I wonder whether a Curia man really stands a chance any more than one of the extreme leftist gentry like Montini. But for the fact that the present Pope came from Venice, I think I would be prepared to take a long shot on Urbani, his successor as Patriarch.

Archbishop Heenan tells me that this evening at the last meeting of his joint Commission, his attention was drawn by one of the others to the new Archbishop of Florence. His companion remarked that there was the next Pope and Archbishop Heenan rightly pointed out that he was not even a cardinal. But there is widespread rumour that a new batch of cardinals will be announced very shortly and inevitably this archbishop will be included. He seems to be a very good theologian and an able pastoral bishop but one cannot help feeling that next time the cardinals will go for someone they know well. And that must apply to every member of the present Sacred College whose views on almost every subject must now be known to their neighbours.

There we are: burying the poor Pope before there is any real certainty regarding the nature of his illness. But there is no doubt that he does not look well and there is also no doubt that he will in any case go down in history for the brilliance of his concept in calling this Council. In spite of all the difficulties, it is most interesting now to find that all the original critics are united in the opinion that the Council can succeed now and will give new life and impetus to the Church.

Then, after describing the return to London before Christmas, he reports the sad end of Cardinal Godfrey not many weeks later. He grieved, though a good deal less painfully than he had mourned Cardinal Griffin.

There is little point in my going into all the details in this diary . . . They were hard days but days during which one's admiration, and indeed, affection, for the Cardinal increased steadily. He seemed quite serene and with a fair anticipation of what lay ahead. He talked more openly with David[1] and myself than he ever had done before but apart from the pair of us and Bishop Cashman, and of course the nuns and doctors, nothing more was said in public.

He had to enter the Westminster Hospital in order to receive cobalt treatment to try to bring the rapidly increasing growth under control. If he had not done so there was a likelihood that he would have a great sore in his thigh and this could have continued until it had damaged an artery. We were told by the doctors that we must face the prospect that this could go on for several months.

Mercifully, at any rate in retrospect, his heart which had always seemed very strong failed. He was immediately anointed[2] and then for the first time we were able to make known to the world outside the extreme gravity of his illness. In accordance with his wishes we gave no indication that he was suffering from cancer but at least we were out in the clear and people were prepared in large measure for what followed. The Cardinal died very peacefully on 22nd January. May he rest in peace.

It was of course a tremendous blow to all of us and in some ways one must have regarded it as a tremendous blow to the Council. There is no doubt that his contribution to the Council, as revealed in these pages, was considerable and I think that all outsiders were surprised by the volume of praise for him and in particular for his speeches in St Peter's. Cardinal after cardinal telegraphed sympathy and made mention of the grave loss which the Church had suffered by his death.

Worlock did not appear to see the contradiction in what he was saying – that a pro-reform consensus had taken hold, and that the die-hard conservative Godfrey had emerged as a leading influence in the Council. A case of 'All is for the best, in the best of all possible worlds' perhaps. Adrian Hastings' verdict on Godfrey is severe.[2] 'Godfrey's years at Westminster were christened by its clergy somewhat irreverently "the safe period". His leadership was hardly such as to grasp imaginatively the undoubted opportunities with which the Catholic Church in England was now confronted.' Opportunities that were about to be opened up by the death of two principal players.

Among English Catholics the progressives' first choice would be Cardinal Montini of Milan for Pope and Archbishop Heenan of Liverpool for Westminster. Montini would continue the direction chosen by John XXIII,[4] perhaps even more single-mindedly. Heenan would change the complexion and public perception of the English Catholic Church more fundamentally than the appointment of Pope John had done. Godfrey's Hierarchy was a conservative leadership, stolidly right of centre on the progressive–conservative theological spectrum and in one or two of its members, far right. It did not see the need for change. Yet it was also capable of change; indeed, by the end of 1962, it did change. About the only one who seemed not to notice was Cardinal Godfrey, but his mind was on other things.

And then, quite remarkably, the tone of Worlock's diary begins to change too. It is as if his loyalty to Godfrey had held him back from entering fully into the rhythm of Vatican II. Even at the end of the first session, he was still calling Cardinal Montini of Milan, the future Pope Paul VI, 'an extreme leftist gentry'. There is little doubt that is what his chief thought. But within a few months, he had become a Montini enthusiast; even more surprisingly and perhaps more tentatively, a few months further on a Heenan enthusiast too.[5]

Freed by the death of his master, he had begun to mature, be more his own man. His diary even begins to sound partisan on the other side. And towards Heenan, he warmed by a minute fraction of a degree as each week passed. A year later, his administrative and manipulative skills were fully deployed for the cause of Church unity, the cause Heenan had made his own, the very cause Worlock had been so disdainful of. Indeed, in the end Worlock proved the more wholehearted convert. Heenan pulled back, while Worlock pressed on. They passed, so to speak, on the stairs. There never was a meeting of minds between them.

> A vacancy is never an easy time and this has proved no exception to the rule. There have been a number of real problems with which I have had to deal in a national capacity and this can sometimes make it difficult with one's diocesan authorities if, as is technically the case, one has no position in the diocese during a vacancy. I am tired of describing myself as overworked and unemployed. So far as the future of the Council is concerned it seems likely that whoever is appointed archbishop, I shall be in Rome for the next session. At the Low Week meeting of the Hierarchy the bishops unanimously requested the Secretariat of State to give me formal recognition as director of their secretariat for the Council.

This was not quite good enough for him. Worlock hankered after an official role within the business of the Council itself, if not as a bishop then as a *peritus*, a consultant or expert attached to an individual bishop to help him with a specific task. But each *peritus* had to be applied for, and approved individually. *Periti* were allowed to attend Council debates, though not to take part in them: if their bishop was a member of a committee or commission, however, then the *periti* went too and were allowed to take part in those meetings – except that from time to time they were ordered to remain silent. Bishop John Petit of Menevia in North Wales had been elected to the Council commission which was preparing a draft document on the laity in the life and mission of the Church. It was a subject close to Worlock's heart, on which he felt he was an expert.

Bishop Petit asked to be allowed to make Worlock his *peritus*, but was refused. He was refused again despite the unanimous backing of the Hierarchy, the reason each time being that there were no vacancies. But Monsignor Glorieux, the secretary of the commission dealing with the laity, had told Petit he was at liberty to consult Worlock and show him any documents. Thus Worlock got to see the first draft document of a schema intended for eventual debate and endorsement by the full Council. He was fairly disgusted with it – 'forty pages of the most high-flown language', he called it.

*　　　　*　　　　*

I called a meeting of the boys a few days later and decided it was quite impossible merely to note a few amendments. It was a case of a complete rewrite, and that, quickly . . .

We then decided to add a completely new fourth part on the formation of the laity for the apostolate. For us it was the old question of spiritual formation, doctrinal formation, social formation and professional formation but it seems that for many it was something completely new. We dealt especially with the need for providing facilities for the further formation of the layman and even the role of the church in establishing training centres. Altogether our document ran to eleven foolscap pages.

Much of the initial work was done by Kevin Muir and he came to see me on Monday evening and we worked on it for a very long time trying to hammer it into shape and it was at this stage that I introduced the section on formation. Just as we had completed this task I received an SOS from the Bishop of Menevia to say that the document must be in Rome before the end of the week and furthermore that we must provide Latin and French versions as well as the English version. This was a terrible headache.

I spent most of Tuesday getting the document into shape and that evening went to Sloane Street where I worked on it again with Yvonne, Philippa and Catherine. On Wednesday morning we set about the task of trying to have it translated into French and into Latin. The Franciscan Missionaries of Mary at the Boltons kindly undertook to do the French version and to my delight sent it round on Thursday morning. Unfortunately they had left all the accents off and so we had a desperate time doing a re-type there. With the Latin we were less successful. The convent at Kensington Square kindly undertook to complete the job, kept the document all day and returned it to me late on the Wednesday evening saying that it was beyond them. That left us two days and I shall not easily forget the labours of Thursday and Friday with Father Anglim and Father Pilkington getting the whole thing put into Latin.

Treasa Carey slaved away with the typing and duplicating and eventually David Norris and I went out to the airport at midnight on Friday night to put 30 copies of the document in Latin, a dozen in French and a dozen in English on a freight plane which bore the lot off to Michael Ashdowne in Rome. By this time I was having to telephone to the bishop who was in the Blue Nuns' hospital and also telephoning to Michael Ashdowne so that he could collect the parcel. The Bishop sent it at once to Monsignor Glorieux, Michael Ashdowne secured a list of the addresses of the members of the Commission in Rome and he and Helen Breen spent the best part of 24 hours taking copies round to ensure that everyone had it by the time the Commission met on the Monday.

This was an astonishing achievement, and, it must be said, a slightly impertinent one. The Commission had not asked for a revised version from Derek Worlock, who had no standing at all in the matter; but wanted merely Bishop Petit's comments on the Commission's own text. But Worlock had a more or less complete theory of the lay apostolate (as he would have called it at that time) which he had worked out over many years with his famous 'Team' – the group he called 'the boys'. He fervently wished this theory, which he was convinced was state-of-the-art, to be adopted officially by the Catholic Church, if at all possible by incorporating it into the documents and decrees of Vatican II.

Worlock did eventually get his *peritus* status, and found himself back in Rome long before the resumption of the Council proper. There he was quickly locked into long and tedious debates with bishops and experts from around the world as they tried to arrive at a global approach to the lay apostolate.

In many Catholic countries the predominant model for lay Catholic involvement in what would be termed 'social action' – a broad Catholic euphemism for politics – was through a structure known as Catholic Action. The principle behind Catholic Action was that lay activity in the name of the Church had in some sense to be directed by the Church – which meant it had to be under the control of the local Hierarchy. Loose control in some cases, fairly tight control in others. It was this link to the official Church that enabled lay Catholic initiatives of this kind to be regarded as an 'apostolate' – missionary work as an extension of the Church's apostolic vocation.

Worlock's model for the lay apostolate drew a clear distinction between what was appropriate for the laity and what was the proper function of the clergy. All the campaigning and organizing of political or trade union life was within the competence of lay people, but outside the competence of priests and bishops. Their job in the first place was to teach lay people the general principles of Catholic Social Teaching, generally as laid down in the Social Encyclicals *Rerum Novarum* of Leo XIII, published in 1891, and *Quadragesimo Anno* of Pius XI, published in 1931. (Two new Social Encyclicals, *Pacem in Terris* and *Mater et Magistra* had been issued by Pope John XXIII, but Catholic Action and the ideas of Derek Worlock both pre-date these newcomers.) In the second place it was to supervise the spiritual formation of lay Catholics involved in this work. They had to be 'good Catholics'. In practical terms that meant seeing that they attended to Bible study, frequented the Sacraments (especially Sunday Mass and Confession), studied Church teaching, and developed their prayer life (saying the Rosary regularly, for instance, or occasionally going on retreats). Part of the unwritten agenda of Catholic Action, as indeed of Derek Worlock's more modern approach, was the combating of Communist influence, particularly in trade unions. He would have regarded the Young Christian Workers as a body close to his ideals; indeed, he had taken that organization under his wing. The Team – Worlock's idea for building up an élite Catholic lay leadership – grew out of it.

He recorded in his diary the reaction in Rome to his first great efforts, and went on for page after page to describe the detailed battle inside the Lay Apostolate Commission over the weeks and months of the summer and autumn of 1963. Among the *periti* present were two of the principal figures of progressive Catholic theology at that time, both German: Bernard Häring and Karl Rahner. In the course of it Worlock put forward his own philosophy of lay involvement in public affairs at considerable length.

Much of the debate arose from the fact that the particular experience of delegates related closely to the situations in their own country, both the state of politics and the place of the Catholic Church. They had, as Worlock had, based on his particular experience of conditions in England, a strong tendency to generalize, to assume that what worked for them would work everywhere. Only slowly did they grasp the point that a general document should not generalize from the particular: but then they fell into the trap of being so unspecific that they were saying nothing at all. But these debates were not meaningless. The involvement of Catholics in political life in England may have been little more than marginal to the main political history of that country at the time. But in France, Spain, Italy, Germany and all the countries of Latin America, Catholic lay movements of various kinds had sometimes wielded decisive influence. The destinies of nations sometimes turned on them.

Their pre-war history still had a major influence on how they saw the world. In all those countries they had been actively opposed by anti-clerical movements of the Left and actively courted by authoritarian movements such as Mussolini's Fascists or Franco's Falangists. But Catholicism was not comfortable in such company, probably because the principles of the 1891 and 1931 Social Encyclicals were egalitarian rather than oligarchic. Fascists tended to glorify violence: Catholic social theory tended towards pacifism. Fascism was willing to subvert the established order, overthrowing it by force if necessary: in Catholic social theory, just laws had divine sanction and were binding in conscience, while the lawfully constituted State could almost be regarded as acting in the name of God. Catholic theory approved of and encouraged trade unionism, opposing it only when it was used for nakedly political purposes: Fascists usually locked up trade unionists at the first opportunity. Catholic theory respected the right to private property; Fascism saw all ownership as subordinate to the interests of State and party. They were agreed on a conservative approach to personal morality, such as support for the family, and on resistance to Communism as the common enemy.

What tended to weaken Catholic lay action was the overarching influence of the Church Hierarchy, which wished to have a veto over leadership and policy and to overrule the membership in the name of some greater good that was more visible to bishops than to anyone else. In at least two cases, Italy and Germany, this desire to control Catholic political movements led the Church authorities to undermine those they could not control. Pius XI disapproved in principle of Catholic parties that were independent of the Church, and in Italy actively encouraged Catholics to join the Mussolini's Fascists as being more amenable and respectful to the Church than the Catholic Popular Party had been. With regard to Germany, Pius XI, advised by Cardinal Pacelli (later Pius XII), had actively collaborated with Hitler in undermining and eventually dissolving the Centre Party, which was in effect the Catholic party, again because the Church could not control it. Arguably this removal of the Centre Party from the stage was one of the principal reasons why German political life was so quickly and completely dominated by the Nazis after they came to power in 1933.[6]

These Catholic parties, from the Church's point of view, were indeed difficult to deal with, as they set up in each society an alternative pole of Catholic leadership to the bishops. No matter how much pro-Church goodwill they may have started with, sooner or later headstrong prelates and headstrong politicians would disagree about something – and eventually, human nature being what it was, about almost everything. So the existence of Catholic parties tended to divide the Church and weaken the authority of the bishops. They were not regarded as a suitable instrument for translating Catholic social theory into action, therefore. Any other body which was to meet this criterion, on the other hand, had to have formal links to the Hierarchy: to be, so to speak, its agent in the world of politics.

A further factor was the influence of Ultramontane theology. Partly in reaction to the unification of Italy and the conquest of the Papal States, the Vatican had struggled throughout the latter part of the nineteenth century to compensate for its loss of political power by increasing its spiritual power. The symbol of this increase was the First Vatican Council, which in 1870 proclaimed both the dogma of papal infallibility and the principle that the Pope had 'immediate universal jurisdiction' over the Church worldwide. Many thought that the decisions of 1870 had made the entire

Church one diocese, even one parish. The Catholic Church was no longer an episcopal Church (except in name) but a papal Church. The job of a bishop was first and foremost to stay loyal to Rome, to transmit its teaching, to support it when it was attacked, and so to draw from this intimate and devoted relationship with the Holy See the strength and inspiration to preach the Gospel. Nowhere was this Ultramontane spirit stronger than in England, where Catholics had suffered and died for their loyalty to the Pope. Disloyalty to the Pope, even in private, was a source of scandal and shame, the defining mark of the 'bad Catholic'.

If the Pope was at the top of the hierarchical pyramid, the next layer down was the episcopate, and below that the priesthood. Power and authority in the Church was envisaged as trickling down from the top, through each of these lower layers. The divine 'entry point', so to speak, was at the peak of the pyramid. The closer one's position was to that, the holier it was. The laity were the bottom layer, not very holy at all. They were neither ordained nor consecrated to higher office; they had not been called. They were assumed to be generally ignorant of the twin Catholic sciences of theology and canon law. They were deemed much more liable, left to their own devices, to get things wrong rather than right. As their status in the Church placed them at a lower level than priests, it was through their priests that they were connected to the total life of the Church. And of course, the laity had sex; some of them were even women.

The bishops were successors to the apostles. It was they, above all, who had an 'apostolate', a mission to spread the Word of God throughout the world. Whether this commission came directly from God, or was transmitted, so to speak, through the office of the Pope, was a moot point which the Second Vatican Council eventually resolved in favour of the former position against the Ultramontanists who favoured the latter.

The priests were sharers in the work of the bishop, under his leadership. They had a share in his apostolate, therefore. What of the laity? They too could share in this apostolate, by loyally assisting the priests and bishops. It was not only a matter of financial support. The lay person was 'out there' in a way priests and bishops were not. The lay person was sometimes the best person, therefore, to fulfil the Church's mission in a particular situation. If he was a good lay person, he would be a humble one, and if a humble one, he would be prepared to take instruction from his Church on what the methods and goals of his lay activity should be.

Thus Cardinal Griffin, in a pastoral letter in 1948, declared:[7] 'The Catholic, from the reading of the Social Encyclicals, has a sound knowledge of the mutual duties and responsibilities of the family, the State and the individual. Problems of education, matrimony, the social and medical services and the rights of the workers – to give a few examples – are bound to recur with regularity in every public assembly.' He urged Catholics to join the Catholic Social Guild, where they would receive the assistance they would need.

De la Bedoyere gave an account of the Catholic lay apostolate in the late 1940s which he said was how Cardinal Griffin saw it. But the words undoubtedly came from Derek Worlock, Griffin's secretary of some three years when these words were written, who had already become the acknowledged specialist in Archbishop's House Westminster on all matters social and political. This was Worlock's charter, if not exactly of how things were, but of how he wanted them to be.

'Active Catholics in this country are organised in a number of societies or associations' wrote de la Bedoyere, 'not for the purpose of trying to insert the Church into public and professional life, but for the purpose of encouraging and instructing Catholics to play a more useful part as citizens in the affairs of the world and the country, and in order to make them spiritually and morally conscious together of their Catholicity.' He mentions the Association of Catholic Trade Unionists, the Association of Catholic Managers and Employers, 'both of which were founded in Westminster under his leadership and encouragement' (and both of which came under the wing of his young secretary Worlock, as did the third body de la Bedoyere lists, the Young Christian Workers). It was by their connection with the Hierarchy that these lay bodies could say they shared in the apostolic work of the Church. It was through the Hierarchy, after all, that they were connected with the fount of wisdom and guidance in these social matters, the Popes and their Social Encyclicals.

What characterized this English version of the lay apostolate, however, was its need to work in the generally unfavourable environment of a parliamentary democracy where the predominant religious ethos was Protestant or secular. It was only by a process of infiltration that Catholics could gain influence for themselves and their ideas. Thus there was a good deal of interest at the time in the idea of a 'cell' structure at local level. This enabled small groups of lay Catholics, with a priest on hand, to meet and discuss mutual difficulties in confidence (and obviously, to a degree, advance each other's interests for the sake of advancing the influence of their shared ideals). This may sound more sinister than it actually was, given that the ideals they were fostering were the well-publicized, and on the whole not very controversial, social teachings of the Popes. They were fairly banal conspiracies to do good.

But on the part of the Continentals and Latin Americans, the type of society they were used to dealing with or wished to deal with (an idealized version of the actuality, perhaps) could be described as *intégriste*. In this there was no theoretical distinction between Throne and Altar. It presupposed a Catholic society, with Catholic citizens, Catholic laws, and an overwhelming influence for the Catholic Hierarchy. The *intégriste* ideal would be monarchist, and indeed the French name for it, the *ancien régime*, referred back to the time of the Bourbon kings before the French Revolution. But it was not entirely incompatible with a Republican constitution, as for instance in de Valera's Irish constitution of 1937.

In an *intégriste* model of the relationship between Church and society, secret cells and quiet infiltration had no place. The lay apostolate had to boast of its presence, and it did so under the banner of Catholic Action. This was the official answer to the 'disaster' of the Catholic political parties of the pre-war years. Catholic Action was an umbrella under which associations of laity could come together, to co-operate and to accept leadership and guidance from the bishops. They acquired from that blessing from the successors of the apostles the necessary formal bond with the work of the Church by means of which they too became 'apostolic'. Worlock thought all this sort of thing far too controlled and controlling, and too visible. He did not like the triumphalism implied by the term Catholic Action. He thought it authoritarian and backwards-looking; he believed his own discreet methods, refined over a dozen years, much more appropriate to the modern age. Whether he would still say that twenty years later is another matter.

*   *   *

There is no doubt at all that the document caused quite a sensation. Bishop after bishop went to Bishop Petit to thank him and to congratulate him and at the same time explain that this document had reached them so late. He truthfully replied that we had only been given about ten days in which to prepare it. It is the old case of Rome imagining that no work can be done outside Rome . . . When they came to the section dealing with the formation of the laity, someone suggested that our section should be adopted completely in place of the few lines given to the matter in the official schema. This was hoping for too much but it was agreed that those who had prepared the original schema should re-write their section with our document in front of them. In fact from the papers which I have seen it seems that they adopted our general headings with regard to the training of the laity and a great deal of other material had been incorporated. One cannot be sure at this stage just how much because we shall not know until the next volume of material arrives from Rome for the Fathers of the Council.

At all events the Bishop of Menevia was delighted with himself and with us and the greatest surprise of all came shortly afterwards and after the Bishop had left Rome to return to this country when he received a letter from Monsignor Deskur, co-secretary of the Commission with Monsignor Glorieux, asking for further copies of our document as it was to be given further study. I sent these off at once and had an immediate and grateful letter back from Monsignor Deskur. It seems quite clear, therefore, that they know we are being treated as *periti* even without official designation. Indeed the Bishop insists that he has been told by the Commission to obtain the views of the English *periti* on this and similar documents . . .

In the early days of April the Bishop of Menevia received a letter from Monsignor Glorieux saying that the revised document on the lay apostolate had been submitted to the Co-ordinating Committee and approved by them with the proviso that two further subsidiary documents be prepared. The first of these is an Appendix dealing with points in the lay apostolate which should find provision in the new Code of Canon Law; and the second is what is described as an 'Instruction for the formation of the laity for the apostolate'. This latter is wonderful news and if the document took the form of the sort of *Instructio* recently issued dealing with the rubrics it would be a most valuable compendium of information. Possibly this is why they asked for further copies of our document bearing in mind the section dealing with the formation of the laity. But one cannot be sure and we await the arrival of the draft of these two additional documents which are apparently being prepared in Rome.

An even more significant document now came Worlock's way, through the same channel. It was the prototype of the Second Vatican Council's crowning achievement, the decree *Gaudium et Spes*, with which Worlock had more and more to do as time went on. Again he set about a fundamental rewrite, again without any formal standing in the matter.

Later in April just at the time of the Bishops' Meeting, the Bishop of Menevia received another long document entitled the presence and activity of the *Church in the World Today*. This one could have been real dynamite in that it has undoubtedly been prepared as a result of some of the remarks made at the end of the First Session to the effect that the Church was concerning itself too much with theological niceties and not enough with the problems of the world. One remembers Bishop Dwyer's address when he said to the Fathers: 'We have been here for two months and not one word has been said about the real problems confronting the world at this time. One third of the world is starving and is there not a danger that they will point their fingers at the Council and ask "Is Christ there?"'

This new document has been prepared by a joint commission drawn from the Theological Commission of Cardinal Ottaviani and the Lay Apostolate Commission. One does not know quite which individuals have been involved but it is quite clear that various sections have been prepared by different persons: the whole style of presentation and of language differs. The Bishop of Menevia passed these papers over to me adding that the views of the English *periti* were required and that the whole job must be in Rome at the beginning of the week commencing 12th May. This would give time for the document to be circulated to the Fathers concerned prior to their meeting in the middle of that week. That gave us just over a fortnight for the whole job including the task of translation and once again we had the most appalling job to finish the work in time.

The document itself consisted of a general introduction and then some six chapters. Slowly I worked my way through it and although much of what it contained was good, it seemed to me to reflect in many places an attitude which cannot be regarded as in tune with the reign of Pope John XXIII. The general introduction itself left me very angry because it was so patronising. It seemed to envisage the Church and the world as two separate entities, the former bending over in its generous goodness to give a word of advice and a little bit of help here and there to the world which knew no better.

Although the Bishop of Menevia was keen that I should consult the Team, I felt that certain chapters called for the advice of experts. In the end I decided to re-write the introduction myself making it a much longer document but trying to show the Church's involvement in any problem which concerns as much as one of her members or indeed one member of mankind. In order to do this I drew largely from *Mater et Magistra, Pacem in Terris* and some of the speeches of Pius XII. I have been told more lately that there is an unwritten rule not to use in any of the *schemata* quotations from the encyclicals. This seems to me to be nonsense, How one can speak of social justice without reference to *Mater et Magistra* defies me. The suggestion is that one should use the same ideas and merely include reference to *Mater et Magistra* in the bibliography. Yet if the Pope has said it perfectly, how can one hope to improve on it? It will be interesting to see what happens about this.

The first chapter was entitled '*De admirabili vocationis hominis secundum Dei*'. This was fairly wordy and not very profound but it was a reasonable statement of the Church's teaching. In its revision I asked the help of Father Waterhouse of the Catholic Social Guild and Father Edward Michinson, but at the end, we decided to recommend only five largely verbal changes. The same can be said of chapter two '*De persona humana in societate*'. Here I used the same men and there were only four changes for which we asked. It seemed important, one should add, that one should not be asking for too many changes unless it was necessary in case they got the idea that we were never willing to accept anything which had come out from Rome. As it was, the introduction was a complete re-write and there was no point in doing the same elsewhere.

Chapter three was '*De matrimonio familia et de problemate demographica*'. Here I decided to seek the help of Father Maurice O'Leary of the Catholic Marriage Advisory Council. I eventually obtained from him what I wanted though I have always found that in dealing with others it is much easier to obtain from them criticism of what has already been prepared rather than the preparation of an alternative paragraph. On the whole Father O'Leary was reasonably pleased with what had come from the Joint Commission but he recommended about nine fairly major changes.

The fourth chapter '*De cultura et progressum*' I turned over to Kevin McDonnell and to two fellow Catholic lecturers at the University of London. The first thing they pointed out was that it contained nothing about progress and they recommended that this word be dropped from the title. They also asked for a clearer definition of culture, bearing in mind that this section should really contain the Church's teaching concerning the use of leisure. I was very impressed by what they prepared and most of all by the fact that David Black turned out to be a Latin scholar of considerable merit. He and Jack Scarisbrick were delighted to be called in for this job. There is no doubt that they regarded it as a tremendous privilege to be doing something for the Council: a lesson for those of us who grow a little tired of it at times. I was very pleased indeed with their points concerning this chapter which showed considerable technical competence and in addition a really apostolic approach to the subject.

Chapter five was '*De Ordine Oiconomico et de Iustitia Sociali*'. And this was a matter that I could safely entrust to the Team. Kevin McDonnell, Denis Maccagno and Mick Foley worked on this and it seems that they were joined by David Black with whom they were much impressed. Their contribution was very sound, giving practical form to a number of theoretical propositions and dealing with some subjects which they had left out such as Youth and Labour and the necessity of ensuring that there was justice in the provision of proper apprenticeship and time off in accordance with their youthful inexperience and need for leisure. They also compiled a useful section on trade unionism, making the point that while Christian trade unions might be the most satisfactory form in certain countries, they should not be regarded as the only form of trade unionism in which Christians could take part. I am a bit fearful of this and we want to make sure that if the layman is really to be encouraged to take his part in society, he should not be prevented from doing so by unnecessary prohibitions which do not apply in neutral or non-Catholic countries. The contribution to this chapter ran to no less than seven foolscap pages and it will be very interesting to see how much notice is taken of what has been said.

*   *   *

2nd June: The next really major issue since the close of the First Session has been the health of Pope John himself. Even as I write these words he is dying and for several days now we have been told that his life hangs by a thread. The similarity between his illness and his death agony with that of Cardinal Godfrey is so remarkable that these last few days have been not merely intensely busy but charged with a special poignancy.

When last I saw him at the beginning of February, immediately following the death of Cardinal Godfrey, he looked so wonderfully restored to his former vigour that it was hard to recall his apparent weakness and appearance of exhaustion at the end of the First Session. One remembers how at that time he seemed to have lost a lot of weight and his whole face had fallen in. His eyes gave the appearance almost of being drugged and it was suggested that he was suffering from anaemia. Now, of course, one knows the real reason, that he has been suffering from cancer and even that he has known this for six or seven months. I cannot help wondering whether he ever spoke to Cardinal Godfrey. It has been suggested in the Press that the Pope's secret was kept within his immediate entourage in just the same way as we kept Cardinal Godfrey's secret. Neither would have been men to bother the other with their own ailments but both apparently came to the same decision, to work on to the end and only when death was proximate to make known to their people their need for prayers. It makes the Pope's interest and kindness to us earlier this year all the more wonderful and it has the additional interest for me in that it gives new meaning to the message of thanks and good wishes which he sent when he received my account of Cardinal Godfrey's illness and death, as written in the special issue of the Cathedral Chronicle.

Earlier this year the Pope seemed to bounce back to good health. In that cheerful way in which he sometimes spoke of the Pope in the third person, he told the people in St Peter's Square 'The Pope was ill and the Pope is better again.' But looking back one can notice a very real change in his appearance. He undoubtedly had lost a great deal of weight and his face appears far older and more drawn looking. Only a fortnight ago Pat Keegan was in Rome for a conference of the International Union of Adult Christian Workers and was called for an audience with the Holy Father. When the Pope came in Pat had to give him a hand up into his throne and then the Pope quite naturally said to him: 'Keep going until I get my breath back.' But the news of his illness really only became public about ten days ago when it was said that the Pope was once more suffering from anaemia. We know now that this was due to a haemorrhage as a result of a tumour in his stomach.

*   *   *

Sunday 29th September 1963: Many busy months have passed since last I took up the story in this diary. Pope John was dying and now it seems almost to have been a different age when in fact he died after a great agony on the evening of Whit-Monday, 3rd June. I shall always remember his anniversary because it was my ordination day. The effect of Pope John's death on the world at large was quite astonishing. Everyone, Catholic and non-Catholic alike, seemed to feel a personal sense of loss and I remember I was very busy at the time having to broadcast and do television tributes to his memory. It was not difficult because everywhere one found a sympathetic audience.

I can remember very well sitting down with David Norris on the night when Pope John died and looking through a copy of the *Annuario*[8] and working out who were the possibles. Without much difficulty one was able to assemble a short-list and I don't think that I wavered from this short-list during the days which followed. The obvious character was of course Cardinal Montini of Milan. I went carefully through the list and worked out that he could be reasonably sure of 40 votes at the very first scrutiny. In assembling these 40 I left out the support of most of the curial cardinals because, after what happened in 1954, one could not be sure that he would receive their support. It seemed to me that if the Curia decided to support him he would be home very quickly. Without their help I could not see how he would amass the necessary 52 votes he would need.

The Conclave itself opened on Wednesday, 19th June, and Cardinal Montini was elected Pope at the fifth scrutiny, on the morning of Friday, 21st June. The announcement was made at 11.35 am. and I was invited by the BBC to do a broadcast on the new Pope at 10 o'clock that evening. I had to spend most of the day at the House of Lords, where the Abse Bill on divorce was being debated and I met Field Marshal Montgomery there, who expressed his delight at the election by saying: 'Absolutely first-class: the cat's whiskers!' It was quite a plum for me to be able to use that in the broadcast that evening. The Cardinal chose the name of Paul VI, which delighted everyone in England, as it was rapidly pointed out that Paul was the Apostle of the Gentiles. Undoubtedly, the sermon which he had delivered in Milan the previous Sunday had had a considerable effect on the vote. During the Council, it was never known exactly where he stood. He spoke so seldom, though, as I have often recorded in this diary, I often saw him giving a brief to some of the other Continental and more liberal bishops. In his sermon at Milan, he declared himself a true follower of 'the incomparable John', whose path must be followed in the new reign. This was enough. And on the whole, the election has been very well received. It will be desperately difficult for anyone to follow Good Pope John and it is important that whoever is elected should follow his own line and be himself. But in the weeks that have passed, Pope Paul does not seem to have put a foot wrong. He has undoubtedly worked exceedingly hard, making the various rounds, and the only setback at all has been an unsuccessful approach to the Orthodox . . .

We had a Solemn Requiem for Pope John XXIII on 12th June, in the Cathedral. Considerable excitement was caused by the fact that the Apostolic Delegate[9] invited Bishop Holland to preach the panegyric, which he did very well. But everyone was wondering whether this meant that Bishop Holland was the Delegate's candidate for Westminster. In fact, he had told Bishop Craven that neither Liverpool nor Birmingham was to be invited, in case it gave rise to speculation. By inviting Bishop Holland, he caused far more speculation. It was obvious at this time that the Delegate was very far from well. He had had a series of heart attacks at the beginning of the year and although he insisted that he had recovered, he was clearly a sick man. The last time I saw him was at the Mass in the Cathedral on the evening of 2nd July to mark the Pope's Coronation, but on the following day, when he was due to hold a reception at Claridges in honour of the same occasion, he had to cry off due to exhaustion. He took to his bed soon afterwards and died on the evening of Tuesday, 16th July. What an astonishing time it had been!

But the death of the Delegate was clearly of very great importance with regard to the election to Westminster . . . I could not help remembering that the Delegate had said on more than one occasion to me – and to others in public! – that if it was Archbishop Heenan, it would be over his dead body. Would this turn out to be a prophecy rather than a threat?

My own schema on the Apostolate of the Laity turned out to be far more satisfactory than I would ever have hoped in the days when we were working on it earlier this year. The re-write has been successfully carried out, except perhaps for the last section which has never been discussed in the Commission. The result was that in this last session, there is a considerable amount of repetition and rambling, reminiscent of what the whole was like originally. The section on the formation of the Laity: this was the one which pleased me most, as it was evident that not only our points had been received but even in the very form in which we had made them. I suppose that this was the first occasion in which the Hierarchy officially used me as their Secretary for Conciliar matters, as distinct from the administration of their joint affairs during the First Session.

*   *   *

By the time I returned to London we had prepared observations which even ran to some two pages of typescript, dealing with about eleven points in this document which we felt needed clarification. Our recommendations were really designed to implement some of the points which we had felt of importance in the *schema* on the Apostolate of the Laity. There were undoubtedly a certain number of subterfuges regarding *Actio Catholica*: a red rag to the Bishop of Menevia. There is no doubt that in one or two cases *Actio Catholica* has been put in wherever references to the organised Lay Apostolate had been used in the original document. We took the line that in a document of this kind and certainly in the new code of Canon Law terminology should be general, whereas *Actio Catholica* was merely one specific form. It was surprising how many paragraphs it took in order to check up on the various twists and turns which had been given to the original document . . . I am quite sure that there is a struggle ahead in the Council about this. The Bishop of Menevia stated his case bravely in the commission last March but it is possible that he over-played his hand and I have heard from Cyril Pickering, newly returned from France, that a number of the French and the Spanish bishops have signed themselves up to deal with Menevia once the Commission gets to work again in September.

The second crisis, though of less rigour, was equally demanding of time and it took the form of a return visit of Cardinal Heard on his way back from Scotland en route for Rome. His stay, 'for the night' lasted from Wednesday 4th September till Monday 9th September. On the evening of Thursday 5th September I got my first inkling that an appointment to the Archdiocese might be proximate. I had noted in the *Osservatore Romano* that Cardinal Confalonieri had had two Audiences with the new Pope in a period of just over a week and I realised therefore that the name could have been submitted to the Pope on the first occasion and the acceptance made known to him on the second. Then it was just a question of waiting for an announcement. On that Thursday evening I had several enquiries from the Press who were looking for photographs of Bishop Beck and Bishop Holland. They told me that the report from Rome – unofficial of course – was that an appointment would be made on the Saturday and that it was one of these two. It certainly was not Archbishop Heenan. The story continued all day Friday. I informed Bishop Craven who received word from Monsignor Torpigliani on the Friday evening that an announcement would be made at midday on the Saturday. As we had Cardinal Heard staying with us, I thought I had better let him know this report but he stuck to his story that nothing would happen till October. When on Saturday morning the *Daily Telegraph* actually announced that Bishop Beck would be appointed at mid-day that day, the Cardinal became most knowledgeable and said that he had always expected it! I received word from the Apostolic Delegation at one o'clock simultaneous to their release of the news through the Press Association that Archbishop Heenan had been appointed 8th Archbishop of Westminster. Cardinal Heard said it was what he had expected for a long time and that the choice was first class. With the latter I came quite quickly to agree.

I had known the Archbishop for eighteen years and he had always been a good friend to me personally, even though at times we occasionally had differed on matters of strategy. However, it is always better to put those things behind one. I had no particular feelings about who it would be as long as we had an Archbishop to lead the Hierarchy at the Council. I have also always held that because someone acts in one way in one diocese it does not follow that he will act in the same way in another. Indeed a big man is able to adjust himself to his surroundings and there is no doubt at all that the Archbishop has made a most spectacular take-over of the Diocese and the appointment has been widely acclaimed throughout the Press and in all national circles. What was more important was that the priests welcomed it and for the first time we had an Archbishop coming to Westminster who is already widely known. This gives him immense opportunities and there is every indication that he has risen to the occasion in a big way.

He met the priests in the Cathedral Hall on Friday afternoon, spoke with them very frankly, giving them in general a go-ahead to do what is best for the flock and not to worry with asking too many permissions. It was all rather like a breath of fresh air and indeed both David Norris and I came to regard it in this light. When we have been going at full pressure during the last week or two, no one worked harder than the Archbishop himself and he had an immense success with television, radio, and the newspapers. The build up towards the enthronement worked far better than these things normally do and we were very fortunate in that the big news containing the Profumo affair and the Denning Report thereon was not released until midnight on the day after the enthronement.

As a result the Press Conferences given by the Archbishop and the enthronement itself occupied the main space on the main pages of the newspapers, both could have been easily crowded out by the long-awaited Denning Report. Before the enthronement I succeeded in taking the Archbishop to Hare Street with which, thank God, he was delighted and which I imagine he will use a great deal in the future. I also took him to visit St Edmunds and realised as I did so that this was the fifth Archbishop I had seen solemnly welcomed at the College in the last 30 years. When Cardinal Bourne came there for his Golden Jubilee in 1934, I was the smallest boy in the school. Under Cardinal Hinsley I was the head Prefect. When Cardinal Griffin came in 1944 I was a deacon awaiting ordination. I took Cardinal Godfrey there for the first time in 1957 and now I was bringing the 8th Archbishop of the Archdiocese in the person of Archbishop Heenan. There are many lessons to be learned from this, not least the heavy demands made on an Archbishop of Westminster and the corresponding high mortality rate!

I had already discovered that, at least as far as written material was concerned, the new Archbishop is much easier to help than Cardinal Godfrey was. It was never very easy to make corrections in what had been drafted by the latter. But methods are entirely different and at least at the present time the Archbishop is dictating most of his correspondence. It is too early to judge just what is the extent to which he will use the machine we have created at Westminster over the past twenty years but on the other hand one can already say that he is a very easy man to work with. It would be idle at this stage to look too far into the future, but he has already made it plain to me that he fully accepts my ideas regarding future developments and the establishment of a National Secretariat for the Hierarchy. Before we left for Rome[10] he had already given me the opportunity of taking him round the entire establishment to see exactly what my redevelopment plan was. In general it is approved; it is just a question of time.

It was hard luck for the Archbishop to leave the diocese so soon after his enthronement, but no man could have done more to secure the loyalty and affection of such a newly-bestowed flock. He decided to leave all the diocesan officials just as they were.

I managed to attend the High Mass in the College Chapel[11] at 9 am and immediately afterwards Desmond Fisher, Editor of the *Catholic Herald*, came to see the Archbishop – and me, before and after he had seen the Archbishop. I have a great admiration for Desmond Fisher both as a man and as a far-seeing journalist, but I do not think he got very far with the Archbishop this morning. I don't know why, except that he must have asked some pretty straight questions as to the position adopted by the English Bishops in the Council. He told me that he thought that the French and the German Bishops presented a pretty clear image but that the image of our Hierarchy was by no means clear. I tried to argue that if, as was my opinion, the Hierarchy stood in the middle of the road, it was perhaps not always necessary or even wise to project a public image, because this tended to restrict the possibility of bringing the two extremes together. I doubt if he was convinced.

My own opinion again is that the Hierarchy are now slightly left of centre but, as I pointed out to him, it would seem to me that the entire Church is slightly left of centre now and has moved that way in the course of the last year. This is not so much due to either a change of Pope, in the case of the Church, or to a change of Archbishop of Westminster, in the case of the Hierarchy. I think it has been a natural process as a result of all that has been discussed, both in the Council and out of it, during the past twelve months. He wanted to know whether we stood for the primacy or for the collegiality, which is the great issue of the moment; but again, to some extent, I think we probably have to reply that we stand for both. This is not just a British compromise: no-one denies or wishes to reduce in any way the primacy of the Pope but I at least have strong feelings on the necessity of bringing the various regions and national hierarchies more directly into the government of the Church . . . I must give credit to the Archbishop, who I do not think really enjoyed this interview, for a first-class answer to the question as to the desires and policy of the Hierarchy. He said that we stood for ecumenism and apostolicity. A good answer.

*　　　*　　　*

Worlock's interest in the substance of the Council's debates never strayed far outside his own concerns: although he was by nature a bureaucrat, the general principles of Church organization, which could have profound implications for the future shape of the Catholic Church, did not greatly interest him. But even he could not ignore the heart of the matter – the change in the role and authority of bishops that was at the core of all the Council's deliberations. The First Vatican Council had ended in a hurry in 1870, its work incomplete. It had established once and for all that the papacy ruled the Church worldwide and had the power to issue infallible teachings.

This left the bishops with no clear standing beyond that of being a channel to and from Rome. Although the First Vatican Council did not actually say so, in practice bishops had come to be seen, and to see themselves, as branch managers exercising powers delegated to them by the Pope. But this was hard to reconcile with the treatment of bishops in ancient theological tradition, for instance the view that the relationship of the Pope to the other bishops of the Church was that of *primus inter pares*, first among equals. The tradition also said that the Pope was Pope by virtue of being Bishop of Rome, occupant of the primary See in the Church which took its ecclesiastical title deeds from Sts Peter and Paul (both of whom were executed in Rome). Clearly the Catholic Church had not yet worked out what being a bishop exactly meant.

The answer that began to emerge was what was termed 'collegiality'. Together, the bishops of the Church constituted a collective body, a college in the medieval sense, through which they exercised a shared and joint responsibility for the Church. That much was still compatible with the idea of a bishop as a branch manager, entrusted by the Church's chief executive with delegated powers – a soft version of the doctrine of collegiality. What gained ascendancy during that second session of the Council was the much harder doctrine, that the bishops held their powers as such and not because Rome delegated them.

In practice that would have transformed dramatically the relationship between the Roman Curia and individual bishops. In theory it meant that the normal government of the Catholic Church could no longer be exclusively exercised by and through Rome, but ought in principle to be shared as a collective responsibility. In deference to the First Vatican Council, this was never put forward as being opposed to the idea of government by popes but as a form of collaboration with them. To the supreme power of the papacy had been added the supreme power of the episcopate.

In its most graphic form, this doctrine represented the assembled bishops of the contemporary Catholic Church as being the successors of the first Apostles, who were, so to speak, the original and prototype College of Bishops. To suggest that the Pope ruled the Church alone was therefore like suggesting that only Peter had held authority in the Church at the very beginning, and the other Apostles were simply his representatives. No Catholic could possibly think that. Worlock records the actual moment when the 'hard' version of collegiality was endorsed by large majorities, probably the critical moment in the entire Council.

*   *   *

It has been a busy day, but I suppose that so far as the history of the Church goes, what was decided in the Council this morning will be remembered long after the petty distractions and disturbances with which my day has been peppered.

In the Council this morning, they had the five test questions. These asked the Fathers to say whether it would be agreeable to them that the revised schema should proclaim that episcopal consecration represents the highest point or peak in the hierarchical order; that every consecrated Bishop is a member of the collective body of Bishops; that this College is a successor to the College of the Apostles and that, in union with the Pope, it is the supreme power in the Church; that this is by Divine right; and that the diaconate[12] should be restored as a separate order in the Church, without its being said whether deacons should be allowed to marry or not.

In spite of all the argumentation which has gone on during these past few weeks, and indeed all the difference of opinions which have been expressed, the five questions received an overwhelming vote in the affirmative. At lunch, Bishop Browne of Galway remarked that it must clearly be the Holy Ghost and

I suppose that we should not be very surprised about that. The suggestion that collegiality is by Divine right seems to have produced 408 negative votes, as against 1,717 in favour. The largest negative vote was 525, against the institution of the diaconate. Nonetheless, there seemed to be fairly general satisfaction today that there was far greater unanimity on the issues than had been expected. These votes were, in no sense, an infallible declaration but they would seem to pave the way for far more definite teaching in the future on the question of the episcopate.

*   *   *

Friday, 8th November: I suppose that today will always be reckoned as Cardinal Frings'[13] day. For this morning the big explosion took place. It was Cardinal Frings who fired the big shots and seems to have laid into the whole Curial system.[14] I think there are many who feel that perhaps he overdid it and that it would have been more to the point if he had kept his remarks to the Holy Office. He seems to have attacked their bullying tactics but it is interesting to record that at least one bishop commented that it was strange that it should be the German Cardinal to attack bullying tactics. 'He did not seem to have much to say about the bullying tactics of Hitler!'[15] At all events, it seems to have been a big speech this morning and one which inevitably drew applause from different parts of the House.

Another interesting sidelight is that Archbishop Heenan seems to have walked out. I cannot determine whether he walked out during or immediately after the speech but Jock Tickle came to my room at about midday to ask if the Archbishop was all right. I said that so far as I knew he was all right and that he was in the Aula.[16] 'Oh, no, he has been seen back in the College a quarter of an hour earlier and then has gone out for a walk.' I asked him about this afterwards and he told me that he was heartily fed up, hearing these puerile attacks which really, in his opinion, achieved nothing.[17]

*   *   *

This afternoon, we had a Press Conference on 'Bishops and the Rule of Dioceses' given by Bishop Dwyer, who, of course, served on both the Preparatory Commission and on the Conciliar Commission in the preparation of this document. It was the least successful of those we have organised during this Session and we had an attendance of barely 40. This was due to a number of reasons. Cardinal Frings undoubtedly gave the Press quite enough to get on with this morning and afterwards they went on to the Americans at 11.30 am, when the panel seems to have elaborated some of the charges laid by Cardinal

Frings. There were the usual gang of representatives of Catholic papers but relatively few others and it was rather disappointing because in some ways the Bishop was very good.

In his address to the Press, the bishop stressed two important aspects in the schema: the first dealt with the relationship between the bishops and the Roman Curia, and the second with National Conferences.[18] He made the point that, so far as the relationship with the Curia was concerned, the point which had to be decided was whether the faculties held by a Bishop were to be considered as a concession on the part of the Holy See, and therefore had to be regularly applied for with the necessary dispensations, etc., or whether they were due to him because of his episcopal rank, with merely one or two reserved to the Holy See.[19]

On the question of National Conferences, the Bishop spoke of the value which such Conferences would hold if there was to be any real delegation of power from the Holy See. He made it clear that he, personally, was against any formal statute which would be of universal application and thought it better that each Bishops' Conference should be able to act in the light of its own particular needs and circumstances. He pointed out that, if it was to have a juridical status, a Bishops' Conference would have powers which might possibly conflict with the views of individual Bishops who, whilst welcoming all this talk of collegiality, were nonetheless – to use his own words – 'monarchical' when it came to the rule of their own dioceses. It was a valuable expression of opinion and it was a pity that there were not more people there to hear him. But circumstances were against us this week. It could have happened any time.

*   *   *

Meanwhile, in the Aula of St Peter's, discussion has been continuing on the subject of Bishops and the government of dioceses. Today, there was some come-back to the attack launched by Cardinal Frings last Friday and, not surprisingly, the defence came from Cardinal Spellman.[20] I cannot help wondering what position Cardinal Godfrey would have been called upon to fulfil had he been alive, as undoubtedly the Cardinals in the Curia regarded him in a special way as their protector. Cardinal Spellman, who of course spent many years here in the Secretariat of State in days gone by, is reported to have said that there were many inexact ideas being set forth on such questions as the collegiality of the Bishops of the Church. The theology which the Bishops had learned in the seminary had taught them that the Pope alone had full power over the entire Church. He did not need the help of others. As far as the Roman Curia was concerned, it was only an executive organ of the Holy Father, and therefore it was not up to us to try to reform it or to correct it. We could only offer suggestions and recommendations. I doubt if this will take them very far.

Shortly before lunch, Michael Ashdowne put his head round the door and handed me an envelope from Bishop Petit. It was a large-sized envelope and Michael was full of sniggers whilst I opened it and discovered that, at long last, I had been appointed a *Peritus*. The document was dated 9th October and signed by Cardinal Cicognani, which makes all his protestations of inability to do anything seem somewhat pointless at this stage. I wonder how long it has been lying on whose desk. It is interesting that, in the corner of the envelope, there is written in pencil Cardinal Marella! The Cardinal who undertook to advance Bishop Petit's plea last February. One thing is quite certain and that is that the appointment was made without the knowledge of Archbishop Heenan, who was as surprised as I, when I told him the news shortly before lunch. The rest of the bishops were very pleasant about this and there were mild congratulations and drinks all round before lunch.

*   *   *

Nothing more clearly demonstrates how far Worlock had moved by the autumn of 1963 than his role in the thwarting of Bishop Beck of Salford, who had failed to read the runes as clearly as the rest. Beck wanted to make an attack on the progress of the ecumenical idea, pointing out that it could discourage individual conversions to the Catholic faith. He wrote out a speech and asked Worlock to get it typed and translated, which was Worlock's job. Worlock realized this was not what Heenan would have wished, and shopped him. Heenan ordered Beck to withdraw his text, which he did. Worlock does not appear to have noticed that he was now acting as policeman for Heenan's policies, imposing that line on any bishops who dissented from it. Nor had he realized that he was acting exactly opposite to the way he would have reacted when he was Godfrey's man. But nowhere does Worlock record a 'Road to Damascus' experience, his realization that the old ways were wrong and the new ways right. He was, as ever, just swimming with the current.

The Archbishop and I were invited to dinner by the Marists tonight . . . There was one rather embarrassing incident during the Father General's speech. He was going round the table with his various remarks and he gave great praise to the Bishop of Salford for his inspiring interventions in the Council and expressed the hope that the Bishop would speak more frequently. Little did he know that, earlier this week, Bishop Beck had prepared an intervention for a forthcoming debate on Unity. But it was the most die-hard and ultra-conservative stuff which I do not think would even have carried Cardinal Godfrey with him.

Although there is a lot of reason in what the Bishop says on the subject of unity work having a restricting influence on conversions, this is certainly not the time in which to labour this point and it is increasingly clear that Archbishop Heenan feels that we must go out into the lead on this whole field of ecumenism and show that we are willing to do whatever the Church wants. This will be his main line for his talk next week. Bishop Beck's speech would have, if anything, put the whole movement into reverse. I was asked to get it typed earlier this week and I had to pass the word to Archbishop Heenan. He persuaded Bishop Beck to let him see the speech and at the end told him quite simply that he must not make it. If anyone was to make it, he must get someone else to do so, but if he made this speech, and it were reported in England, we could say goodbye to any hope of Government help for our schools as Bishop Beck was so much associated with the whole of the field of Catholic Education.

I think Bishop Beck is sad, and perhaps smarting a little under this but he has accepted the Archbishop's ruling. It was therefore particularly unfortunate this evening that this high tribute to his interventions – which in any case have not been particularly numerous – should have been made. It is hard to see just where Bishop Beck stands in all this and I sometimes wonder if he is acting as a spokesman for Bishop Wall, who undoubtedly is the main leader of the opposition on this whole question of unity and our relations with non-Catholics in England.

*   *   *

Worlock's visit accompanying Heenan to a dinner given by the Polish bishops was remarkable chiefly for his noticing the new Archbishop of Cracow, an acquaintance he was to invoke on many occasions in the future as the latter became first a cardinal and then the first-ever Polish Pope.

The College is quite a modern building and through the big glass doors of the main entrance I could see drawn up the serried ranks of the Polish Hierarchy – about twenty of them. I just had time to warn the Archbishop that the Polish Bishops were likely to hold any representative from England in awe and reverence as the result of the work of Cardinal Griffin,[21] when we were swept inside and were treated to a greeting in Polish. The Archbishop replied in English that he was sorry he knew no Polish[22] but mercifully he remembered some Polish phrase he must have learned at one stage during the war and he finished up by trotting this out and there were loud bursts of applause. We were then swept off to supper and I viewed the prospect with some anxiety as it was evident that there was scarcely any one of the Polish Hierarchy, other than my friend Bishop Bednorz of Katowice, who had a word of English.

One of the things one always notices with Polish Bishops is their immense sense of hierarchy or seniority, and on this occasion pride of place seemed to be given to Archbishop Baraniak, the Archbishop of Poznan. There were, in all, about twenty Polish Bishops present . . . I was treated almost like a relic and it was interesting to me to see the surprise of Archbishop Heenan at the terms of high esteem with which the memory of Cardinal Griffin was held by these Polish Bishops. When it was time for the Archbishop to reply, he spoke in English, with the Rector interpreting. He was generous in his praise of Polish Catholicism, offering every form of help. This followed on various suggestions which had been made at the table, principally by the new Archbishop of Cracow,[23] a young Pole with an immensely strong face. They had spoken with pleasure of the books which we had sent to them and they seemed to emphasise over and over again the importance which English writers could be to them, in the very delicate task which lay ahead. There is no doubt that they are anticipating further trouble when they get back and, whilst they want all sorts of information made available to the English people through the Press, they are most anxious that care should be taken not to divulge its source.

*   *   *

Archbishop Heenan's anxiety to suppress Bishop Beck's speech was partly a desire to maintain a united front in public, for he had his own quite different contribution to make. After much drafting and redrafting involving Dwyer and Holland (and Worlock too, obviously), Heenan had written a passionate speech full of praise for the ecumenical movement which he delivered on behalf of the whole Hierarchy. (Beck and other dissenters such as Bishop Wall just had to lump it – clearly this new idea of collegiality sometimes rode rough-shod over the rights and views of individuals.) Worlock took exceptional measures to publicize this speech and to make sure it was reported fully and accurately. Rather than rely on the Vatican Press Office, for which he had little time, he duplicated many copies in English and handed them out to the Press himself. It was a speech that would have had Godfrey turning in his grave in despair.

Heenan stated that he was speaking for the whole Hierarchy of England and Wales and that they accepted with joy the schema, since it provided a direction for the future from the supreme authority of the Church, without which ecumenical action could hardly flourish. In the past, some had considered Catholics in England indifferent to the Ecumenical Movement. Some of our separated brethren had even gone abroad in order to exchange in dialogue. But, whilst we would not wish to restrict their freedom to attend any international ecumenical gathering, we hoped that the Council would recommend that in future the dialogue be carried on normally within the region of those taking part and, so far as Catholics were concerned, under the authority of the local Hierarchy. The reason for this was that it was fitting that the dialogue should take place in the context of the local conditions shared by all parties; and, if final unity were to be obtained, they must all live together . . .

The obligation to preach the full truth should be affirmed in the schema. This should not offend our separated brethren because it proceeded from fidelity to Christ's commands. Further, a clear-declaration would aid ecumenism, since it would allay the doubts of some Catholics and bring them to a true religious dialogue. It was not enough for Catholics merely to work with others in social and charitable efforts. We, of England and Wales, thanked God that the days of mutual recrimination were passed and, in the name of the Hierarchy, the Archbishop declared that we were prepared to do anything, short of denying the faith, to obtain the union of Christians. We desired the fuller and more frequent dialogue with all Christians, of whatever denomination.

When the Archbishop closed, there was a tremendous burst of applause and there is no doubt that, quite apart from what he had actually said, the sincerity with which he had spoken shone through the amplified tones of his voice. Needless to say, I was delighted, and found myself receiving reflected glory . . . I met Bishop Holland, who was bubbling with joy and I asked him what had been the reaction in his part of the Aula. He smiled in a rather ashamed way and said that he did not know because he had not been in the Aula at the time. 'I was down at the tomb of Pope John' he said, 'I could hear it all down there and I was pleading my heart out.' This is one of the nicer memories to take way from the Council.

Perhaps one may interject at this point a comment on the relationship which seems to exist between the Archbishop and Bishop Holland, who, because of the dry and mostly good weather throughout the Council, have walked together to St Peter's each morning.

*   *   *

Then once again the outside world intruded cruelly on the Council's proceedings. Worlock supplies his own answer to the celebrated question: 'Where were you when you heard of the assassination of President Kennedy?' He heard it from the BBC's man in Rome at the time, Patrick Smith.

At about twenty minutes to nine, Patrick Smith was called to the telephone and I went out with him. I saw him look very shocked when he received the message by a telephone in the Porters' Lodge and he came out to me and said, quite simply, 'Something terrible has happened. Kennedy has been shot.' Even then I don't think I realised that Kennedy could be dead. It seemed quite unbelievable. I asked if he was badly hurt and Patrick Smith then told me that he had been assassinated and had died at about 1.30 pm local time in America, and presumably about one hour before, so far as our time was concerned. The BBC had telephoned to tell Patrick to get out into the streets and to try to gauge reaction, as he would be needed on television later that evening.

We went back into the Refectory and told the Archbishop. The Archbishop was speechless for about ten seconds and then tapped his glass with his knife. He told the bishops that there was grave news and that President Kennedy had been murdered. There was absolute silence all round the room, broken only when there were expressions of incredulity. Thank goodness the Archbishop had the presence of mind to say 'Eternal rest give to him', to which we all added 'May he rest in peace.' Patrick Smith was almost more moved by this reaction than he was by the news itself, but he left at once to carry out his job . . .

Needless to say, this terrible news cast a great cloud over the evening . . . I always had a great admiration for Jack Kennedy, who appeared to me utterly sincere and, so far as his faith went, he never seemed to put a foot wrong. I and most of the bishops will be offering Mass for him tomorrow morning and one's heart goes out to his wife, who apparently was next to him at the time when be was shot from a window as he passed below in a car. May he rest in peace.

Saturday, 23rd November: Somehow, the whole of today has been over-shadowed by the news of Kennedy's death. There is no doubt that Rome and, so far as one can judge, the whole world is in mourning and is shocked by something which one thought that, in civilised countries, had been relegated to the past. All the flags are at half-mast in Rome and, of course, there have been special editions of the Italian papers bringing us all the latest details of the arrest of Lee Oswald, the Communist sympathiser, and it is reported that the Dallas police have full evidence that it was he who shot the President.

*　　　*　　　*

Occasionally Worlock gave rein to the schoolboy in him, which he enjoyed especially when it meant poking fun at symbols of authority he did not like, such as the Vatican security police. They upheld rigorously a 'no filming' rule, which Worlock believed existed merely to protect the privileges of the official Vatican photographer, Felici, for whom he had no time whatever.

He had agreed to help the Revd Vernon Sproxton, a BBC religious department producer, get some exclusive footage at St Peter's.

This morning we were also engaged in what we came to call Operation Sproxton. I wrote last Friday of the preliminary observation I had made in the
Piazza, so as to see where was going to be the best place for Vernon Sproxton
to get his Council shots. We smuggled him in to the Square in the green Fiat,
driven by Michael, at about a quarter to twelve. We got through the barricade
quite easily. We had a Council badge on the car and I flashed my *tessera*,[24] and
once through we drove over by the fountain on the left where the cars are
parked and swung the car into position so that Vernon was able to get quite a
good long shot of St Peter's itself, sweeping round by the Holy Father's apartments and down to the massed buses, parked below the bronze doors on the
right-hand side of the Piazza.

When he had got enough film of this, we drove over and he and I disem-
barked by the colonnade and sent Michael on up to the side-door to await
Bishop Beck. I asked him to call back into the Square as I thought we might
have difficulty in getting out through the barricade afterwards.

As things seemed relatively quiet and the police seemed disinterested, we
boldly set up Vernon's cine camera on a tripod just inside the colonnade and
with the lens directed on the main doors of St Peter's, through which the
Fathers of the Council would be streaming at 12.15 pm. We had just completed our task when one of the police came over and became inquisitive. I put
my hand into my breast pocket, as if I was going to produce a document, and
he saluted and withdrew. At 12.05 pm, one of the plainclothes men came over
and started to wave his hands in front of the lens, to make it perfectly clear that
we could not use the camera there.

I put my hand into my pocket again and this time produced the tessera and
the man smiled and said 'Scusi' and withdrew. It seemed almost too good to be
true and Sproxton was quite impressed, though a little anxious. 'It might just
as well have been your laundry book' he said. But then another complication
almost led to our downfall. The Moderators inside misjudged the timing of a
speech and at a quarter-past twelve there was still no sign of the Fathers and
by then the crowds had started to gather at the barricades and the plainclothes
men were busy, keeping everyone out of the Piazza. To my horror, I saw the
bald-headed head man heading in our direction and I muttered to Sproxton
that, if we got into difficulties, I would try to lead the head man away whilst he
could bolt with the camera, to make sure that it wasn't confiscated and, if possible, try to set up somewhere else. The man came over and again waved his
hand in front of the lens and told us that this was forbidden, though the truth
is that Felici, the photographer, has the monopoly and will not agree to anyone

else being admitted. The theory is that one can get a pass, but one knows that in practice, it is never granted in time. I produced my *tessera* but this time it failed to work. He told me, quite truthfully, that my *tessera* as a *peritus* had nothing whatever to do with the use of the camera in the Piazza.

I started to walk away and he came with me and I thought that Sproxton would have to run for it. But then I tried another line and I told this character that I was the Director of the Information Services of the English Hierarchy. This, in my best Italian, seemed to shake him a little and he asked me if I would repeat it. I even added a few superlatives here and there and rolled it out with great authority and, to my delight, he just shrugged and went off. For a time, he stood at a distance and watched us and when someone came and stood in the way of the lens, he even moved them on so that we could have a clear view. At last, at 12.25 pm, the Fathers started to stream out of the doors and I had briefed our Bishops to walk over to where we were, and Bill O'Brien had got the Bishops' bus parked at a convenient place nearby. Sproxton kept filming, until he had used the whole of a long run of film and then had to change the film in the camera.

Meantime, the bishops were all assembling by their buses and when Sproxton had re-loaded his camera, he whipped it off the tripod which I was left holding, and he rushed out into the middle of the Square, starting to take close-ups. Immediately, all the plainclothes men moved in on him and I had to grab him and advance towards the bus. They came along in hot pursuit after us but were completely taken aback when, bless them, all our bishops trooped out of the bus, lined up, formed a nice group of smiling faces and waited to have their photographs taken. The plainclothes men just shrugged and went away, whilst Sproxton got another good shot. It was only when the bus had driven away that I realised we were once more alone in the middle of the Piazza and the centre of all eyes, and that it was only a matter of time before we were called to order once again. My embarrassment was increased still further when Sproxton got down by the obelisk and was more or less lying on his back, taking upward shots of a few passing bishops who were leaving the Square on foot.

Again, the police started to move in on us and I saw that it was impossible that we should get through the barricade without the camera and film being confiscated. There was no sign of Michael, who had failed to re-enter the Square as all the traffic was being diverted out via the Holy Office. So I took Sproxton by the arm and we moved off to where the last of the cars was leaving on the other side of the Piazza and the police walked slowly after us. He got one or two more shots of 'beards', as he kept calling them and, when it finally became too hot to stay in the Square any longer, I took him once more into the colonnade on the opposite side from where we had been filming and together we jumped the barricade and got out by the Holy Office. Sproxton was in terrific form and was lying down in the road, getting upward shots of buses passing, packed full of bishops, and I should imagine he had a wonderful scoop of film.

Finally, we walked round towards where the Carozzas were parked so that he could get his last shots of the Roman cabbies and horses, and who should we walk into but Canon Pawley and the Bishop of Ripon. I asked Sproxton if he knew Ripon and he replied that he did. Ripon took one look at him and asked him what he was doing here. Sproxton is a Congregational minister and his father was a parson. But by this time, he was in such good spirits that he cheerfully told Ripon 'Oh, I've converted.' I think that Ripon took him quite seriously and he looked rather anxiously at me 'I suppose Worlock did it' he said, with some venom, I thought. And to my horror Sproxton said 'Yes, that's right.' I decided that this conversation had gone far enough and I dragged Sproxton away and was almost relieved to hand him over to his secretary who was waiting in the Press Office. He is beside himself with joy, having succeeded in taking about 260 foot of film, which he will be able to use in the television programme which is to be canned out here on Friday.

*　　　　*　　　　*

In connection with the making of this film for the BBC a party of English VIPs had arrived, which included the Tory MP for Chelmsford and well-known lay Catholic, Norman St John Stevas.

I was a little embarrassed by Norman Stevas, who started to rush up to every Cardinal within reach, kissing his ring and claiming some acquaintanceship which at least surprised those whom he greeted. I told him to quieten down and to come with Agnellus, Kenneth Lamb and myself, to the box where those admitted merely for the Mass are allowed to view the scene. Hardly had I said this than he rushed off towards the centre of the Aula, starting to approach some of the Cardinals at the Presidents' Table. I went after him and told him, quite sharply that if he continued in this way, he would undoubtedly be put out by the ushers. He then knelt at the Confessional of St Peter and someone distracted my attention. When I looked back, Stevas had gone and I never saw him again. I watched quite clearly to see whether he came out with the others at the '*Exeant omnes*' but I saw no sign of him. I have a horrid fear that he smuggled himself into the building somewhere and stayed there throughout the morning – a privilege to which his pass did not entitle him and I hope I am not misjudging him. Certainly, he was not with us for the Mass, as had been arranged.

*   *   *

By now Worlock was becoming absorbed in the business of the Council, especially his duties as a *peritus* in the Commission preparing a draft of a new document, *The Church in the Modern World*. His description of the way this vital work was tackled is quite extraordinary, and captures a flavour no other account of the Second Vatican Council has achieved.

> I think I should say briefly that the Commission Meeting achieved the right result but was about the most frustrating and shattering experience that I have had for a long time. I suppose that there were about forty Bishops and two dozen *periti* in the room and the meeting was presided over by Cardinal Cento, now eighty-odd and quite definitely ga-ga, and Cardinal Browne who seems to have gone downhill a lot in the last year and now is completely inaudible when he ignores the microphone and unintelligible when he succeeds in hitting it. I had always imagined that he would be a great orator but in fact he yammers to such an extent that one does not know where one is. Very different from some of the Bishops speaking from lower down the table.
>
> The Commission Meeting started with a real show-down. Fr Tromp, SJ, who is secretary of the Theological Commission, came to the microphone to explain that there were now two documents, one prepared by the mixed Commission last May and one submitted by Cardinal Suenens.[25] Mgr Glorieux[26] had claimed that Cardinal Suenens had been commissioned by the Co-ordinating Committee[27] to carry out this work of re-writing but he wanted to know by whose authority this document had been prepared and circulated. This was a direct attack on Cardinal Suenens and I must say that I objected to the document but for reasons different from those put forward by Fr Tromp.
>
> Fr Tromp's argument was that there was nothing we could do in this mixed Commission: only the Co-ordinating Committee and Cardinal Confalonieri could decide which document should be considered by the mixed Commission. Cardinal Cento had not the least idea what was being spoken about and sided with each speaker in turn. Amongst the *periti* on the far side of the room were a number of men of Cardinal Suenens' school. Mgr Philips decided to defend the value of Cardinal Suenens' document which he had almost certainly written himself, on scholastic grounds. Another youngish priest, who said quite plainly that he was Cardinal Suenens' private secretary, attacked those who had attacked Cardinal Suenens and said most hotly that he had been directly commissioned by Cardinal Confalonieri to write this document.
>
> It looked as though we were going to be put to a most embarrassing vote

but Bishop Hengsbach succeeded in steering it away and leading the discussion towards the type of document which was required. He thought that the Conciliar document was more practical, though some parts of the old text upon which the present one was based were perhaps better. Even now, at regular intervals, members of the Suenens group were leaping up to defend their master and eventually Cardinal Cento said that there could be no doubt that the job had been given to Suenens and therefore there could be no further discussion on the point.

Bishop McGrath, from Panama, who is a great linguist then came out in favour of the Conciliar document and then Fr Rahner, the Jesuit, gave us an almost Hitlerian performance from the bench of the theological *periti*. He thumped the table and said that what was needed was a practical directory for the guidance of the people in the modern world and that no Conciliar document could possibly give these people the kind of advice which they required. This was neatly steered away by some of the other speakers to suggest that it would be better if these important questions were not dealt with in the Council at all. Tromp stood up and slammed Rahner and Rahner[28] was back on his feet immediately to reply to Tromp. At first it was amusing and then it was rather disedifying but we were no nearer any solution.

Eventually, Cardinal Koenig moved some definite resolution, more or less suggesting that the Suenens document should form the *proemium* and first chapter, dealing with man's vocation, and then that the Conciliar document should be used for the other chapters dealing with practical matters. But there was a lot of opposition to the Suenens document and again it looked as though the whole thing was going to be steered away. I was delighted when de Rabicht, the leader of the Auditores present for the first time, said quite simply, and in French, that the world awaited this document. The Church must give an answer and if the Council failed to give that answer, the world's faith in the Church would have been betrayed. He spoke well.

By this time, Rahner was leaping to his feet after each speech, trying to gain the floor, but the most useful intervention we had was from Monsignor Pavan, whom many think was the force behind the two great social encyclicals in the last reign. We were meant to be dealing with the position of the Church in the world today. Theological principles about the Church's position would apply to the Church at any time, but we were concerned with the problems of today and therefore we must give a practical answer. We had been at this for over two hours when finally we managed to force a vote on the suggestion that a steering committee be appointed, made up of three persons each from the Theological Commission and the Lay Apostolate Commission, their task being to prepare the *proemium* and the first chapter.

*   *   *

The second session staggered to an end, with almost nothing finished but the internal debate having moved to a point where the conservatives were on the defensive on every front. Pope Paul VI closed the session with a speech which cut through much of the debate, announcing what his future policy would be on a number of matters that the Council had yet to resolve – and exercise of the power of the papal absolutism in defence of collegiality, ironically enough. In particular the Pope forecast that after the Council, some machinery would have to be devised so that collaboration between the Holy See and the worldwide episcopate would be on a permanent basis. That pre-empted much of the debate on collegiality; it was probably the moment the conservatives were truly defeated.

> However, apart from the Commission for the Revision of the Code of Canon Law, this is, I think, the first time the Pope has spoken about post-Conciliar Commissions . . .
>
> This leads one to the second important point which is that he seems to have accepted the idea of collegiality, without anywhere actually referring to this term. He said that in the revision of the Code of Canon Law, he would set up Commissions, both for the Latin and for the Oriental rite, the members of which he would himself select. 'Naturally, it will be a source of joy to Us to choose from among the bishops of the world and from the ranks of the religious orders, as was done for the Preparatory Commissions of the Council, distinguished and expert brethren, who, along with qualified members of the Sacred College, will bring us their counsel and help to translate into fitting and specific norms the general decisions of the Council.'
>
> And now comes the important piece where he appears to be accepting the idea of a Senate or body of Episcopal Advisers, who can help him without in any way diminishing the primacy of Peter, which he stressed elsewhere in his address. 'And so experience will show to us how, without prejudice to the prerogatives of the Roman Pontiff, defined by the First Vatican Council, the earnest and cordial collaboration of the bishops can more effectively promote the good of the Universal Church.'

Notes

1 Norris.
2 Given the last rites.
3 *A History of English Christianity 1920–1990*, SCM, 1991, p. 479.

4 Heenan (*Crown of Thorns*, p. 385) observed many bishops consulting Montini during the first session of the Council, just as Worlock had done, but did not attribute it to a left-wing conspiracy. 'Although he gave only one speech during the first session he was consulted by many bishops to find out the mind of Pope John' wrote Heenan. 'Cardinal Montini was known to be his intimate friend.'

5 Godfrey died on 22 January 1963. John XXIII died on 3 June 1963; Paul VI was elected on 21 June 1963. Heenan was translated to Westminster on 2 September 1963. Part of the delay in replacing Godfrey was caused by the death of the Apostolic Delegate, the abrasive American Archbishop O'Hara, not long after Godfrey. It was he whom Worlock had reported as saying Heenan would go to Westminster 'over my dead body', which turned out to be true.

6 For a fuller treatment, see *The Vatican in the Age of the Dictators 1922–45* by Anthony Rhodes, Hodder and Stoughton, 1973.

7 *Cardinal Bernard Griffin* by Michael de la Bedoyere, Rockliff, 1955.

8 Vatican Year Book.

9 Archbishop O'Hara.

10 For the opening of the second session of the Second Vatican Council in September 1963.

11 They had returned to the routines of life at the English College.

12 This was an entirely separate issue. Deacons, along with priests and bishops, are in Holy Orders; but in the Western Church they had become merely a preliminary stage to the priesthood. The proposal before the Council was to re-establish deacons as a permanent class of male clergy, not necessarily bound by the rule of priestly celibacy. (Whether woman can become deacons has never been officially resolved.)

13 Archbishop of Cologne.

14 Reining in the power of the Curia was intimately connected with the assertion of the power of the episcopate, a determination no doubt strengthened by the vote in favour of a 'hard' theory of collegiality a few days before.

15 Worlock was never entirely free of a certain anti-German bigotry characteristic perhaps of his generation of Englishman.

16 The main debating chamber.

17 Worlock is beginning to notice Heenan's reaction against the progressive tendency he had hitherto identified with. This got far stronger once the Council was over.

18 The proposal had been made that each Hierarchy should become a National Conference of Bishops where local collegiality could be exercised.

19 This was the heart of the collegiality issue.

20 Archbishop of New York and the most famous American Catholic prelate of his generation; also an arch-reactionary and supporter of Senator McCarthy.

21 Griffin had helped the Polish exile community in London and spoken out in favour of an independent Poland just as it was being sucked into the Soviet orbit after the war.

22 He had passed through Warsaw in 1937, cutting short an intended visit of three days in protest at being attacked by a Polish soldier in the street. Apparently it was the law at the time that citizens had to remove their hats when Polish troops marched past. He refused to accept an official Polish apology to the effect that the soldier had mistaken him for a Jew, which Heenan did not think was an adequate explanation. (*Not the Whole Truth* by John C. Heenan, Hodder and Stoughton, 1971.)

23 Karol Wojtyla, later Pope John Paul II.

24 Pass.

25 Archbishop of Malines-Brussels and one of the chief progressives of Vatican II.

26 Secretary of the Commission on the Lay Apostolate, one of the two bodies represented on the new joint Commission, the other being Tromp's Theological Commission. Tromp was Ottaviani's man.

27 This was responsible for liaising between different Commissions, preventing overlaps and conflicts.

28 This episodes paints Karl Rahner SJ, one of the most distinguished and influential Catholic theologians of the century, in a new and unexpected light.

6

Good Catholics, and Stepney

By the beginning of 1964, the Catholic Church really had changed direction. The Second Vatican Council still had a lot of work to do, and there were still skirmishes to be won and lost. But the war was over – the war, that is, between two different conceptions of Catholicism identified (by Worlock among others) by the labels progressive and conservative. When asked in the middle of the Council by a journalist to say whether the English Catholic bishops were now 'left of centre' in theological terms, Worlock replied that the entire body of bishops at the Council could now be so described. Hence the English were not different from the rest. Nor had they been different at the outset, when they, and the rest of the bishops at the Council, could fairly be described as right of centre. (These metaphors imply that there is a 'centre' that remained constant throughout, to measure Left or Right from. In fact that could not have been so. If the whole body had moved, then logically the centre must have moved too.)

One issue preoccupied Derek Worlock most of his lifetime, and became more and more important to him at the Council itself – the role of the Catholic laity. He brought to the Council wide experience of a field he regarded as central to the work of the priest: supporting lay people in their daily lives and daily work. He had pioneered what he called his Team, a small and élite corps of committed and devout lay Catholics from various walks of life. These represented his ideal model. But he would also have put forward the Young Christian Workers, as a national and international institution, and the Grail, as a Secular Institute,[1] as examples of good solutions to the problem of the laity. And there was indeed a problem, both real and perceived. It is summed up in a term very current before and for some time after the Second Vatican Council: the 'Good Catholic'. The laity problem was about encouraging the former to be more so, and the latter to become like the former. The method Worlock preferred was called 'lay

173

formation'. The concept was modelled on the 'priestly formation' which was the business of the seminary.

At the Council, he wanted to see his ideas reflected in the results, especially in the two documents most appropriate for this purpose, the *Decree on the Laity* and the *Decree on the Church in the Modern World*. He was, once he had been appointed as a *peritus*, a member of the small group of priest-consultants attached to both of the Commissions which were preparing these documents. He played a significant part in their meetings; and being who he was, that included a willingness to go away after a meeting to draft and draft again, far into the night, then to return to the fray at the next session to see his drafts dissected or rejected, or merely swamped by the volume of other people's drafts and redrafts. That is the kind of battle Worlock relished. But it was for his idea of what a layman was, and of how the Church ought to behave towards him, that he fought his corner.

There is little sign in all these meetings that Worlock felt he had anything much to learn from others present. Nor was he very interested in the theological question of 'what a layman is'. There was an *impasse* at one stage of the Council over whether the definition of a layman should appear in the text being produced by the Theological Commission or the one being worked on by the Commission on the Lay Apostolate. Which it was to be interested Worlock more than what it was to be. He thought he knew what a layman was, and so did everybody else. A layman was not a priest. And a layman was either a Good Catholic or a Bad Catholic.

This approach comes straight form the Council of Trent, whose Catechism, under the heading 'The Members of the Church Militant' goes on to declare:

> The Church militant is composed of two classes of persons, the good and the bad, both professing the same faith and partaking of the same Sacraments, yet differing in their manner of life and morality . . .
>
> The good are those who are linked together not only by the profession of the same faith, and the participation of the same Sacraments, but also by the spirit of grace and the bond of charity. Of these St Paul says: The Lord knoweth who are his. Who they are that compose this class we also may remotely conjecture, but we can by no means pronounce with certainty. But although the Catholic faith uniformly and truly teaches that the good and the bad belong to the Church, yet the same faith declares that the condition of both is very different. The wicked are contained in the Church, as the chaff is mingled with the grain on the threshing floor, or as dead members sometimes remain attached to a living body.[2]

These concepts were so all-pervading in their influence that few bothered to examine their content. They were everywhere to such an extent that they were invisible. When Worlock drops into one of his early diaries a remark that a certain MP is thought to be a Catholic but no one is sure whether he is a good one, he is taking for granted a common shorthand and sees no need to say what he means any more explicitly.

'Good' in this reference does not always necessarily mean morally good, as in 'a good man'. It means 'good at being a Catholic', as in 'good musician'. Like a good musician, a good Catholic had to be specially 'formed'. It was even possible, within this terminology, to be a 'good' man and a 'Bad' Catholic simultaneously. However, a certain odium was inevitably connected with being a Bad Catholic (that is to say, with being bad at being a Catholic). Bad Catholics had broken the rules in some respect, and keeping to the rules was itself deemed morally good even if the rules had no objective moral content, such as abstinence from meat on Fridays. Divine sanction was attached to them. Missing Mass on Sundays, taking part in a Protestant church service, getting married without the blessing of a priest: all these actions, morally indifferent or even conceivably positive in themselves in certain circumstances, became sins when they involved deliberate disobedience of the Catholic Church's authority.

In English terms the twilight zone between the Good and Bad Catholic was more often explored by novelists than by theologians or sociologists. The most celebrated Catholic novel of the post-war years was Evelyn Waugh's *Brideshead Revisited*;[3] and the most celebrated Catholic novelist was Graham Greene. Both of them found rich material in the Good Catholic/Bad Catholic dichotomy. Their popular success could not have depended solely on Catholic readers, even less in Waugh's case on an élite wealthy snobbish clique which would have recognized itself in *Brideshead*, because there were not enough of them. They appealed to the non-Catholic English public at large partly because they transcended this narrow and esoteric caste system of Good Catholics and Bad Catholics in order to say true things about the human condition and the divine spark therein; but partly also because the English were able, through these novels, to get an idea of what a religion would be like if those who belonged to it believed every word of it (something they could not learn from contemplating the internal affairs of the Church of England). The perils of Catholic damnation or the miseries of Catholic guilt could be enjoyed vicariously. Indeed, they had a powerful attraction.

The Bad Catholic, as Worlock would have used the term, was a somewhat home-grown idea. It did not equate with the Continental idea of an anticlerical. It may have had its origins in the seventeenth-century divide between 'church-papists' on one side and 'recusants' on the other – two ways of coping with the severe penalties that were attached to the practice of the Catholic faith in England at that time. Recusants refused to attend the services of the Church by Law Established, and were regularly fined for their defiance. For some of the period, assisting a Catholic priest to go about his duties was a capital offence. Recusants were not allowed to be MPs or magistrates, to hold a commission in the services, or even to go to Oxford and Cambridge.

Church-papists, who were so numerous that their alleged influence over the court of Charles I was one of the causes of the Civil War, were secret Catholics who outwardly conformed to the State religion. Recusants saw them as disloyal to the Catholic faith, putting self before duty. Puritans and others disliked them for their disloyalty to the Anglican Settlement. They were the 'enemy within'; they were having their cake and eating it. English Catholics had to grow acutely sensitive antennae to distinguish between recusants and church-papists. Thus arose the searching question one Catholic would ask another about a mutual Catholic acquaintance: 'Is he *completely* loyal to the Church?' In other words: 'Is he a Good Catholic?'

On top of the political issue there was also the influence of Jansenist spirituality in English Catholicism. It had been well rooted in Ireland, though the movement started in France in the mid-seventeenth century as a protest against the alleged moral laxity preached by the Jesuits. It was strict; it did not like the human body and its functions, and it did not like people enjoying themselves because of the ever-present danger of sin. It had some of the characteristics of Calvinism in its insistence on the initiative of God in human salvation – 'by grace alone'. Its influence on popular Catholic piety was to foster the feeling that salvation was a precarious prize easily lost, and that God was fearsome and only to be approached with extreme trepidation. It discouraged regular Communion almost as much as it discouraged human contentment. It was the source of a lot of Catholic anguish.

Aside from this intensification of spiritual nervousness caused by Jansenism, orthodox moral theology of the Counter Reformation era already taught that mortal sin destroyed the relationship with God and could only be restored by confession and absolution. One who died in a state of mortal sin went straight to Hell. One who was not in a state of mortal sin was said to be in a state of grace. Though it was not part of the teaching of Cornelius Jansen[4] as such, the Jansenist outlook made it seem that mortal sins were easily committed and the state of grace was forever in danger of slipping away. It was necessary to be very watchful, even scrupulous, if this was to be avoided. Like Calvinists, Jansenists strongly believed human beings were naturally wicked and left to their own devices much more likely to prefer the wrong to the right.

Priests influenced by this spirituality naturally encouraged lay Catholics to stick to the rules of the Church as rigorously as possible, as the only safe course. It was accepted, for example, that to eat even a morsel of meat on a Friday was a mortal sin, damning the soul to Hell. There were, of course, escape routes. In Graham Greene's *Brighton Rock*,[5] the young thug Pinkie ('the Boy') torments himself with the thought that he might die in a state of mortal sin and burn in Hell for ever; but is comforted by remembering that even 'between the stirrup and the ground'[6] it is possible for the sinner to repent and still get to heaven. The Good Thief was the Patron Saint of Bad Catholics. Crucified with Jesus, the Good Thief repents of his sins and asks to be admitted into heaven even as he dies. Jesus tells him his wish is granted. It is symptomatic of a certain style of Catholicism that with various murders and other crimes on his conscience, Pinkie is also worried by his false marriage to the girl Rose, yet another mortal sin for which to be damned. It was against the law of the Church; and the power of the Church is not to be mocked.

'You a Roman?' the Boy asked.

'Yes,' Rose said.

'I'm one too,' the Boy said. He gripped her arm and pushed her out into the dark dripping street. He turned up the collar of his jacket and ran as the light-ning flapped and the thunder filled the air. They ran from doorway to doorway until they were back on the parade in one of the empty glass shelters. They had it to themselves in the noisy stifling night. 'Why, I was in a choir once,' the Boy confided and suddenly began to sing softly in his spoilt boy's voice: *'Agnus dei qui tollis peccata mundi, dona nobis pacem.'*[7] In his voice a whole lost world moved – the lighted corner below the organ, the smell of incense and laun-dered surplices, and the music. Music – it didn't matter what music – *'Agnus dei'*, 'lovely to look at, beautiful to hold', 'the starling on our walks', *'credo in unum Deum'*[8] – any music moved him, speaking of things he didn't understand.

'Do you go to Mass?' he asked.

'Sometimes,' Rose said. 'It depends on work. Most weeks I wouldn't get much sleep if I went to Mass.'

'I don't care what you do,' the Boy said sharply. 'I don't go to Mass.'

'But you do believe, don't you?' Rose implored him, 'you think it's true?'

'Of course it's true,' the Boy said. 'What else could there be?' he went scornfully on. 'Why,' he said, 'it's the only thing that fits. These atheists, they don't know nothing. Of course there's Hell, Flames and damnation,' he said with his eyes on the dark shifting water and the lightning and the lamps going out above the black struts of the Palace Pier, 'torments.'

'And Heaven too,' Rose said with anxiety, while the rain fell interminably on.

'Oh, maybe,' the Boy said, 'maybe.'

In Evelyn Waugh's *Brideshead Revisited*, Lord Marchmain makes that final movement of the hand on his deathbed, the sign of the Cross, which signals to those watching that he has repented of his long-time rejection of Catholicism at the last possible moment. It is the climax of the novel. But neither Pinkie nor Lord Marchmain are proposed as models to be followed; they are interesting because they defy the rules until the last possible minute and get away with it (or in Pinkie's case, perhaps not).

Nowhere does Waugh work the seam of Bad Catholics/Good Catholics more effectively than in the final scene, where he has Lady Julia explain to her one-time and would-be lover Charles Ryder why they cannot see each other again. She is trapped in a loveless match to a faithless husband, but divorce is forbidden to Catholics. 'I've always been bad. Probably I shall be bad again, punished again. But the worse I am, the more I need God. I can't shut myself out from his mercy . . . I saw today there was one unforgivable thing . . . the bad thing I was on the point of doing, that I'm not quite bad enough to do; to set up a rival good to God's.' If she gives up thought of marrying Ryder, 'if I give up this one thing I want so much' then 'however bad I am, He won't quite despair of me in the end.' Thus a Bad Catholic stands on the threshold of becoming a Good Catholic again; so the devious church-papist becomes an honest recusant; so the sinner grasps at grace instead of relying on good works – 'a rival good to God's'.

There were two essential points about being a Good Catholic. The first was the importance of observing all the rules of the Catholic faith, not just some of them. Being approximately Catholic did not count. Large acts of virtue did not compensate for small acts of sin. The state of grace was easily broken – missing Sunday Mass once was enough to put an individual into mortal sin. This was specially true in the matter of sex. Nowhere did this perilous Jansenist threat of instant damnation loom larger than in connection with impure thoughts and wilful motions of the flesh. A mortal sin could be committed in an instant by failing to check one's spontaneous physical responses when contemplating a picture of a partly clothed woman. Even contemplating it in the mind was enough; no actual picture need exist. The redeeming aspect of this supercharged landscape of instant damnation was the ready availability of the prescribed antidote. Confession to a priest made good the harm done at once, restored the life of grace, washed away the sin (though not, in theory, all the punishment due for it). *In extremis*, as Greene often noted in his novels, an individual could be rescued from imminent damnation by saying to himself a perfect 'act of contrition' – repenting totally of all his sins, and throwing himself entirely on the mercy of God.

The second crucial aspect of the life of grace of a Good Catholic, therefore, was maintaining a relationship of good-humoured and respectful submission to the clergy. It was permissible to feel that a particular priest was, as a man, a bit eccentric, or boring, or even overfond of the bottle; but as a priest he was closer to God than a lay person and therefore to be looked up to. His closer-ness to God came partly from the fact that he celebrated the divine mysteries, above all the power of consecrating bread and wine so that 'it becomes for us the Body and Blood of Our Lord Jesus Christ'. But it was partly his membership of the hierarchical Church, albeit at a level below that of bishop but above that of layman. The notion that grace, authority and spiritual power flowed down from the top through the various strata of the Hierarchy did not just make the priest special: it also made him necessary. A willing dependence on priests was therefore the mark of a Good Catholic.

Worlock's emphasis on the lay apostolate and the importance of lay formation was an attempt to make the best of this situation, not to change it. Indeed, this is more or less the line taken in the eventual outcome of the Second Vatican Council which most concerns the laity, the decree *Apostolicum Actuositatem* (on the Apostolate of Lay People). It bears all the hallmarks of having been assembled from different sources, as Worlock's own account of the Commission meetings confirms. Some of the compromises that were necessary seem to have consisted of running alternative versions of the same ideas one after another, when finding a synthesis became too difficult (or the climate in the committee became too heated).

In places its conception of the lay apostolate is strictly hierarchical: the laity act within and as part of the Mystical Body of Christ and must be governed accordingly. But that is the pre-conciliar stress. Elsewhere, the distinctive voice of the Second Vatican Council can be heard when it talks of the laity as part of the People of God, of their equality with other members of that People, and of their autonomy in the secular sphere. Their apostolate comes from their baptism, therefore, not from being commissioned or sanctioned by the Hierarchy. These two ways of talking about the role of lay people sit ill together. The Council refused to choose between them: to that extent the decree reflects an argument begun but not finished.

Nowhere is the difficulty more acute than in the matter of lay formation. The model suggested is definitely the pre-conciliar one, but updated: that of lay apostolate as an official extension of the Church's general apostolate. Hence it is under the Church's control and direction, if not directed by the Hierarchy then through priests the Hierarchy has appointed for such work. It is a very churchy conception, tending to produce a clericalized laity.

What the Council was doing in following this model was no more than 'encouraging best practice' as found in the Counter Reformation pre-conciliar Church, especially (in a long section all to itself) Catholic Action. The section on Catholic Action in the final document was little more than an uncritical description of the work of Catholic lay institutions in the pre- and post-war period. There is nothing proposed that is innovative.

But Worlock's dreams did start to come true. 'Training' in the lay apostolate 'is indispensable' said the final document, and 'besides spiritual formation, solid rounding in doctrine is required, in theology, ethics and philosophy.' The decree concedes: 'While preserving intact the necessary link with ecclesiastical authority, the laity have the right to establish and direct associations and to join existing ones.' But 'the hierarchy's duty is to favour the lay apostolate, furnish it with principles and spiritual assistance, direct the exercise of the apostolate to the common good of the Church, and see that doctrine and order are safeguarded.' By means of lay formation, the gap which had been opened up between priest and people at the time of Trent was to be closed again, not by lowering the priesthood but by lifting the people, making them less 'lay' (in the common, slightly pejorative sense) and more like priests.

What Derek Worlock seemed to want was to convince the Hierarchy, including himself, that the laity could be trained up well enough to be let loose on their own. But the training was crucial. Thus the Good Catholic was like a well-bred sheepdog, who had been by its master's side long enough, and been trained well enough, to learn its master's ways and so to be trusted with the care of a flock of sheep when the master was away. That was a step forward from the conservatives' conviction that the laity could never be trusted on their own but must always be kept on a lead, lest they maul the sheep (which it was their nature to do).

But it was still only one step. Worlock's ideas of the role of the laity were yet to adapt to the deeper insights of the Second Vatican Council. It was not immediately obvious what would be the full implication of the substitution of a 'People of God' model for the Church in place of the more hierarchical 'Mystical Body' model. In the terminology of 'lay apostolate', this ultimately must mean that the right and duty of lay people to spread the message of the Gospel in the secular world came directly from their baptism, not from their receiving transferred powers from the clergy. But this was hotly contested in the Lay Apostolate Commission as it struggled to present an agreed document for discussion by the Council when it resumed.

Worlock's theological stance at this time could be described as that of a very progressive type of conservative, rather than of a progressive *per se*. In his Vatican II diary entry for 5 March 1964, when he was involved in an intense series of meetings of the Lay Apostolate Commission in Rome, he still seemed to feel that the laity could be dangerous if not kept under control. 'It was the layman who represented the Church in the world and . . . unless he were properly formed and trained for his task, he could be a menace', he reported himself as arguing.

Formation of the laity to equip it for this role so that it did not become a menace was at the time for him an *avant-garde* concept. It was certainly a great step forward from the idea that the laity had nothing much to do but 'hunting, shooting and fishing' – that as far as the Church was concerned their proper place was to be the passive and grateful recipients of the ministrations of those in Holy Orders. But it still put the laity in a subordinate relationship to the clergy, who were still, so to speak, the professionals. One factor in this attitude may well have been the overhaul of priestly training that had been undertaken after the Council of Trent in the mid-sixteenth century.

As a result of much longer and higher quality training, priests were far better educated than they had been at the time of the Reformation. They were knowledgeable in philosophy, Scripture and theology; and they were expected to have a sophisticated prayer life, saying the Daily Office, celebrating a daily Mass, studying sacred literature and so on. By such means they were 'formed' into the kind of spiritual life appropriate to their status.[9] They gave far more attention to their own sanctification, and to their own understanding of the Catholic faith, than a layman could be expected to give. Inevitably, the status of layman came to be regarded as second class. This attitude was revealed in a sharp exchange in the Lay Apostolate Commission, when a fellow member doubted whether lay people could ever achieve spiritual perfection. Worlock seemed to think the possibility could not be ruled out, for instance in the case of a member of a Secular Institute.

'Lay formation' was an idea modelled on the formation given to priests, but in an adapted and abbreviated form. There obviously was not time to equip a layman with all the knowledge a priest had, so a priest had to be available to him as a convenient repository of this expert knowledge. The spiritual formation was just as important – deepening the layman's prayer life, so that he became more humble and virtuous, indeed more Christ-like. Humility was probably the quality Worlock had most in mind when he talked of lay people becoming a menace without proper formation.

Humility would make him receptive to the guidance of a priest rather than reliant on his own opinions. If he was receptive to the guidance of a priest he would be unlikely to become a troublemaker, one who criticized the policies of the hierarchy. It is in this area that the idea of a 'Bad Catholic' held most dread for Church officials of Worlock's background and experience. Bad Catholics could mislead Good Catholics into sinful and rebellious ways. The thought of what they might do was enough to induce a shudder of horror. A Bad Catholic was worse in every way than a merely lapsed Catholic. One thing a Bad Catholic might do, for instance, was to challenge such settled doctrines as the one that said that the use of contraception was a mortal sin.

None of these thoughts were ever spelt out in the Lay Apostolate Commission as it put together its draft document for consideration by the Council itself. Everyone knew them and they could be taken as read. But what happened at the Council, and what happened in the years shortly afterwards, cannot be understood without reference to them. The Bad Catholic/Good Catholic divide may have emerged unscathed from the Council. But it did not long survive the crisis in the Church that broke out three years after it ended, arising from the publication of the papal encyclical on birth control, *Humanae Vitae*.

Another novelist who has explored the Bad Catholic/Good Catholic territory was David Lodge, though he deconstructed it rather than used it as a fictional framework. In his *How Far Can You Go?*,[10] he described a group of lay Catholics who travel through the time of Vatican II and the *Humanae Vitae* crisis and emerge with a transformed and modern idea of the Catholic faith that would surely have horrified the Derek Worlock of 1965, but with which he would be familiar and at home twenty years later. The group started to campaign for the kind of Catholicism they now believed in, calling themselves the 'Catholics for an Open Church' movement.

> 'Where we went wrong, of course,' said Adrian, 'was in accepting the theology of mortal sin.'
> 'No,' said Miriam, who had been listening quietly to their comments.

'Where you went wrong was in supposing that the Church belonged to the Pope or the priests instead of to the People of God.'

They nodded agreement. 'The People of God' was a phrase the Catholics for an Open Church approved of. It made them sound invincible.[11]

No doubt this was not what Derek Worlock had in mind in 1964, as he went into the lists to fight for what he regarded as the proper place of the laity in the Church. It is clear from his detailed record of the debates – almost blow by blow – that in the collision between his more advanced ideas and the far more cautious stance of some of the Continental bishops and theologians, Worlock was gradually being pushed further forwards. That was the logic of the position he had adopted. The amount of detail he recorded, not one-tenth of which is reproduced here, indicates just how fundamental to the future of the Catholic Church he felt these battles to be.

Not everyone who is passing over a watershed is aware of it at the time. The emotional intensity of his efforts suggests that those months spent battling in Commissions and Sub-Commissions of the Council were his own personal turning point. This was when he became a real progressive, a true believer in the Second Vatican Council. This was when he finally let go of the Counter Reformation mindset of the preconciliar churchman, the mindset he was now having to fight almost line by line to produce a document on the laity which would, in his opinion, do justice to the gravity of the issues. It is at this stage in the diary that the reader begins to meet the modern Worlock, the man who became Bishop of Portsmouth and later Archbishop of Liverpool, the man who was only a whisker away from making cardinal, the man who came to represent in his very person all that the Second Vatican Council eventually stood for, faults and all.

Maybe he was not quite ready to let go of the universal preconciliar notion of the laity as consisting of Good Catholics and Bad Catholics. But he found it less and less useful. It didn't say what he wanted to say. It is not surprising he was one of the first to abandon it in the crisis of 1968. That theory would have required him to reclassify some of his closest friends, some of his own personal Team, the very best Catholics he knew, people who were the actual model on which parts of the Second Vatican Council's teaching on the lay apostolate were based, as Bad Catholics.

This is how he fought the battle.

Towards the end of the morning session, I raised the point which had come up on Tuesday, of the layman as a '*pons*' – a bridge between the world and the Church. I asked for the inclusion of my paragraph emphasising that the layman must be in contact with the world and that it was his function to show the teachings of Christ and of the Church before the world and to represent the needs and cares of men to the Church.

This was welcomed by Bishop Menager and Bishop Guano but Father Moehler[12] saw difficulties. I became rather tired of his opening remark '*Habeo difficultatem unam!*' which usually meant he had several. Was I making a separation between the Church and the layman? Was my principle theologically sound? When I explained the importance of this he said that mine was merely a pastoral consideration and I said it was for this reason that I wanted it incorporated here. All seemed to be settled when he and Father Papali[13] pointed out that another Commission was dealing with the section on the field of the apostolate and that my ideas would be incorporated there. I argued that I wasn't talking about fields of the apostolate. It was part of the layman's vocation to represent the Church to the world and vice versa. Bishop Necsey then declared for lunch and I had a strong suspicion that I had lost my point. We returned to do battle at a second session at 4.30 and I at once asked Father Papali whether my point was settled. He said that it would be dealt with by the other commission, but I said that unless it was included in the draft that I had been asked to revise I would raise the point immediately. He gave me the assurance that it would be included and it will be interesting to see tomorrow whether he has done it.

This afternoon we were meant to be dealing with two sections on the fundamental basis for the apostolate and on formation. Much of the conversation this afternoon was led by Father Moehler with whom I had two clashes. I said that I thought we should explain that Christ's call to the apostles to 'go and teach all nations' was the basis of the call to all Christians to exercise this apostolic task. I then made my distinction between '*praedicare*' and '*docere*'. But Father Moehler insisted that this instruction was given only to the apostles and not to all Christians. All argument on this point was inconclusive but if the scripture scholars hold that I am wrong, then a good many other writers I have read are wrong.

In considering these fundamental principles, I found the continental mind was set on nice distinctions between various forms of the apostolate, even seen in the form of theological principles, e.g. the apostolate of prayer, the apostolate of suffering, etc. In the end we scrapped a good deal of what the Commission had proposed in favour of a *votam* sent in by 25 French bishops.

My first stand was on the question of formation, where to my horror I found that Father Moehler suggested that the whole matter be left over to the Directory[14] and that as all formation was specific it would be pointless to try to include it in the general principles which we were formulating. I let them drift away on this for a while and then said with great emphasis that I thought that in many ways this was the most important section of the whole document. In non-Catholic countries especially it was the layman who represented the Church in the world and unless he were properly formed and trained for his task, he could be a menace. There were certain general principles of formation which could be set down and I indicated certain paragraphs in my propositions. These seemed largely acceptable when Father Moehler started again to say that these were designed again for specific formation and that anything more general was nothing more than teaching the catechism to those who wished to follow the Christian life. He did not think there was any point in mentioning the instruction given by parents, teachers or priests. I told him that with so much emphasis on the People of God there was a real danger of anti-clericalism and that the parents' role in the formation of the layman must be mentioned. In this I had the support of Bishop Guano and of Cardinal Cento who sat in for part of this afternoon session.

Friday 6th March: This morning the meeting of our sub-commission started at 10 o'clock . . . We started with the *Proemium* and it was beautifully written; but I objected to the fact that the whole stress on the need for the lay apostolate was based upon the alleged shortage of priests in the world today. I argued that whilst this might be true in many territories, it was also true that with improved education and formation there were many lay people who desired to give themselves to the apostolic service of the Church regardless of the shortage of priests and who were anxious to fulfil a specifically lay role in the Church's mission. The German supported me on this but we could do nothing with the Czech Bishop Necsey. I feared that the text, as it now stands, will inevitably come in for criticism on this point at least from the Americans. And I must say I shall feel inclined to support them.

There were many small verbal changes to be made but I was on the look-out to see whether my sentence or two from my propositions on the idea of the layman representing the Church to the world and bringing the cares of the world to the Church was included. Father Papali proudly pointed to a sentence which he claimed conveyed this idea, but I felt unable to accept it. We must have spent nearly half an hour trying to find a phrase which would satisfy everyone, but the version they produced was totally unsatisfactory to me as it indicated only that the layman exercised his apostolate in the world and served as the world in the Church: an extraordinary statement which I felt endangered the whole idea that the layman was part of the Church.[15] In the end it was more or less suggested that we should accept my well-known principle that if in doubt we should leave it out. But I tried, whilst saying that I would bow to the majority, to impress upon them that in a non-Catholic country the people judge the Church from the laymen and not from the priest, and it was in that sense that the layman represented the Church to the world. The Italian agreed that this might be so but Bishop Fernandez from the Argentine argued that in a Catholic country the Church was known from the priest and layman.[16] In the end I had to let it go, but Bishop Guano and Bishop Menager both undertook to see that in the full text of the Schema this idea was incorporated elsewhere. We shall see.

There was one further point in which I was concerned when it was stated that the layman, whilst he must try to show the Christian way of life by his example, should also, on suitable occasions, by word preach Christ to his neighbour. I said that I thought this was a very difficult thing to ask any layman to do, especially if one envisaged the working conditions in which many of them had to exercise their apostolate. I tried to secure, and had some success, in seeing that the phrase was turned to mean that on suitable occasions he should try by word to lead his neighbour to a knowledge and a love of Christ's truths. After all in many cases where it is impossible to teach one's neighbour about Christ, one can lead him towards a knowledge of Christ by giving expression to Christian social teaching.

On the whole it was a fairly satisfactory if laborious morning. Father Papali had not completed the paragraph or two about formation but he showed me his component parts which included a sizeable extract from my propositions. He wanted to go off and complete his re-write this evening, but it seems that Monsignor Glorieux caught hold of him immediately after our meeting and took all the papers off him so that the whole document could be prepared for the plenary session due to take place tomorrow morning.

Saturday 7th March: Today's meeting began at 9.30 and Bishop Condé was given the task of presenting the work of our sub-commission on the *Proemium* and first chapter. On the whole things went not too badly. Archbishop Castellano proved to be the most able mover of amendments and most of his arguments were accepted. When it comes to this kind of discussion, the presence of 30 bishops, most of them with differing ideas, makes the actual formulation of propositions almost impossible. But in the end Archbishop Castellano managed to get a number of his ideas clarified and he played what was, on the whole, a fairly welcome part. During the morning we were also issued with new extracts from *De Ecclesia* dealing with *De Laicis*. They seemed to have tried to deal with his function under varying headings but it is hard to say that they have produced any hard and fast logically sound definition. Largely the work is descriptive of layman under various roles and from varying aspects.

There followed certain other amendments to the text and finally we came to a third section dealing with Formation. Father Papali had prepared a contribution which was ludicrously small and Monsignor Cardijn protested that this treatment was so small it was better that there should be nothing at all. He then left the session of the Commission. We turned back to the discussion of further points in the second session and I waited patiently to see whether we would reach the third section on Formation again.

When at last it was reached, none of the bishops had anything to say, so I raised my hand and went to the table. I said that I wished to support the contention of Monsignor Cardijn. He had said that it would be better to have nothing than just these few lines. Clearly we could not have nothing and therefore we must have more. We had already agreed to prepare a document which was greatly in excess of what we had been allowed by the Co-ordinating Commission, let's be devils and add at least one more page and have a separate section on Formation. I said that I thought this would go some way to meeting the difficulty of the previous evening and Archbishop O'Connor, who was in the chair, put it to a vote. There were no objections and it was announced then that our sub-commission must have a new chapter on Formation ready by ten o'clock on Monday morning. The sub-commission varied in its reactions to this extra task but it was agreed that we would meet at 9.30 on Monday to see what could be done. Finally Father Moehler said that he and I and Father Papali should meet tomorrow morning and prepare something.

Archbishop O'Connor who was in the chair decided to close the meeting at this point and announced that our sub-commission must have the new text on Formation ready when the Commission met in plenary session at ten o'clock on Monday. By this time Father Papali had gone and Bishop Fernandez Condé, who by now calls me Urlock, said 'Urlock, come'. I went with him to Bishop Menager, who agreed that the bishops on the sub-commission were unable or unwilling to meet on Sunday and that Father Papali and I should prepare the new text. Monsignor Glorieux said that he would tell Father Papali that we were allowed one page.

*　　　　*　　　　*

Derek Worlock had his hands on the steering wheel at last. That spring and summer his energies were directed to his two important Council projects, the Lay Apostolate and *The Church in the Modern World*, while he continued to act as Secretary to Archbishop Heenan, now of Westminster. But he was no longer at home in that job. He said of that relationship in a reflection he wrote in 1981 (quoted more extensively later in this chapter): 'In no real sense was it a partnership. He scarcely used me and never told me what he was up to.'

His secret diary begins to wander away from the affairs of the Second

Vatican Council to record other aspects of his life, above all his appointment to a large Catholic parish in Commercial Road, Stepney. Heenan had
raised various possibilities for Worlock's future: Rector of the Venerable
English College (after Tickle had been made Bishop for the Forces); President of St Edmund's College, his old school; or the fashionable parish at
Warwick Street, by Piccadilly Circus. There was concern among his
friends that Commercial Road would be viewed as a demotion, though
Worlock insists it was his own idea. This impression was enhanced when
Heenan refused to make a public or Press announcement about the
appointment, saying it would be sufficient to mention it in the next list of
appointments that were sent out from time to time.

Worlock claimed he had chosen Commercial Road himself as his next
move. It says a lot about him that he volunteered for what was one of the
most challenging jobs in the diocese. It was the first time since 1944 that he
would do regular pastoral work in a parish, and he must have known that
his qualifications to be made a bishop in due course would have seemed a
little short of practical experience, for which a spell in a tough parish in the
East End of London would more than compensate.

> On Sunday morning I saw the Archbishop and asked if he had any views at all
> about a statement to be sent to the Catholic Press. He told me that he really
> didn't think it was necessary to send any statement, that the inclusion of my
> name in the appointment list would be sufficient and that everyone would
> appreciate what a great honour had been conferred on me. Little did he under-
> stand the reputation of the East End parishes in the last few years and there has
> been great despondency there in the general belief that the East End had been
> lost in the post-war years, especially when the young people moved out.
>
> On the Monday morning Pat Casey[17] again approached me with regard to
> the wording of an announcement and I told him that in view of the Arch-
> bishop's reaction the previous day, I really did not feel able to raise the matter
> again. Pat then decided to go to the Archbishop himself and told him quite
> plainly that the reputation of the East End was such that he must be very
> careful lest by apparently removing me from a position of trust in Archbishop's
> House, he incurred the displeasure of a number of priests who might feel that
> I had been hardly treated. I think that the Archbishop was a bit shaken by this
> but I must admit that by this time I was heartily sick of the whole business.
> Canon Fitzgerald was due to come in to see the Archbishop at four o'clock that
> afternoon and so at three I went out for a walk and when I returned at four it
> was to find a note on my desk which was the wording of the announcement
> which was to be sent to the Catholic Press. It stated that I had been appointed
> to succeed Canon Fitzgerald as Rector of the parish of St Mary and St

Michael, Commercial Road, following the Canon's resignation owing to ill-health. At the same time I should retain an office in Archbishop's House in order to continue with my work for the bishops in connection with the Council. There was a frightful scene going on in the office and both the girls were in tears. The Archbishop had cheerfully walked up and handed them this note seriously believing that they would be in a high state of jubilation.

I had to put up with poor Canon Fitzgerald for about three quarters of an hour after the Archbishop had gone. He came into my room to tell me to have no illusions about the East End, that it was no longer a reputable part of the Catholic life of the diocese, etc. etc. He also told me of a considerable problem in the youth club which I should have to settle and altogether did his best to make the picture as gloomy as possible . . . I had then to go out to St Patrick's Soho for the blessing of the shamrock and I shall never forget the embarrassed silence with which the Archbishop's announcement was greeted when he solemnly informed the priests at supper of the honour which had been done me. Make no mistake. I was personally delighted at the thought of Commercial Road but the reaction of my brethren was such that it took the Archbishop completely by surprise. Puzzled priests would come to me and ask whether they were meant to congratulate me and it became quite a burden to keep this thing up . . .

The weeks that followed at Westminster were increasingly difficult. As soon as my appointment was announced, even though it was made clear that I was to retain my position until 1st May, my new colleague Bruce Kent[18] quietly but firmly assumed control. It was delicate in the extreme on more than one occasion, especially as he made it pretty clear that in spite of the fact that the Archbishop had asked me to pass on all information to him, he did not really consider that this was the least bit necessary. It takes two to effect a hand-over and I can honestly say that if there were any shortcomings at the end it was not my fault . . . The time could not pass quickly enough . . .

Meantime things were blowing up in Commercial Road and I paid a couple of visits there to see the Canon and on Wednesday 15th April I went and had dinner with him and the curates. I think that that was one of the worst days I can ever remember. I had been pushed around so much in Archbishop's House during the previous week that I was near breaking point and I was also desperately tired. The Archbishop chose that morning to see me about a number of matters, suggesting that I should resign all the various offices which I hold in order to leave myself free for the parish and for the work in Archbishop's House. Things had been difficult enough at the Bishops' Meeting the previous week, when bishop after bishop was coming to me to say that they hoped very much that this appointment which mystified them would not mean that I would have to drop my work for the Hierarchy. I said that we should just have to see how it all worked out but when the Archbishop began to make these demands the worm in me suddenly turned and on that Wednesday morning after a further push around went to Pat Casey and asked him outright whether he thought that the Archbishop wanted me out of the house for good, for if so I had no desire to retain any office there whatsoever. Casey was perplexed and without my knowledge went back to the Archbishop who for the first time really got the wind up. He sent for me that evening and told me that he understood how I must feel but at the same time he assured me that I had his full confidence and what was more he knew from the bishops that I had their confidence as well and that there would be an unholy row if I abandoned my national work. On the whole the incident seems to have done no harm, though it is the first time that I can remember really standing up to an Archbishop and arguing my own position. It is not a situation which I should like to repeat but perhaps it proved worthwhile in the end . . .

I returned the following Tuesday in time for the dinner which the Archbishop was giving in my honour. To this we had invited my various friends from days gone by and at the end of the meal the Archbishop stood up and made a speech which, in the light of what had happened the previous week, I found thoroughly embarrassing . . .

Slowly the days passed. Needless to say there was an enormous amount to be packed and a whole lot more to be put through the 'stripper'. The sisters helped with the packing, the rest I had to do alone. It was a tremendous strain . . . I know that I can be hypersensitive but the watching and waiting tactics were almost unendurable. Somehow by the night of Tuesday 28th April I had everything packed away, had moved what I needed of 'national' things to the old VG's office which was now mine and the next morning I got out quickly to the airport and flew to Rome for the sub-commission meeting on Schema 17.[19] It was the end of an era and when the time came it was a relief as well as a wrench. I could not held wondering how many of my labours to build an efficient office would be tipped out of the back door.[20]

*   *   *

Some seventeen years later Worlock, while summer holidaying in Cornwall, looked back on this period as his own turning point. He set down on paper a long and introspective account of his feelings and experiences, perhaps with a view to eventual publication or simply because he found writing therapeutic. This is an edited version of that document. It is more self-conscious than his secret Vatican II diary, which was written at the time of the events it describes. His 1981 account is much more discreet about his problems with Heenan.

Musing on the theme of change in other people, I suppose it is only honest to try and face the same question about myself. One is, of course, much less conscious of change in oneself. In spite of momentous events and turning points, the whole process is so gradual that one is not conscious of the degree of change in outlook, and perhaps even in character, which will be apparent to others.

I have to accept the fact that people have said that I changed. I tried to explain it away by saying that before 1964, when I left Archbishop's House, Westminster, people did not know me as I was in myself, only in so far as I tried faithfully to reflect and transmit the views of those I had to serve. And you could scarcely find three more different characters than Cardinals Griffin, Godfrey and Heenan. There is a lot of truth in that explanation but yes, if I look back, I have to admit that my outlook changed in those critical years at the end of the council immediately before I was made a bishop.

Some of it was due to opportunity to self-expression, some was due to the development of ideas over the years which reached fruition in the council, some was due to the council itself (which, as Nick France[21] says, was a conversion experience for me), but I think most was due to those months at Stepney, to the priests I was with then, and the laity, especially the dockers and their families, with whom I worked in undoubtedly the happiest time of my life, March 1964 to October 1965.

Before trying to analyse these influences in the Stepney era, it is only fair to say that having learned something about social justice in the years immediately after the [Second World] War through my involvement with Cardinal Griffin and his dealing with the labour leaders – Bevin, Bevan, Tomlinson, Isaacs and of course the great Dick Stokes – I began to get involved with the lay leaders of the Young Christian Workers (YCW). They not only introduce me to the practical problems of the worker apostolate, they also began to open my eye to the true role of the laity in the Church. I suppose that was the real beginning.

In the early 1950s, when Cardinal Griffin was either sick or in diminished activity, I took a number of initiatives in his name or with his backing, for example drawing together a group of representative young laity to attend a first World Congress for the Promotion of the Lay Apostolate (COPECIAL). As a result of that in 1952 there was formed the National Council for the Lay Apostolate (NCLA). That was quite an important step because it was the first time I know of when what was the called 'the Church', i.e. central administration, paid for the expenses of a delegation of representatives of organisations which chose who would represent them. Hitherto it had largely been a case of giving some authorisation to whomsoever chose to go in a representative capacity and could pay for themselves.

In this way I was drawn into close relationship with nearly all the lay movements but, through Pat Keegan [a founder of the Young Christian Workers], more especially with the YCW, and with the various lay leaders who came to Clapham Road[22] for training. It was in the late 1940s and early 1950s that Pat, Frank Lane and Kevin Muir came to me about the formation of a team to comprise the totally committed who, at the completion of a fixed term of service with some movement, wanted to commit themselves to apostolic work and needed mutual support, especially of a spiritual nature. It was essentially directed to the worker apostolate, to the service of God's poor.

They asked me to become their chaplain: at that stage it meant a monthly meeting and Mass, and continuing spiritual counsel. Now, over 30 years later, the team still exists. It has been a long and enriching relationship which enshrines some marvellous friendships, as with Kevin Muir and Austin Winkley, but with no one more than Pat Keegan himself. I shall never forget the night we celebrated in Rome Pat's making the first lay intervention in the council. As we met for a meal we got a telegram from Kitty Foley in London to say that Maurice[23] (ex-YCW) had just been made Parliamentary Secretary to George Brown, the Foreign Secretary. It all seemed to be happening at once.

That night, after a meal in the Hotel Columbus, Archbishop Gillie Young of Hobart made an inspired speech about the caravan of God, trundling forward, some pulling ahead, some pulling back, some hanging on like grim death to the sides. It was the Church we were to know so well in the years following the council.

All this was part of my increasing involvement in the general work of what we called[24] the lay apostolate. When the council came I was appointed a peritus and attached to the Commission for the Lay Apostolate. In time this led to my role with the Holy See's Council for the Laity.

So, in that sense, even in the hidden years at Westminster, I was preparing (or being prepared) for my later role, which found fulfilment in the implementation of all the insights and recommendations of *Lumen Gentium*.[25] This may seem to be development rather than change, but it must at least be true that certain people, events and influences hastened and sharpened up the process.

Nevertheless, the turning point was March 1964, when I escaped from Westminster and went to St Mary and Michael's, Commercial Road, Stepney, in London's East End. The transformation from the marble halls of Archbishop's House probably put the spotlight on things for others. For me it was just the change I was looking for.

It came about in this way. After nearly nineteen years at Westminster I was not anxious to begin a new and third commitment as Private Secretary, least of all to John Carmel Heenan, whom I had known at Manor Park when he was parish priest, even before he went to the CMS. In one sense I knew too much, but I also knew our methods and approaches were quite different. He was appointed in September 1963, just before the second session of the council. He asked me to see him in, and of course I had to be in Rome with him. But in no real sense was it a partnership. He scarcely used me and never told me what he was up to.

We returned in December 1963 and after Christmas he talked vaguely about the future. Perhaps I would be made an auxiliary to Westminster in a few years' time, but first I must have pastoral experience in a parish. Some of the bishops were also insisting that I retained my role as unofficial secretary to the bishops' meetings. So perhaps I could take on some West End parish and come into an office at Westminster as occasion demanded.

I think he was surprised when I asked to go to the East End. Morale was at its lowest there, lapsation overwhelming and Canon Fitzgerald under pressure to retire. Heenan doubted if I knew enough about the area and its goings-on. As luck would have it we had had some meetings in Poplar, and to his astonishment he found that I knew more trade union leaders and politicians there than he did. He agreed, and without too much seriousness agreed to my request to choose a new team of priests to work with me and try out new ways for perhaps five years.

As dean I was even able to choose new priests for neighbouring parishes, and, marvellously, it all began to come alive.

We instituted team programmes and team living in a way accepted today but quite unknown to that time. It brought me great joy. We had about 7,000 parishioners with a Mass attendance of under 1,000. In the eighteen months I was there the Mass attendance rose to 2,800 but it was the quality of our parish community which was so rewarding. We based our tactics on pastoral visiting and the establishment of small groups.

In a systematic way we got round all the homes in about six months at a time. The family groups of six couples each grew to nine groups and these proved the basis of apostolic formation of men and women alike. Most worked in the docks, Billingsgate or shops and offices. But a family spirit grew up in the parish which achieved such an effect that the media attention probably won us as many enemies as friends.

But the effect on me was tremendous, and I suddenly found myself being labelled as the leader of a group of 'progressives', for that was the new word in the Church. Of course it was fascinating to be doing all this interspersed with frequent visits to Rome in the final stages of the council: talking to the dockers about Rome and bishops, and to such fellow council commissioners as Karol Wojtyla (now Pope John Paul II) about my dockers and their work and their homes. What a transformation for me at a key time. Not that my friends all welcomed it.

Cardinal Heenan was sceptical of my pastoral policies, which differed from his in Manor Park in 1945. Priest friends found it hard to reconcile my views and works with the Westminster days where my 'hidden' apostolic life had largely been unknown. Lay friends could not understand that I had gone politically Left: in Stepney it was unthinkable to think or vote save as a socialist – the alternatives were Communists or near-Fascists. I think that I can honestly say that I revelled in the new-found ideas with which I was being fed by my new companions, whilst they were obviously glad to use my professional and organisational expertise – not to mention my entrée to Westminster (which officially they wrote off as out of touch and irrelevant, but in practice were only too glad to use).

We certainly learned to share our life, our (usually my) possessions and eventually our spirituality. Here was the most profound influence of all. How well I remember Brian Nash, at the end of a day's pastoral planning, hitting the table and saying: 'How can we really work together if we don't bloody pray together?' That was the turning point. It was not easy, but it was at that stage we discovered true brotherhood in priesthood – but without separation from our good parishioners whom we regarded as real friends, and whom we desired as a group to try to lead and serve.

Looking back, I can say that learning to pray together, or just listening to the prayers of others and trying to pray aloud in front of them, probably did more to enrich my relationship with God and my brother priests than anything else. I believe that it was this sharing of our spirituality which accounted for most of the change which others detected in me – even though I have retained to this day a reputation for being a bit aloof or reserved personally, even if pastorally I am a 'sharing' person.

Or so I'm told. As I say, it is difficult to trace or detect such lines in oneself. Looking back, the most interesting thing is the way different trends and events all came together to give me direction for the greater responsibilities which I have now but could not have foreseen at the time. The link between my Westminster job and the developments in Clapham Road (YCW) and Pinner (The Grail), led also to the combination in Stepney of pastoral initiatives and theological expression which were viewed with suspicion and disenchantment[26] at Westminster.

I began to wonder if we would be left together for the promised five years. The move to Portsmouth after eighteen months put an end to it for me and cast a damper on the whole movement in Stepney. History will judge. Other events and other persons led other ways. If it was critical for me, it was also approaching the most critical time I have known for the Church.[27] As always on such occasions, there were many casualties, some of whom were people who had really influenced me during these years. It is now I want to acknowledge their role among so many others in what I call my development, and others see as the time when I changed.

*   *   *

It is clear from the diary that Worlock's marginalization by Heenan, together with the work in Stepney and the two specialist areas which dragged him away from there to Rome (the Commission on the laity, and on *The Church on the Modern World*) had taken his mind off the main currents swirling round the Council. Though as *peritus* he was entitled to attend any debates he wanted to during the 1964 and 1965 sessions, his record becomes disjointed and less useful to a historian. It can still be admired as journalism, however: and by the end of the third and penultimate session of the Council Worlock was doing a regular BBC radio broadcast describing the highlights of the Council's business. He reported to his listeners the big row that broke out just before the session ended, when, as Bishop Alan Clark was to put it later, the curial cardinals were at last eclipsed and the American bishops had finally emerged from their 'divided ineffectiveness'.

The issue that aroused them to open rebellion was religious liberty. This was, as Worlock observed elsewhere, something they regarded as their speciality. The American contribution to the drafting of the final document is apparent, for there are deliberate echoes of the American Constitution in its discussion of the need to preserve an appropriate distance between Church and State. But there were far bigger issues at stake. The concept of religious liberty was a major departure from the Catholic tradition – or major 'development' to use the slightly coy way changes tended to be described.

For instance Pope Pius IX's Encyclical known as his *Syllabus of Errors*, published in 1864, listed a number of propositions in favour of religious liberty and described them as errors the Catholic Church denounced and anathematized. Under 'Indifferentism', and 'Latitudinarianism' he condemned the views that 'every man is free to embrace and profess that religion which, guided by the light of reason, he shall consider true'; that 'man may, in the observance of any religion whatever, find the way of eternal salvation, and arrive at eternal salvation'; and that 'good hope at least is to be entertained of the eternal salvation of all those who are not at all in the true Church of Christ'. As 'Errors Having Reference to Modern Liberalism' he denounced the view that: 'In the present day it is no longer expedient that the Catholic religion should be held as the only religion of the State, to the exclusion of all other forms of worship'; and equally condemned the logic of religious pluralism, that is to say, the view that 'it has been wisely decided by law, in some Catholic countries, that persons coming to reside therein shall enjoy the public exercise of their own peculiar worship'.[28]

The *Syllabus of Errors* is significant evidence that 300 years after the Council of Trent, its spirit – the spirit of the Counter Reformation itself, in other words – was still the dominant one in the Catholic Church. Nevertheless a hundred years further on, when Vatican II began, Catholic practice in most parts of the world had evolved considerably in the direction of tolerance, and pressure to update Catholic theory in line with this was becoming irresistible. But even in 1962 the Catholic Church would not have been generally regarded as an outstanding friend of liberty, nor were the consciences of those of different religious persuasions considered by it to be in need of protection. No single issue more clearly symbolizes the modernization of Catholic doctrine that John XXIII had called for at the outset.

In its final form, promulgating at the end of the Council in December 1965, the declaration *Dignitatis Humanae* stated:

> This Vatican Council declares that the human person has a right to religious freedom. This freedom means that all men are to be immune from coercion on the part of individuals or of social groups and of any human power, in such wise that no one is to be forced to act in a manner contrary to his own beliefs, whether privately or publicly, whether alone or in association with others, within due limits. The council further declares that the right to religious freedom has its foundation in the very dignity of the human person as this dignity is known through the revealed word of God and by reason itself. This right of the human person to religious freedom is to be recognised in the constitutional law whereby society is governed and thus it is to become a civil right.

and much more of the same.[29]

Not surprisingly, this part of the project not only had powerful supporters, especially in the United States, but also powerful enemies behind the scenes.

'You remember', Worlock said in his BBC report of the matter,

> that it came up for discussion a year ago and there was widespread disappointment when, at the end of the second Session, the document was not put to a vote because there was no time. Last September saw it back again, though cast in rather different form, and after the debate it went back to the Secretariat for Christian Unity, charged with its revision in the light of opinions expressed at that time.

For some time now there have been those strange Roman rumours about strange Roman happenings which always seem to add up to delay.

Once more there seemed to be an attempt to block it. The report in his secret diary is even more dramatic than the version he gave the public:

Thursday 19th November will rank as one of the historic dates in the history of the Council both for good and for evil. After the Mass a series of votes were taken and the first was the final vote on *De Ecclesia*. Of the 2,145 Fathers voting, 2,134 voted *placet*, there were ten *non-placets* and one null vote. Needless to say this result was greeted with applause as it represented at least the penultimate stage with regard to the Council's most important document so far.

The morning's debate was divided into two parts, first of all on Christian Education and secondly on the Sacrament of Matrimony . . . But the whole debate was completely overshadowed by the rumpus on the question of the document on Religious Liberty. I had spent the early part of the morning at my desk at the College and didn't arrive at St Peter's until just on eleven o'clock. By then things were really boiling. It seems that before the debate started Cardinal Tisserant, acting in the name of the Commission of Presidents, announced that the Council would not after all proceed to a vote on Religious Liberty. The previous day he had said that a preliminary vote would be taken to see whether or not the Fathers wanted to deal with this matter during the Third Session. But today he announced that a sufficient number of persons had asked for more time to consider this new Declaration that the President decided to postpone further discussion on the matter until the next Session.

One recognises of course that the new Declaration did contain a certain amount of new matter but the manner in which this thing was handled was certainly sufficient to set off the furore which followed. It seems that as soon as Cardinal Tisserant had made the announcement, Cardinal Meyer[30] got up from the table and went to Cardinal Tisserant to dissociate himself from this announcement made on behalf of the Presidents. His objections were obvious and clearly and quickly spread into the Aula itself. Nearly all the American bishops trooped out of the benches and moved into the side aisles and they were followed by a large number of others who were gravely disturbed at what was reckoned to be a calculated attempt by possibly the Curia and some of the right-wing conservatives – the Spaniards were named, though they subsequently denied that they were responsible – to block this contentious matter once again. When I arrived it was in time to find the American *periti* setting up shop in the side aisles where they had large sheets of papers and bishops were queuing up, one behind the other, to sign a petition to the Holy Father to beg that a vote be taken on this Declaration this Session. It was an incredible sight.

The story went round that in order to prepare the petition, one of the *periti* had slipped into the office and pinched Felici's typewriter.

Be that as it may, the organisation of this protest petition was remarkably efficient, even though one could regret the vehemence with which the whole matter was being tackled. It soon became clear that the majority of the bishops present were prepared to sign this petition but could anything be done about it? Meantime Bishop de Smedt had been called to the microphone in order to read the *Relatio* for the Declaration, even though it was not to be voted upon. This of course was just the opportunity that was needed for high drama. Bishop de Smedt[31] started off by saying that it was with feeling that he introduced the Declaration – and here he changed his text from 'which is now to be voted upon' to 'which is now not to be voted upon'. As he began his impassioned plea for a matter which is thought generally to be closest to his heart, his full flights of oratory soared around the ceiling of St Peter's. He sobbed, his voice broke, and he delivered the most impassioned appeal that I have ever heard, even from a Continental. As he was drawing towards his end, those bishops who had been out in the side aisles all packed in round the President's table and the Confession of St Peter's and looked down the Aula to where this lone figure was standing in a state of high emotional tension.

To an Englishman it was all rather embarrassing but there is no doubt that the cause was served by this Continental oratory on this occasion. Archbishop Heenan told me afterwards that he squirmed as he listened to his friend but I do not think that it was a put-up performance: he really felt as he sounded. Finally he regained control of his voice as he reached the end of his text. In a complete monotone, which was the more effective in that it followed after the high oratory of the earlier parts of the *Relatio*, he quietly said that the Secretariat for Christian Unity had finished with this document and passed it to the Co-ordinating Commission some three or four weeks ago: I forget the exact date which he mentioned. It seemed that nothing had happened about it until a short time before and then it had been suggested that the Vatican Press, which has to do all the printing of the official documentation for the Council, had become absolutely jammed up with the various documents which had to be given to the Fathers. He left it quite open as to whether one accepted this story or not and he merely gave the date on which the document had reached the Fathers, earlier in the week. Then with great deliberation he said: 'Let us pray at this moment for the guidance of the Holy Spirit in an issue which is of supreme importance to the Church.'

There was thunderous applause, quite the loudest I have ever heard in St Peter's and after a while one realised that it was going to take a long time before it died down. When eventually it showed some sign of flagging, it rose once more from the far end of the Aula and it became evident that what had started as applause for a feat of oratory had now turned into a positive attempt to pass the document by acclamation. Cardinal Meyer was standing in the side aisle with some of the other American Bishops and the atmosphere was quite electric. On several occasions the Moderators tried to break in over their microphones but the applause did not cease. In fact it continued for about four and a half minutes, so far as I could time it, but when at last it did die down Cardinal Döpfner, the Moderator, called the first speaker for the debate on the remaining document of the Sacrament of Matrimony.

Once it was realised that the Presidents had carried the day, the atmosphere changed from one of exhilaration to one of acute bitterness and disappointment. Cardinal Meyer went back to the Presidents' table, clearly in two minds as to what he should do. He was beckoned once more to the side and I saw Father Molinari, an Italian Jesuit and a very good man, advising him quite straightly that he should take the petition directly to the Holy Father. Word evidently reached Cardinal Ritter and Cardinal Léger, both of whom left their places in the Aula and came down to join Cardinal Meyer. The petitions were brought in by the *periti* from the various parts of St Peter's and Cardinal Meyer rolled them up and put them under his arm. It was reckoned that there were over 800 signatures already and later that day we were told that the number had risen to over 1,000. It was a straight request for a vote of some kind on the Declaration before the Session stopped.

As poor Cardinal Gilroy laboured away, almost without anyone seeming to listen, on the subject of Matrimony, the three cardinals with some other bishop whom I could not recognise in attendance walked slowly across behind the Confessional and away up the stairs towards the Holy Father's apartments. I could not help wondering what would have happened had the cardinals walked the whole length of St Peter's before making their way out to the doors to go to the Pope. I fancy that half the bishops would have stood up and gone with them. Perhaps it was as well that they didn't but even so it was a moment of great tension and drama: something which one is unlikely to see again . . .

Rome buzzed all that day with the excitement of the morning and not without reason. Some of the *periti*, notably Monsignor Osterreicher, could be seen after the morning Congregation giving a full account to the Press and inevitably the thing was blown to fantastic heights in the Press reports which followed the next day. (When I got back to London I found this incident described widely as a 'punch-up' which it certainly was not.) But there is no doubt that it was all very regrettable and, though one must question the policy of Cardinal Tisserant and the General Secretariat in the decision which they made, there was little evidence of approval of the bitter vehemence of the American bishops. They seem to think that they have a corner in this question of Religious Liberty but I suppose that they were so disappointed in their failure to take the document home at the end of the Second Session that this third delay was just the last straw.

I believe that there were wild scenes of excitement at the Press Briefing at the USO that afternoon . . .

After supper that evening I heard that old Cardinal Heard[32] wanted to see me about the Jews and I could not think what was worrying him. I had heard earlier that the Pope had summoned all the Cardinals that evening in order to discuss with them the troubles of the morning but I could not think that this had anything to do with Heard's message. When I got to see him he told me that he thought that there had been some row with the Jews in the Council that morning and what insufferable people they were! He asked me if I would let him have any documentation that I might have on the subject as apparently the Pope had asked him to give a judgement about it in the morning. I was very perplexed and I went back to my room and looked over my notes and came to the conclusion that he must be thinking of the row over Religious Liberty, which of course had nothing directly to do with the Jews.

I checked with the Archbishop[33] who was of the same opinion and then went back to Heard. Gently I tried to tell him that it was not a Jewish issue which was at stake. I told him what had happened in the morning and it seems that the old man was so deaf that he had very little knowledge at all of what had gone on. What made it even more remarkable was that during the audience with the Pope, the Holy Father had apparently decided to refer the protest received from the American bishops to the Tribunal of which Heard was a member. They were to meet before the following morning's session and give judgement on the point which had arisen.

It was a most extraordinary anticlimax to all the high-level excitements of the day that I should have found myself trying to explain to the old judge just what it was all about. So far as I could I remained dispassionate but it was remarkable how, once the old man had got a picture of what had happened, the judge in him returned to the surface. He said that it was a perfectly simple issue. Had Tisserant (whom he profoundly dislikes) exceeded his powers in giving the decision which he had given? If the powers were provided for in the *Regolamento*, then so far as the Tribunal was concerned, they had merely to give judgement that the Presidents had acted within their powers.

If the Presidents had no such powers in the *Regolamento*, then they would have to go back on it the following day. It was quite clear cut in the old man's mind and I left him looking into his red-bound copy of the Rules. The question of whether or not the decision was a good one or a bad one did not enter Cardinal Heard's mind. The fact that a thousand bishops might have wanted to vote on the matter was again beside the point. It was a question of the Presidents staying within the powers. It might have been interesting had he been able to determine whether the President of the Commission of Presidents, i.e.

Cardinal Tisserant, had adequately consulted the other members of his Commission. But this did not seem to have entered into the matter and I had little doubt which way the decision would go the following morning.

In public his view of Bishop de Smedt became more flattering than the one confided to his diary. 'One of the greatest orators in the Church today, who rose to the occasion' was his BBC description of what he privately regarded as more an unseemly outburst than a speech. Worlock was ever sensitive to the Church's public relations image.

The Declaration on Religious Liberty was indeed safely passed by the Council in its fourth and final session the following year, 1965. English Catholics having been in no position to persecute anyone for more than 400 years, it perhaps seemed an academic point. But getting the English Catholic community out of the mental ghetto into which it had retreated in that time, largely as a result of being denied its own religious liberty, was a more pressing concern. It touched on the one Council issue which was to occupy him for most of the rest of his life – getting right the relationship between the Catholic Church and its lay members. At the end of the Council in 1965, he would probably have said that the Decree on the Laity, which he had helped to draft, was the most important document to come out of the Council from an English point of view. He would have regarded it as the last word on the matter. But his opinion gradually changed – or developed.

Inside Information by Derek Worlock. Courtesy of Liverpool Roman Catholic Archdiocesan Archive at St Joseph's, Upholland, Lancashire.

Notes

1 There was always great difficulty in defining a Secular Institute. (Secular in this respect has a special Catholic meaning of 'not clerical', rather than of 'having nothing to do with religion' which is its more common meaning.) It was a body of dedicated lay people sharing a common life and bound by rules, recognized as such by the Church and overseen by the bishops. It was neither a religious order like the Jesuits nor a monastic order like the Benedictines, nor even a half-way house between them and the lay state. Worlock spent some time at the Council seeking proper recognition of the place of Secular Institutes, and for the Grail in particular.

2 This is to some extent designed to curb predestination, as taught by the Calvinists, and also against the Protestant doctrine of assurance, which maintained that an individual who has been saved by faith may possess an inner certainty that he is among the elect.

3 First published 1945.

4 The Dutchman whose ideas, based on St Augustine, were popularized after his death by the writings of Blaise Pascal.

5 Published 1938.

6 From 'Epitaph for a man killed falling from his horse' by William Camden (1551–1623), 'Betwixt the stirrup and the ground/Mercy I asked, mercy I found.'

7 From the Tridentine Mass: 'Lamb of God who takes away the sins of the world, grant us peace'.

8 'I believe in one God . . .' from the Latin Creed.

9 The Reformation having happened before the Council of Trent, the pattern of clergy education in the Church of England is actually pre-Tridentine and closer to the medieval pattern, being shorter and less intensive. This may explain the cult of the gentleman-amateur which is still sometimes encountered among the Anglican clergy.

10 Secker and Warburg, 1980, p. 80.

11 Paragraph 31 of Vatican II's Dogmatic Constitution on the Church (*Lumen Gentium*) states: 'These faithful are by baptism made one body with Christ and are constituted among the People of God; they are in their own way made sharers in the priestly, prophetical, and kingly functions of Christ; and they carry out for their own part the mission of the whole Christian people in the Church and in the world.'

12 General of the Pallottine Fathers.

13 Worlock called him 'a Carmelite who looks like an Indian and speaks Italian with the accent of Peter Sellers'.

14 An angry argument developed later about this proposed Directory, which was intended to be a more detailed set of guidelines for the lay apostolate but not actually a document from the Second Vatican Council as such. Some wanted it to be discussed by lay organizations before it was issued. Worlock himself felt the Directory was a distraction from the job of getting the schema right.

15 He is clearly becoming influenced by the 'People of God' model of the Church.

16 This is a Worlock slip, according to the sense he must mean 'priest and bishop'.

17 A senior priest of the archdiocese, later Wall's successor as Bishop of Brentwood.

18 Monsignor Bruce Kent, subsequently Catholic Chaplain to London University, and later General Secretary of the Campaign for Nuclear Disarmament (CND).

19 *The Church in the Modern World.* Worlock was a *peritus* on the Commission preparing the draft of this document, for debate when the bishops returned for the next session of

the Council in the autumn.

20 This is literally what happened next, and Worlock never forgave Bruce Kent, nor Heenan.

21 Canon Nicholas France, his Secretary when Bishop of Portsmouth and lifelong friend.

22 YCW headquarters in SW London.

23 Maurice Foley, Labour MP, who had been on the outer fringe of the Team activity.

24 His use of the past tense implies he had abandoned this term by 1981.

25 He is primarily referring to its recommendations for involving priests and laity in the work of the diocese.

26 It is clear that the ill-feeling he described at the time of his move from Archbishop's House, Westminster continued long afterwards. The phrase ' . . . at Westminster' can really only refer to Heenan.

27 He may be referring to the *Humanae Vitae* crisis of 1968, and the fact that this led directly or indirectly to many priests he had known leaving the priesthood.

28 Clauses 15, 16 and 17; and 77, 78.

29 This topic was also addressed in the Vatican II decree *Nostra Aetate*, more usually cited for its repudiation of anti–Semitism. On the salvific value of other faiths, *Nostra Aetate* said: 'The Catholic Church rejects nothing that is true and holy in these religions. She regards with sincere reverence those ways of conduct and of life, those precepts and teachings which, though differing in many aspects from the ones she holds and sets forth, nonetheless often reflect a ray of that Truth which enlightens all men.'

30 Edward Meyer, Archbishop of Chicago.

31 Of Bruges.

32 Still living at the English College.

33 Heenan, presumably.

7

A Vatican II Bishop

St Edmund's College, Ware, Hertfordshire, was Derek Worlock's *alma mater*. With its junior school, St Hugh's, it was both a public school and a junior and senior seminary of the Archdiocese of Westminster. It was named after a medieval miracle-worker, monk, saint, scholar and statesman who had taught at Oxford and who is credited with having introduced the English to Aristotle. Worlock claims to have been the youngest pupil when Cardinal Bourne visited the College in the 1920s, head prefect when Cardinal Hinsley visited it the following decade, and cardinal's secretary when both Griffin and Godfrey came there in their turn. He was never content to be ordinary.

The town of Abingdon, Oxfordshire, was in the Roman Catholic diocese of Portsmouth, a huge area which also included the southern half of the university city itself. It was also his home diocese, and the diocese whose bishop, William T. Cotter, had refused to sponsor him for ordination training because he had a policy, so Worlock later claimed, of only appointing Irish priests. It could just as well have been because Cotter, one of the old school, thought the Worlock family, converts from Anglicanism, were too Tory, lower middle class and minor public school for their son to fit into a mainly working-class immigrant Irish culture centred on the dockyards and docks of Portsmouth and Southampton.[1] That form of inverted snobbery was, and still is, not unknown among the Catholic clergy. Nor was snobbery *per se* unknown among the *petit bourgeois* strata of society from which the Worlocks came. Worlock's father, Harford Worlock, liked to use his former army rank, Captain – something someone of higher social class would have regarded as 'not done', and something not provided for in military etiquette (though acceptable for naval captains, being a much more senior rank). Those who finished the war with the rank of army captain had as likely as not started their military service in the ranks, and become a 'temporary gentleman' for the duration, after most of the 'permanent gentlemen' had succumbed to German machine guns. Using the title was a claim to be a little grander than the common herd, and it also betrayed a fear that his superior status might not otherwise be noticed. This is just the kind of English lower middle class insecurity that would have been despised as much from above as from below in class-conscious 1930s England.

St Edmund Rich of Abington[2] was not only a distinguished scholar but an outspoken Archbishop of Canterbury (appointed directly by Pope Gregory IX), and one of the most virtuous and attractive figures of the medieval English Church. It would have been well known to Worlock that Edmund Rich's influence as archbishop had been undermined by clerical intrigue, particularly involving the papal legate, Cardinal Otho, whom the Pope had sent to England at the request of King Henry III. No doubt this increased the attraction for Edmund that Worlock already felt. He too considered himself hampered by intrigue in his career, some of it involving the Vatican, some involving Cardinal Otho's twentieth-century successor, Archbishop Bruno Heim, who was Apostolic Delegate at the decisive span in Worlock's career, 1975–76. And Worlock did his own share of standing up to the powers of the realm. He had chosen his spiritual patron well.

In July 1987 Worlock described in his private notebook the events surrounding his appointment as Bishop of Portsmouth in 1965, and his non-appointment as the next Bishop of Menevia, which would have taken him to Wrexham, North Wales. Bishop John Petit, who was 70 at the end of the Council, had been a member of the Commission on the Lay Apostolate at the Second Vatican Council, and Worlock had been his *peritus* (though his own records of those meetings do not depict him consulting his superior to any great extent, but playing his own cards). Feeling his age and having to cover a vast area of rural Wales, Petit had apparently asked the Vatican for a coadjutor bishop with right of succession. Between them, it seems, Heenan and Petit had requested that it be Worlock, Heenan to get rid of him, Petit because he had already worked with Worlock on the Lay Apostolate Commission and liked him. They reckoned without the power of saintly intervention.

Ever since I went to the Junior Seminary, St Edmund Rich has somehow been a part of my life, a very special sort of patron. He was of course the name-patron of the College where I received my schooling and preparation for the priesthood,[3] and it was in the chapel which was his shrine that as boys we often heard Mass and had spiritual conferences.[4] As important was the fact that, having prayed to Mary in the Lady Chapel, I would go each morning and evening to the shrine and would recite that prayer 'O Glorious Saint Edmund, most highly exalted among the friends of God,' which I rapidly came to know by heart and which I still recite each morning.

During the war, when I was in the Senior seminary, I was given the task of College Air Raid Warden, which meant that I had to walk round the entire property each night. Often I went privately into the College Chapel and shrine chapel, technically out of bounds as part of the school. There I would pray to be a priest and also for those who had been in the school with me and who had been killed or were missing in action.

Towards the end of my studies I became ill, with severe sinusitis and a chronic condition which required surgery. This had a double effect. I was told that I must do no more 'head-work' and that I would never be fit for more than part-time duty, perhaps as an assistant in a country parish. That put an end to the plan that I should go to Cambridge with a view to teaching subsequently in the seminary. It also led to a summons to the President of the College who told me to go into hospital and, for the time being, to forget about the proposal that I be ordained priest with the rest of my year in Westminster Cathedral a few weeks later.

The effect of such a setback after eleven years of training was immense. I turned to St Edmund, my patron, for help. As a boy I had heard about his miracles, about how his relic was carried to a dying student who had been restored. Yet no-one made any suggestion in my regard. The night before I left for hospital, during my round of duty as air raid warden, I went secretly to the shrine chapel, climbed the steps behind the altar and duly placed the relic against my forehead. I was a deacon at the time, so, in those days, I did not feel I was breaking too many rules.

Next day I left for hospital. Unknown to me my fellow seminarians began a Novena[5] to St Edmund on my behalf that I might be cured in time for ordination. Gory details are unnecessary. After the operation I had a haemorrhage but a remarkable Blue Sister, Raphael, was determined to help and gave me large quantities of Guinness. Even that would not have done the trick, but for the Novena of which at the time I was ignorant. One day I began to feel much better and confidence returned. The surgeon agreed shortly afterwards that I might return to the seminary and I arrived back just a few hours before the pre-ordination retreat[6] began. Later it transpired that the students' Novena had concluded that day when my strength had returned.

I was ordained with my fellow deacons by Archbishop Griffin on the appointed day. I was told by the surgeon that I must have a good holiday before my threatened appointment to a country parish. I was given six weeks: and then presumably authority forgot. I was appointed curate at Our Lady of Victories in Kensington and less than a year later the Archbishop ordered me to become his Private Secretary – a post I held at Westminster for nearly twenty years. The role of that Novena in what has subsequently happened to me is startling. On one of my many visits to St Edmund's for the feast day, 16 November, my old Spiritual Director told me I must write it down. I belatedly do so but with due reverence for my patron's heavenly powers.

For the next 21 years I was fortunate. Being for almost all that time the secretary to successive archbishops I was present in most years at St Edmund's College for the patronal festival. So my devotion to St Edmund grew no less. In 1964 I left Archbishop's House to go to Stepney. Meantime the Second Vatican Council was in progress, and as a *peritus* I was almost a commuter to and from Rome, even in between sessions.

In September 1965 I was preparing for the final session. As Secretary to the Bishops' Conference (to which post I was appointed as I left Westminster and the Conference as such came into existence) it was my duty to take many papers to Rome and prepare the way for the bishops. So I drove down to Hare Street House, about five miles from the College, to see Cardinal Heenan who was holidaying there and to check the final arrangements. At the end of the afternoon, as I was about to return to Stepney, Cardinal Heenan told me to sit down and then said straight to me: 'There is a secret which you must keep for the time being. After the next session of the Council, you will not be returning to Stepney. You are likely to be a bishop, but you need not imagine that you are going to be one of my auxiliaries here. You will be much further away. Now, no questions. I can say no more, and what I have said is secret.'

I was deeply upset at the thought of leaving Stepney, where I had been parish priest for less than eighteen months. I was bewildered as to where I might be going and when. And I could talk to no-one about it. Heenan refused to say more but expected me to be grateful for the warning, about which I could do nothing. On the way back to London I called as St Edmund's College and went into the Shrine Chapel to ask St Edmund to help me. There was no-one about, and it was strangely like that earlier occasion in 1944 when I had prayed to be ordained a priest on time. I found now that I had no desire to be advanced to the next Holy Order,[7] least of all if it was to take me away from London.

I was still further puzzled when I arrived in Rome, by cryptic remarks from various bishops. One I remember asked: 'What's all this madness about sending you so far away? So much more sensible to keep you closer to London.' This did nothing for my peace of mind. Another said: 'We must get them reversed. What on earth is Heenan up to?' Only one (Petit) seemed reasonably content and said: 'We must get you made a bishop before the Council's over.' So much for secrecy and discretion. In mid-October I had a phone call from Cardinal Ritter of St Louis who remarked that he had just attended a meeting of the Consistorial Congregation (now the Congregation of Bishops) and 'Good luck'.

A few days later in St Peter's I was handed by Cardinal Heenan a solemn letter informing me that Paul VI had appointed me Bishop of Portsmouth. It was made public a few days later and, though I have never attempted to confirm my suspicions, it was announced simultaneously that Langton Fox had been appointed Coadjutor to the Bishop of Menevia in North Wales.[8] The Bishop was Bishop Petit, who had worked with me in the Council's Commission for the Lay Apostolate. It was he who had expressed a desire that I be a bishop before the end of the Council. Had I been appointed to Menevia all the remarks of the previous weeks would have made sense. Subsequently John Petit told me that he had never heard of Langton Fox.[9] I think that I attached more significance to the fact that, with Our Lady, the principal patron of the diocese of Portsmouth is St Edmund of Abingdon.

So I came home to the Hampshire of my upbringing and to the diocese where Edmund Rich was the name patron of so many churches and institutions. When after just over ten years I had to go north, not to N. Wales but to Liverpool, I found that he was almost an unknown saint, save in Waterloo where there is a parish in his honour, an offshoot I imagine from the neighbouring parish of St Thomas of Canterbury.

Worlock was later to use his position as Archbishop of Liverpool to have a comprehensive school renamed St Edmund (but 'of Canterbury' rather than Abingdon because 'no-one had heard of Abingdon'). And when he rearranged the interior design of the private chapel in Archbishop's House, Liverpool, he dedicated it to St Edmund. He had a special statue carved for it which was a replica of the statue of St Edmund at the shrine chapel at Ware, 'in his hands the staff which he held before me in the years of my training. Each morning when I say my prayers to my patron I clutch hold of this staff. I owe much to his intercession. His staff is a symbol of the help I need to support me each day', he wrote.

How much supernatural support he needed can be glimpsed from some of his private correspondence, particularly when he first went to Liverpool. It was a dismal time. In a heart-felt letter to his old Portsmouth secretary Canon Nicholas France, writing from Lancashire in January 1976 shortly before news of his appointment as Archbishop of Liverpool, he remarked: 'We were 30 minutes late as someone pulled the communication cord somewhere near Crewe. (Not guilty, though I felt like it.)' Of the former seminary known as St Joseph's College, Skelmersdale, then called the Upholland Northern Institute (UNI), he commented: 'This place is worse than I had imagined.' (He was attending a retreat for bishops). 'The team from UNI are pleasant enough but very northern', he went on, 'i.e. antisouthern. God help any southerner who comes up here. I would think the clergy united on that one.'

He was made Archbishop of Liverpool on 7 February 1976. By July his mood was little better. Again on retreat, and again writing to France this time in reply to him, he confessed:

> I suppose it all helped to make me face the reality of the situation. You know me and how I find myself still feeling. I really have tried during this retreat and perhaps because I am trying to face it, I suppose it is easier. But initially I made comparisons to myself all the time and realise how much I miss . . . For myself it has really been a test. Of course I accept it but it is (still) all so foreign and for the most part I have almost sensed some part of me dying. It's so unusual and 'not me'.

Worlock said he was trying to lose himself in activity –

> profitable, I hope, but I so much need to draw more deeply spiritually. As I sit and prepare homilies, I feel that I am at the bottom of a well and I thirst. I know enough and I think I love enough – or at least desire to do so – but I am so dry. And seeing this must be because as yet I am not able to share it, to share myself, to draw on the strength and ideas of someone like you . . . God knows I am willing to make this sacrifice, yet I find it so hard, especially in view of the last ten years and even before, to come to just 'Him[10] and me' which I know it should and must be . . . I count on your prayers to help for I think you alone have perhaps understood the test it has been and still is.[11]

He found the appointment of Dom (later Cardinal) George Basil Hume OSB to Westminster, and his own move to Liverpool instead, hard to accept. It had been his conviction for some years that he was himself a fairly obvious choice to succeed Cardinal Heenan at Westminster, on the latter's death or retirement. He felt he had earned it and would have been right for it: no man on earth had a more detailed insight into the demands of such a job. Indeed, during the illness of Griffin and Godfrey, he had virtually run the place single-handed.

But if Worlock's bitterness was understandably human, his public manner towards Hume was always truly Christian. Thus for the afternoon of Basil Hume's installation as Archbishop of Westminster in the spring of 1976, the authorities at Westminster Abbey had issued an unprecedented ecumenical invitation to the Benedictine Order in England – some dozen communities of monks – to sing Solemn Vespers according to the Benedictine rite in that once-Benedictine Abbey. It was to be their dramatic 'return' after an absence of almost 450 years. Just before the long line of hooded monks filed slowly into the abbey, as the whole congregation held its breath, a small silent procession took place from the main door to the altar consisting of an Abbey mace bearer, a chaplain, and the Roman Catholic Archbishop of Liverpool in full regalia (himself an archbishop a mere matter of weeks).

Worlock was the only English Catholic bishop present. It was not scene-stealing; it was magnanimity. He had come to offer his full public support to the man who had beaten him to the prize; and to do so in a striking ecumenical context. His gesture also seemed to be his acknowledgement that there were some tricks up Basil Hume's sleeve, by virtue of his Benedictine background and Establishment connections, that were beyond even his own extraordinary repertoire. This doesn't mean he felt the better man had won. At times, it seems, he clearly felt the contrary. But he did not blame Hume for the outcome. He blamed the Church, and all the more keenly as he loved the Church. It was like a rejection by a lover. In the long term, this gave Worlock an experience of injustice and suffering that softened him and made him more sympathetic to others who felt they also had been wronged by the powers-that-be (or indeed, rejected by a lover). It may even have helped him understand and sympathize with Liverpool itself, which has a long and strongly felt history of condescension and exclusion by the London Establishment.

It was in 1975 that events started accelerating for Worlock. The two most important Roman Catholic archdioceses in England were becoming vacant. George Andrew Beck announced his intended retirement from Liverpool (which technically took effect when Worlock succeeded him). And John Carmel Heenan announced that he did not think it too soon for the people and clergy of Westminster to begin to look for his own successor. In fact he never got to retire; he died in office in November 1975. But the public consultation process had already begun.

This was very unusual. The appointment of a new archbishop or bishop is organized by the Pope's personal representative in Great Britain, known in 1975 as the Apostolic Delegate, since 1982 as the Apostolic Nuncio.[12]He occupies a fine house overlooking Wimbledon Common, in south-east London. His job involves discreet trawling for suitable candidates, canvassing support for various names, and preparing and vetting the short-list of three, known as the *terna*, which is then sent to the Congregation for Bishops in Rome. They can ask for further enquiries or even further names, and finally they make a recommendation to the Pope, who may also ask for more work to be done. It has always been true that both papal representatives and the Vatican itself are open to suggestions for such nominations. But they do not usually advertise vacancies, even by proxy. Heenan's announcement implied that a new and more open policy was henceforth being pursued. He encouraged anyone in the archdiocese who had an opinion on who the next archbishop should be, to communicate their thoughts to the Apostolic Delegate in Wimbledon, including names. To set this in its context, the new 'policy' of wide consultation did not seem to apply to the hardly less important appointment to Liverpool. Very few people were consulted and it is almost inconceivable that any of them would have suggested the Bishop of Portsmouth.

In other words consultation was a Heenan ruse to keep out Worlock, not a new policy at all. That Heenan did not like Worlock was clear from all sorts of evidence, not least the abrupt way he had cleared him out of Archbishop's House, Westminster, in 1964 and tried to have him packed off to North Wales a year later. As Worlock reported in the private note quoted above, he was told not to imagine he was likely to be made an auxiliary bishop of Westminster (which was another way of saying 'I don't like you and I don't want you succeeding me').

Though he does not seem to have been aware of it at the time, Worlock was not very popular among the clergy in Westminster. Later he was to attribute this to the fact that he had had to do unpopular things in the names of the cardinals he had served – their 'hatchet man'. He felt there had been a conspiracy to do him down among some of the Westminster clergy,[13] and it seems likely he would have regarded Monsignor Bruce Kent as having a hand in it.[14] Heenan would have been well aware of this level of feeling, and his announcement of a more free and open consultation to find his successor was really a signal to the Westminster clergy to make their anti-Worlock feelings well known to the Apostolic Delegate. He gave them permission, so to speak, to do something that many of them would have found difficult without such encouragement.

Worlock's personal papers contain only a passing reference to how the battle went against him, which does not quite do justice to the evidence. In some contexts, he blamed 'Westminster priests' for blocking his appointment. In a long essay primarily about Cardinal Griffin, however, he suggested that opinion turned against himself as part of a more general pattern of disenchantment with Heenan. (Hence it wasn't Worlock's fault, except for the way he had stayed loyal to the dying cardinal right to the end.) The general discussion of Heenan is also interesting, as much for its selectivity as for its candour. He seems to be subtly engaged in bolstering Griffin's reputation by indirect unfavourable comparisons with Heenan. Why he should set down these thoughts at such length, preceded by a note 'In this volume I am not thinking of print or publication; just what I wanted to write', is not at all clear. Anyone reading Worlock's private writings would be well advised to heed the warning that he was prone to self-deception and to the revision of his own memories for the sake of self-justification. The strongest example of this is his private account of the events leading up to the papal visit to Great Britain in 1982, given in a later chapter. But this account of Heenan should carry the same Government Health Warning. And the same applies to the 'not for publication' remark quoted above. Not everything Derek Worlock says should be taken at face value. Of Heenan, he wrote:

> For most of his life he was rightly regarded as 'progressive' and a real leader in pastoral initiatives and experience. In the late fifties in Liverpool he was the leader of new thought. He had come to terms with ecumenism, reconciled it with his well-known form of apologetics,[15] and there seemed no-one better fitted to lead our Church in England and Wales into the Council and renewal.[16] But the truth was he was an individualist. The collective wisdom of the Council left him cold. Its long-drawn-out procedures gave him little opportunity to sparkle, and when he could speak in St Peter's – as in the famous intervention about *periti*[17] – he had recourse to his CMS and Hyde Park Corner tactics of destroying one's opponents. In this he alienated many who had admired his brilliance and pastoral zeal. By the end of the Council I did not dare to put him up at the weekly Press Conference. Those who turned up were hostile to him for the sweetly paternalistic way in which he could turn a question to make the questioner [look] naïve or ridiculous.
>
> He was thankful when the Council was over but then he found himself faced with the implementation of the various structures decreed by the Council, not least the Bishops' Conference. Try as he would, he could not be other than a one-man band: I had dreadful troubles as Secretary to the Conference. He simply could not believe that anything of consequence existed off his desk. Sharing responsibility was meaningless, Commissions[18] at best lip-service to an idea which would not survive. Yet in spite of that he never lost the magnetism of personal charm and sparkling brilliance. So he always had a wide range of very influential friends who were utterly committed to support of his one-man apostolate. Whilst he was fit, it was at least a way of going about things. When he became ill it was very difficult. Really only in the last two or three years of his life would he let people help, notably David Norris and myself.
>
> Once again our involvement with him at the end of his regime meant that when he went to God – it was a holy and humble death at 3 pm one Friday afternoon – we were both identified with a way of doing things at Westminster which a group of Foreign Office and Wimbledon-loving[19] true-bloods (untypical of our Church in the past as now) decreed must be swept to one side. At the end he was faced with a choice none of his predecessors had known: to die

in harness run-down, or to retire (unthinkable or even forbidden to pre-Council cardinals). He announced his intention to retire, set things in motion, and then died. Retirement for John Heenan, always at the centre of things, would have been unthinkable.[20]

So he was one who got caught in the middle – the last volume of his auto-biography[21] is one of the saddest books I have ever read.

This is certainly fair comment, and Worlock is not just referring to the fact that he is not mentioned by name in either of the Heenan autobiographies. Heenan saw the post-Conciliar Church in drastically apocalyptic terms. 'We are still too close to events to be sure what went wrong', he wrote in 1973.[22] 'The way many Catholics both lay and clerical reacted to Pope Paul's decision to leave unchanged the teaching of his predecessors on contraception was the greatest shock the Church has suffered since the Reformation.' Heenan seems unaware that he had added to that shock when, as vice-president[23] of the Papal Birth Control Commission set up by the Pope to review Catholic doctrine in this area, he had himself indicated that change was likely. He was not a last-ditcher. Worlock was not the only person who adjusted his memory to suit his prejudices.

'Yet it was only a symptom of a far more serious disorder in the Church', Heenan went on.

> Theological revolutionaries, mainly in Europe but with eager disciples in North America, claimed that the Council was a failure because it had not really changed the Catholic religion. They contended that its only real function had been to serve as a stepping stone to real theological reform. Selective theology under the name of pluralism became the fashion . . . This was the situation Pope Paul had to face. He had to implement the decrees of Pope John's Council in the face of the self-appointed leaders of anti-Catholic renewal. In the golden days of Pope John, Catholics had not talked about the 'institutional' Church nor had they been obsessed with 'structures'. Pope John had departed this life before structures became the rage in ecclesiastical, academic and even political circles. Many lay theologians left the Church while new-style priests and nuns began to practise the evangelical virtues unhampered by vows. Outraged by the lack of love in their own communities they sought Christ in each other's arms.

and so on. It is unlikely that the author of this unbalanced rant against 'progressives' and their 'structures' would have had much time for Derek Worlock, the normative Vatican II progressive, the ultimate structures man.

Worlock confessed in another of his private papers that two theologians who had greatly influenced him were Hubert Richards and Charles Davis. They gave him new sympathy and understanding for the new ways of studying Scripture he had encountered at the Second Vatican Council. Davis, whom Heenan had appointed to the staff of Heythrop College, later resigned from the priesthood and the Catholic Church, and married. Richards was sacked from Corpus Christi catechetical centre in the West-minster diocese after a row with Heenan (who appointed him too) over whether to invite the famous Swiss liberal theologian Hans Küng to give a lecture there. Richards also resigned from the priesthood and indeed married a former nun. But they were not the anti-Catholic monsters of Heenan's fevered imagination. Küng remained a priest, but was stripped of his right to teach Catholic theology after refusing to retract his attack on papal infallibility. There can be little doubt that these were the sort of people whom Heenan regarded as betraying the Church after Vatican II. In no way did they deserve his sneers: in no way were they that important, even.

When the search began for Heenan's successor, there were numerous possible candidates apart from Worlock, including Bishop Alan Clark of East Anglia, who was proving a success as Catholic co-chairman of the Anglican-Roman Catholic International Commission (ARCIC), Father Michael Hollings, a priest of Westminster of good connections and great charisma, and Bishop Basil Christopher Butler OSB, former Abbot of Downside, who had been present at the Second Vatican Council as head of the English Benedictines.[24] The senior and most obvious candidate was the Archbishop of Birmingham, George Patrick Dwyer, who had become something of a moderate progressive under the tutelage of Heenan. But despite the support of several senior bishops, including, it is said, Bishop Clark, Dwyer announced fairly publicly that he did not wish to be consid-ered. He was nearly 70; it had become customary for bishops to retire at 75. The attitude of the other bishops to Worlock at that time could more accu-rately be described as respect rather than as affection. He was not generally easy in their company. Neither among his fellow bishops, nor among the senior clergy of Westminster, was the prospect of Worlock as head man regarded as enticing. Some members of the cathedral chapter made their misgivings known to Archbishop Heim at Wimbledon. It was probably what he wanted to hear, indeed what Heenan had told him to expect. Worlock never really forgave them, and years later friends were surprised to hear him complaining bitterly about these priests. 'It seemed so sad', said one of them.[25]

The 'dark horse' candidacy of Abbot George Basil Hume of Ampleforth, then 53, was supported by a group of influential laymen including the Tory MP Norman St John Stevas and the editor of *The Times*, William Rees-Mogg, with the Duke of Norfolk said to be a late convert. A small group went to Rome to press Hume's case. When Worlock heard this his old friend Patrick Keegan went to Rome to do some counter-lobbying, but to little effect. Hume has since said that none of this discreet diplomacy on his behalf was done with his knowledge or permission.[26] Indeed, on hearing the news he tried to decline the appointment. He only changed his mind on being told personally by Pope Paul VI that he must consider it a direct command from God.

Hume's candidacy, unwitting though it was, had two advantages over the others. The Archbishop of Canterbury, Dr Donald Coggan, had got to know him well when he was Archbishop of York, and let it be known that he thought Hume would make an excellent choice for Westminster.[27] And Hume's brother-in-law was Sir John Hunt. As Secretary to the Cabinet and head of the Home Civil Service, he was the most powerful civil servant in the British Government. These were unusual qualifications. Not since Manning's relationship with Gladstone had an Archbishop of Westminster been so close to the peaks of the British political landscape – closer in fact than any recent Archbishop of Canterbury.

But there are deeper reasons even than these. In overstepping Worlock, indeed in moving him to the totally unsuitable archdiocese of Liverpool, the Apostolic Delegate, Archbishop Bruno Heim, was rejecting the best of the available candidates produced by the usual machinery. Heim had been close to Cardinal Angelo Roncalli, later Pope John XXIII, and had served him in a junior capacity (1947–51) when Roncalli was nuncio in Paris after the war. It would have been obvious to any Vatican observer of the English bishops at the Council that they were converted to the reforms of the Council more by their loyalty to the Church than because they saw the necessity for them. This would have been no less true of Worlock than of any other. He was a busy bishop, an activist and administrator, who on being asked what he proposed to do to relax on holiday, replied that he would be revising the statutes of the Bishops' Conference.

In a television interview in 1985 William Rees-Mogg gave his explanation for supporting Hume, which was not entirely convincing as it ignored the fact that the Abbot of Ampleforth's primary rival, Worlock, was no more Irish than he was. Indeed, there were no obvious candidates that fitted the 'Irish' criteria Rees-Mogg said would have disqualified them. But there was one obvious one who fitted the 'administrator' category, and it is a fair bet this is who Rees-Mogg had in mind.

'I thought that we needed in Britain to have a change from the type of Archbishop we'd had to another type', he said.

> We had had Archbishops who had come up the ladder of bishoprics, who were very strongly administrative. We'd also, with Cardinal Heenan, whom I liked and admired and thought a very fine man, had a strongly Irish Archbishop, and it seemed to me that we had become rather over-administered, that there was a feeling that there needed to be a personality primarily seen in spiritual terms. I think he got the job because the Vatican realised, through the agency of the Apostolic Delegate, that something fairly radical needed to be done, that the English Catholic Church was in bad shape, that the congregations were declining, that the presence of the Church in English life was a diminishing presence and that the voices who spoke for it were not heard.

The body of English bishops in 1975 was not so different from what it had been at the Council. With one or two exceptions, they can all be regarded as products of the Counter Reformation tradition of priestly formation. Professor Adrian Hastings[28] states that Godfrey had used his influence as Rector of the English College (the *Venerabile*), as Apostolic Delegate and then as Archbishop of Westminster to 'transform the English Hierarchy into a Roman clique by the steady appointment of a single sort of bishop'.

He goes on:

> Up to the 1930s only a handful of English bishops had been old boys of the *Venerabile*, and those not the most important. The English Hierarchy had become more homogeneous than it had ever been: Griffin, Masterson, Heenan, Grimshaw and Dwyer – five archbishops appointed in the forties and fifties in Godfrey's wake were all from this one stable, as were Rudderham of Clifton, Restieaux of Plymouth, Ellis of Nottingham, Holland of Salford. The *Venerabile* spirit was that of a clerical élite, isolated by seven long years in Rome with little personal contact permitted outside the circle of fifty fellow students. It was a regime of strict rules punctuated by Christmas theatricals and long summers playing cricket. It cultivated polite disdain alike for Anglicans and for continental theology. Rome was adored but Italian was seldom learnt. Insularity was as important as ultramontanism. From the Second World War until the Second Vatican Council the Church in England was entirely controlled by priests of this particular formation, while those of other traditions, both secular and religious, felt themselves excluded from the centre of power and under suspicion as not being quite the real thing.

The Restoration of the Catholic Hierarchy in 1850 was a direct fulfilment of the strategy of the priest-missionaries who had laboured so long and dangerously in England since the reign of Mary. It was a clerically-based ideal of the Catholic Church. And for all his efforts to find a proper role for the laity within it, Worlock only managed to show how to produce a clericalized laity, not an emancipated one.

One of the greatest problems faced by post-Vatican II Catholicism was that of spirituality. The piety expected by the Counter Reformation was, at best, deeply impressive when it worked on priests, disappointing when applied to the laity. The *Garden of the Soul* kind of piety was indeed capable of being profound, but it was passive: the laity were the led, not the leaders, the taught, not the teachers. The celebration of Mass in the Tridentine Rite was at its best a brilliant spiritual explosion, which may explain why some of the greatest treasures of the canon of classical music are settings of that ritual. But more often, a typical Tridentine celebration would consist of a priest muttering to himself in Latin, back turned to the congregation whom he ignored and who ignored him, except for the genuflexions and adorations prescribed by the rubric. The rest of the time – following the pattern of the *Garden of the Soul* itself – they would fumble with their Rosaries, praying to Our Lady or a favourite saint, lips moving to an entirely different rhythm from the priest at the altar.

English Catholicism from the 1560s to the mid-1950s was Counter Reformation Catholicism, uncritically so. In every direction in space and time, Catholicism was the same: and that was how it was supposed to be. It was serene, numinous, beautiful and immutable, indeed eternal. It was a sublime blueprint, a universal formula for personal salvation. In that respect as in so many others, the model for the Counter Reformation Church was the triumphant militarism of ancient Imperial Rome, a homogeneous monolithic civilization spreading to all corners of the known world with the same laws and customs in every part of it. To the papal Curia of that era, putting down the Reformation was akin to putting down local rebellions and fratricidal wars in the Roman Empire. So closely did the first Counter Reformation Popes identify themselves with the emperors of classical Rome, they busied themselves, as those emperors had done, with the erection of public monuments (and the adaptation of pagan ones) and the improvement of public services, such as the supply of clean water, to the citizens of Rome. They were, of course, great patrons of the creative arts.

Calling themselves *Pontifex Maximus*, the very title used by the emperors, they thus emphasized the continuity between the spiritual empire of the Roman Catholic Church and the political and military empire of pagan

Rome. And this was a crucial part of their policy of reforming the Church to make it more resistant to the spiritual insurgency of Protestantism. As Rome had once been the centre of the known civilized world, so it had become so again. It was in the same spirit of expansion that the Counter Reformation papacy launched Jesuit missions into Latin America and the Far East, especially Japan and China, dividing the unchristianized areas of the world between Spanish and Portuguese spheres of influence. But the Counter Reformation had set the cultural forms of Catholicism in stone: they were never to be changed, and therefore not to be adapted to local conditions. On this principle of inflexibility the sixteenth-century Jesuit missions to India, China and Japan were eventually to founder. Permission to adapt Catholicism to local custom was refused by Rome, even though that adaptation was the necessary price for missionary success. In this respect the Counter Reformation, which had provided the explosion of spiritual energy for this great missionary expansion, turned out also to be its own greatest obstacle. The conversion to Christianity of half the world's population could have been within the Church's grasp.

As Bishop of Portsmouth, Derek Worlock had become the very essence of 'Vatican II man'. He seemed to be presenting himself as almost a Moses, bringing the tablets of stone down from Mount Sinai to the people. On his arrival, he wrote later,

> I was not unnaturally asked by the priests and people of my diocese what they were to expect and where my priorities would lie. With a somewhat superficial over-statement I replied 'We shall try to do the lot. Neither you nor I will pick and choose.[29] We will follow each decree and all subsequent implementing legislation. In a time of change, "to stay with Peter" is the best touchstone of orthodoxy'.

He commented he had 'no idea of the full measure required by that first undertaking I gave'.[30] It meant attending many meetings and creating many new structures; also giving many speeches.

But he can be criticized, not only for this remark, but for the attitude it exemplified. From the way he spoke of it, the Second Vatican Council was another kind of inflexible formula or blueprint for a new Church, which was to be constructed by 'doing the lot'. Indeed, he did the lot, in Portsmouth and in his national work, both as a key member of various committees and also later as the episcopal secretary of the Bishops' Conference. Yet formula or blueprint was precisely what the Second Vatican Council was not. Worlock thought it was a new way of talking about the Church. In fact, as George Basil Hume intuitively understood, it was a new way of talking about God. Talking about the Church was what Worlock was good at: talking about God was what Hume was good at. In terms of his appeal to the British public, talking about the Church (even in a new way) scored very low, compared with talking about God. Worlock exemplified a man in love with the Church; Hume, a man in love with God. There is no doubt, in such terms, Hume's appeal was wide, Worlock's narrow.[31]

It is true the Second Vatican Council represented in very many ways the close of a Catholic era, the completion of the unfinished business of the First Vatican Council, even the reform of the reforms of the Council of Trent, and hence the end of the Counter Reformation. That Council had been divided into two camps. There were those who wanted to take a tough line with the new Protestant Reformers, invoking ecclesiastical powers to excommunicate them and even invoking the civil powers to suppress them. And there were others who wished to adopt a conciliatory response to the Reformation. The hard-liners won the day, though the conciliators gained some concessions.

The Second Vatican Council, especially in its Decree on Ecumenism but also by its fundamental adjustment of the Catholic Church's self-definition, seemed to be an attempt to go back to the very time of Trent, to reopen those old debates and this time reach a different verdict, with the conciliators now coming out on top. What the Council of Trent actually said or implied about the Protestant Reformers under the influence of the sixteenth-century hard-liners, and what the Second Vatican Council said or implied about them under the influence of the twentieth-century progressives, cannot both be true. Nor can it be a question of what was true in the sixteenth century somehow becoming untrue in the twentieth. Thus the Second Vatican Council cannot honestly be seen as a sequel to the Council of Trent, a 'development' or 'adjustment' rather as Einsteinian physics developed from or adjusted Newtonian physics.

The Second Vatican Council was an implicit admission that many of the decisions made at Trent were mistakes, an admission that in various important respects the Counter Reformation had taken the Catholic Church in the wrong direction. Yet both Councils, in Catholic theology, were regarded as safeguarded from error by the Holy Spirit. A minimalist reading of that safeguard would understand it as meaning only that the Catholic Church cannot formally define as infallibly true any dogma that is contrary to the Gospel. The Second Vatican Council made no such definitions at all; Trent did, but in such areas as transubstantiation and the number of sacraments. But they were not the real problem. Because of this aura of authority, policy decisions of a General Council which do not involve any dogmatic definition were nevertheless assumed – at least in popular piety, and by Church officials not over-concerned with the more subtle nuances – to be guaranteed by the Holy Spirit too.

This is of course untenable. Such examples as the Fourth Lateran Council's decree on the Jews in 1215, forbidding them public employment, confining them to ghettos and requiring them to wear yellow stars in public – policies so sinisterly followed seven and a half centuries later by the Nazis – were manifestly not inspired by God in any sense. There is no guarantee in Catholic doctrine that a General Council of the Church will reach decisions that are sensible and wise, prudent and compassionate. As Lateran IV illustrates, they can even be morally wrong. In fact its measures against the Jews were a signal for an intensification of Jew-phobia across Europe, culminating in the cruel expulsion of all the Jews from England by the end of that century.

The Second Vatican Council's decree *Nostra Aetate* specifically states that the Catholic Church repudiates all persecution, adding: 'Moreover, mindful of her common patrimony with the Jews, and motivated by the Gospel's spiritual love and by no political considerations, she deplores the hatred, persecution, and displays of anti-Semitism directed against the Jews at any time and from any source.' That is an implicit but unambiguous repudiation of the particular instruction of Lateran IV regarding the treatment of the Jews in the thirteenth century. No one would try to argue that Lateran IV on the Jews was justified according to the values and needs of its time, or that *Nostra Aetate* of Vatican II was in any sense a development of it. The only honest view is to say that Vatican II repudiated it.

The contrast between Trent and Vatican II is no less sharp in the case of what the former calls heretics and schismatics, the latter, separated brethren. In the *Dogmatic Decree on Baptism* issued by Trent, Canon VIII read: 'If any one saith, that the baptized are freed from all the precepts, whether written or transmitted, of holy Church, in such wise that they are not bound to observe them, unless they have chosen of their own accord to submit themselves thereunto; let him be anathema.' Thus all the baptized were under the jurisdiction of the Catholic Church, whether they acknowledged it or not. The consequence was that they were bound by the rulings of the Council of Trent, and could be punished for disobeying them. This is as anti-ecumenical as it is possible to be.

Vatican II's decree on ecumenism, *Unitatis Redintegratio*, stated:

> For men who believe in Christ and have been truly baptised are in communion with the Catholic Church even though this communion is imperfect. The differences that exist in varying degrees between them and the Catholic Church –

whether in doctrine and sometimes in discipline, or concerning the structure of the Church – do indeed create many obstacles, sometimes serious ones, to full ecclesiastical communion. The ecumenical movement is striving to overcome these obstacles. But even in spite of them it remains true that all who have been justified by faith in Baptism are members of Christ's body, and have a right to be called Christian, and so are correctly accepted as brothers by the children of the Catholic Church.

It is recognizably the same doctrine about baptism, but in the former case used to denounce and condemn, in the latter to embrace and encourage.

In most respects, however, those charged with the duty of spreading the teaching of Vatican II preferred not to stress the contradictions but to emphasize the continuities between the Church before and the Church after. One who did not was Archbishop Marcel Lefebvre, former Archbishop of Dacca, who as Derek Worlock had noted had been a leading figure in the attempt to recruit Cardinal Godfrey to the ultra-conservative faction at the start of the Council. Lefebvre later started his Confraternity of St Pius V, named after the Pope who promulgated the Tridentine Rite Mass after the Council of Trent and who had declared it unalterable for all time. Lefebvre took particular exception not only to changes in the Mass but to the Vatican II documents on ecumenism, the Jews, and religious liberty, especially the latter. They were, he maintained, 'heretical', 'anti-Christ', and 'satanic', being contrary to the traditional teaching of the Church, above all as exemplified at Trent. When he proposed to ordain new bishops so that his association could carry on after his death, Pope John Paul II ordered him to desist. When he defied the Pope in 1988 he was formally excommunicated – the only time excommunication was used to silence a critic of the teachings of Vatican II.

The other criticism of Worlock's all-or-nothing approach to the implementation of Vatican II arises from the uneven quality of the various documents issued by the Council, and from the fact that to understand them properly it is usually necessary to place them in their historical context. The first decree to be issued, on the mass media, is by general consent the worst document of them all. It was brought forward in 1962 when the Council business started to seize up after the initial clashes between conservatives and progressives, when there were no documents of greater weight ready for processing. So bad was it that a Vatican department had to set to work not long after the Council ended to produce a substitute document on the same theme which, though having less authority, made better sense. Also only 'good in parts', like the curate's egg, were the decrees on education, the priesthood, the missions, and the religious life.[32] Even Worlock's own baby, the Decree on the Lay Apostolate, has not entirely stood the test of time. The concept of lay apostolate it relied on went out of fashion, and the locus of 'lay formation' became the ordinary parish. Thus lay formation became less understood as the special preparation of a particularly dedicated group of laity – the meaning implied by Worlock's remark in the Vatican II diary that unformed laymen are a 'menace' – and more the universal duty of every individual and the responsibility of every priest. So 'lay formation' came to mean the same as 'living a Christian life as well as possible'. It would be fair to say that Worlock's theology of the lay apostolate, which he argued for at Vatican II and which the Decree on the Lay Apostolate promulgated, contained the seeds of its own destruction. It became no longer tenable to regard a lay person as an adjunct of the hierarchical 'apostolic' church, and as such able to exercise an apostolate only as an agent of the Hierarchy. The new theology of Vatican II emphasized the fundamental importance of baptism, which lay people received equally with clergy, bishops and Pope (and for that matter, with members of other Christian Churches). It was by virtue of their baptism that they had a duty to live and spread the faith, therefore, not because they had been specially commissioned to do so by the Hierarchy of the Church. This concept was what had usually been implied by the term 'lay apostolate', which is why it was dropped.

One Vatican II text whose interpretation became problematic, once it was no longer seen in the context in which it was created, was paragraph 25 of the Dogmatic Constitution on the Church, *Lumen Gentium*. As Worlock faithfully records in his Vatican II Diary,[33] the key issue being debated when this section was under consideration concerned the relationship between the teaching authority of the Pope and the teaching authority of the bishops.

The First Vatican Council had declared papal authority to be the supreme arbiter and standard of orthodoxy, the fount of the Church's special *magisterium* or teaching office which was deemed to be protected from error (papal infallibility). The Council had been adjourned in 1870 as an army hostile to the papacy marched on Rome; and it was never reconvened. Thus no further consideration had been given to the teaching authority of the bishops. It was, so to speak, unfinished business. When the Church returned to the matter in the course of debating *Lumen Gentium*, the idea of the *magisterium* had to be set forth in much more explicit detail, to make it clearer what part the Pope played and what part the bishops played. The papal *magisterium* had been a relatively simple idea. Once bishops were involved, however, the *magisterium* became more complicated. The document had to spell out different degrees or measures of authority, to meet the various combinations and permutations created by the possibility of episcopal participation in the *magisterium*. But there appears to have been very little attention given to the way these actual degrees or layers were described, or what the responsibility of the faithful was towards them, as that was not where the controversy was centred at the time. The descriptions were taken as read.

However, rather in the way in which the decrees of the Council of Trent and the First Vatican Council had been regarded almost as Holy Writ – as prescriptions to be applied literally – so this became a common approach to the interpretation of the Second Vatican Council too. Vatican II was read with a Vatican I mind. This applied with particular force to *Lumen Gentium* paragraph 25, after the publication of the papal encyclical on birth control, *Humanae Vitae*, in 1968. The countries which adopted the most literal and legalistic interpretation of *Lumen Gentium* 25 were the ones that had the greatest problem with *Humanae Vitae*. They were, primarily, the so-called Anglo-Saxon countries, where the law is assumed to be a precise instrument, any technical infringement of which brings a sanction, rather than a general guide to good conduct.[34] Countries without the Anglo-Saxon approach to law seemed to take *Humanae Vitae* much more in their stride (in most cases, it would seem, stepping over it as if it wasn't there).[35]

'Bishops are preachers of the faith', declares *Lumen Gentium* 25, at last supplying the episcopal balance to papal authority which was stressed by the First Vatican Council in its decree *Dei Filius*

> who lead new disciples to Christ, and they are authentic teachers, that is, teachers endowed with the authority of Christ, who preach to the people committed to them the faith they must believe and put into practice, and by the light of the Holy Spirit illustrate that faith. They bring forth from the treasury of Revelation new things and old, making it bear fruit and vigilantly warding off any errors that threaten their flock. Bishops, teaching in communion with the Roman Pontiff, are to be respected by all as witnesses to divine and Catholic truth. In matters of faith and morals, the bishops speak in the name of Christ and the faithful are to accept their teaching and adhere to it with a religious assent.

This is a hugely significant clarification, making it clear that bishops also have a teaching office 'by divine right' – that is to say, not delegated to them by the Pope but derived directly from the fact they are bishops. It was by virtue of this passage that bishops ceased to be seen as 'branch managers' of the Catholic Church, mere local agents of Rome. They were seen (again) as apostles in their own right.[36]

As if to avoid giving the impression that this passage somehow diminished papal authority, however, *Lumen Gentium* 25 goes on to restate it:

> This religious submission of mind and will must be shown in a special way to the authentic *magisterium* of the Roman Pontiff, even when he is not speaking *ex cathedra*; that is, it must be shown in such a way that his supreme *magisterium* is acknowledged with reverence, the judgements made by him are sincerely adhered to, according to his manifest mind and will. His mind and will in the matter may be known either from the character of the documents, from his frequent repetition of the same doctrine, or from his manner of speaking.

It is still vague in parts, perhaps deliberately vague; for it puts the onus on the individual to decide what weight to put on a particular papal statement by its somewhat indeterminate references to the Pope's 'repetition' and 'manner of speaking'. Nevertheless after *Humanae Vitae* many a Catholic conscience – particularly in the Anglo-Saxon world – went into overdrive to wrestle with the precise meaning of phrases like 'religious submission of mind and will'. All this passage was doing, in fact, was demonstrating that the new emphasis on the teaching office of the bishops was not meant to contradict the previous emphasis on the teaching office of the Pope. It is clear from what Derek Worlock says in his Vatican II diary that that was the sole purpose of this text. It was never meant to bear the enormous weight that was later put on it. He admitted as much when he gave a television interview in the aftermath of *Humanae Vitae* and remarked: 'Birth control is not the acid test of Christianity.' With that remark, Worlock was no longer reading *Lumen Gentium* with a Vatican I mindset. For him, the Counter Reformation was over.

Notes

1 What Worlock wrote in a personal notebook about this was 'We were informed that the then Bishop of Portsmouth, Timothy Cotter, originally from County Cork, normally drew his priests from Ireland or Irish immigrant families in his diocese. The apparent unsuitability of my background suggested that it was useless even to apply. Subsequent experience confirmed the accuracy of this advice. . . .'
2 1175–1240. Abington is the old form of Abingdon.
3 He also studied for the priesthood at Allen Hall, the senior diocesan seminary.
4 They would have been a standard part of religious education in Catholic colleges at that time.
5 A special form of petitionary prayer repeated on nine consecutive days.
6 A quasi-monastic period of prayer, the sacraments, sermons and spiritual readings,

often in preparation for some major spiritual event.

7 Holy Orders in episcopal churches are broken up into three degrees: deacon, priest and bishop.

8 Centred on Wrexham, North Wales, at that time; boundaries since rearranged, and now centred on Swansea, South Wales.

9 Worlock later told his secretary Nicholas France that Heenan claimed he had intervened to make sure Worlock got Portsmouth and Langton Fox Menevia. When Heenan first saw the two appointments they were the other way round; he realized this was 'nonsense' and had the Congregation for Bishops swap them over. That does not entirely square with the version of events given above, but is the more flattering to Worlock's ego.

10 He means a personal relationship with God in prayer.

11 Around this time Derek Worlock told the author, in a private conversation, that he was under medication for depression. No doubt it eased later, as he started to make new relationships and to overcome the sheer loneliness of the job which is so transparent in this letter. But it may also have become chronic, and may have helped to make him at times paranoid towards his associates.

12 For a brief period he was called the Apostolic Pro-nuncio, as Britain had opted out of the Vienna Convention under which Nuncios automatically became Dean of the Corps Diplomatique, and the title Pro-nuncio did not carry that implication. The Holy See later renounced this right under the Vienna Convention.

13 Handwritten letter to the author c. 1976.

14 His successor as Archbishop of Westminster's private secretary whom he accused of throwing out all his files, who later became RC Chaplain to London University and eventually General Secretary of the Campaign for Nuclear Disarmament, before leaving the priesthood.

15 A Catholic expression, meaning 'explaining and defending the faith in debate.' Before becoming a bishop, Heenan had run the Catholic Missionary Society (CMS), a body which evangelized on behalf of the Catholic faith in Britain.

16 This is not what he said at the time, see the Vatican II diary.

17 Heenan had attacked the arrogance of some theological advisers at the Second Vatican Council.

18 The Bishops' Conference set up a series of mixed Commissions, mainly clergy and laity but headed by a bishop, to offer expert advice to the Conference on issues of the day. They were largely Worlock's doing.

19 Not a reference to tennis. 'Wimbledon-loving blue-bloods' appears to refer to those well-born Catholics whom Worlock considered had insinuated themselves into undue influence over the Apostolic Delegate, who was based at Wimbledon. 'Foreign Office' is unclear, none of the group who supported Abbot Hume's candidacy are covered by that description.

20 Twenty years later, exactly the same could be said of Worlock. He tried hard to get the Holy See to extend his retirement date beyond his 75th birthday in February 1995, and was crestfallen when his pleas were rejected.

21 *A Crown of Thorns* by John C. Heenan, Hodder and Stoughton, 1974.

22 *Ibid.*, p. 390.

23 Heenan maintained he was really 'Pro-President' of the Commission, perhaps a distinction without a difference.

24 Much later, the retired nuncio Archbishop Bruno Heim said he could not imagine

himself appointing someone who wore his lunch on his shirtfront, implying Butler was a messy eater. On such small details do great outcomes depend.

25 Letter to author from Monsignor Ralph Brown of Westminster.

26 Conversation with author.

27 Coggan was later irritated to find himself compared unfavourably with Hume, which, in view of his role in the appointment, was most unfair.

28 *A History of English Christianity*, SCM, 1991, p. 479.

29 This unconsciously reflects the well-known observation that in the Catholic Church something forbidden one minute becomes compulsory the next.

30 *Give me Your Hand* by Derek Worlock, St Paul Publications, 1977.

31 In conversation with the author afterwards, Archbishop Bruno Heim said he would always appoint a 'man of God' over a good administrator.

32 Used in a Catholic context, this phrase refers to people who live the life of a dedicated 'religious' (used as a noun) who is subject to vows, such as a monk or nun.

33 See p. 157.

34 The following anecdote may illustrate the difference. Three priests from the English College were driving in a car in Rome with a visitor from London, not long after the *Humanae Vitae* crisis. The car stopped at traffic lights, which quickly appeared to be stuck at red. As they waited, to left and right they were overtaken by Italians, who slowed down to ensure the junction was safe to cross but did not feel it necessary to wait and see if the lights would eventually change. After sitting there a while, the driver turned to his visitor and remarked '*Now* do you understand *Humanae Vitae?*'

35 The distinction has also been made between countries whose legal system is based on the *Code Napoléon* or something like it, and those whose legal system is based on common law. The distinction still crops up from time to time concerning different national approaches to European Community legislation. It is said Mediterranean countries are used to seeing laws and regulations as goals, while Northern European countries see them as binding to the letter.

36 Pope John Paul II, asked in an interview about his traditional title 'Vicar of Christ' replied 'The Pope is not the only one who holds this title. With regard to the Church entrusted to him, each bishop is *Vicarius Christi* . . . Thus, if with this title one wants to refer to the dignity of the Bishop of Rome, one cannot consider it apart from the dignity of the entire college of bishops, with which it is tightly bound, as it is to the dignity of each bishop, each priest, and each of the baptised.' *Crossing the Threshold of Hope*, Alfred A. Knopf, Inc., 1994.

8

'The Greatest Shock'[1]

The issue of birth control does not appear to have occupied Worlock seriously until about the time he became a bishop at the end of 1965. Even before his ordination – the use of the more traditional term 'consecration' for the making of a bishop was dropped soon after Vatican II – he was approached by a young priest of the diocese, Father Joseph Cocker. He had been expelled from his position as a curate in Ryde, Isle of Wight, by the Vicar General of Portsmouth diocese, Monsignor Sidney Mullarkey (the previous bishop, John Henry King, had died in March that year). Cocker had remarked to a local newspaper that he agreed with a priest in Birmingham who had been suspended for questioning the Church's teaching on contraception.

In the mind of many conservative clergy, this was rank disloyalty verging on heresy. After a period of uncertainty he was given a new temporary position under close supervision, but the terms were mutually irksome and he told Worlock 'I gather there were very few PPs[2] willing to have me.' He appealed to Worlock to help him. His letter was later filed among the many letters of congratulation that Worlock received on the news of his appointment as a bishop, including a particularly warm one from the Archbishop of Cracow, Karol Wojtyla,[3] and a decidedly cool one from Heenan. Cocker was most warmly replied to by Worlock, who told him: 'We need not imagine that I shall find overnight a complete answer to all your problems. But be assured at least of my great desire to help. Until then try to be serene and patient and let us pray for one another.' He interviewed him, reinstated him and moved him to a parish in the city of Portsmouth. He was advised not to raise the issue of contraception in public while the Papal Birth Control Commission was still deliberating.

The Commission[4] had been set up by Pope John XXIII not long before his death in 1963. A fashionable preoccupation at that time was the so-called 'population explosion' in the Third World – the fear that the world's population would soon outstrip food resources. Demographers were therefore among those to be consulted.[5] The Pope's purpose was partly to avoid an embarrassing debate on the floor of the Council, though the theology of marriage was bound to arise sooner or later. The Commission was also welcomed because the recent invention of the contraceptive pill was said by some commentators to have changed the terms of the argument, and hence it needed fresh expert study. When the Council ended in December 1965 the Commission had by no means finished its work.

In the English-speaking world the storm had broken with the publication in 1963 of *The Time has Come*[6] by Dr John Rock, an American Catholic gynaecologist. The time had come, he argued, for a reconsideration of the Catholic ban on contraception. Not long afterwards it was reported that Dr Anne Biezanek, a Catholic GP in the Shrewsbury diocese who agreed with Dr Rock, was being placed under ecclesiastical sanction by her bishop – in effect, denied access to Holy Communion – unless she stopped prescribing contraceptives in her surgery. She refused. On the Continent, controversy centred on an article and radio interview by Bishop Bekkers of 's-Hertogenbosch in Holland suggesting the invention of the Pill had changed everything. The argument was that as the Pill induced temporary sterility by altering the hormone levels, it was more akin to 'mutilation' than to contraception. Catholic moral theology allowed mutilation, e.g. amputation of a diseased limb, for the good of the patient as a whole. He had said: 'Most commentators have forgotten to ask themselves seriously whether these progesterone hormone products really belong to the same category as the more traditional, well known contraceptives.' He had also remarked that 'surprisingly sound new arguments arise from the modern phenomenology of man and from new insights into human sexuality, however much they are scorned by scientists of the traditional school.' As this debate filtered through to English Catholics, anguished argument broke out in such places as *The Spectator* and the *New Statesman*, two secular weekly magazines, a sign that the issue was still regarded as too hot to handle in the Catholic papers (except, perhaps, in defence of the *status quo*[7]).

This began to change when a small circulation magazine called *Search* published a serious challenge to the Church's official position by Archbishop Thomas Roberts SJ, formerly a missionary Bishop of Bombay and a member of the English province of the Jesuits. He was himself a member of the Second Vatican Council and he could not be ignored. In essence, he said he was unpersuaded by the usual Catholic objections to contraception on the basis of natural law – the 'ethical argument' – and so had to fall back on the 'argument from authority': that the Church had divine authority to preach true morality, and had consistently exercised this authority to condemn birth control. But he listed a series of issues where the Catholic Church had adjusted its moral teaching down the centuries, for instance on usury, slavery, the possibility of salvation for pagans, and the literal inspiration of the Bible. 'Only a few months ago, the Fathers of the Vatican Council were given statements on freedom of conscience which I personally find extremely difficult to reconcile with the *Syllabus* of Pope Pius IX', he wrote. If the Church had changed its mind on some issues, might it not do so on contraception? He did not exactly give the answer 'Yes', but he certainly wrote in such a way as to invite that reply from the reader.

The English Hierarchy issued a hasty statement in repudiation of Roberts, the kernel of which was the sentence: 'Contraception itself, however, is not an open question for it is against the law of God.' The bishops added caustically: 'The faithful are not incapable of the high degree of virtue which the observance of God's law sometimes demands. Let them beware of false leaders. "If the blind lead the blind, both fall into the pit" (Matthew 15:14)'. This is very characteristic of Heenan's style, and though the statement was issued in the name of all the bishops, the Press attributed it, not unfairly, to Heenan.

It may have been this clear judgement in favour of resisting change that led Pope Paul eventually to appoint Heenan as a vice-president of the newly enlarged Birth Control Commission, the president being Cardinal Ottaviani of the Holy Office and the other vice-president Cardinal Döpfner of Munich. In a statement to the cardinals at about this time, the Pope insisted that despite the review he was initiating, people must continue as before. 'We say frankly that up to now we do not have sufficient motive to consider out of date and therefore not binding the norms given by Pope Pius XII in this regard. Therefore they must be considered valid, at least until we feel obliged in conscience to change them.' The definitive Catholic condemnation of birth control in the twentieth century was the papal encyclical *Casti Connubii* of Pope Pius XI issued in 1931, but Pius XII had restated the position in an *Address to Midwives* in 1951, and it is to this that Paul VI referred. (Pius XII had specifically accepted the legitimacy of the so-called 'safe period'.) He also insisted that nobody should make official statements contradicting the official position. 'And it therefore seems opportune to recommend that no one, for the moment, takes it on himself to make pronouncements in terms different from the prevailing norm.'[8]

Nevertheless the possibility of change was clearly advertised by this statement. Nor were the English bishops at the Council unaware of this possibility. Worlock's diary describes a long lecture on the contraception issue given by the German moral theologian Father Bernard Häring at the

English College in the course of the Council session in 1964, at the invitation of Archbishop Heenan. It was introduced – in masterly fashion, according to the diarist – by George Patrick Dwyer. Worlock did not think much of Häring or his arguments, but was impressed by Dwyer's open-mindedness. He also reported an excited conversation in the English College concerning the possibility that the world had misunderstood what Pius IX had been talking about in 1931. It was usual to use extreme euphemisms in papal documents discussing sexual matters, and one school of thought among the students was that he was merely denouncing *coitus interruptus,*[9] but had beaten about the bush to such an extent that no one realized it.

More public debate went on when Cardinal Suenens, visiting the United States, gave a Press conference which was reported in *The Times.*[10] 'Acceptance by the Roman Catholic Church of a pill that would aid family planning has been predicted here by Cardinal Suenens, Archbishop of Malines-Brussels', it reported.

> He said that such a pill is nearing perfection and that its use would conform to the Church's doctrine on birth control.
>
> Noting that population increase is becoming a major problem throughout the world, he observed that the Church must accept a new situation. The Cardinal said: 'There are really two questions involved. One is medical, the other moral. Medically the question is whether the pill in question is a direct sterilising agent or whether it merely regulates natural functions, so that a woman will know three or four days in advance when she is able to conceive a child. The moral answer depends on the medical answer.' The Cardinal also indicated that he had given the Revd Louis Janssens 'liberty of research' to study the possibilities of such a pill.

Suenens' expectations turned out to be a red herring, except in one slightly bizarre respect. The contraceptive pill did turn out to have a secondary effect. After taking it for a while and then stopping, the rhythm of a woman's natural cycle seemed to become more regular. Menstrual irregularity was one of the major difficulties of the rhythm method. But during the actual course of treatment, the pill would give a contraceptive effect. That allowed pharmacists and GPs in Ireland, where the sale of contraceptives as such was illegal until the 1980s, to claim that the contraceptive pill was merely a cycle-regulator, and hence to prescribe and dispense it lawfully. It is to their credit that nobody thought this was anything but an ingenious device to get round the law.

But Worlock was by now fully committed to his own Vatican II agenda, and he reports the growing crisis over the birth control issue only in passing. He was much more exercised by trying to stop an amendment in support of Catholic Action creeping its way into a document on the duties of bishops. 'One is astonished at their naïvety and their persistence and I suppose in the end they will probably win through', he grumbled. He reckoned he could easily muster 200 votes to block the amendment but feared he would need 700, which would be more difficult. This does show a man confident that he possesses considerable influence over the proceedings, and still not yet a bishop. He obviously did not possess enough, as Catholic Action is commended by name in the Vatican II document *Christus Dominus* (on the role of bishops). But he also notes an important decision in the course of the final debates on the document *The Church in the Modern World* to treat the two 'ends'[11] of marriage – procreation, and the mutual support and love of the spouses – as of equal value. While this drew broad support, some misgivings were expressed that this might result in married people treating mutual support and love as more important than procreation if these ends of marriage came into conflict, and this could open the door to contraception. Although there were several important speeches at the Council suggesting the Church had to reassess its position, it seems likely that the great majority of bishops would have voted for no change had they been given the chance. The withholding of the contraception issue from the Council chamber was not necessarily a conservative manoeuvre.

Once the Council had finished at the end of 1965, however, the expectation of change was greatly enhanced when it became apparent that the original Commission had run into difficulties. It had to be enlarged by bringing in more bishops and experts. Meanwhile leaks began to appear suggesting not only that there was disunity among the members of the Commission but also that a majority no longer supported the argument against contraception based on natural law.[12] This was getting close to the position taken by Archbishop Roberts in 1964 that had provoked such a ferocious counter-attack from Heenan and his fellow bishops.

To some extent Paul VI tried to address the argument of the 'No contraception equals population explosion equals world starvation' lobby with his 1967 encyclical *Populorum Progressio*. This linked poverty to unjust relations between rich and poor nations, and the solution was therefore to put in place fair international terms of trading bolstered by direct wealth transfers from rich countries to poor ones (international aid and development). But he also asserted:

There is no denying that the accelerated rate of population growth brings many added difficulties to the problems of development where the size of the population grows more rapidly than the quantity of available resources to such a degree that things seem to have reached an *impasse*. In such circumstances people are inclined to apply drastic remedies to reduce the birth rate. There is no doubt that public authorities can intervene in this matter, within the bounds of their competence. They can instruct citizens on this subject and adopt appropriate measures, so long as these are in conformity with the dictates of the moral law.

What those dictates were, of course, was the business of the Birth Control Commission, though by the time *Populorum Progressio* appeared, it had reached its conclusions.

The Commission had existed in various guises; by its definitive meetings in May 1966 it had another sixteen cardinals and bishops as well as the earlier 55 members. It worked in a series of specialist groups of which the most important were the moral theologians, more than twenty of the total. It was there the crisis was deepest, with some fifteen votes in favour of change and four against.[13] They produced a majority report to the main Commission, while the four dissenters (or loyalists) also submitted papers. These documents later leaked into the Press, first in the *National Catholic Reporter* in America (April 1967) and thence into *The Tablet* of London. In some circles, apparently including Archbishop's House, Westminster, change in the Catholic line on birth control was coming to be anticipated.

On 23 June 1966 the bishops and cardinals on the Commission met separately from the experts, and voted by secret ballot on a series of questions. The answers to the basic question 'Is contraception intrinsically[14] wrong?' were Yes – 2; Yes, with reservations – 1; Abstention – 3; No – 9. Heenan appears to have abstained. This majority of bishops and cardinals went on to approve the report to be submitted to the Pope recommending a change in teaching. Cardinal Ottaviani, leader of the minority among the bishops and cardinals, also supplied the Pope with a paper prepared by the dissenting minority of four theologians. The majority report contained a long discussion, headed 'Pastoral Introduction', which set out in plain language what the majority thought the new position ought to be, and how it was to be explained in the light of what had gone before. It was designed for public consumption. In effect it would have been a substitute for the encyclical *Humanae Vitae* which was in fact issued by Pope Paul VI two years later, and which took the opposite line.

The majority's 'Pastoral Introduction' attempted a somewhat retrospective reinterpretation of the Church's teaching, in order to try to demonstrate that the proposed new teaching allowing contraceptives was not entirely inconsistent with it.

> What has been condemned in the past and remains so today is the unjustified refusal of life, arbitrary human intervention for the sake of moments of egoistical pleasure; in short, the rejection of procreation as a specific task of marriage. In the past the Church could not speak other than she did, because the problem of birth control did not confront human consciousness in the same way. Today, having clearly recognised the legitimacy and even the duty of regulating births, she recognises too that human intervention in the process of the marriage act for reasons drawn from the finality[15] of marriage itself should not always be excluded, provided that the criteria of morality are always safeguarded.

From whatever point of view it is looked at, this cannot be regarded as a completely honest summary of the history of Catholic teaching on this point. By refusing to accept that they were in fact proposing a fundamental development on the key point rather than a slight adjustment, they were refusing to face the one objection to the course of action they favoured which was most persuasive and which eventually prevailed – namely that Catholic tradition and the authority of the *magisterium* might be undermined by such a move. It was not necessarily an unanswerable objection, but it required a lot more theological work on the issue of the Church's teaching authority than the majority gave it. Most of them were from the wrong theological specialities to have opened the issue up in a positive and creative way. They needed some first-rate ecclesiologists – specialists in the 'theology of the Church' – and perhaps an ecclesiastical historian or two.

One of the most important new theological ideas of the nineteenth century was John Henry Newman's notion of 'the development of doctrine'. He first put it forward in his final days as an Anglican, in order to answer the Anglican objection to Roman Catholicism that it had invented 'new' doctrines not explicitly found in Scripture, such as the primacy of the Pope. He and his Anglican friends were primarily interested not in the Protestant Reformation but in the patristic period of Church history, running from approximately the first to the seventh century. He believed that there was a continuity between the teachings of these early fathers and latter-day Catholicism, but they were not exactly the same. Buried within the old tradition, so to speak, were treasures waiting to be unearthed. The job of discerning true gold from false was for the Church authorities to perform, according to certain principles.

This meant it was no longer enough to reject a particular item of

Catholic doctrine as untrue simply because it was absent from the Fathers and absent from Scripture, if it could be shown to be a legitimate development subsequently approved by the Church. 'Development' implies a tangible connection between the new thought and the old one. But the term could cover what might look to ordinary mortals like a complete reversal. Thus it would be perfectly possible for the Catholic Church to teach, as it did until the nineteenth century, that slavery was under certain conditions permitted by natural law, and yet for it to teach, as it did by the middle of the twentieth century, that slavery was contrary to human rights. This was 'development'. In fact the underlying principle in both cases would have been the dignity of the human person made in the image of God. The argument that slavery might be compatible with natural law would be based on a theoretical model of what slavery could ideally entail – slavery with human dignity intact. Nice distinctions would have to be drawn between owning in perpetuity a person's person, so to speak, and owning in perpetuity the right to their labour. The fact that very few examples of such 'moral' slavery may actually have existed did not rule out the possibility. (In this case, slavery would seem to be condoned by Scripture, so this doctrinal development would be away from Scripture.)

But Newman's idea, though necessary to the defence of Catholicism against Anglican criticism, was in turn highly subversive of the Counter Reformation image of Church doctrine as unchanging and permanent. To prove an idea wrong it was enough to show that it was not the same as the teaching of the Council of Trent or an earlier council of equal weight. Before Newman, there was no real concept of development as a rational historical process. If the Church had any new ideas at all, they came from the Holy Spirit (if they were deemed correct) or the Devil (if not). There are striking parallels between Newman's theory of development and Darwin's theory of evolution (and they appeared within ten years of each other). In the Catholic sense of the term, species 'developed'. In the Darwinian sense, doctrines 'evolved'. In neither case did they suddenly arrive fully formed as a gift from the Creator, as had previously been supposed.[16]

The Second Vatican Council was rich in developments of this kind, some of which looked (to people like Archbishop Roberts, for instance) like reversals. Developments had taken place even in the specific area of contraception, such as Pius XII's approval of the use of the rhythm method in 1951. Paul VI's *Humanae Vitae* of 1968 was itself a development in some respects: it took a very different tone from that adopted by Pius XI in 1931. Given a Church awash with doctrinal developments as the Catholic Church was in the middle of the 1960s, the objection to a new policy on contraception on the grounds that it might undermine the weight given to tradition or weaken the authority of the Pope began to look unconvincing. Tradition and papal authority had both been recast by the Council. And hadn't generations of Catholics been taught to believe that St Pius V in the sixteenth century had ruled out changes in the Tridentine rite of Mass for ever and ever?[17]

Promising though such avenues might have been, they were left unexplored. Once the cardinals, bishops and theologians of the Papal Commission had done their work (however inadequately) and returned to their dioceses or universities, all went relatively quiet in the Catholic Church, at least on the surface. The world was waiting for the Pope to speak; no one actually jumped the gun. But nowhere in the world came nearer to doing so than Liverpool, in the unlikely form of the new Archbishop, the successor to Heenan – George Andrew Beck. He was not a moral theologian but a former headmaster and he was certainly not a radical. Heenan had even forbidden him to make a speech at the Council against ecumenism. But now he nearly split the Church wide open, and a spectacular resignation must have been on the cards.

In November 1967, in conditions of secrecy, Archbishop Beck drew up a document headed 'Statement for Council of Clergy'.[18] Whom he consulted is not clear, though some clue may be gleaned from the fact that when he owned up to his 'misdemeanour' at the Bishops' Conference the following year, he listed three moral theologians as having had copies: Maurice O'Leary (of the Catholic Marriage Advisory Council); Kevin Kelly (of Upholland); and Enda McDonagh (of Maynooth). Only the latter two would have been sympathetic to the line Beck took. It is unlikely, though not impossible, that Beck drafted all this himself. What had clearly moved him to act was the growing evidence (he mentioned the leaks in *The Tablet*) that the Birth Control Commission had rejected the natural law argument against contraception. Such actions could still be wrong, but not invariably wrong, wrong *per se*. In other words there may be cases where the use of contraceptives could be justified, for instance if that was the only means for safeguarding the good of the children of the marriage and the love and support between their parents.

Beck began what he called his 'Statement for Council of Clergy' with an explanation of why he thought it necessary. 'A letter from one of the deanery conferences draws attention to the acute pastoral problem caused by the present birth control controversy', he stated. 'It was appreciated that Pope Paul had said that Catholic practice in this matter should remain unchanged, but guidance at local level was asked for. After much thought and advice I have decided that it is my pastoral responsibility to offer some guidance to the clergy of the archdiocese . . . What I now say is – at least for the present – confidential to the clergy and not in any way for publication.'

He then put forward an exposition of the Catholic theology of marriage, based on tradition and the teaching of the Second Vatican Council's decree *The Church in the Modern World*. As a result of that, he said, the Church no longer talked of the 'procreational' and the 'relational' aspects of sex as primary and secondary. They were now seen to constitute an 'intrinsic unity'. So the Church's teaching was open to development, which would occur to the extent that it deepened its understanding of these values. He went on to quote from the leaked Majority Report of the Papal Birth Control Commission, and then asked the crucial question: 'What is the position of the priest whose advice is sought on this matter?' There were, he said, various alternatives. It was possible to say the rule against birth control was now doubtful and therefore did not bind. He hesitated to go that far. Nor was he happy with the simple solution, that a priest may advise a penitent simply to 'follow his own conscience'. 'In this matter many people will interpret this as meaning, Never mind what the Pope says, follow your own conscience'. To give this impression could easily undermine the whole authority of the Church's *magisterium*.' But he was no more attracted by the opposite, the minority report of the Birth Control Commission. 'A logical conclusion of this view would seem to be that no contraceptive practice can be allowed and consequently reception of the Sacraments must be refused to any who continue in the practice.'

He explained: 'The important point is that the absolute inviolability of the law on contraception has been drawn from its interpretation as a demand of the Natural Law. The axiom has always been – if a thing is intrinsically evil it cannot be done in any circumstances and for any good reason. The absolute inviolability has been drawn from its Natural Law character, not from its character as a demand of the Church.'

But this was longer sustainable.

The present state of theological thinking seems to be overwhelmingly in favour of rejecting the view that contraception is against the Natural Law, that it is intrinsically evil. This means that it is legitimate for us to see only one source for the binding force of the Church's teaching on contraception and that is the directive of the Church . . .

No priest should ever say: 'The Church is wrong in forbidding contraception', just as he should never say that the Church is wrong in commanding Sunday Mass. But he can say to an individual – 'I do not think you are committing sin by missing Mass in your circumstances'; and likewise it is suggested that he can equally say to an individual 'I do not think you are committing sin by practising contraception in your circumstances.'

With this view Beck agreed, and commended it to his clergy.

The Church's awareness of the essential values of marriage especially as a 'community of love' has undergone remarkable development in the recent past. If in a given case these values are seriously endangered by following the Church's traditional teaching on contraception, an individual couple may judge that they are excused from the observance of the concrete directive which is embodied in this teaching.

He set out the detailed criteria priests should apply when asked their advice or when dealing with these matters in the confessional. In essence, his answer was: nothing without good reason, rhythm where possible, contraception where necessary, sterilization rarely, abortion never.

'If the rhythm method is impossible or uncertain, and if the priest is satisfied that the penitent or person consulting him has a proper concern for the essential values of Christian marriage, and a true respect for the authority of the Church, he would be justified in not condemning as sinful a couple's decision to use some means of contraception, for example the contraceptive pill.' He also pointed out that it was the pastoral duty of the priest 'to assist others to make their own judgement of conscience, not to make the judgement for them'.

Beck read this 2,800-word statement to a select group of clergy in Liverpool but did not hand out copies; and then he fielded questions. One priest asked from the floor: 'Is anal intercourse still out?' and Beck said it was. This was not wholly absurd, as one of the arguments used by the minority of four theologians in the Birth Control Commission had been that allowing the use of condoms could logically lead to allowing oral and anal intercourse – in that chaste and celibate company, a knock-down argument. Traditionally, oral and anal intercourse had been lumped with condoms, masturbation and *coitus interruptus* as things which deviated from the natural use of sex. If the natural law argument was no longer applicable against condoms, did it any longer apply to other actions which had been condemned on the same theoretical basis? This 'How far can you go?' question – once contraception is allowed – is one the Church of England, for instance, has still not resolved. The four theologians clearly had a powerful point. It was one of the major defects of the 'Pastoral Introduction' in favour of change that it never properly addressed this objection.

Beck then sent his copies of his statement to Cardinal Heenan, who appears not to have responded, and to the Apostolic Delegate in Wimble-don,[19] whom he also went to talk to in person. The Delegate asked him to send a copy of his text to Rome. Two months later – not exactly in haste – he had a letter from Cardinal Cicognani, Vatican Secretary of State. (The file copy is somewhat dog-eared, showing every sign of having been carried round in Beck's jacket pocket for some time.) It stated:

> His Holiness bids me assure Your Grace that he is well aware of your devotion and loyalty to the Holy See, and that he can well understand the concern in conscience which prompted Your Grace to make known to your clergy certain practical norms regarding the pastoral treatment of the present problem of family limitation. His Holiness would have me, nonetheless, communicate to you that, while awaiting an authoritative statement of the supreme *Magisterium* in this delicate matter, Catholics should be advised that the norm hitherto taught by the Church, and integrated with the wise instructions of the Council, is to be faithfully and generously observed. For this reason the 'Statement for Council of Clergy' which your Grace has prepared should not be published or distributed.

Beck wrote back saying he would scrupulously respect the Holy Father's wishes, and appears to have taken no further action (not even to withdraw the guidance he had given members of the Council of Clergy. They knew he had not followed up his meeting by circulating the document, but none of them knew the Vatican had intervened to stop him.) He reported all this to the spring meeting of the English and Welsh Bishops' Conference, not many months before the storm broke. This was not the first time, of course, that Beck had been forced to withdraw a paper he had carefully worked on – as when Heenan (tipped off by Worlock) had stopped him making a speech at the Council against ecumenism.

The publication of *Humanae Vitae* on 28 July 1968 was preceded by a private letter to all Catholic bishops throughout the world, signed by Cardinal Cicognani, in which he passed on the Pope's hope that they would loyally support him in the coming crisis.[20] Cicognani told the bishops that the Pope 'knew full well the bitterness that his reply may cause many married persons who were expecting a different solution'. He went on to appeal, on the Pope's behalf, for all the bishops to 'stand beside him more firmly than ever in this circumstance, and to help him present this delicate point of the Church's teaching to the Christian people'. The two-page letter, presumably drafted by Pope Paul himself, was a revelation of extra-ordinary papal anguish and vulnerability that was bound to move his fellow bishops to rally to him out of solidarity and loyalty as best they could. But it was also very firm: neither in the confessional nor in the pulpit could any ambiguity be tolerated concerning the Catholic Church's view of birth control.

The encyclical did not get a good press, even in the normally loyal Catholic weeklies. *The Tablet* began its leader on 3 August 1968 'Crisis in the Church' with the words: '*Gaudium et Spes*, the famous pastoral constitution of Vatican II, is more frequently cited than any other authoritative document in the Pope's encyclical on birth control *Humanae Vitae*. We must honestly confess that neither joy nor hope can we derive from the encyclical itself.'[21]

Once the encyclical had appeared, Beck issued a pastoral letter to his archdiocese, to be read in all churches in Liverpool, in which he commended the encyclical for its 'far-sighted and noble vision'. He did not beat about the bush, quoting in his opening words the decisive judgement of *Humanae Vitae* which ruled out birth control: 'Each and every marriage act must remain open to the transmission of life.' In what may have been a slight hint of his own difficulties, he concluded: 'I pray earnestly that all our people in the archdiocese will listen to the words of the Vicar of Christ, and that we shall all have the grace and courage to accept them with sincere loyalty.' But he also added, a little disingenuously in view of his statement of the previous year, that 'the Pope has thus brought to an end the long period of waiting for an authoritative statement – a period which may well have allowed wishful thinking by many to assume that there would be a change of doctrine in this matter'. Despite this, he was subsequently to give a long interview to the *Catholic Herald*[22] in which he raised expectations of change (or development) once more. 'The Holy Father has given a lead in this matter', he said. 'I don't think he has closed the door absolutely and perhaps with careful thought to what he has said there may be movement in the mind of the Church to a full realisation of Christ's purposes in the whole institution of marriage.'

In fact Beck had not really altered the position he put out in his 'Statement to Council of Clergy' of the previous November. Indeed, nothing in *Humanae Vitae* disproved the points he had made in his Statement except that it was no longer possible to deduce anything from the silence of the Pope. A year after that débâcle, four months after the encyclical, he received the following heartfelt handwritten letter from a married couple living in Liverpool:

I am a teacher aged 35 with four children ranging from 10 years to five months in age, living in a small semi. We are in good health thank God, and enjoy a comfortable if non-luxurious standard of living; this may give you a picture of our situation. My wife and I feel that our young family is enough to cope with, to care for with patience and individuality, to wash, clean and mend for, to clothe, feed, educate and shelter – another child would mean moving to a larger house, and this is beyond our means. My wife has gone through 36 months of pregnancy and has had ten years of baby-minding with another ten to come. We honestly believe that to have another child would be to stretch our capabilities, economic, mental, physical and most important emotional, too far.

We have used the safe period on and off for about six years and yet our two youngest children, wonderful though they are, were 'unexpected'; it could be said that two failings in 72 months is a good record, but we feel that one more failing would be too much.

We were deeply disturbed by the Encyclical. We cannot see that, after having four children, we must now be banned from showing each other our love, from worshipping each other's bodies. We don't want an easy affluent life – there is too much positive work to do for Christ in this lop-sided cruel lonely world for that. And so, after much prayer, reading and thought, we approached a priest, separately, and discussed our dilemma. The result was that he agreed that, as long as we felt in conscience that we were doing right, we may practise contraception, and are not only allowed but urged to receive Holy Communion; and that, as we feel we are doing right, it is not a matter for the confessional. Consequently we now practise contraception: we use the sheath as we fear an eventual health hazard with the Pill. We have found that, free from the worry of conception, our sexual act is attaining a happiness hitherto unknown to us; far from encouraging faithlessness it is drawing us closer together. In the joy of our new freedom we use it perhaps to excess, but no doubt we shall achieve a pattern of moderation.

We are worried, however, that we are acting against the command of the Pope, the inspired Vicar of Christ. I can't help feeling that, as I reject this command, I should forfeit the right to the benefits of our Church and should leave it; but how else can I maintain a right conscience? This comes hard on me who usually attend Mass three times a week – this is not boasting, but showing the depth of my concern. We obviously must go on praying for guidance. I am sorry to have written at such length in such detail, but I think it right that the lay view should be put before you. May we humbly take the opportunity, Your Grace, to thank you for the compassionate attitude towards your people, priests and lay, which you have adopted throughout this difficult time. We would like to wish you good health and assure you of the prayers of our children and ourselves.

Beck replied immediately, saying:

> I am bound as your archbishop to proclaim objectively the teaching of the Holy Father, and I am quite sure he has expressed an ideal of Christian marriage which needs to be kept constantly in mind. On the other hand, both the Holy Father and the bishops of this country have recognised that there may be many people who find themselves unable in conscience to accept the teaching of the encyclical, or while accepting it in principle find that they cannot adhere to it in practice. It seems clear to me from what you tell me that you and your wife have conscientiously fulfilled your duty in discussing your problem with a priest, and I think you may accept his guidance. I am sure it would be a mistake in the present circumstances to think of leaving the Church or of abandoning the sacraments, though, as you say in your letter, you must continue to pray that the Holy Spirit will enlighten you fully in this difficult and delicate matter.

In fact *Humanae Vitae* specifically rejected the argument that its ruling was merely an 'ideal' to be aimed at. In assuring this couple that they may use contraceptives, and by implication applauding the priest who told them this, he was driving a coach and horses through the encyclical.

Meanwhile, in Portsmouth, Derek Worlock was facing a not dissimilar outbreak of dissent from the faithful. He said later it virtually took over his life for a whole month. In a sense his immediate constituency covered the whole country, for he was President of the Laity Commission, a post-Vatican II 'structure' that had been set up so that bishops could hear what a select but not unrepresentative group of lay Catholics had to say on the issues of the day. Several members were well known to Worlock from the days of his 'Team', showing that he had been given considerable discretion over picking his friends for membership of the Laity Commission. In the light of his views of the importance of lay formation, and of the 'menace' of the untrained layman, it may be assumed that he had every confidence in its members as exemplary post-Vatican II lay apostles.

And they revolted too. The dissent was unanimous. A working paper attacking *Humanae Vitae* and clearly emanating from the Laity Commission was leaked to *The Times*.[23] (Laity Commission minutes record that one unnamed member admitted he had been the unwitting sources of this leak, and his offer of resignation was declined.) Dr Paul Black, Chairman of the Laity Commission (Worlock was President) then wrote to Cardinal Heenan, saying that if *Humanae Vitae* was to be understood by the laity, 'a fuller explanation than the document itself provides is required'. That was a veiled criticism of the papal text: in other words it did not prove its case.

Black went on:

> We have particular concern for certain people who are placed in special diffi-
> culties by the encyclical. Those include: those who cannot in conscience accept
> all of its teaching and who at the same time have professional responsibilities
> affected by it; those priests who are experiencing a conflict between the disci-
> pline of their ministry and their own conscientious views: and those Catholics
> who because of difficulty in understanding the teaching, feel that they cannot
> conscientiously accept it, and that therefore they have no alternative but to
> leave the church.

This last point was a new one, and likely to be very telling. It may not be
fanciful to see Worlock's hand in it, as he had great skill in asking questions
that seemed courteous enough but in fact went to the heart of the matter.
It was his habit to advise groups he was involved with on how to make their
point to best advantage and a minimum of acrimony. In the mental equip-
ment the bishops brought to bear on the problem of adverse lay reaction to
Humanae Vitae, they would have been guided by the old distinctions
between 'Good Catholics' and 'Bad Catholics'. From time to time they had
tried to apply those categories to the public debate, especially in the
approach many of them had chosen to adopt – that coming round to an
acceptance of papal teaching was bound to take time. That is to say good
Catholics had been led to become less good, because of the uncertainty of
Church teaching, misguided leadership, the Press, whatever. Their recovery of their full 'Good Catholic' status would not happen overnight.
Patience was required.

The bishops were treating the use of contraception, so to speak, as a
habitual sin. This was familiar territory to experienced practitioners of the
confessional. The very presence of the habit reduced the element of free
will and hence reduced culpability. Priests were encouraged not to treat
reliance on birth control as a mortal sin (which required full moral
consent). The appropriate analogies in the confessional would be with, say,
masturbation or alcoholism. The individual may have to fight the sinful
tendency over a period, would need constant encouragement, would fall
and be forgiven in the confessional, and fall again, and be forgiven again;
until eventually, with prayer and the grace of God, the sinful habit was
mastered. It is possible the bishops were recollecting their own struggles
with various temptations against chastity when they were young seminarians. This is precisely the kind of spiritual counselling they would have
been given.

Quite what sort of thing the bishops imagined going on in the bedrooms of the faithful was not clear. It is hard to see how anyone can succumb to the use of contraception in a moment of temptation, under the influence, say, of addiction or sexual arousal. Contraceptives, whether by the condom or the Pill, require a certain amount of cold-blooded pre-planning. The only form of contraception likely to be used on the spur of the moment was *coitus interruptus*,[24] which is not what everyone was talking about. This argument – that Catholics who used contraceptives did so out of moral weakness – was often bolstered by the observation that self-control was an important Christian virtue, with the implication that those who use contraceptives, especially men, did so mainly out of selfishness. 'Is it too much to ask Catholic couples to abstain from sex for a few days each month?' was typical of the sort of comments made by bishops at the outset,[25] and an indication of how wide the gulf was.

What the Laity Commission was saying did not begin to fit this pattern of temptation momentarily and selfishly succumbed to. In particular a 'Good Catholic' who felt driven by his own conscience to quit the Catholic Church, because of a disagreement over a point of teaching, was a contradiction in terms. Theory said it was 'Good Catholics' who followed their consciences and stayed in the Church; 'Bad Catholics' who didn't.

While the Laity Commission took the subtle approach, its sister body, the Bishops' Conference Social Welfare Commission, simply kicked down the door. It wrote to the Bishops' Conference Episcopal Secretary (Derek Worlock again, wearing another hat), saying:

> The Commission for Social Welfare of the RC Bishops' Conference of England and Wales regrets the publication of the Encyclical *Humanae Vitae*. Its sincerity is not in doubt. But the encyclical's failure to develop an adequate concept of responsible parenthood in Christian marriage defeats its own ends: responsibility demands informed choice, which can be guided but not directed. The positive aims of the encyclical – to support the family and to encourage the adoption of creative social policies – are unattainable without first educating the consciences of peoples and governments. This the encyclical signally fails to do. Men of good will were looking for guidance in facing an increasingly uncertain future. They have been told how they must behave: they have not been taught how to evaluate their own evolving experience. We cannot regard the publication of the encyclical as closing the debate. We propose in consultation with other relevant commissions to prepare a detailed statement of our position.

The bishops who received this critique were remarkably good humoured about it – the Conference minutes merely record that a little more care might be taken in appointing members of such commissions in future.

There is an important truth revealed by this language. Lay people who were senior enough in their lay professions and respected enough in the Church to be appointed as members of a national commission of the Bishops' Conference thought they were being treated like naughty children. It is in this respect that a serious misreading of their own relationship with the clergy and laity had finally caught up with the bishops. The bishops had shared the experience of the Second Vatican Council together. They had, by and large, travelled with it a long way and were still on board. They saw their next task as passing on to the laity the fresh wisdom and new insights the Council had assembled. Some of them, like Worlock, had gone at this with great gusto. But virtually all of them had failed to see that many of the laity were already ahead of them. Dispensing with the regulated 'lay formation' so beloved of Worlock, a certain type of educated lay person in Britain had studied, bought books, talked, attended lectures, joined societies, and above all pored over the secular and religious Press for every detail of the Council's business, every twist and turn of the debates. If anything, they were ahead of the bishops and knew more. They had read the progressive Continental theologians that the bishops had only passed by in the Vatican II corridors. They had become well versed in the terms of the contraception debate. They weren't ready for the bishops to patronize them.

The Newman Association, the official society for Catholic university graduates, was a typical lay organization of this type. Immediately after *Humanae Vitae* appeared, its Executive Committee wrote to the Bishops' Conference to say it was 'gravely concerned' by the encyclical, not least that 'the manner of the promulgation of the encyclical . . . appears to disregard the principle of collegiality'. Translated from theology into English, this was tantamount to crying 'Foul!'.

There were of course those who knew little of all this, and they stood just about where the bishops thought everybody stood: needing to be told. There were also groups who bitterly opposed the agitations of the progressive laity, saw it as rank disloyalty to the Pope and regarded the bishops' failure to suppress it with gunfire, so to speak, as wicked collusion with the Church's enemies. Bishops' postbags filled with letters from all types.[26]

Meanwhile some members of the Laity Commission formed a protest group, known as the London Ad Hoc Committee, with a number of other Catholics. Their concern was to campaign on behalf of various priests who had been quoted, in the days immediately after the publication of *Humanae Vitae*, as saying they did not agree with it and who faced being disciplined for it. Some of them had already been summarily removed from their parishes. One, Father Kenneth Allan of Coulsdon, Surrey, quoted Canon Law back at his bishop (the late Archbishop Cyril Cowderoy of Southwark) to the effect that he could not be removed without due process, on conviction of a *crimen* (an offence against Canon Law). Told that in that case he would be suspended instead, pending due process, he said that was unlawful under Canon Law too; and promptly returned to his parish.[27] Every day the newspapers were full of such stories, the latest round in what had become a bitter struggle between bishops and dissenting priests. Priests would come straight from angry interviews with their bishops, and give Press conferences in the street outside. For at least a fortnight it was Fleet Street's favourite story: it remained a front page item all summer. Reporters interviewed Catholics coming away from Sunday Mass; they doorstepped bishops' meetings; they organized opinion polls; television cameras turned up to cover routine meetings of organizations that had never seen the light of day before.

One priest was suspended by the Portsmouth diocese Vicar General while Worlock was away on holiday that summer; but promptly reinstated without fuss when he returned. That was the limit of the damage in Portsmouth. Writing not long afterwards from Rome, where he was attending a meeting of the *Consilium de Laicis* (Council of the Laity), in a letter addressed to his clergy dated 2 October 1968, Worlock contrasted the coolness of the Italian reaction to *Humanae Vitae* with the heated British reaction.

There is no obvious evidence of concern, certainly nothing to compare with what we have known since the end of July. I have noticed that in recent years speakers have occasionally slipped up by saying 'Before the War' instead of 'Before the Council'. Now we have a new point of departure: 'Before the Encyclical'. It is almost as if there had never been another; clearly there has never been another to compare with it so far as reaction is concerned. For weeks it has moved in and out of the main headlines of the newspapers. What a London curate had or had not said outside his church became the principal item in the television news. To discover a BBC magazine programme when the encyclical was not featured was almost an achievement. I doubt if there has ever been anything like it in this age of mass media. There is a saying in Fleet Street that no summer story survives the beginning of October. The radio this morning suggests that *The Times* today is endeavouring to prove this wrong. My fellow members of this *Consilium* all confirm the major part played by the Press throughout the world in keeping up the pressure on this issue. Last week there were reports of many representatives of Continental magazines present in London to fan the apparently dying flames of controversy.

In the same letter to his clergy Worlock set out his own tolerant and patient approach to these problems and commended it to his priests. He recalled the two conferences he had held in Portsmouth diocese for them, which appeared to have gone harmoniously enough although there were the same divisions of opinion as elsewhere in the Church. He added: 'Let us not be too ready to put heads through nooses, our own or anyone else's. And let us try to get a little joy back into living the Gospel.'

The event reported on the radio that morning was a sensational letter published in *The Times* signed by 55 priests. 'We respect the decision on birth control made by our Holy Father the Pope according to his conscience', they wrote.

> We realise the possible grave dangers that can result from the indiscriminate use of artificial means of birth control. We deeply regret, however, that according to our consciences we cannot give loyal internal and external obedience to the view that all such means of contraception are in all circumstances wrong. As priests we feel that our duty towards Catholic people compels us to bear witness to the truth as we see it.

The letter was organized by three priests, Kenneth Allan, already mentioned, together with Nigel Collingwood and Peter De Rosa. They had offered *The Times* a longer list of names but only had the signatures of the 55 whose names appeared, and it was the paper's policy to insist on original signatures in every case.

Worlock's insouciance in his letter to priests may have been somewhat forced, judging from his files. The preparation of his own pastoral letter on *Humanae Vitae*[28] caused him a great deal of anguish and uncertainty. He started it again and again, amended his manuscript radically, and covered page after page with second thoughts and third thoughts. He switched targets, blaming at one point the Press, then substituting 'irresponsible commentators'. As the pastoral letter took shape, his amendments seem to indicate that he was not sure what the real issue was. He was fairly sure what it wasn't – contraception. A phrase appears in the early drafts, which is honed as he rewrites. First: 'And all this about a matter touching, it is true, the very origin of life, yet scarcely the test of being for Christ or against Him.' This becomes: 'Clearly other wider and more fundamental issues are also indirectly involved. Yet it is important that we should see this question of the regulation of births within the wider context of the Christian life, for it is scarcely the acid test of being for Christ or against Him.' This latter phrase, with slight variations ('not the acid test of Christianity' being one) became the Worlock media sound-bite of the *Humanae*

Vitae crisis, and it certainly helped to defuse the row. Heenan's equivalent to this was given in a television interview with David Frost, who asked what the Cardinal would say if a person in the confession box admitted using contraceptives but claimed to be doing so with a good conscience. 'I would say God bless you', replied Heenan. Frost was not a Catholic, and failed to follow up with 'But would you give him absolution?' which was the real issue.

Worlock had decided that the central issue was about authority, and how it should be exercised. His answer to that is made clearer by his actions: no priests were suspended in Portsmouth for voicing dissent over *Humanae Vitae*. As the dust began to settle, he came under pressure from the Laity Commission, of which he remained President, to do something about priests suspended in other dioceses. The most obstinate case was Nottingham under its particularly hardline bishop (Edward Ellis), who had suspended five priests and refused to reinstate them. Asked by someone in Nottingham diocese to intervene in the dispute, Archbishop Beck agreed that it was damaging the reputation of the Catholic Church but added that Bishop Ellis was 'a man of integrity and of delicate conscience' who was unlikely to alter his views. As months and years went by the item 'Nottingham Five' reappears again and again in the minutes of the Laity Commission, usually with such remarks as 'President still dealing with it' or 'President to speak again to Cardinal', meaning Worlock. Eventually, the trail peters out: it has even been suggested that Worlock had some of them moved to his own diocese but preferred not to put that fact in writing. In any event, they ceased after a while to be a *cause célèbre*.

What helped Worlock deal with these articulate lay people was a surprisingly conciliatory statement[29] from the Bishops' Conference in mid-September of 1968. The first draft[30] was prepared by Bishop (formerly Abbot) Basil Christopher Butler, who was their best theologian, albeit not a specialist in moral theology. The paper by Bishop Butler pleased Beck, who wrote back saying 'I am very much in sympathy with all that you say' and in return forwarded a copy of his aborted 'Statement for Council of Clergy' that the Vatican had stamped on the previous year. In the privacy of this correspondence between bishops, Beck did not explain that he had since changed his mind. On the contrary, he wrote: 'I cannot see how specific actions in, for example, the use of marriage can be regulated in detail by the natural law.' It is not clear why, but a different copy of Beck's 1967 document appears in Worlock's files, apparently typed on the same typewriter used for official papers for the Bishops' Conference September meeting. This strongly implies Heenan (or Worlock himself, as episcopal secretary) had decided that it should be circulated to all the bishops. It also implies that the bishops knew that at least one of their number, a much-liked and respected senior figure, was having considerable trouble coming to terms with *Humanae Vitae* himself. This was something the Press never even began to realize: the controversy was entirely reported as pope-and-bishops versus priests-and-laity. The very solidarity between bishops that had made them want to stand by the Pope, must now have moved them to want to stand by Archbishop Beck. This goes a long way towards explaining the conciliatory tone of the September statement.

Butler's paper had been amended into a second draft,[31] which shows evidence of input from Heenan. Rumours circulated afterwards that the meeting had been a heated one, but no record of the discussion is in Worlock's files. Clearly there was no inclination among the bishops to reopen the key doctrinal point. They knew they could not alter it. The question was how to appear to endorse the encyclical without on the one hand driving into a corner those like Beck and Butler, who had serious reservations about the papal ruling, while on the other hand demonstrating their loyalty to the Pope and his teaching office. Butler was useful because of his grasp of the issue of authority, having worked on *Lumen Gentium* during the Council. To assist them they asked two moral theologians, Monsignor Lawrence McReavy and Father Jack Mahoney SJ, to prepare answers to a series of questions.

The most significant and original passage of the bishops' statement, paragraph 6, declared:

At one time not only Catholics but all Christians held contraception to be abhorrent. In recent years, however, doubts have been expressed about the Church's interpretation of the moral law. The very fact that the Pope created a commission to review the question tended to confirm their doubts. It was soon widely believed that a change in the Church's attitude would be announced. Understandably many wives and husbands, anticipating the promised statement of the Pope, have come to rely on contraception. In this they have acted conscientiously and often after seeking pastoral advice. They may now be unable to see that, at least in their personal circumstances, the use of contraception is wrong. A particular difficulty faces those who after serious thought and prayer cannot as yet understand or be fully convinced of the doctrines as laid down. This is not surprising in view of the discussions of recent years which have resulted in the present controversy.

For others the problem of putting the doctrine into practice in their lives seems insuperable because of ill-health or other serious obstacles, sometimes because of a conflict of duties. All should bear in mind the great weight which attaches to a pronouncement the from Holy Father . . . It is not unreasonable to ask all to practise the Christian virtue of humility and acknowledge the duty of every Catholic to listen with respect to the voice of the Vicar of Christ.

It was a remarkably liberal exposition of the case, and its circulation round the international Church may have been the first moment that Catholics elsewhere realized that English Catholicism was going through, or had gone through, a sea-change (more or less from conservative to progressive; though Heenan, for one, came to hate those terms).

McReavy's defence of the encyclical, in one of his answers to the bishops' questionnaire, may serve as one of the best explanations of how and why the bishops became convinced that the encyclical's crucial ruling was the right one, aside from their instinct to think so out of sheer loyalty. Like Beck, they were well aware that the argument from pure reason – the natural law argument – had been found wanting by the majority on the Birth Control Commission. They were also aware that the encyclical's own statement of that argument was weak. In one of his less convincing passages, Pope Paul VI had asserted:

> They must also recognise that an act of mutual love which impairs the capacity to transmit life which God the Creator, through specific laws, has built into it, frustrates His design which constitutes the norm of marriage, and contradicts the will of the Author of life. Hence to use this divine gift while depriving it, even if only partially, of its meaning and purpose, is equally repugnant to the nature of man and of woman, and is consequently in opposition to the plan of God and His holy will. But to experience the gift of married love while respecting the laws of conception is to acknowledge that one is not the master of the sources of life but rather the minister of the design established by the Creator. Just as man does not have unlimited dominion over his body in general, so also, and with more particular reason, he has no such dominion over his specifically sexual faculties, for these are concerned by their very nature with the generation of life, of which God is the source.

Those not already convinced would quickly come to a stop in such a passage as they waded through a deepening pile of *non sequiturs* and begged questions. *Non sequiturs* are a give-away – they do not matter, and may even be invisible, to those for whom the truth of the argument is already obvious. But they loom ever larger in the mind of someone trying to see the point but failing to do so, as his intellect screams with ever-increasing exasperation at the text – 'Yes, but why . . . *why?*' It appears that the Pope could not imagine anyone in good faith disagreeing with him. He actually stated at one point: 'If each of these essential qualities, the unitive and the procreative, is preserved, the use of marriage fully retains its sense of true mutual love and its ordination to the supreme responsibility of parenthood to which man is called. We believe that our contemporaries are particularly capable of seeing that this teaching is in harmony with human reason' – which must be the one statement in the whole encyclical that everybody could agree was manifestly not true.

McReavy, in his paper for the bishops, put the Pope's essential case much better. He gave an answer to the 'Why?' He wrote:

> Though the morality of contraception is a question of the natural law, the Church's doctrine is not based simply on human reasoning . . . Right reason can discern in the conjugal act a twofold significance, procreative and unitive, but I doubt whether it can prove that the one may never be sacrificed to the other. When however the sexual faculty and its use in marriage are examined in the light of man's revealed destiny, they emerge as something very much more than a natural function. We are confronted by an astonishing divine con-descension on which *Humanae Vitae* touches in its opening words (I regret that it did not develop them further). We know from revelation that the ultimate purpose of the whole of this visible and temporal creation is to build up the divine family of adopted Sons who, made partakers of the divine nature, are destined to live in an eternal union of love with God their Father.
>
> The astonishing truth, implicit in Genesis 1–3, is that the Creator has chosen to make His own creatures His free and responsible collaborators in the working out of His design. Not only that, He has made the achievement of His design dependent on their free collaboration. Only when, as a result of their preliminary mutual action, natural forces have brought about a conception, does He create and infuse another spiritual and immortal soul who turns the product of their union into a potential son of God. When the procreative ori-entation of the conjugal act is seen in this light, it acquires a sacred character which no amount of natural reasoning will ever discover . . . Only in this light can one assess the extent of man's moral obligation to respect the procreative as well as the unitive significance of the conjugal act. It is, I suggest, these supernatural considerations, the viewpoint of faith, which have led the church to regard the procreative orientation as sacrosanct.

That certainly elevates the argument to a higher plane. What McReavy does not do, however, is to demonstrate why this principle has no excep-tions whatever, in any circumstances. The idea that the rule against contraception had no exceptions derives in part from the way Catholic moral theology handles the natural law. The evil of an act contrary to the natural law was intrinsic, contained within the act itself, not taking its moral character from any external consideration. And 'one may not perform an evil act, even if good may come of it'. This was the difficulty on which the Catholic approach was impaled, unable to break free. It may have seemed like a small difference between the two sides, but in practice it was an unbridgeable one. On one side of the gulf, it offered a way out for the Catholic father of four from Liverpool whom Beck had dealt with so sympathetically. On the other side of the gulf, it simply told him 'No'.

What was never resolved in 1968 was how to handle the case where the natural law theory could only be applied in a suggestive or indicative way, but needed a supernatural law, so to speak, for the teaching to be completed. Did the philosophical logic of no exceptions, built into the natural law theory, still hold? Was it still correct to isolate a particular element in the human drama of sexual loving, and then to say that the frustration of its biological consequences was always and invariably an 'intrinsic evil'? It is not surprising that one of the suggestions Father Mahoney put to the bishops was for a 'working party of qualified priests' to explore the implications of the encyclical in confessional practice. He raised a number of issues still unclear, most of all the case of the 'drunken and/or overdemanding husband'. He asked: 'Can a wife defend herself from at least the consequences of such an attack? Is this contraception? It is not arbitrarily separating the generative from the unitive aspect of the act, as there is no true unitive aspect.' The questions Mahoney[32] was asking were risky, from the point of view of Church executives trying to shut down a quarrel rather than stoke one up again. No such working party was ever set up.

Nowhere in the controversy did the question arise – is it biologically correct to speak of the unitive and creative aspects of sexual love as belonging to a single act? The argument was conducted mainly between theologians rather than biologists or doctors. (And it is noteworthy that theologians were invariably male: female voices were absent from the considerations of the Papal Commission.) The Catholic theological tradition against contraception goes back to a time when ejaculation and fertilization were assumed to happen at the same moment.[33] It was not until well into the nineteenth century that medical science identified the two components, ovum and sperm, that had to come together to create a new embryo.[34] Until then the sperm had been assumed to be the only active component (*semen* means seed) and the female role was to be receptive and nurturing to it – fertile soil, as it were. In fact the meeting of sperm and ovum, leading to fertilization, may not happen for up to two days after intercourse; the woman will not be aware it is happening; and it is not part of the sex act. Nor is the readiness of an ovum for fertilization, and its presence at the right place at the right time in the woman's body, caused by the sex act (unlike ejaculation in the male case). It seems nature has already separated what Catholic doctrine insisted must be inseparable: a case of Nature contradicting Natural Law, perhaps. But it was not primarily the biological separation of intercourse and conception that fuelled the debate. It was the emotional separation.

Husbands and wives may feel strong and passionate physical attraction drawing them into an act of sexual love; but except in the sense of something to be avoided, their feelings are unlikely to be equally engaged with what the Church called 'procreation'. In the experience of sex itself, it is the 'unitive' (to use another Church word) which dominates. The stronger the sexual feelings, the less room there is for any other kind. Nor is it a coincidence that while the act of sex is commonly known as 'making love', it is rarely called 'making babies' (except as a kind of joke). In these respects too, the Church seemed to be insisting on not separating what in the experience of ordinary married people was already separate. And what underlined the sense of a natural separation between the 'unitive' and the 'procreative' purposes of sex was the fact that the Church permitted married couples to have sex while the woman was pregnant, after her menopause, after hysterectomy or similar surgery, during lactation, and at and near the time of menstruation (and elsewhere during the 'safe period'). In some such cases, fertilization was improbable or impossible; and if the latter, the famous *Humanae Vitae* phrase that sex must always be 'open to the transmission of life' had no possible meaning or relevance. It was as futile as suggesting that the eyes of a blind person must be 'open to the transmission of light'. Furthermore, neither the male nor the female sex drive seems to be altered in intensity by the time of the month (unlike with most other mammals), and hence it was independent of fertility. And the female orgasm itself seems to play no role in reproduction – it does not trigger, nor is it triggered by, the release of an ovum. An orgasmically frigid woman can be healthily fertile.

Worlock must have had to sit through many hours of discussion of topics such as these, though probably tailored to spare his celibate blushes. The Catholic atmosphere was thick with them. And never once did he say or imply that he thought that the Church could one day win this argument. He must have realized, from lay Catholic married couples he knew exceedingly well, how utterly convinced they were that *Humanae Vitae* was wrong. But throughout this time he never gave any hint that he thought so himself. He was loyal to the Church and its teaching: speculating on the truth or otherwise of a particular doctrine was not his forte.

The bishops' September statement began to pacify the laity, but did not solve the problem of priests who had been suspended, whose ranks had grown as a result of the '55' letter to *The Times*. This required another bishops' meeting and another statement. The evidence from the files is that Worlock played little part in the preparation of the September statement, but was crucial in the one that followed concerning the disciplining of recalcitrant priests. Considering that he was President of the Laity Commission, and that it was the Laity Commission which was officially raising this question, that is not surprising. Worlock's files show an earlier version of the final resolution, not dissimilar to it, in his own handwriting with his own amendments. That suggests he was the original drafter. This was not so unusual – ten years before, he used to draft all the bishops' resolutions.

It required priests 'to refrain in preaching, teaching, in the press, on radio and television or on public platforms, from opposing the teaching of the Pope in matters of faith and morals', adding 'if a priest is unwilling to give this undertaking it is for the bishop to decide whether, without scandal, he can be allowed to continue to act in the name of the Church. He need not, however, be required to cease celebrating Mass.' It went on: 'A priest cannot normally be allowed to hold faculties to hear Confessions unless he undertakes to declare faithfully the objective teaching of *Humanae Vitae* in the confessional and in giving spiritual guidance.'[35]

The bishops also resolved to let Cardinal Heenan draw up a standard letter to the clergy, containing these points, and if necessary to release it to the Press. Worlock later complained that he had been absent for that part of the meeting, and the 'No statement' decision at the start of the resolution was contradicted by the later decision to release Cardinal Heenan's letter.[36] That he was the primary author of the resolution is clear from a letter to Monsignor David Norris, who had taken the minutes, complaining that they were not quite accurate. 'It may be that an attempt has merely been made to tidy up my English; in fact some of the changes have changed the meaning . . .' he acidly remarked. How much change is not clear. The fact that Worlock was claiming authorship of the resolution's wording, and that he had been thought to be one of the most liberal of the bishops, seems like a contradiction. It even gave rise to a suspicion that Rome had said it did not like the conciliatory tone of the September statement, and wanted something tougher. There is no evidence for this, and Worlock's role makes it even more unlikely. He may have been taken by surprise by the adverse reaction to this statement; he, like everybody else, was sailing in uncharted territory.

The terms of this resolution seemed tough, but they were in fact only as tough as the local bishop wanted them to be. Heenan led the way in interpreting them tolerantly; most bishops followed his example. The principle behind the restriction on preaching was logical, in that a priest was technically a representative of the Church and had a duty to put forward the Church's policy, rather as an MP might be expected to put forward his party's policy, regardless of what private misgivings he might have had. In the confessional, penitents had a right to have the Church's line explained to them. But nothing the bishops said prevented a priest giving an honest answer to the question: 'That is what the church says – what do you think yourself, Father?' The Catholic Tory MP Norman St John Stevas, who had become a focus for anti-encyclical feeling in the country, put out a statement interpreting the statement that way and was not contradicted. In any event, there are no publicly recorded cases of a priest being refused faculties to hear confessions on the grounds mentioned in the bishops' statement.[37]

There was another unwritten implication behind the bishops' statement that was by no means apparent at the time, even to the bishops who voted for it. It was a tacit acknowledgement, at least for the time being, that there was nothing to be gained by an aggressive policy of promoting the teaching of *Humanae Vitae* in the parishes. This was where the statement was most eloquently silent. A bishop issued his carefully worded pastoral letter, and in many cases also a private letter to his priests,[38] and then left the subject alone. After a while, this became a difficult silence to break. And the habit of silence turned into a habit of trying to prevent all further discussion, on either side of the argument. Throughout the 1970s one of Derek Worlock's tasks was to keep the lid on the National Conference of Priests, where there were always liable to be priests clamouring to reopen the issue. His other task was to keep the lid on the laity.

Worlock had a hand in framing the request from the Laity Commission for discussion with the Bishops' Conference's own Theological Commission on the subject of *Humanae Vitae*. (Offering theological discussion to dissident laity became a standard tactic in defusing the row.) The Laity Commission, as well as the Social Welfare Commission, were raising questions about the encyclical that went far beyond issues of discipline. They were, in fact, questioning its truth. After some stopping and starting, a meeting was eventually arranged between representatives of the Laity Commission, the Social Welfare Commission (which did not seem very interested, but went along with it), and a team from the Theological Commission under George Patrick Dwyer, by then Archbishop of Birmingham. It was Dwyer whose analysis of the birth control issue Worlock had so much admired five years earlier.

The minutes of this meeting record very little. Indeed, the next Laity Commission meeting requested an expanded account of the proceedings because the minutes were so scanty – a request that was never met. While the Laity Commission was approaching these discussions with great seriousness, circulating, debating and agreeing position papers beforehand, the Theological Commission was less interested in debate. One Laity Commission working draft has amendments in Worlock's handwriting on it. The best description of the paper's attitude to *Humanae Vitae* would be 'deeply sceptical'. The effect of the amendments was to make it only slightly less so.

The promised series of follow-up meetings between laity and theologians never materialized. One lay participant later recalled:

> Archbishop Dwyer set up the meeting as a tutorial with lengthy papers given by the theologians, who seemed to assume we knew little, while our agenda was seeking responses or approaches to specific questions based on our experience. It was not entirely a surprise when the draft record of the meeting spent a long time on the corner of Archbishop Dwyer's desk and then seemed to fall into a waste bin. We were pretty fed up about the way the joint meeting was handled, and even more so about the loss of the record.

This matter was still dragging on at the start of 1970.

Playing it long and letting the dust settle may have been sound tactics, but it is doubtful whether they were deliberately chosen by the bishops. More likely they did not know what to do and were playing it by ear. There is nothing cynical about the bishops' tone when they discussed these things among themselves. They were genuinely flummoxed: they had their own agonies of conscience. One further factor may have influenced how they felt. They were very attracted by a thesis on *Humanae Vitae* put forward by the editor of the *Clergy Review*, Father Michael Richards, first in an article in that journal and later in various talks he gave to clergy groups. A version of his argument was circulated to all the bishops. Father Richards was a member of the group representing the Theological Commission in discussions with the Laity Commission. His analysis seemed to let the bishops off the hook, at least in the short term. It was, in summary, that an understanding of *Humanae Vitae* could not be expected on the basis of the natural law argument alone, but would gradually come about as the couple developed their spiritual lives and reflected prayerfully on the natural law argument in the context of Revelation (the issues raised by Monsignor McReavy's paper). This explained why it was possible to be a 'Good Catholic' and not accept the encyclical. For that, it may be necessary to become an 'even better Catholic'. The danger that this gave *Humanae Vitae* an almost occult status, and turned its central doctrine into a kind of Gnostic mystery accessible only to a chosen few initiates, was outweighed by the fact that the theory allowed business as usual to be resumed with an easy conscience.

Michael Richards had stated it thus: 'Reason alone, or an appeal to natural law, thought of as a body of doctrine which would be self-evident or sufficient in itself, does not in fact enable us to arrive at certain conclusions in this matter . . . We need the illumination of faith in the Christian revelation if certainty is to be found.'

This he supplied:

> Love between the sexes, while it often appears to be exclusive of all other love in the early stages, is nevertheless other-directed as well, in the sense that the couple must arrive at a situation of loving together, in a profound harmony of the whole of their being, an object beyond themselves: God Himself, their children, their joint purpose in fulfilling God's plan for their lives. Contraceptive intercourse, in removing one aspect of their openness, limits the outgoing nature of the love of the couple and therefore keeps them at a lower level of maturity in Christ.[39]

Meanwhile the Laity Commission was pursuing its own analysis of what had gone wrong. It seems likely that Father Richards had read his paper to the Laity Commission representatives at the joint meeting with the Theological Commission, without making the slightest impression on them. They were as closed minded as he was: *Humanae Vitae* was simply wrong. This was because, they decided, those making the decision had allowed themselves to become dangerously cut off from what married lay people were thinking. Elaborate theories of married life had been constructed, including the dos and don'ts of sexuality, which were logical and consistent within themselves but remote from reality, out of contact with the actual experience of marriage. Thus the Laity Commission started to look for ways to educate theologians in 'what marriage was really like'. It wrote to a dozen of them, and got mainly sympathetic replies.

This developed in turn into a theological explanation of where the Church had gone wrong, albeit a somewhat speculative one: the pastors of the Church had omitted to consult the *sensus fidelium* before giving their ruling. This raised a complex ecclesiological question, one of many not properly resolved by the Second Vatican Council. Where did the faith of the Church ultimately reside? Not exclusively, it seemed, in the papacy, nor even in all the bishops. It resided in the whole Church, the entire body of those who are baptized and in communion. To use an inadequate but almost literal translation of *sensus fidelium*, that was where the 'sense of the faithful' was to be found. The ultimate test of whether something was

Catholic or not was its conformity to the *sensus fidelium*. But the official answer to the question 'How do we know what the *sensus fidelium* is?' was simply 'Ask the *magisterium*'. The bishops, speaking through their representative and leader the Bishop of Rome, could infallibly define what was or was not part of the Catholic faith.

But nobody would quite go so far as to suggest that ordinary Church members had no role but to listen and obey, at least not since Vatican II. They were also baptized; they were also the People of God; they were also influenced by the Holy Spirit. In the case of marriage, furthermore, they were in receipt of the grace of the Sacrament of Matrimony (which priests were not). The Council of Trent, no less, had said so. So did they have a role within the *sensus fidelium* beyond that of being told what to believe and believing it, the role for instance of helping to shape it? The Laity Commission thought so. The Second Vatican Council did not deny it. But the theologians behind *Humanae Vitae* did not seem to think it was even theoretically possible for there to be a discrepancy between what the official *magisterium* taught and what the *sensus fidelium* contained. One of the weaknesses of this objection to *Humanae Vitae* is that the consensus of the faithful, however it was measured, had supported the Catholic position against contraception down the centuries, though not for consistent reasons. Only in the 1960s did the consensus start to break up. Indeed, until the twentieth century there was a consensus against contraception in all Churches, Protestant as well as Catholic. It was not until 1931 that the Anglican Communion, through a resolution of the Lambeth Conference, altered its view. Until then 'birth control' had been a favourite nostrum of the eugenics movement, and was campaigned for by those who thought the race was being degenerated by the excessive breeding of inferior classes.

This argument about the *sensus fidelium* would rumble on for twelve more years (indeed, it has never been resolved) and it came for a while to threaten a breakdown in relations between the Bishops' Conference (who knew exactly what was being suggested, and objected to it) and the National Conference of Priests (who would not let go of *sensus fidelium* language). The chief and official liaison officer between the Bishops' Conference and the National Conference of Priests was, of course, Derek Worlock.

His technique was not to answer the problem theologically but to administer it out of harm's way – as it were, to get it into the footnotes out of the text, and then out of the footnotes into a covering letter, then into a postscript. Another technique, which was by no means his own invention, was to disguise the dispute by talking about it in shorthand. The very phrase '*sensus fidelium*' had rapidly become Catholic code for

'*Humanae Vitae* was wrong'. Unfortunately the Press kept breaking the code.

The Catholic bishops of England and Wales had been through a most difficult trial, and by and large they came out of it with great credit. It was not for them to reverse the papal decision on birth control. The most they could have done, had they thought it utterly mistaken, was to resign, which would have achieved nothing more than another shocking newspaper headline and further damage to the Church they loved. It is true they misread the crisis over *Humanae Vitae* at the outset. But as it unfolded, they showed, as they had shown during the Second Vatican Council itself earlier in the same decade, remarkable adaptability. They were quick learners and shrewd pastors.

One thing they first misjudged was the mood and motivation of the dissenters, lay and clergy. The overall temperament of English Catholicism, due to a long history and clear collective memory of persecution and discrimination, was characterized by loyalty to the Pope. It was for the successor of St Peter their treasured English Martyrs[40] had died. They came out of the tradition of the Counter Reformation, which had been a vast centralizing influence on world Catholicism. Many of the clergy had trained in Rome itself; many of the laity had gone there as pilgrims.

Though there were important exceptions (including Cardinal Newman), English Catholicism took naturally to the trend in theology in the eighteenth and nineteenth century called Ultramontanism.[41] Cardinal Manning had been a leading proponent of the ultimate Ultramontane doctrines of papal infallibility and universal papal jurisdiction at the First Vatican Council (1869–70). His successors right up to Cardinal Basil Hume were Ultramontanists too. So were virtually all the bishops.

Ultramontanism is usually represented as a conservative force – it was seen as 'digging in' against change – but it could just as well be on the side of liberal causes. Pope John XXIII, for instance, was followed and appreciated in Great Britain as least as much as anywhere else in the world. His great encyclicals, *Mater et Magistra* and *Pacem in Terris*, had come as a liberating breath of fresh air in England, not just because of what they said but because they were said by a Pope. Thus the English were on the way to becoming what might have seemed a contradiction in terms, liberal Ultramontanists. They wanted to follow the Pope loyally as their forefathers had done, but they wanted to be led in a more progressive direction.[42] While the rest of European Catholicism seemed to greet the encyclical in 1968 with little more than a Gallic shrug (or Italian shrug, as Worlock had noticed), many English Catholics were grievously disappointed, even shattered by it. They were still basically in the Ultramontane camp. They wanted desperately to be loyal. This the bishops began to understand.

It was for such reasons that articulate lay Catholics such as those on the Laity Commission were so eager to discover 'what had gone wrong'. They wanted to belong to a perfect Church, not one that made mistakes. Being Anglo-Saxons[43] they had a conscientious attitude to law. They wanted a Church which made rules which were the right ones, capable of being followed. They didn't want to have to cheat, and if cheating was the way in which foreign Catholics dealt with *Humanae Vitae*, then so much the worse for them. They did not want to be let off lightly, easily pardoned, shown compassion. All the bishops' early responses were of that kind, and they missed their mark.

The encounter between the Laity Commission, mainly married lay people, and the Theological Commission, celibate priests and bishops, was the one attempt that was made at a serious theological dialogue over *Humanae Vitae* in this whole period. But it was essentially at cross purposes from first to last. The episcopal side were not interested in demonstrating why *Humanae Vitae* was right: that they took for granted. The line they were selling was that if loyal Catholics followed the teaching willy-nilly, while immersing themselves in the pursuit of spiritual perfection, it would gradually become clearer and clearer to them why the teaching was right, as they progressed. But this was not objective proof. Indeed, it begged the evidence.

Thus when Michael Richards argued that 'contraceptive intercourse . . . limits the outgoing nature of the love of the couple' he was certainly not basing this on sociological or psychological evidence. He was arguing thus: contraceptives were wrong: therefore they must do some harm; what harm might that be? – well, harm to the couple's capacity for outgoing love, perhaps (for that would be true of anything that made anyone a worse Christian). But to tell this to a group of lay Catholics who had been specially selected on behalf of the bishops to be the most exemplary representatives of their kind, whose capacity for 'outgoing love' nobody had ever before called in question, was ill-judged.

The lay side, on the other hand, were convinced *Humanae Vitae* had made a profound mistake. Taking it on trust was the opposite of what they were prepared to do. They wanted to argue with whomever would listen as to why it was wrong. Everything they heard added to their conviction that those defenders of *Humanae Vitae* who were pontificating over the place of sex in marriage did not know what they were talking about.

There must be some sympathy for them. All the theological texts circulating at that time on behalf of *Humanae Vitae*, including those quoted above from McReavy and Richards, seemed to be engaged in reducing married love to its constituent parts. Nothing they had to say seemed to come even near the reality. For instance, Pope Paul VI, McReavy and Richards had all expressed the fear that contraception would obscure from married couples the extraordinary co-operation with the will of God that human reproduction entailed.

They had obviously never held their own newborn child. With the overwhelming miracle of human procreation warm, wet, breathing and beautiful in one's arms, there is no need to theologize in order to get the point. One is in the presence of an awesome mystery, at once humbling, frightening and inspiring. That is why people cry on such occasions, or shout with almost inexpressible joy. Insofar as natural law has anything to do with it, it is surely at such moments that Nature takes over and writes the script herself.

Nor had they – or at least nor should they have – ever experienced the heights and delights of the love between a man and a woman; the total disorientation, the sense of being turned completely inside out, entailed in the experience of falling in love; the transcendent presence of something ennobling, sublime and beautiful that yet belongs to and is contained within the person beloved. They had never tasted the conquering power of erotic attraction, the quasi-mysticism of sexual passion, ecstasy and union, the sense of being translated beyond time and space to another dimension where angels sing; the outer circle, surely, of the Beatific Vision itself. Otherwise they would not have talked, as Richards did, of 'love . . . which often appears to be exclusive of all other love in the early stages'. The love of a new lover embraces the whole universe, excluding nothing. A lover knows something of the Divine in the only way the Divine can be known.[44]

The last thing a lover needs is a theological paper pointing out the relationship between the experience of love and the Force that created and controls the universe. Such knowledge is overwhelming and intuitive. Perhaps these theologians needed to read more love poetry, before rushing in where angels feared to tread.

How, after more than 30 years, can one characterize the Catholic crisis over contraception? It was not a clash between faith and a secular ideology, but an argument within faith itself. It seems to belong to its own time and place, in that it affected a once-and-never-to-be-repeated change in Catholic self-consciousness. The Church that emerged from the crisis could not have another one, just like it. The sort of people Catholics were in the period 1965–68 do not exist any more. Worlock was right to speak of 'Before the Encyclical' and 'After the Encyclical', and this was a more distinct watershed than 'Before the Council' and 'After the Council'. In that respect, as Bishop Butler later suggested,[45] the crisis brought Catholics to question things they needed to question, such as the relationship between individual conscience and the authority of the institution they belonged to. That questioning goes on, and can now never stop. But it cannot coexist with the spirit of the Counter Reformation, the unquestioning obedience to the rulers of the Church which was like the unquestioning obedience to superior orders expected of soldiers in an army (or indeed, the unquestioning obedience of subjects to monarchs).

Secondly, the debate was about real issues, not how many angels can dance on the end of a pin.[46] These issues were in their own way characteristic of modernity – the relationship between the sexes, the place of sex itself in those relationship, and the freeing of woman from 'the tyranny of their own biology'. Marriage as an institution grew up over a very long period as a civilized, but traditional, solution to the taming of that tyranny. If a new solution has been found mechanically, or indeed chemically, is there still a social and moral need for the old solution? How do these two answers to the same question exist side by side?

Western society still faces the challenge that confronted the Catholic Church in 1968, the integration of what it coyly called at the time the 'unitive' and the 'procreative' aspects of human sexuality. What else is the fuss about single motherhood about, what else the increasingly draconian attempt by successive British governments to pursue feckless males who father progeny without the slightest sense of responsibility for mother or child?

Thirdly, the debate was a public display of agony of conscience by an entire community, conducted according to rules which all had to play by and with an intense seriousness and care for truth that – at the time – brought it considerable and unexpected credit in the eyes of many uninvolved spectators. The internal decision-making processes of the Catholic Church suddenly became public property, and so they have remained. It was seen under intense media scrutiny to be a careful and honest process.

Fourthly it paraded a way of doing business by the leadership of the Church that had reached the end of the line. The initial reaction of some of the bishops – to crack the whip – was exactly how their predecessors would have reacted. But they quickly discovered that somehow, probably connected with the new thinking of the Second Vatican Council, the principle of 'government by consent' had become a limiting factor in the way they exercised authority. If they pushed Catholics too hard, they discovered, eventually there wouldn't be any Catholics around to push. The encouragement of a self-critical and mature Catholicism among lay people meant the end of unthinking docility. In the English context, furthermore, the idea of obedience was inexorably caught up with the tactics of survival. The one condition necessary for the total disappearance of Catholicism in penal times was a serious conflict between the leaders and the led – spiritual proof of the military aphorism that the one thing a commander must never do in battle is to divide his forces in the face of the enemy. The charge has to be laid against Pope Paul VI that he committed that fundamental tactical mistake; though he is entitled to answer that he was only doing his job. The Catholic bishops of England and Wales did realize that danger, and acted just in time to avert the consequences. After a certain amount of blundering about, by some kind of silent and unstated agreement between bishops, priests and people, the debate arising from *Humanae Vitae* was in effect adjourned *sine die*. It was in a sense too dangerous.

This issue was 'not the acid test of Christianity', as Worlock memorably said. However, the election of Pope John Paul II in 1978 was not just the end of an unhappy decade for the author of *Humanae Vitae*.[47] It was also the beginning of a new age of certainty at the top of the Catholic Church. One of the things the new Pope seemed sure of was that the issues raised in 1968 were indeed the acid test, of nothing less than being for God or against Him. This immediately put in peril the 'English solution' to the birth control crisis, of which Worlock's remark was the foundation. Worlock was to spend much of the rest of his career defending it – not in battle or debate, but in holding at bay a set of absolute and unflinching attitudes and policies that were fundamentally irreconcilable with the English solution.

There were those in Rome who would have liked to see strongly conservative bishops appointed to English dioceses, gradually to replace the compromisers and reconcilers of 1968 with men of harder iron. The fact that there were no men of quality on site with those requirements would not have stopped them. There were plenty of places in the world that had to suffer the promotion of second-rate candidates to the episcopate simply because they could be trusted to be loyal to the party line, when better men were too independent-minded for Rome to trust them. English Catholics did not suffer that fate, and one of the reasons was the educated and informed laity were 'in on the deal', and knew what was expected of them. If they rocked the boat, they would end up being tipped out of it. If that meant 'living with hypocrisy', as some of the more scrupulous (on the Right) or radical (on the Left) complained from time to time – that is something the English were good at. The English call it the Nelson touch, after the occasion when that famous admiral put a telescope to his blind eye in order not to see a signal commanding him to alter course. Or as Nelson's twentieth-century successor, the great Admiral Jackie Fisher, once remarked: 'Any damn fool can obey orders.'[48]

Notes

1 'The greatest shock the Church has suffered since the Reformation'; Cardinal J. C. Heenan, *A Crown of Thorns*, Hodder and Stoughton, 1974, p. 390.

2 Parish priests.

3 The future Pope John Paul II told him: 'On the occasion of your nomination to the Bishop's Office, I am happy to join with you in extending my sincere congratulations. I wish to say a special word of thanks to you who always were good to Poland and all Poles. To you, your Excellency, I renew my warm and heartfelt congratulations and good wishes on this occasion.' There was also a telegram from Archbishop Thomas Roberts, formerly of Bombay (see below), saying 'May the spirit of St Thomas be with you.' No doubt he meant 'Doubting Thomas'.

4 Officially the 'Pontifical Commission on Population, Family and Birth'. Apparently there was a desire not to put 'birth control' into the title.

5 One original member was Dr John Marshall, an English Catholic neurologist who had specialized in understanding the cycles of female fertility and had written books explaining the so-called rhythm method.

6 Published in the UK by Longmans.

7 Once the ground had been broken, both *The Tablet* and the *Catholic Herald* published articles in Britain implicitly critical of the official position.

8 *The Pill and Birth Regulation*, edited by Leo Pyle, DLT, 1964.

9 This unsatisfactory birth control method, traditionally condemned by the Catholic Church, involves the man withdrawing his penis from the vagina just before the moment of ejaculation.

10 9 May 1964.

11 What it is for.

12 One of those who had changed his mind on this point was Dr Marshall.

13 This summary is by Jan Grootaers, editor of *De Maand*, Brussels, and taken from *Mariage Catholique et Contraception*, Éditions de l'Épi, 1968 quoted in *On Human Life*, Burns and Oates, 1968. Though unofficial, it has never been contradicted.

14 'Intrinsically' here means 'of itself' and hence 'regardless of circumstances'. The thought here was that behaviour which is intrinsically wrong can never be justified or excused; there can be no exceptions. Not many actions fall into this category – even killing can be justified in self-defence. Another example of an intrinsically wrong act, which no circumstances could possibly justify, would be sex with young children.

15 'Finality' is an inadequate translation of the French *finalité*, and refers to the 'ends' of marriage, its ultimate purposes. In this case, the *finalité* being referred to is the love and mutual support of the spouses, which the Second Vatican Council, in its document *The Church in the Modern World*, had recently elevated to the same status as the more traditional *finalité*, procreation. This is exactly what some of the critics of this Vatican II document had feared.

16 Perhaps not surprisingly, Newman was very relaxed about Darwinism and certainly did not see it as undermining the Christian faith.

17 In fact, at almost exactly the same time the bishops of England and Wales were trying to sell the 'no change' policy on birth control to dissatisfied lay people, another group of dissatisfied lay people were bitterly protesting about changes to the Mass (and using arguments from tradition similar to those the bishops were having to resort to in

defence of *Humanae Vitae*).

18 This document has never before been published nor its existence alluded to in public. Beck later told the Bishops' Conference that there were only six copies in existence, and he knew who had each one. The full text is given in Appendix I, Document 1.

19 By then Archbishop Cardinale.

20 The *Catholic Herald* commented in September that *The Times* (for which the author then worked) had 'an uncanny eye and sensitive ear for any exclusive Roman scandal, but what is more important it also has extremely good contacts, although some are not as infallible as one would expect from those doing business with Printing House Square. Remember how The Times fell for the alleged secret letter that accompanied *Humanae Vitae?*' The 'alleged secret letter' is indeed in the archive.

21 The Latin title of the document frequently described as simply *The Church in the Modern World* comes from the document's opening words: 'The joys and the hopes, the griefs and the anxieties of the men of this age, especially those who are poor or in any way afflicted, these are the joys and hopes, the griefs and anxieties of the followers of Christ.'

22 23 August 1968.

23 In a plain brown envelope addressed to the author, who was then an assistant news editor on that newspaper, with no covering note.

24 In fact this crude method spoils the sexual pleasure of the couple, and hence the temptation is more likely to be *not* to use it having decided beforehand to do so, rather than to use it on the spur of the moment. But this was not the sort of things Catholic bishops were expected to know.

25 'Christian marriage is not a farmyard' was how the Bishop of Brentwood put it in a television interview, rather missing the point that unbridled copulation is not what farmyards are about either.

26 Though opinion against *Humanae Vitae* may have hardened in the following twelve years, some indication of the climate of opinion in 1968 may be gleaned from a survey conducted by Gallup, published in 1980, which recorded that only 13 per cent of Catholics disagreed with the statement: 'A married couple who feel they have as many children as they want are not doing anything wrong when they use artificial methods of birth control.'

27 He received a supportive letter from Archbishop Beck.

28 Appendix 1, Document 5.

29 Appendix 1, Document 2.

30 Appendix 1, Document 3a.

31 Appendix 1, Document 3b.

32 Jack Mahoney SJ went on to become a leading English expert on the moral theology of medical ethics, and when there turned out to be questions it was too dangerous to ask in that field too, he became the first Professor of Business Ethics at the London Business School (where the dangerous questions were all aimed at the values of businessmen).

33 *Contraception*, J. T. Noonan, Harvard University Press, 1986.

34 The Encyclopaedia Britannica attributes the discovery to Oskar Hertwig (1849–1922) of Berlin.

35 Appendix I, Document 4.

36 In the event, Heenan's letter only contained a short passage from the statement, and did not identify it as such.

37   At a debate at the National Conference of Priests six years later – attended by Worlock
     – one priest declared: 'The problem is that the decisions we make privately in the con-
     fessional are not the decisions we would make publicly to our bishops. There are two
     teachings in the Church on contraception – the official teaching, and what is said pri-
     vately.'

38   Known as an *ad clerum*.

39   This approach could eventually have one useful result for the supporters of *Humanae
     Vitae*. If the doctrine was founded exclusively on natural law, it was outside the scope
     of papal infallibility. If it was based on revelation, however, infallibility could cover it.
     At the time of the promulgation of *Humanae Vitae*, the Vatican had insisted that the
     condemnation of contraception was not an infallible teaching. That may have been
     based on its presumed natural law status. The direction in which Richards, McReavy *et
     al.* were taking it – as a doctrine rooted in revelation – could eventually lead to that
     judgement being altered. So far the Vatican has resisted the temptation.

40   Forty of whom had been canonized by Pope Paul VI in 1970.

41   Literally 'over the mountains' – the mountains in this case being the Alps. Ultramon-
     tanism emerged as the opposite to Gallicanism – the belief, prevalent in the French
     Catholic Church before the Revolution, that a national Church should not be subordi-
     nate to Rome. (This theory was attractive to Anglicans too.)

42   There was a significant, but as the years went by, declining minority of English
     Catholics who regarded Vatican II as a disaster. But they too were at heart Ultramon-
     tanists and they too had their conflicts of loyalty.

43   This literal-minded attitude to law may also explain why the other country most
     affected by post-*Humanae Vitae* outcry was the United States, especially, perhaps
     because of a hardline Archbishop, in Washington DC.

44   This notion that in marriage, sex itself had a sacred aspect was expressed twelve years
     later in a document called *The Easter People*, following the National Pastoral Congress
     in Liverpool in 1980. Worlock quoted it at the subsequent meeting of the National Con-
     ference of Priests, saying it showed the way ahead. It stated that 'sexual love in marriage
     is a relationship in which the couple affirm each other's identity . . . and through which
     they make Christ sacramentally present to each other.'

45   See next chapter.

46   After his retirement as Archbishop of Canterbury, Lord Runcie, in his Gore Memorial
     Lecture, declared: 'The acceptance of artificial contraception represented and indeed
     continues to represent a revolution in the Church's attitude to sexuality . . . because its
     effect is to separate sexual enjoyment from procreation and set the two impulses on
     divergent paths. That has affected the whole of Western sexuality.' (Quoted by
     Humphrey Carpenter in *Robert Runcie*, Sceptre, 1996.)

47   He never wrote another encyclical.

48   Author's personal footnote. In the files relating to the bishops' *Humanae Vitae* meeting
     in October 1968, in Worlock's handwriting, is a piece of paper with my name on it –
     'Cliff Longley'. There is no clue what it is in connection with, and Worlock and I had
     not been in touch for many months. But it might have had a bearing on an incident that
     happened soon after. Heenan attended a public meeting at about that time, at which it
     was thought likely that *Humanae Vitae* would come up. The Press was present, includ-
     ing a reporter from *The Times* (for which I then worked as an assistant news editor). In
     the course of his remarks, Heenan stated that there was a journalist on *The Times* who
     was a Catholic – but not the editor, William Rees-Mogg – who took every opportunity

to write stories damaging to the Catholic Church. (In those days *Times* news items rarely carried bylines.) After the meeting the reporter, Ronald Faux, approached him, and asked, in view of the seriousness of his allegation, if he could say who he meant.

Versions diverged at this point. Heenan later claimed he had never heard my name before, and had to turn to his accompanying priest and ask who it was they had been told about. The reporter himself, Ronald Faux, said Heenan answered immediately – 'Clifford Longley'.

On Faux's return to the office this conversation was reported to the acting editor, Iveragh MacDonald, who consulted the night lawyer and was told the allegation was defamatory. He advised him that it could only be published in *The Times* with my permission, provided there was also a denial from me. MacDonald rang me at home and asked me for my consent, adding that he had been advised that my right to take legal action against Heenan would not be compromised. I gave him a suitable denial, to the effect that in my position as an assistant news editor I did not write anything at all. The allegation made by Heenan was duly published, with my denial and MacDonald's own endorsement of it. And it was indeed the case that while assistant news editors did initiate coverage, albeit only with the news editor's blessing, they had no influence over the resulting copy.

Heenan's denunciation, at such a sensitive moment, caused a furore. The editor of the *Catholic Herald*, Desmond Albrow, published a signed leading article attacking Heenan for attacking me, together with comments in the same vein from Norman St John Stevas, at the time Tory MP for Chelmsford. Rees-Mogg wrote a strong letter to Heenan, and through his good offices a meeting was arranged. This was to enable Heenan to apologize to me in person.

When we sat in his study at Archbishop's House drinking tea he was fully contrite and very charming, and gave me permission under Canon Law to sue him for libel. Catholics are not allowed to take legal action against bishops in the civil courts without their permission, though St John Stevas had apparently told the Cardinal that refusal of such permission could place a bishop in contempt of court. He said he understood it might be necessary for me to sue in order to protect my professional good name, and he quite understood if that was so.

Heenan agreed to write an article for *The Times*, retracting his allegations against me in full. Rees-Mogg agreed to pay him over the odds for it; and it was agreed that Heenan would immediately pay the fee to any charity I nominated, as a sort of damages. So a few days later a cheque for £200 (about £2,000 in 1999 terms) reached a very puzzled Society of St Dismas in Southampton – a shelter for homeless ex-prisoners – in Heenan's name, with no explanation. And the matter was closed.

Subsequently I was in touch with members of the newly formed Ad Hoc Committee, who invited me to be co-opted onto it to advise them about publicity. At times the Committee seemed to be acting as a sub-committee of the Laity Commission, according to the way the matter was treated in the Commission's minutes. Worlock obviously knew all about it, and was instrumental in arranging for a deputation from the Ad Hoc Committee to meet Cardinal Heenan. I was present. Heenan told us he accepted that we were motivated by concern for the truth and love for the Catholic Church, and were not, as he had at first thought, mere trouble-makers out to cause the Church harm.

He was capable of great magnanimity, and a little while after this he personally nominated me to be a member of the new Mass Media Commission of the Bishops' Conference. At a general meeting for all members of the new Commission, around

1970, he declined to sit at the top table but rather conspicuously chose the seat next to mine. With Derek Worlock, Heenan played a considerable part in fostering this spirit of Christian reconciliation between bishops and laity. Later on, sadly, he turned rather sour. I have always imagined that my restoration to grace had something to do with Derek Worlock's intervention.

After a while the Ad Hoc Committee left it to the Laity Commission to pursue these issues, and it turned itself into the 'Catholic Renewal Movement' with a national membership and an annual conference. David Lodge's novel *How Far Can You Go?* (Secker and Warburg 1980) included a fictionalized account of this movement, which he renamed 'Catholics for an Open Church'. The original outfit was a little harder headed than its fictional version.

9

Abraham's Tent or Solomon's Temple?

After the Second Vatican Council drew wearily to a close in December 1965, the world's Catholic bishops might have hoped for a peaceful and studious period in which the various reforms instigated by the Council could be digested piously, gradually and calmly. Events quickly told them they were going to enjoy no such luck. In Northern Europe in particular – Holland above all – the end of the Council signalled not an end to the pressure for change but an acceleration of it. The progressives felt they had an unfinished agenda. If it was possible, for instance, for the Catholic Church to change its mind after 400 years and admit that the liturgy of the Church ought normally to be celebrated in the language of the people – one of the cardinal demands of the Reformation – what else was it capable of changing? *Ecclesia reformata – semper reformanda*?[1]

The answer was not entirely to be found in the Council texts themselves. The documents of the Second Vatican Council are sometimes spoken of as if they constituted a seamless and coherent whole, whereas they bear all the evidence of many unfinished conversations with loose ends everywhere. Some of the major breakthroughs in thinking happened relatively late, as Worlock described in his diary. By then, other documents were already in their final stages, too late to undertake a wholesale revision. People were getting tired, reaching the limit of their capacity to sustain this intensity of debate. Here and there bits of text were added, therefore, that were not wholly consistent with what had been agreed before. According to Worlock, for instance, at one point a gap was left in the draft document on the 'lay apostolate' waiting for a new theological definition of a layman to be agreed as a result of the deliberations over *Lumen Gentium* (the draft document on the Church). It was then dropped into the text, but the effort to align the rest of the document with this new – in some respects radically new – teaching was not entirely successful. It was a move away from the definition of lay people as simply those not ordained, to those who, by baptism itself, are admitted to the common priesthood of the People of God. Baptism was thus the defining characteristic of a Christian, shared by lay people equally with priests and bishops – and shared by Catholics with members of other Churches whose baptism the Catholic Church normally recognized as valid. The theory of a 'lay apostolate' delegated from the bishops and clergy to the laity (and needing to be closely supervised by them) thus became somewhat obsolete; and so did the term itself. Even the section of *Lumen Gentium* (section 25) that was to be pored over with such care in connection with *Humanae Vitae* (to see what relief it could offer for troubled consciences) can best be understood as two versions of the same doctrine bolted together, without ironing out all their differences of nuance and emphasis. Is the ultimate authority in the Church the Pope alone, or the Pope with the bishops, or the bishops with the Pope? *Lumen Gentium* seemed to give all three answers.

The authorities in the Curia badly wanted to call a halt. In 1966, not long after the Council ended, Cardinal Ottaviani circulated a highly confidential document to bishops' conferences throughout the world, asking about the prevalence of certain 'errors' among Catholics and demanding to know what the bishops were proposing to do about them. Cardinal Heenan replied, more or less, that everything was under control (which it wasn't). 'We recognise the danger of these errors', he wrote back,

> and shall continue to be watchful so that the faithful under our care will not be led into false ways of thinking and acting . . . As yet England and Wales have few faculties of philosophy and theology of university status.[2] To a large extent, therefore, we do not have any breeding grounds of new theories. Most of the dangerous writing published in our territories is a repetition or translation of what has appeared abroad.

This highly reactionary document could have been written by Cardinal Godfrey – or maybe that was precisely the impression the bishops wanted to give.

Against the perception that the Council was the last and final word on disputed matters of the day (much in the way the Council of Trent had been regarded) there was an alternative reading of the Council as merely the beginning of a process and the setting of bearings for the future. Catholicism was never again going to be set in concrete (*à la* Counter Reformation) but would henceforth be in a state of permanent reform (*à la* Reformation itself). This was a conflict of attitude and approach that was to provide plenty of material for storms and divisions in the internal life of the Catholic Church for years to come. One version of this contrast was between the model of a 'pilgrim church', an untidy procession of hurriers-up at the front and pullers-back at the end, but all going in the same direction; and the model of a 'fortress church', well disciplined inside and looking out at the world suspiciously from behind its ramparts, with the drawbridge up. Fortresses, of course, don't move.

The questions the progressives were asking as the Council finished went further than any raised in conciliar debate. What else had the Reformation got right and the Counter Reformation wrong? Clerical celibacy? The infallibility of the Pope? Contraception was high on their list, but further down was divorce, homosexuality, the election of bishops, the radical updating of religious orders, open communion with members of other Churches (and reunion all round not far off). Even the issue of women priests could be detected lurking in the undergrowth ahead. Ancient dogmas about the divinity of Christ and more recent dogmas about the Virgin Mary, all seemed in need of re-examination. So did Marxism. There was a flight from Catholic social teaching based on the encyclical *Rerum Novarum*, which was accused of attempting to discover non-existent middle ground between implacable enemies, capital and labour. The originators of liberation theology were inspired by the Latin American Bishops' Conference in 1968 at Medellín, Colombia. The seminal work, *A Theology of Liberation*, was published by Gustavo Gutiér-rez, a Peruvian priest and theologian, in 1971. If he was right, there was no longer any middle ground for the Church to occupy nor safe observation balloon where prelates could float above the struggle. All was now class war, and the Church was either on the side of the capitalists or the prole-tariat. Here was much further material for future turbulence. It was a *Runaway Church*,[3] to use the title of a book by Peter Hebblethwaite not long after he left the Jesuits, married, and embarked on a career as an Oxford don and religious journalist and author. He was part of the phe-nomenon.

The *Humanae Vitae* crisis had concentrated attention on one issue, but the firmly conservative line taken by Pope Paul VI on that was an early sign that the Vatican was in the mood to apply a brake, not to accelerate, in all other areas too. Before his election as Pope, Worlock had had Montini down as a Vatican II progressive, even as the string-puller in that camp. But once in the papacy he was surrounded by the very Curia the progres-sives so disliked. And he kept them on, even old Ottaviani at the Holy Office (though it was renamed the Sacred Congregation for the Doctrine of the Faith).

In England, once the dust settled over contraception, Heenan decided that things had gone far enough. Bishop Butler, meanwhile, gave it as his considered verdict on the *Humanae Vitae* crisis that 'there is a good deal of evidence that since 1965 the old habits of autocratic action in Rome have survived the Council. A great many Catholics and some non-Catholics, whatever they may think of the actual teaching of the latest encyclical, are profoundly disturbed by the history of its genesis and the mode of its promulgation.'[4]

Butler speculated that good might come of it nevertheless. The crisis 'is already compelling the Catholic Church to face internal criticisms of the encyclical, thus making Vatican II a living reality. The Council itself is the only genuine answer to such internal criticism.' Butler was by then one of Heenan's auxiliary bishops in Westminster; but Heenan was in no mood to face up to anything. 'His ultramontane training, never questioned, left him helpless', later wrote Adrian Hastings, himself one of the many distinguished priests who separated themselves from the formal structures of the Church. 'It was a tragedy of a whole generation of able priests – perhaps the ablest the Catholic Church in England ever had – who went down leaderless between Rome and their people; but it was a personal tragedy too of John Carmel Heenan.'[5]

Although the greatest acceleration in the rate of loss was between 1968 and 1969 – disillusionment over *Humanae Vitae* may have been a factor – it was the 1970s that saw the most devastating losses, including mature priests who could one day have made good bishops. The gap in the ranks of Catholic clergy of a certain age, then and now, has been likened to the shortage of young men in Britain in the 1920s, the generation that fought and died in the trenches of the First World War. Many of these priests married, most seeking 'dispensation' (release) from celibacy and formal reversion to the lay state, though Hastings himself, as a protest against the celibacy rule, did not do so on principle. Diocese by diocese, bishops made strenuous efforts to hold back the losses, none more so than Worlock. The Pope wrote to bishops everywhere, warning them that if they did not do their utmost to stem the losses, they 'would be guilty before God for their grievous consequences'. Priests who failed to live up to the rule of celibacy caused 'sorrow, dishonour and unrest' in the Church, he said. Despite his reluctance to denounce them in such terms as this, Worlock found it hard to sympathize beyond a certain point – at no time in his life did he seem to feel the slightest temptation to leave the priesthood himself, to get married or for any other reason. When the Vatican introduced stricter rules about who may be laicized[6] and who not, he wrote back appreciatively, saying it was about time. Faced with one priest announcing his intention to leave the priesthood to marry, he lamented to a friend, perhaps not entirely jokingly: 'Why couldn't he just have an affair with her?'

Not that he encouraged licentiousness. He merely thought a tendency to fail in the strict observance of celibacy was part of the fallen human condition. It was repairable. Like many other bishops at that time, he took this line with priests guilty of child abuse as well as with those guilty of lapses between consenting adults, a policy which disastrously failed to take into account the obsessive and probably incurable nature of paedophilia, though at the time that aspect was by no means fully recognized. At least one child-abusing priest in Portsmouth was given the standard treatment by Worlock – a period of psychiatric counselling, with apology and repentance accepted as genuine by the Church, and then the offer of a clean sheet in a new parish (where the child abuse may have started all over again). The custom of sweeping such things under the carpet was actually condoned by the police in those days: just before Worlock arrived in Portsmouth, the ·Chief Constable of Hampshire had given the diocese 24 hours to get one seriously child-abusing priest out of the country (he went back to Ireland) or risk seeing him arrested.

Apart from such policies, which were by no means unique to him, Worlock was good, pastorally. He would go a long way to help a priest in trouble, and they knew it.[7] His kind and understanding treatment of Joe Cocker at the beginning became the norm.[8] His policy towards any priest who admitted to a sexual relationship with a woman was to try to wean him off it, not to throw him out.

As ever, his loyalty was to the Church rather than to any particular school of theology. Indeed, his erstwhile friends from Westminster days felt he had betrayed them by his wholehearted acceptance of Vatican II, while many of them were still clinging to the triumphalism of an earlier Westminster. Meanwhile in Portsmouth ecumenical initiatives began to flourish; Catholics and members of other churches eyed each other warily for the first time as new and as yet untested friends.[9] Worlock revived the old structure of deaneries – local groups of parishes in one town or city – and had them set up pastoral councils where handpicked lay people and selected clergy could discuss the problems of the Church in that area. He drew from these deanery councils the membership for a new diocesan pastoral council, probably the first and certainly the most effective attempt to involve priests and laity in the administration of any Catholic diocese in Britain. It was the very model of a post-Vatican II diocese, a state-of-the-art affair. Worlock was very proud of it.

This combination of hierarchical or quasi-monarchical government with democratic clergy and lay participation was never entirely natural or harmonious, however, probably because 'the people' had no real power. In any serious disagreement with the bishop they would always have to back off. But probably this degree of reform was as far as things could be allowed to go at that time.

One sign of Worlock's liberalism was his willingness to let the City of Portsmouth deanery set up a working party of laity and clergy to study the birth control issue at length, once the controversy had died down. (No other bishop allowed anything like this.) Its report *Catholics and Contraception in Marriage*, published in 1975, concluded that while the rhythm method was the ideal for Catholic married couples, fewer and fewer of them seemed to be using it. Couples who felt they should use artificial birth control – the great majority, presumably – should continue to receive Holy Communion and 'it is understood that they would not confess it as a grave sin.' The report tried hard to say many good loyal things about *Humanae Vitae*, but there was a strong sense about it of shutting the stable door after the horse had bolted. The appearance of the report, and the lack of any further rancour over the issue, was a vindication of Worlock's conciliatory approach in his own backyard. Worlock's record as a liberal helped to retain the confidence of those who might otherwise have rebelled, and it was they who by and large provided the enthusiastic post-Vatican II laity to fill his new diocesan structures. Morale, in other words, was higher than might otherwise have been expected. He felt *Humanae Vitae* had been a distraction from his real work.[10]

He claimed some personal credit for having pulled the whole Church back from its preoccupation with that issue. In a lecture in 1995,[11] he recalled a conversation he had had with Pope Paul VI in 1972 in which he had pleaded with him not to devote the 1974 International Synod to the subject of the family 'lest it should revive the crisis which had followed *Humanae Vitae*'. The Pope reacted 'almost as if I had struck him; the look was a mixture of pain, perplexity and compassion'. It was a measure of the Pope's humility

> that within days he had accepted my suggestion . . . that the Church should get over its identity crisis, start looking again at the work of the Gospel, and devote the next synod to the study of Evangelisation. I was a very young bishop at the time, still at Portsmouth, and I am thankful to have witnessed a far-sighted and courageous decision by Pope Paul, courageous because the pressure for a synod on the family was considerable. It is my conviction that this proved to be the turning point for the post-conciliar church.

Worlock was in effect praising the Pope for taking his advice, thereby saving the Church. He was never a man to let modesty deny him his rightful place in history. In fact the document that was written by Paul VI in the light of that synod, *Evangelii Nuntiandi*, was one of the best of his entire reign. It achieved a theological synthesis between the Church's involvement in justice and peace issues, and the preaching of the Gospel.

No doubt on his departure from Portsmouth to Liverpool, some of the more entrenched conservatives among the clergy felt Worlock himself had been a distraction from their real work. The Irish tradition, dating from Cotter, lived on, and with it a firm independence of spirit among many older parish priests – independent both of the bishops and of the laity. When Worlock's successor, Bishop Anthony Emery, showed no great enthusiasm for parish and deanery councils, they began to fall into abeyance and some priests welcomed the end of what they regarded as lay interference. But the diocesan pastoral centre Worlock had set up at Park Place, near Fareham, in Hampshire, continued to function. Many of the young priests Worlock had brought to the fore, such as Nicholas France and Patrick Murphy O'Connor (his brother Cormac, Worlock's secretary before France, became Bishop of Arundel and Brighton in 1977) were encouraged to continue the Worlock Vatican II project, and even let off the leash a little more than Worlock would have allowed.

The verdict on his Portsmouth decade must be that he achieved most of what he wanted but learned less than he might have done. Unlike what was to happen in Liverpool, there was no particular ecumenical partnership forged in that period, partly because the Portsmouth Roman Catholic diocese covered all or part of about six Anglican dioceses.[12] Though he made representations to various local authorities from time to time on such matters as housing policy or city redevelopment, these were little more than came to be expected from a modern bishop (though perhaps more than was expected locally of a Catholic one, given the policy of non-involvement followed by his aged and eccentric predecessor John Henry King). The Portsmouth years did not see any great development of his thinking on issues of politics and social justice domestically – it took the influence of David Sheppard to trigger that – though he was keen to see the success of Cafod[13] which he had helped to start while at Westminster. Worlock was sufficiently concerned with political matters to forge a friendship with the local Labour MP Frank Judd, who for a while was Parliamentary Private Secretary to Harold Wilson, Leader of the Labour Opposition. Judd's special interest was overseas development. Portsmouth diocese began a tradition of supporting priests in Catholic missions in the Third World, mainly Cameroon in West Africa. But Worlock had not really got to grips with the deep conservatism of an old-guard Catholic clergy, educated before the Second Vatican Council and not very interested in finding out about it nor seeing what it had to do with them. He was still blueprint-minded – his faith in structures and plans was intact. The fact that they only went skin deep in Portsmouth, and began to fade once his energy was no longer applied to them, did not discourage him from trying the same things in Liverpool.[14]

There was a structural blueprint for Liverpool too: an archdiocesan development plan, launched with some flourish at a meeting of clergy not long after he arrived in 1976. He relaunched his development plan in 1980, this time insisting that he did not believe in blueprints (probably because he had been criticized for believing in them too much), and demanding that parishes and deaneries should have another try at setting up pastoral councils. The 1976 plan involved closing several city parish churches and merging parishes to produce larger areas with team ministries. There was much grumbling and some real resistance, though something of the sort was entirely necessary. But he had not quite won over the hearts and minds of all the clergy, who noticed that he had started to do what he had first tried at Portsmouth – dropping into parishes unannounced during a Sunday service, and standing at the back to observe. Although his intentions were the best, they felt he was snooping on them.

So he never completely overcame the resistance to a 'southerner' which he had detected during that visit to Upholland at the start of 1976, and which resulted in his motives being viewed unfavourably. Catholic bishops play a surprisingly important role in the emotional lives of their priests even when they do not see each other very often – an aspect of the psychology of celibacy, perhaps – and some clergy develop an almost neurotic preoccupation with 'what the bishop thinks of me'. Worlock was not the type to defuse such feelings; on the contrary he could exacerbate them by his own insensitivity which at times, in the opinion of some, had a hint of paranoia.[15] (He was preoccupied with what other people thought of him.) In psychological terms an archdiocese like Liverpool was an immensely complex task of man-management. Given his disadvantages, personal and circumstantial, it is hard to see what more he could have done. It was not long before Liverpool absorbed him, and he it. He began to talk of himself as an adopted son of the city, never more proudly than when he received the Freedom of the City in 1995.

David Sheppard wrote about him just after he died in 1996:

Derek Worlock was very proud that as a southerner he felt himself adopted as an 'honorary Scouser'. The granting of the Freedom of the City last year was for him the most special of honours. His love for the city and its people, coupled with his gentle and lively humour, was reflected in his acceptance speech. With a voice choked with emotion he spoke of 'our Liverpool home'.

This was a home he loved and valued. He wanted to end his days in Liverpool, amongst the people he has loved and served so faithfully.[16]

And so he did.

Whether they loved Derek Worlock as much as he thought they ought to is a fair question. There were perhaps three kinds of affection for him: among those who knew him very personally, like David and Grace Sheppard; among local civic and business leaders, who knew how tirelessly he had tried to serve the whole community and to stand with it during some very bad moments; and among his own flock, who loved him because he was their archbishop, and Liverpool Catholics have a tradition of taking archbishops to their heart. (Uniquely in England, it was customary for substantial crowds to gather at Lime Street Station for the departure of an archbishop leaving for duties elsewhere, or a new one arriving to take over.) Nevertheless the obvious reserve of the shy English middle-class southerner probably set a limit to the public enthusiasm for Worlock on the streets of his adopted city. There were those who found him pretentious. There were those who wondered if he wasn't in fact more comfortable among the local (mainly non-Catholic) political and business élite, to which his friendship with David Sheppard gave him access, than with his own people.

The relationship with the Sheppards went far deeper than most people in Liverpool had realized. Even so, to call it 'the Mersey Miracle', as Worlock was sometimes wont to do (usually attributing the epithet to an unnamed third party), rather implausibly suggests the overcoming of immense improbabilities and difficulties. It also ignored the groundwork laid by previous Liverpool church leaders, Heenan above all on the Catholic side. In fact it was easy. It may have started for tactical reasons which suited the interests of both men, but it became a strong bond of real affection. Grace was very much part of it. In the end, the ecclesiastical relationship between the two men became almost irrelevant. It was a kind of adopted family kinship: they were like brother and sister to him. Grace Sheppard wrote for publication in 1990,[17] the year of his 70th birthday, about 'the warmth and welcome of his home during mealtimes, and the stillness and simple elegance of his chapel the three of us have shared over the years. I shall always be grateful for his generosity in offering me his writing desk in Archbishop's House for six weeks, so that I could complete my first book in peace. On the desk was a postcard of welcome in his absence.'

She went on:

Once I decided to consult him as a priest when I was wrestling with a particularly painful and private problem, and needed someone a little more detached than my own husband. In a way I needed to 'confess' my deep anger and hurt over something which was becoming destructive. He provided a still place in which I could unwrap my pain, and he enabled me to feel accepted and to see beyond the pressing problem. I did not feel patronised, judged or bombarded with advice. He did not allow his professionalism to part company with his own humanity: not always an easy balance for a priest to find. I felt he had been there too. And he listened.[18]

The relationship between David Sheppard and Derek Worlock was eventually strong enough to survive a particularly difficult test. Both the Sheppards had been brought up strict Evangelicals, which put them on the Protestant wing of the Church of England. In 1988 Jenny Sheppard, beloved only daughter of David and Grace Sheppard, decided to become a Catholic and to marry her Catholic boyfriend Donald, at a Catholic wedding. She had been instructed by Father Michael Hollings of St Mary and All Angels parish in Bayswater, West London – one of the priests who had been gossiped about as a possible successor to Heenan – and he was to conduct the marriage service, which was to include a nuptial Mass. For the Sheppards, it was not so much their daughters' conversion that caused the difficulty and her departure from the Church of England in which her father was a leading figure (though it is not hard to speculate about their feelings on that) as the fact that the Catholic Church's rules did not allow those who were not Catholic to receive Holy Communion at such a service.[19] It would have felt as though the families were being torn apart by religion at precisely the moment they should have been coming together. And for the Sheppards, not being allowed to receive Communion at their daughter's wedding, just after she herself had done, would have been a very painful moment.

The families devised what they called a 'three Eucharists' solution. First, at St Mary and All Angels in Bayswater, Hollings said Mass in the presence of both families, and the Catholics present, apart from the bridal couple, received Communion. Then at an Anglican parish church in Notting Hill, in the presence of both families, David Sheppard celebrated Holy Communion according to the rite of the Church of England. The Anglican members of the family received Communion. The parties later reconvened at Hollings' church again for the Catholic marriage ceremony and nuptial Mass, at which only the bride and groom received Holy Communion.

What astounded them was the fact that Derek Worlock cancelled an important engagement in York in order to make a special journey down to London to be present for David Sheppard's Anglican Communion service before the wedding. At the time for distributing Holy Communion he came forward to receive a blessing from David Sheppard. It was a sensitive act of true friendship that moved the Sheppards beyond measure. Jenny herself later became a staunch friend of Worlock.

Worlock sometimes stated that he reached Liverpool with specific instructions from Pope Paul VI – his 'double mandate', he called it – to take care of the people's social and material needs and ensure that Liverpool did not become 'another Belfast'.[20] This was a convenient papal authorization, if one were needed, for the priority Worlock was to give to the building up of ecumenical relations on Merseyside, though this did tend to overstate the actual danger of sectarian violence in Liverpool by the mid-1970s.

His close working relationship with Bishop David Sheppard caused them to talk at length at least once a week, sometimes by phone or in person on a Sunday evening, and again when necessary during the week. David Sheppard has stated[21] that even at the times of maximum tension in Northern Ireland, as during the IRA hunger strikes in the early 1980s, Worlock never once raised with him anxieties about a possible outbreak of Catholic–Protestant violence in Liverpool. It may safely be assumed that if any parish priest had detected signs of coming trouble on the streets, he would have informed Archbishop's House immediately. Indeed, when violence came, it was from another direction altogether – the disadvantaged and alienated black community in Toxteth, central Liverpool. The mainly Catholic population of nearby Vauxhall remained calm, and even pro-IRA wall-graffiti was a rarity. Unlike in Northern Ireland, a concentration of Catholics in Liverpool did not represent a great threat to Protestant political interests. Protestant institutions in the city were a pale shadow of what they were across the Irish Sea. The Protestant party on the city council had long been wound up, and Archbishop Richard Downey[22] had himself shut down an equivalent Catholic party. (It is said in return he did a deal with the Labour Party to give him an unofficial right to veto the selection of Labour candidates in mainly Catholic wards and constituencies, to ensure no 'Bad Catholics' were appointed.)

Although Downey and his Anglican opposite number had taken to exercising their dogs together, even that degree of fraternization had drawn criticism from the more Orange-minded Liverpool Protestants. Not surprisingly there had been no ecumenism during Godfrey's time at Liverpool[23] – this was the man who had banned Protestant Bibles from the English College when he was rector there – nor much of it anywhere else in the country. In contrast Heenan's ground-breaking ecumenical work in Liverpool became legendary, and won him a place on the Secretariat for Christian Unity in Rome. (It is sad that Worlock never paid adequate tribute to Heenan's achievements in Liverpool in this respect.) His successor George Andrew Beck[24] had developed a reasonable working relationship with Stuart Blanch, the Anglican bishop and David Sheppard's immediate predecessor (though Beck's lack of enthusiasm for ecumenism has already been noted). Before Beck's retirement, Sheppard (appointed in 1975) had had a private conversation about Liverpool's needs with the Apostolic Delegate, Archbishop Heim, a 'chance' meeting set up for him by Bishop Mervyn Stockwood of Southwark. Sheppard already knew Worlock, though not intimately, having been Bishop of Woolwich at the same time Worlock had been parish priest in Stepney, just over the Thames.

The significance and influence of the warm friendship between Worlock and Sheppard lies elsewhere. Firstly, it seemed to suit a particular trait in Worlock's character. His former secretary Nicholas France,[25] who was a lifelong but not uncritical friend, felt Worlock was aware of the need to have somebody close to him who could challenge him, as his secretaries had done when they were at Portsmouth together.

> This in some ways shows that it was just as well he wasn't at Westminster and that there was someone else, in the person of Basil, to challenge his sense of always being right. Deep down I believe he liked being an effective number two, an *éminence grise* working behind the throne. Perhaps the same can be seen in Liverpool in his relations with David Sheppard, who as the establishment man always took slight precedence over Derek.

By gently hinting that their relationship was what had kept the lid on the sectarian pressure cooker in Liverpool (even if that was not entirely true), Worlock was able to encourage better personal relations between leading Catholic and Protestant churchmen in Northern Ireland. They set an example, and it may well have had a good effect. (There is correspondence that suggests it did.) Similarly, when national ecumenical relations needed moving to a higher level of energy, the example of Liverpool, as well as the actual working relationship between Sheppard and Worlock, also had an encouraging effect. That higher level already existed on their patch, they could say, and it worked to their mutual benefit. For Sheppard, it gave him a positive profile in the one larger Merseyside Christian denomination, especially one that had strong roots in the working class – Worlock often introduced him to local Catholics active in Labour Party politics or local government who had a background in the Young Christian Workers. For Worlock, the relationship with Sheppard gave him access to a circle of professional and business leaders, of whom few were Catholic. Furthermore the fact that each of them, separately, was a key player in the affairs of his own Church gave each of them a level of access, insight and input into the affairs of the other which could not have been achieved by mere observers or joint committees. If the Catholic Bishops' Conference, for instance, wanted to know what the Church of England House of Bishops was really thinking, 'Derek' could talk to 'David'. Nevertheless there was a constant background of grass-roots criticism on the part both of Anglican and of Catholic parish clergy that despite this good example at the top, ecumenical co-operation at neighbourhood level had not everywhere developed much beyond habits of mutual courtesy.

The extent of sectarian feeling has always been difficult to fathom in England. It has often been assumed to be greater than it actually was. Prior to the issuing of an official invitation to Pope John Paul II to visit Great Britain in 1982, this unfathomability was a major concern. It was assumed that England in particular was still generally anti-Catholic, and inviting the Pope to visit – the first ever by a reigning pontiff – looked to some like a considerable gamble both with his safety and with public order. There was a suspicion in the Church that police forces all over Britain were vastly overestimating the extent of their task in policing the papal visit (and the Catholic Church had some liability to contribute to the extra costs of policing). Gallup was commissioned to conduct a survey to get the measure of public feeling, and the results were unexpected. There was much less anti-papal feeling in the general population than had been anticipated.

The standard model for English Christianity was of a spectrum, with Roman Catholics at one end and Nonconformists (deemed the most Protestant) at the other, with Anglicans in the middle. The Nonconformists, on this theory, were the group to be watched most closely. The Gallup survey produced a different result: those most in favour of the papal visit were, unsurprisingly, the Catholics, but the next most favourable group was within the Free Churches. Members of the Church of England were decidedly less keen. Thus the 'spectrum' theory was not valid. The survey also identified another group which had not previously been considered relevant – there was significant resistance to the papal visit among Left-leaning *Guardian* readers, though presumably not on grounds directly connected with the old Catholic–Protestant quarrels. But none of the opposition to the visit justified the extreme fears that had been expressed in some circles (and many chief constables were left holding large and unnecessary bills for police overtime afterwards).

The one explosion of sectarian feeling of any significance happened in Liverpool in March 1982, and was directed not primarily at Catholics at all, but at the Established Church. Possibly because they were numerically small on a national scale, the Gallup survey failed to detect the remnant of the old Orange tradition of anti-Catholicism on Merseyside. This made its last public appearance at a service at an Anglican parish church in Liverpool, when they interrupted and halted an address being given by the Archbishop of Canterbury, Dr Robert Runcie, in the presence of David Sheppard. Runcie had strongly welcomed the prospect of the papal visit, due to take place that summer, and added to it a personal invitation of his own for the Pope to take part in an ecumenical service at Canterbury Cathedral. Knowing the papal visit was a few weeks away, he started to talk about the relationship between the papacy and England, saying it was Pope Gregory who had sent St Augustine to Canterbury in the sixth century.[26] But his voice was drowned by shouts and jeers from a group of Protestant protesters among the congregation, the rest of which was on his side. Though there was violence in the air, no violence was committed. Runcie had to abandon the service. But the publicity, and the dignified way he had handled himself, swung public sympathy his way.[27] It had the opposite effect to the one intended: when the Pope reached Liverpool on his five-day tour of Britain that June, the warmth and enthusiasm of the welcome that greeted him as he entered Liverpool Anglican Cathedral exceeded any that had been displayed elsewhere during the entire visit.

The papal visit was the culmination of a long process in the Catholic Church in England and Wales which dated from the *Humanae Vitae* crisis in 1968 and the general climate of controversy around at that time. That year all over Europe authority of every kind was being called in question; this was the spring of the Paris riots and the climax of the anti-Vietnam war movement in the United States and elsewhere. This began to affect the Catholic priesthood. A group of French priests declared their solidarity with 'the events of May', and started to organize themselves as a protest movement against Church authority. When an official conference of European bishops was held at Chur in Switzerland the following year – Worlock delivered a paper on 'Priests in the Renewal of the Church' in which he called for 'courageous and responsible experimentation' – a somewhat more raucous and newsworthy unofficial conference of priests was held nearby at the same time. Similar stirrings were reported from America. It became normal to read articles about 'the crisis in the Catholic Church' or 'the crisis in the priesthood'. A nucleus of priests in England and Wales decided they too needed a meeting, and among the issues they had in mind to discuss were some that had been unresolved at the time of the birth control crisis two years earlier – the rights of priests and their security of tenure *vis à vis* their bishops being among them.[28] They also wanted a procedure for arbitrating in disputes between a bishop and one of his priests, for instance where there was a difference of opinion on a matter of moral theology (clearly contraception was what they had in mind).

Worlock was quick to spot what was going on. He appointed himself unofficial (later official) liaison officer between the priests and the bishops, who accepted his advice that the best way of preventing a revolutionary spirit developing among English priests was to allow 'structures' where they could let off steam. The one-off meeting of English and Welsh clergy in 1970 clearly fulfilled a need, and with Worlock's encouragement its leaders moved towards setting up a national institution, which became known as the National Conference of Priests. Thenceforth it met annually, and with the approval of the bishops each diocese put in place procedures for selecting those who were to represent its priests at the annual conference. From the outset it was clear that opinions among the clergy ranged from strongly conservative to mildly radical (mild at least by overseas standards), and varied very much with age-range. The NCP devised a method of selecting representatives, therefore, with each major age band represented by some of its own. Not every diocese adopted these procedures: Heenan in particular resented the way they side-stepped his Senate of Priests.

Worlock attended annually, taking part in debates sometimes to defend official policy but also to advise how to prevent confrontation getting out of hand, either internally or between priests and bishops. In a letter to Archbishop Dwyer in 1972, he was unhappy that not enough bishops were involving themselves in the NCP.

When I visited the final stages of the Liverpool meeting a year ago, I was struck by the obvious hostility of a number of delegates towards bishops in general. All kinds of allegations were made during the week that could easily have been denied, countered or explained had someone from the Bishops' Conference been on the spot. The Cardinal's letter, which should have been read at the opening session, was ignored and I found myself at the end of the meeting having to put right a whole number of points. If I had not been there, certain resolutions would probably have been moved, even if not passed, which could have proved disastrous for future relations between the National Conference of Priests and the Bishops' Conference. On the other hand several bishops had looked in to the meeting during the week. With none of them had there been any real contact.

As well as annual debates on a particular theme, in 1971 the NCP also embarked on an ambitious plan to devise a 'national pastoral strategy' for the Catholic Church in England and Wales. On the principle that showing a willingness to participate was the most likely course to keep tempers cool, the Bishops' Conference consented to set up a joint working party with priest representatives, to draw up detailed proposals. This gradually became the Catholic Church's major strategic initiative in England and Wales for the rest of the 1970s. Early on, but gradually becoming more solid, was a demand for a national conference or assembly to be held at which a strategy for the future of the Catholic Church could be discussed and endorsed by bishops, priests and laity, and could be given the momentum it would need if anything was to happen subsequently on the ground.

The first fruit of the joint working party was an interim report called *The Church 2000*, which was ambitious in millennial vision but a little limited in detailed proposals. The National Conference of Priests asked the working party to continue to work towards the holding of a major national event. But it added a new term of reference that quickly caused major problems for the bishops – the working party 'should give special consideration to the problems of married life in the contemporary world, taking note of the *sensus fidelium* concerning contraception and divorce in particular'. The episcopal members of the working party could not accept it because they knew that what it really meant was that '*Humanae Vitae* was wrong'. (*The Guardian*'s report of the debate at the NCP in 1974 had made that perfectly clear.) Worlock and various other bishops quickly became involved in a wrangle that dragged on for years, generating a good deal of bad temper. In 1976 the whole exercise was very nearly abandoned. One priest member of the joint working party who took a great deal of shifting on the point was Father Michael Hollings of Bayswater, he who later conducted the wedding of Jenny Sheppard. But gradually a compromise was found. Even so, the Archbishop of Birmingham, Dwyer, while welcoming the compromise formula, was still warning Worlock 'This is of great importance but we must take care that if a National Pastoral Council comes off it doesn't become a debate on contraception.' Worlock reassured him: 'The offending reference to *sensus fidelium* has gone.'

The bishops did accept the idea of a National Pastoral Congress – indeed it became an official venture of the Bishops' Conference rather than of the National Conference of Priests. Worlock became chairman of the committee preparing the Congress, and its secretary was Father Tom Shepherd, Chairman of the National Conference of Priests. One reason why the bishops took it over may have been to give them better control – as Worlock wrote later to Dwyer: 'At the Low Week meeting[29] we agreed that any future Conference to discuss these matters should be an initiative of the Secretariat of the Bishops' Conference, so I think we can at least ensure that the issue of contraception is not on the agenda – even though we can never quite be sure that this matter is not mentioned in any individual's speech.' Such confidence did not last long. All the issues facing the Catholic community in the late 1970s were to be discussed and in that context questions concerning marriage – 'the tensions connected with the problems of married life', as the new wording put it – had to be allowed an airing. Furthermore the new Pope, John Paul II, was keen to have issues of family, marriage and sexuality debated at a meeting of the International Synod of Bishops which was due to be held in the autumn of 1980.

With that event just ahead, trying to stop a discussion of the issue at Liverpool in the summer would be virtually impossible. It was regarded by some as a useful opportunity to try to reopen the ruling given by *Humanae Vitae*. Derek Worlock, in charge of the day-to-day preparations of the Congress,[30] had the consent of Cardinal Hume for a full section of the Congress to discuss marriage and family matters. Dwyer, who wanted it kept off the agenda, ceased to be President of the Bishops' Conference of England and Wales in 1979, when Cardinal Hume took over the presidency. The willingness to allow, even encourage, a debate on contraception seems to date from then. Worlock, of course, was loyal to both positions. Where Pope John Paul II stood on these matters was not at that time entirely clear, though he was very interested in interpersonal relations and desired to see some philosophical underpinning to the discussion. There was a certain cautious optimism that the time had come for some modest progress.

The 1980 National Pastoral Congress in Liverpool was widely judged a great success, though Worlock soon discovered that the message was not getting through to Rome. Archbishop Bruno Heim, the Pope's representative in Great Britain, had been present in person and generally supportive. But his deputy at the Apostolic Delegation in Wimbledon, Monsignor Mario Oliveri, was deeply suspicious. While Heim was away ill, he allowed himself to become a channel through which some extremely conservative Catholics could denounce the Congress to the Vatican. One paper he forwarded was headed 'REASONS WHY THE NATIONAL PASTORAL CONGRESS OUGHT TO BE STOPPED', and another complained that the Congress delegates 'appeared to be drawn, on the whole, from either those holding progressive views or from amongst those who know little or nothing about the nature of the Church'. It went on to appeal to the Pope to visit England in person, to 'help English Catholics to defend the Faith of their Fathers,[31] for the sake of their children'.

Worlock complained that these papers had gone to Rome without the bishops being given a chance to comment on them. Oliveri replied that the bishops had to take seriously the complaints of the people who had written to him. A damage limitation exercise was arranged forthwith, with the co-operation of Archbishop Heim, who had now taken charge again. A number of bishops (including, according to Worlock, David Konstant[32]) organized letters from delegates in support of the Congress, asking that they be forwarded to the Holy See through the Apostolic Delegation in Wimbledon. The affair blew over with a handwritten note from Heim to Worlock in July 1980, in which he said: 'I am so sorry about all this trouble which has arisen during my absence. I believe that Rome is now properly informed and that any damage has been undone.' At about that time, Worlock wrote to a correspondent in Australia saying: 'The situation has not been helped by almost inevitable right-wing delations[33] to Rome, but I hope that my visit last week will at least have reduced the danger from these. It is as well that the Pope knows me.'

The possibility of disloyalty to the papal policy on birth control was one of the things uppermost in the critics' minds, even though the debate on that constituted only a small part of the work the Congress had to get through. In the event, after some discussion, 322 delegates in this section, 93 per cent of the total, voted for the proposition: 'There is a widespread lack of understanding and widespread disagreement amongst Catholics about the present teaching on contraception'; 281 (81 per cent) voted for: 'The Church's teaching on marriage is at an *impasse* because of confusion, uncertainty, and disagreement over contraception, which affects the whole sacramental life of many Catholics'; and 299 (87 per cent) for: 'The Church's teaching on marriage can only develop through a fundamental re-examination of the teaching on marriage, sexuality and on contraception.' The proposition that 'Non-contraceptive intercourse is the ideal for which everyone should strive' received 52 votes.

But the Congress was about much more than that, even if the secular Press concentrated on the one issue that would be most likely to interest the general reader – this was where the *frisson* was. The Congress was also the occasion when something very important happened in the post-war history of the Catholic community in England and Wales that is not recorded in any of the resolutions. It was when the post-Vatican II bishops of England and Wales encountered the post-Vatican II laity as they truly were for the first time: not as troublemakers over *Humanae Vitae*, not as customers of the Catholic schools system, not as docile clients of the insti-tutional Church, not as mere pew-fodder and payers-up. They saw them as equals, as fellow Christians, and above all as the primary evangelizers of the world they lived in. And very impressed the bishops were too. One remarked afterwards: 'I felt I had met the modern Catholic layman for the very first time. Phew!' (And it was Derek Worlock, of course, who had arranged the introduction.) Another, regarded as rather conservative, was asked if he had learnt anything from the Congress and dryly replied: 'It has caused me to rearrange my prejudices.'

Among the lay people from all over the country who attended the Congress were many who were prominent in their own careers and professions, experts in their field and well informed theologically. Worlock, as chairman of the preparatory group, had worked assiduously to make sure each diocese, and each representative Catholic lay organization, sent forward good lay delegates. This was reflected in a generally high quality of debate which produced a mature and open exchange of view. (The Duke of Norfolk found himself adopted by a small group of Cockney black girls, who thought he was sweet but weren't sure who he was.) The discussion on family life did indeed include contraception, but the tone was moderate and responsible. A series of questions were put to the delegates at the end of it. Options offered to them ranged from wanting the Church's teaching to 'change', through wanting it to 'develop', to leaving matters as they were. The largest vote was for the 'develop' option, but it was clear by this that delegates meant the absolute ban on artificial birth control should be relaxed. Because it was safer, 'develop' was rapidly becoming a codeword for 'change'.

As often happens, the Congress was as important for the informal contacts made and private conversations had as it was for the business conducted. Apart from the call for a 'development' on birth control, two other Congress decisions were to have a long-lasting influence. There was a strong opinion in favour of the Catholic Church seeking full membership of the British Council of Churches, a bone of contention since Heenan's time. And as well as concern over birth control, there was considerable criticism of the current Catholic policy, stemming from the Vatican, of treating a person who had remarried after divorce, or who was married to somebody in that position, as being in a state of sin and therefore excluded from Holy Communion. These were, in fact, the two messages from the Catholic Church in England and Wales for the international synod on the family. The bishops appointed Cardinal Hume and Archbishop Worlock as their two delegates, the latter being accompanied by Monsignor Vincent Nichols. Hume was to deal with contraception, Worlock with divorce. Hume had attended the Congress discussion on contraception, sitting modestly at the back. He seemed impressed by what he heard, and at the final Press conference stoutly defended the right of delegates to say what they had said (and the right of the Press to report it). His remarks to the synod faithfully reflected what he had heard at the Congress.

After the Congress Worlock organized the writing of the official report, and the draft of the bishops' response to it. He took over a room above his garage for a team that mainly consisted of Jack Mahoney, the Jesuit moral theologian, Pat Jones, a young laywoman Worlock had got to know from both her parents being full-time YCW workers, and Monsignor George Leonard, a Shrewsbury diocese priest who was press officer and public affairs assistant to Cardinal Hume in Westminster. They had six weeks to prepare for the Bishops' Conference a draft statement of response to the Congress, for it to amend as it pleased. 'In the end it was a composite job, largely from my pen', Worlock wrote later to Hume. In fact it went through the Bishops' Conference more or less as drafted, and was published under the title *The Easter People*.

The most delicate passage of all was on marriage, contraception and divorce. Prior to the international synod, Cardinal Hume and Archbishop Worlock visited the Pope in Rome to present him with a personal copy of *The Easter People*. They clearly felt it was nothing to be ashamed of. But Hume later described how he handed it across, deliberately opened at the page on birth control, and drew it to the Pope's attention. The Pope merely waved it to one side. It was an unfavourable omen. Yet the bishops' document was hardly radical. It declared unhesitatingly that 'The encyclical *Humanae Vitae* is the authentic teaching of the Church.'[34] If it was possible to reconcile fidelity to *Humanae Vitae* with what the Congress had decided, then this was the way.[35] That could not be said – or Archbishop Dwyer declined so to say – about a report which the bishop's Theological Commission had prepared (drafted by Jack Mahoney) on the contraception question as an aid to the English delegates at the synod. It was apparently never issued officially as such, because Dwyer objected to it on the grounds that it did not do justice to *Humanae Vitae*. He threatened to write a minority report.

In the middle of all this Worlock found himself anonymously denounced to the Holy See and accused by Cardinal Ottaviani's successor at the Vatican, Cardinal Seper of the Congregation for the Doctrine of the Faith, of authorizing an official document that was 'unsound' on birth control. Two years earlier he had written an introduction to a marriage preparation course prepared by the Catholic Marriage Advisory Council. 'Some passages in this material do not completely comply with the teaching of the Church as set out in the encyclical letter *Humanae Vitae*', Seper wrote. Worlock passed the complaint on to the chief executive of the Council, Father Peter Rudman, in the most defiant and scathing terms. He did not feel obliged to treat it with great urgency. 'It is rather sickening to know that such denunciations continue', Worlock added, 'but at least we can stand together on *The Easter People* and if the Sacred Congregation wants to take exception to that, they will have to take on all 48 bishops. But one is left wondering who made the denunciations in the first place.' Small amendments were made to the text, but the Vatican was informed that most copies of the material had by now been distributed.[36]

At the same time Worlock was fending off complaints from the Congregation for the Doctrine of the Faith concerning a document, *The Pastoral Care of Homosexual People*, which had been issued by the Bishops' Conference Social Welfare Commission. The document was considered moderately liberal, too much so for the Vatican, though it did not condone homosexual practices. He referred the Vatican to the bishop who had chaired the commission responsible, Bishop Augustine Harris,[37] adding 'though I must say that its general tone and content appeared to enjoy a positive welcome from other members of our Conference' (in other words 'You might find yourself fighting all of us'). Worlock also batted back a complaint about Dr Jack Dominian, a prominent Catholic psychiatrist who was a noted critic of the Church's teaching on birth control and unofficially held in high esteem by the great majority of English bishops, including the Cardinal.

It is clear that Worlock felt on safe ground in adopting this robust tone with the Vatican, and the most likely explanation is that he knew Cardinal Hume felt similarly. There was not much of a lingering trace of Ultramontanism about them by now. 'Exasperationism' would be nearer the mark. Among English Catholic bishops, the Vatican's policy of taking anonymous denunciations seriously was (and indeed still is) the most keenly resented of all its practices, being contrary to natural justice and the English sense of fair play. It enables disgruntled factions in the Church, invariably self-righteous ultra-conservatives who are convinced the bishops are deliberately undermining the Catholic faith, to mount a constant barrage of irritating, uncharitable, ill-informed and time-consuming complaints.[38]

Worlock tended to follow Heenan's custom of sentimentalizing the papacy for public consumption, always giving the impression that everything was for the best in the best of all possible worlds. This in a speech on the work of the Anglican–Roman Catholic International Commission in Croydon in 1982, he does not repeat Hume's account of them visiting the Pope to hand over a copy of *The Easter People*, deliberately drawing the section on contraception to the Pope's attention and seeing him wave it aside dismissively. Instead: 'With Cardinal Basil Hume I flew to Rome and we handed the first copy to Peter's successor, John Paul II, the symbol of unity. To him we said: "Here is our church in England and Wales. Now, will you come to visit us?"' etc.

The Pope said yes, though there are various other versions of who first invited him. His acceptance, and the fixing of a date for the summer of 1982, immediately took attention away from the National Pastoral Congress and its aftermath. It presented a new battleground, concerning the tone and content of the papal visit. Even in 1980 it was becoming clear that Pope John Paul II was no Western European progressive; in fact he had little time for them. Vatican II Catholicism (or his reading of it) held the answer to all the problems of modern society, and had little to learn. Because of the assumption in popular Catholic piety that the choice of a new Pope is an exercise largely guided by the Holy Spirit, the opinions and attitudes of the former Archbishop of Cracow quickly became the new orthodoxy. The fact that the same cardinals, and presumably the same Holy Spirit, had chosen another man as Pope not much more than a month earlier, a man with a rather different set of attitudes and opinions, did not fit well with this theory of divine inspiration and so tended to be overlooked.[39]

The 1980 synod was a highly delicate moment in the life of the Church. The briefing papers circulated beforehand held out little prospect of movement in the direction desired by the National Pastoral Congress. The Pope himself had made some preliminary remarks that seemed to toughen, rather than soften, the position over contraception. Worlock and Hume delivered their messages, as requested by the National Pastoral Congress and endorsed by the bishops of England and Wales (more or less).

Worlock told the synod that marriage was changing, and the changes were producing new tensions. He continued:

Personal factors increasingly today include the desire for genuinely interpersonal communication and relationships in marriage and in the family, the ability of couples to control fertility, and the changed status of women, and therefore also of men, in society and the family.

External, or social, factors which endanger the family today are frequently cited as including a spirit of materialism, hedonism and other secular values. It would, however, be more accurate, and perhaps more just to many Christian couples, to point also to lack of adequate housing, poverty, unemployment and enforced leisure arising for many from economic recession or from the microelectronic revolution. These social factors are the more damaging to families insofar as they condemn them to living conditions which are unworthy of their dignity, increase the pressures on the family from within, and prevent it from

giving positive Christian witness to love, fidelity and security, and from resisting materialistic values . . .

But the Church cannot turn a blind eye to the many family tragedies which
are increasing in society, and no less in the Church itself. To these victims of
misfortune, not necessarily of personal sin, or of sin which has not been forgiven, the Church, both universal and local, must have a special healing
ministry of consolation. Nor can the Church neglect those Catholics whose
first marriage has perished and who now find themselves in a second more
stable and perhaps more mature union which may have many of the desirable
qualities of the Christian family. Many acknowledge that their union is irregu-
lar in the eyes of the Church, and yet nevertheless feel, even if inarticulately,
that they are not living in a state of sin, that they love God and may in some
mysterious way be living according to his will, even if against, or outside, the
Church's legislation. The number of such members of the Church is growing
daily, and very many long for full Eucharistic communion with the Church
and its Lord.

As is well known, many pastors, and many theologians, are of the view that
such Catholics may be admitted to Holy Communion, under certain conditions, notwithstanding the danger of scandal, namely that other Catholics,
either about to marry or living in a weakened marriage, may disregard the
Church's teaching on the fidelity and indissolubility of Christian marriage,
with ruinous results. But what is most interesting and calling for close consideration, is that many married laity, moved by pastoral compassion, are of the
same opinion, and do not fear that Christian marriage will be destroyed by
such a practice. They seem to consider that fidelity and indissolubility are
human and Christian values on their own account, and do not derive their
force from being regarded as necessary dispositions for receiving Holy Communion. In this, as in every other aspect of marriage and the family, it would
be desirable to listen to the voice, experience and Christian wisdom of married
couples themselves.

It was a bold plea for Catholics who were divorced and had remarried in a
register office (they were not allowed to remarry in the Church itself), or
those married to such persons, to be allowed to receive Holy Communion
at Mass. Many speakers at the synod had alluded to the problem, but none
with more clarity than Worlock. In future years, these remarks defined his
pastoral approach to the problem, though he never again set it down in
writing.

Hume meanwhile had tackled the even more controversial issue of contraception. He admitted that many married Catholic couples did not accept
the total prohibition of contraception. But some had had no difficulty in

accepting it, and through living strictly within the limits laid down by *Humanae Vitae*, had discovered new richness in their married lives.

> Others cannot accept the total prohibition of the use of artificial means of contraception where circumstances seemed to make this necessary or even desirable. Natural methods of birth control do not seem to them to be the definitive and only solution. It cannot just be said that these persons have failed to overcome their human frailty and weakness. The problem is far more complex than that. Indeed, such persons are often good, conscientious and faithful sons and daughters of the Church. They just cannot accept that the use of artificial means of contraception in some circumstances is *intrinsice inhonestum*[40] as this latter has been generally understood.

A third category, he went on, were those who were confused. They did not want to be disobedient to the authority of the Church but at the same time they were not convinced by the arguments which were given to them to observe the norms laid down. Concentrating on that controversial issue had hindered that development of the teaching on marriage which would bring out all the riches already contained in the Church's teaching.

He concluded:

> I have not come to this synod with solutions to the difficult pastoral problems created by the controversy. But as a pastor I, like you, am much concerned for the spiritual welfare of all the people about whom I have spoken. I hope and pray that as a result of this synod, and with the help of the synod fathers, I shall be able to give better guidance to those married people who are looking to the Church for help.

This mood of optimism did not last. Hume later delivered a much quoted extempore speech, speaking only on his own behalf, in which he praised *Humanae Vitae* but then – rather obliquely but very powerfully – talked of the dangers of the Church not being able to communicate the will of God in these matters. It was not so much the teaching, as the growing attitude of intolerance towards those who differed from it, that worried him. Judging from his mood at the end, he had grown more and more despondent as the synod progressed.

He told the delegates he had nodded off during the synod and had a dream.

> I heard a voice speaking and it spoke of the Church; and I saw in my dream a vision. It was a vision of the Church. I saw a fortress, strong and upstanding.

Every stranger approaching seemed to those defending to be an enemy to be repelled: from that fortress the voice of those outside could not be heard. The soldiers within showed unquestioning obedience – and that was much to be admired: 'Theirs not to reason why, theirs but to do and die.'[41] It seemed thus in my dream, and then I remembered, upon awakening – it was only just to do so – that dreams distort reality. They exaggerate.

Then I had another vision. It was of a pilgrim, a pilgrim through history and through life. That pilgrim was the Church. The pilgrim was hastening towards a vision, towards all Truth. But it had not yet reached it. It limped along the road. But meanwhile there were signposts to show the way, or rather they told you that this or that road was not the right one. The pilgrim is always in search, I reflected, and that can be painful. The leaders, too, of the pilgrimage are often themselves not always clear. They may sometimes co-agonize with the other pilgrims. Co-responsibility[42] will always involve co-agonizing. The fortress was a temple, but the pilgrim lived in a tent. It is sometimes better to know the uncertainties of Abraham's tent than to sit secure in Solomon's temple.[43]

Then I had another vision: I saw with great clarity that the insight of Paul VI in the encyclical *Humanae Vitae*, confirming the traditional teaching of the Church, was surely right. But alas we did not know how to speak to the people. The road-signs point the way, but signposts become weather-beaten and new paint is needed. It takes time to get the work done. My dream became a nightmare, for I saw the wrong paint being put upon the signposts and the last state was worse than the first.

We must never fail to listen to the other pilgrims. And they need encouraging. We must speak gently, compassionately, co-agonize with them, lead them gradually and speak a language that enables them to say: 'Yes, that is right; and is now clear: we accept the teaching.' I saw the pilgrims happy because they had been led nearer to him who is all Truth, and they sang their joy in praise and thanksgiving. I awoke and I said 'Vidi, gratia'.[44]

The object of the synod was to make recommendations to the Pope. Hume, and even more so Worlock, both felt that the synod had been steered towards foregone, and basically closed-minded, conclusions. Indeed, some members of their official party were briefing the Press afterwards that the two English Catholic leaders had felt badly let down by the outcome. Particular exception was taken to the hand-picked lay people present, primed to sing the praises of *Humanae Vitae* in the most triumphalistic manner. There was very little tolerance on display towards those who had difficulties with it. Worlock had tried to have the final message completely redrafted, and offered his own version instead. He argued that 'the drafters of the official text have attempted the impossible in trying to give some account of the work and mind of the synod fathers before the propositions have been submitted or agreed'. He was ruled out of order.

After the National Pastoral Congress but before the Rome synod, *The Easter People* had been published and the National Conference of Priests had met to consider it. They passed a 'declaration' welcoming it. Then they began to learn what had happened at the synod in Rome, and been disappointed. They felt the English delegation, from what they had read, had not been bold enough.

So a meeting was arranged at which leaders of the National Conference of Priests could put their misgivings to Worlock and Hume, and hear first-hand what had happened. Monsignor David Norris was present as secretary of the Bishops' Conference, to draw up a report to be circulated to the bishops. What was said was extraordinarily frank. Hume told them that the liberal shutters were going up in the Church. If the English Catholic community was to hold on to what progress it had made so far, it was going to have to proceed very carefully in future. Already there were signs of their own positions being under attack.

This was inflammably dangerous stuff, as Worlock immediately realized. No doubt Norris had already been told to be careful what he reported. The reality of the conversation must have been a good deal more candid.

Even so: Worlock to Norris (6 November 1980): 'I hope you will understand when I say that I think it would be disastrous if this report were circulated to the Bishops. Indeed I must confess I am most unhappy about the whole of the first page and I doubt very much whether the cardinal would want his remarks reported. The reference to the attacks upon himself and myself could throw our meeting of the Conference later this month into all kinds of chaos . . .', and so on.

Worlock to Hume: 'I enclose a copy of a letter I have written to David Norris on the subject of his report of the meeting with the standing committee of the NCP. I think the report would be disastrous if it goes to the NCP. It would be even more disastrous if it is sent out with the papers for the Bishops' meeting. It will probably be best if I prepare a single sheet.'

Hume to Worlock: 'I am in full agreement with what you say about the report concerning the NCP.' This was the passage they agreed to suppress:[45]

REPORT OF MEETING WITH MEMBERS OF THE STANDING COMMITTEE OF THE NATIONAL CONFERENCE OF PRIESTS

Present: The Cardinal and Archbishop Worlock, Frs R. Spence, J. Carter, Mgr J. Buckley, Frs J. Breen and D. Forrester. Mgr D. Norris (Secretary).

A. Declaration from NCP

(1) General

The Declaration accepted wholeheartedly the findings of the National Pastoral Congress and welcomed the bishops' message *The Easter People*. However, the National Conference had some problems with the bishops' message for they felt that the bishops had moved away from some of the resolutions of the Congress. The bishops appeared to give up their right as a local Church and to be too willing to give way to the Roman Curia.

The Cardinal replied that he considered that conservatism was succeeding in many parts of the world and was also rising in Rome. We had to remember that Western Europe was now a minority in the Church and places like Africa and South America were very conservative. Our local church has to find its way in the present circumstances and it is not always clear how it should proceed.

The Cardinal was sure that it would not help to have public calls on our bishops to act by themselves. There were some conservatives in this country who were already attacking what had already been done by himself and Archbishop Worlock.

The Archbishop was more optimistic – he compared the Synod with the last Council – then the minority had proposed renewal and had managed to become the majority by the end of the Council. Now there had been a change during the four weeks of the Synod, though perhaps not a full acceptance of the minority view. The Pope, too, had attended all the plenary sessions and had made no attempt to interfere with the freedom of those taking part. In his closing speech, the Pope had not closed the door and had in fact welcomed the propositions. Nor had he rejected the famous law of gradualness; what he had condemned was a graded law.[46]

The rest of the document was much less contentious; but none of it saw the light of day. Worlock's optimism that the message was starting to get through may have been for the encouragement of the National Conference of Priests rather than his private view: he did not tell them he had tried to have the final message entirely re-written. Hume's remarks minuted by David Norris, and the eagerness of Hume and Worlock subsequently to suppress the record in order to conceal what they really thought, strongly implied that the two of them had agonized long and hard about the situation in the Catholic Church at that time, and realized they were in some difficulty. Their dismissal from office was almost inconceivable; but the Vatican had other ways in which it could have wrested control of the Bishops' Conference of England and Wales out of the hands of people it did not trust to promote the party line. Before and since, it had shown itself willing to use those powers in countries such as Switzerland, Germany, Austria, the United States, and above all Holland, where a progressive and popular hierarchy had been gradually replaced by a highly conservative and very unpopular one. Often, the tactics involved using ultra-conservative Catholics in the country in question to raise a barrage of complaints, suggesting certain bishops were not loyally obeying the papal line (especially on issues like sex). This evidence was then used as a weapon inside the Vatican to discredit the individuals concerned. What Cardinal Hume was saying to the priests, in effect, was that 'we cannot do all the things we might like to do because Rome would intervene, not only to stop it but eventually to reverse the whole direction of our policy'. This was the most likely reason why *The Easter People* never really became what it was supposed to be, a development plan for the next ten or twenty years. In the short term, the impending papal visit turned attention elsewhere; in the longer term, *The Easter People* was largely forgotten. That is not to say it was a failure, or the exercise was not worthwhile. The National Pastoral Congress was one of two key events in the life of the Catholic Church of England and Wales since 1965, the other being the papal visit of 1982. Together they represented the turning point when the whole community of the Church, bishops, priests and people, saw themselves as the Church that the Second Vatican Council had described, and adopted that as their definition and *raison d'être* henceforth. It may be said to be the moment that Vatican II was 'received' into the *sensus fidelium*. This was the goal Derek Worlock had set before himself when he became the first new 'Vatican II' bishop in England in 1965. This was the Worlock project. That it was achieved, and that the Catholic community did not tear itself apart in the process, owes more to him than to any other individual. If the situation in England is compared with the less successful trajectory over this period of the Scottish Catholic Church, and the far less successful, indeed in some ways disastrous, performance of the Irish Catholic Church over a similar obstacle course, and if the question is then asked what distinguished English Catholicism from the other two cases, then the answer may very well be – Derek Worlock.

But what had been achieved had then to be defended, against those who would undo it if they could. It was not necessarily a wise move to allow Worlock to think he had enemies, as his active imagination might start to find them everywhere. The reference to attacks on Hume and Worlock may have referred, at least partly, to the letter from Cardinal Seper about the Catholic Marriage Advisory Council (which had also gone to Cardinal Hume), which Worlock had already complained was based on the anonymous 'denunciations' which annoyed him so much. But the nervousness about giving this report to the rest of the Bishops' Conference suggests they had another worry in mind. Two of the bishops, Thomas Holland of Salford and Hugh Lindsay of Hexham and Newcastle, had complained that the English delegation at the Rome synod had not been faithful to the line agreed with the other bishops. Holland had apparently cabled to Rome repudiating some of Worlock's and Hume's reported remarks. Lindsay had assisted Holland in getting their reservations into print in an article in *The Universe*, though it had not worked out as he wanted. Worlock's correspondence files contain a copy of a letter in which he bluntly accused Hugh Lindsay of 'a gross act of betrayal'.

There was also a phone call from Worlock in Rome to Lindsay in England in which he remonstrated severely about the *Universe* article. In fact, 'possibly unwisely', Bishop Lindsay had tried to get Holland to modify his attack on the English delegates, while conceding that their reported remarks were not necessarily the view of every one of the bishops. Why Worlock was so hard on Lindsay over this, and did not tackle Holland directly, is not clear. Holland had ceased being regarded as an ally, perhaps, while Lindsay still was. A storm in a tea-cup; but symptomatic of Worlock's state of anxiety, even paranoia – and also of the excessive loyalty he sometimes expected from associates. He could be unthinkingly cruel. As a fellow diocesan bishop, Lindsay was certainly entitled to his own opinion and under no obligation to agree with Worlock. The publication of the article in *The Universe* was tactless, though probably not harmful. The matter blew over, and they resumed their working relationship on the various committees and projects on which they served together. But for Lindsay it remained a painful memory. He did not think Worlock had been fair.

And so the Catholic Church in England and Wales travelled trepidatiously (beneath the surface) but confidently (to all appearances) towards the ultimate Catholic happening – a personal visit by the Pope. It was a great upheaval, requiring many clergy to leave aside their familiar tasks and undertake entirely new and strange ones. Canon lawyers became temporary business managers, seminary lecturers became Press officers, hospital chaplains police liaison workers. One group had to negotiate with car companies for the manufacture of a right-hand-drive 'popemobile'; another to strike deals with insurance companies, another to supervise the growing trade in 'official souvenirs' of the papal visit and extract the appropriate rake-off for the Church. Amateurs though they were, they turned out to be very good at all this.

In no sense was this to be a State visit, or anything official at all, but it involved almost every element of that short of the actual status – a formal welcome at Gatwick, a special train to Victoria, streets closed and crush barriers in place, motorcycle outriders on duty, wall-to-wall television coverage and vast acreage in the Press, an 'informal' visit to the Queen, even a call on Margaret Thatcher at 10 Downing Street. In the light of the assassination attempt in 1981, British security regarded the visit as a major project, no smaller in scale than a State visit as far as their role was concerned, and armed officers were discreetly briefed.

Preparations went ahead for a series of papal visits to London, Wales, Scotland and the English regions, each event to be a major celebration of the Catholic faith likely to be attended by tens, if not hundreds, of thousands of people. The Catholic Church is not established by law in Britain, and enjoys no large holdings of property, neither estates nor investments. Its assets are its people and physical plant, mainly schools and churches, and though as prime sites many of these would have been immensely valuable on the open market, they were all in use. Thus the Church had to borrow from the banks – the total budget was more than £6 million in 1982 values – and raise the money to pay for the visit afterwards, partly from church collections, partly from royalties on branded goods (which quickly became a minor industry). For an institution which traditionally lived hand to mouth, usually more interested in its overdraft limit than its cash in hand, there was a lot at stake.

It was decided, and the Vatican concurred, to make the theme of the visit the seven sacraments of the Church, one for each occasion. Thus on one occasion the Pope would baptize an infant and preach on the sacrament of baptism; on another occasion he would anoint the sick and preach on that; and so on round the country and round the sacraments. A special event would be his joint ecumenical pilgrimage with the Archbishop of Canterbury to the site of the martyrdom of St Thomas à Becket at Canterbury Cathedral, which was expanded into a major Church of England service with the entire membership of the General Synod of that Church being invited. The Pope was to meet members of all the other denominations afterwards. Not only was the theme idea acceptable to Rome, but exceptionally, papal advisers agreed to allow very substantial British input in the briefing of the Pope and the preparation of his addresses. This enabled some careful downplaying of one or more of the most sensitive matters. It was widely felt among English Catholic leaders, for instance, that if the Pope went round the country berating the population for the looseness of its sexual morals, especially in the use of contraception, the visit would rapidly turn into a public relations disaster which English Catholics would have to live with for a long time to come.

Worlock reported in one of his recollections of the papal visit that 'when the rather delicate matter of briefing the Pope was raised, I moved that the matter be left with the Cardinal and subsequently he got a team of three or four together under George Leonard'. Worlock was asked to prepare a couple of drafts himself.[47] Apart from Leonard, Hume's group preparing draft texts for the Pope consisted mainly of Vincent Nichols, Alan Clark and James Hook (Leonard's deputy), working under the Cardinal's supervision. When Worlock discussed progress with a senior Vatican official

> it was evident then, as it was proved by the eventual texts, that the briefings were most acceptable. With the guidance of George Leonard, who had helped me with *The Easter People*, the combined teaching proved more than we had dared to hope for as a validation of the National Pastoral Congress and its recommendations, although he was to refer to the Congress only once, and that at Liverpool.

In other words the English bishops were allowed to tell the Pope what to say, and not surprisingly it turned out to be what the English bishops wanted the people to hear.[48]

There was certainly a sense in the Vatican that this visit had to be approached with special caution, and if the English advised for or against a certain course of action, they were probably correct. One senior Catholic official who was a little slow to catch on that for once the hosts were in the driving seat, was Archbishop Paul Marcinkus, the Vatican's financial adviser and popularly described as the Pope's bodyguard because his build reflected his past as an American football player. He came to Britain to troubleshoot, and ruffled some feathers. But he did not get his way.

The major threat to the event came not from would-be assassins nor even from truculent papal bodyguards but from an entirely unexpected direction: the Argentine invasion of the Falkland Islands in the South Atlantic. A British naval and military taskforce was rapidly assembled, totalling more than a hundred ships and including two aircraft carriers.[48] It set sail at the beginning of April to try to reverse the invasion 8,000 miles away. Though the Catholic Church never made the mistake of regarding its own difficulties as anywhere near as important as the impending war in the South Atlantic, with probably loss of life on all sides, it was nevertheless faced with a serious predicament of its own.

Cancellation was obviously an option from the start, but not necessarily the easy way out. In certain right-wing circles in Latin America, the invasion of the islands they called the Malvinas was being hailed as the correction of an historical injustice committed by a Protestant nation against a Catholic one. If the Pope was seen to cancel his visit because Britain was exercising its rights in international law and the UN Charter of defending its territory from invasion, would that be seen as a neutral and fair thing to do, or as an expression of Catholic bias? The thought occurred in the Vatican itself, and it suggested caution; the thought also occurred in Britain, and it suggested leverage. The idea had to be fostered that cancellation would be treated as a hostile act – 'the British public would not understand . . .' etc.

There had to be a strategy for saving the visit, but who was to be in charge of it? Cardinal Hume thought *he* was; but Derek Worlock thought he was. This misunderstanding became acute as the weeks went on.

It left Worlock with a residual feeling of resentment, or possibly even obsession, as shown by the fact that he devoted part of his holiday in 1982 *and* in 1983 to recording his version of events in 46 ruled A4 pages of long-hand. Implicit beneath the surface of this long and complex chronology is his conviction that he, personally, 'saved' the 1982 papal visit from cancellation. As he tells it, not the least of the problems he had to contend with was an erratic contribution from Cardinal Hume, whose behaviour at times nearly defeated Worlock's own accomplished efforts.

It is true that as the military expedition to the South Atlantic progressed – the arrival off the coast of the Falkland Islands of British sea power, the duels with aircraft, the first landings, the losses of warships on both sides – the visit seemed less and less likely to go ahead. Hume expressed his own doubts at a Press conference, to Worlock's consternation. Would the Pope not be seen to be favouring one side against the other, if he visited it under such conditions? As the date got nearer, however, the Catholic Church in Britain was incurring ever higher financial liabilities. Insurance would have covered the first £1.5 million, but costs were mounting rapidly towards the £6 million which had been the overall budget. Each new day with no cancellation raised the stakes; contractors were starting work, bills were having to be paid, hundreds of coaches booked; everything from temporary lavatories to emergency lighting to first aid to helicopter landing pads had to be settled according to a strict schedule of dates. To Worlock, having to pay for a papal visit that never happened would have seemed like the ultimate catastrophe. He had the connections and the guile, all the diplomatic skills required, to bring about a near impossibility. To Hume, however, it was just one of those things; the visit would surely take place another time. What worried him, it seems, was that Worlock was doing deals to save the visit at all costs, when there were other, higher, issues at stake, and principles that ought not to be compromised.[50]

At the outset of his record, Worlock declared:

> Time might soften certain recollections but can also confuse the memory. Already folklore and political loyalties are taking over and although I am not trying to remove the so-called glory from those to whom it is now attributed, it seems right to set the record down somewhere for future historians. Judgements and assessments can follow later.

Later on the same page, perhaps. There are times when Worlock's attitude to Hume is scathing. Thus they both went to visit the Pope to hand him a copy of *The Easter People*; they invited the Pope to come to England; the Pope consented. 'When we got back', wrote Worlock in the first of these long handwritten essays, 'Basil had to contact the Queen at Balmoral, the Foreign Office, the Archbishop of Canterbury (on holiday in the Greek islands) and Cardinal Gray for the Scots. Unbelievably, he had failed to take any of these steps in advance, as had been agreed between us.'

The word 'unbelievably' is an early hint of a tone of exasperation that gets more intense as the story unfolds. But it does not take much reading between the lines to deduce that Worlock had been manipulating and manoeuvring to get Hume to agree to do all these things, and Hume wasn't responding. A 'Maybe' had been taken for a 'Yes'. The man for whom things were plain, who wanted quick results, was getting impatient with the man with the more subtle mind, who wanted time to think things over. And he was the more senior. It was a situation ripe for a personality clash: the canine versus the feline.

Furthermore, it appears that some of the bishops were unsure about the justice of the whole British enterprise. 'Undoubtedly under the influence of George Leonard, and of his brother-in-law Lord Hunt and Foreign

Office friend Sir Michael Palliser, GBH[51] fell into the role of "supreme hawk".' There was a quarrel about whether the Catholic Church should make a statement for or against the Task Force, or keep silent, with Worlock plainly leading the doves. Hume lost the vote at a bishops' meeting, and Worlock was left to draft a statement calling for prayers for a peaceful settlement. Hume was left to issue it when he felt the time was right, and it never was. The opposition to the British military action was not at all out of any sympathy for Argentina and its claims, but seemed to come from a near-pacifist sentiment shared by some of the bishops, and a feeling that the justification for Britain's action was somewhat undermined by Britain's conduct prior to the invasion (a feeling widespread enough in the country to lead to the resignation of the Foreign Secretary, Lord Carrington).

So Worlock left a long and exhaustively detailed description of what happened in the two months leading up to the papal visit, the crisis period after the Argentine invasion of the Falkland Islands. Taken as a completely fair and accurate account, and discounting the probability that Hume himself would have had a radically alternative version of the same events, it seems as unfavourable to Cardinal Hume as it is favourable to Worlock. But once its value as a straightforward eyewitness account of what happened is called in question, as it must be, does it have any historical merits at all?[52]

The answer has to be that, read in a certain careful way, it illuminates what we know about Worlock as much as what we know about Hume. It reveals Worlock, for instance, as unable and unwilling to make any effort whatever to see if there was any point to Hume's instinctive difficulties with the proposals he had put to him. Worlock often assumed for himself an air of infallibility. He seemed in this case to have assumed – infallibly – that Hume was being foolish. There is one thing Hume really could not stand, and that was being treated as stupid. It was also fairly well known in his immediate circle that he occasionally had a hot temper. When Worlock refers to Hume's angry mood, therefore, he is probably to be believed. When he supposes that Hume's mood is the product of his stubbornness, lack of imagination, or failure to acknowledge the brilliance of Worlock's arrangements, he is ignoring the more likely explanation – that his own manner was provocative. He seemed to have no respect for Hume's misgivings; nothing that he reported himself as saying or doing was designed to offer Hume the reassurance he needed. At one point he calls him an imperialist hawk; at another, a warmonger. That was a serious miscalculation. When the St Paul's Falklands Service was being planned after the conflict, Hume threatened to pull out because he found the tone of what was being proposed too militaristic and triumphalist. It was he who insisted on prayers being said for the Argentine dead and injured.

Worlock had gone to Rome to use whatever influence he had to devise some sort of package deal that would have allowed the papal visit to go ahead in the summer of 1982, despite the approaching military climax in the South Atlantic. He noticed that some Vatican officials – 'Latins', he called them – were not over-impressed with British policy. He returned to Britain to report back.

> Basil Hume was waiting at the airport when we flew in and for a long time could talk of nothing else but an article which he had in *The Times* that day which he described as a bit 'hawkish – not a bad thing when the Church is being shown on television as Argentine bishops blessing their forces etc.' I had not seen *The Times* that day. When I did I had grave misgivings about what had appeared under his name. It was pure 'George Leonard',[53] trying to apply the well-worn just war principles to the present situation and of course in clear support of Britain's position and the measures taken. It certainly attempted to justify the use of military force to regain possession of the islands. It produced an indelible picture of GBH as an imperialist hawk. GBH was very tense when we met, convinced that everyone in the airport both recognised him and had read that day's *Times*.

The source of Worlock's irritation was more that the tone of Hume's article would offend the dovish circle advising the Pope, some of whom had made plain their feeling that Britain was overreacting to the Argentine invasion, than because he was convinced that the use of armed force was not justified. This was precisely what Hume feared – that Worlock had no feeling for the principles at stake. 'Wherever I went,' said Worlock later, 'I picked up the report that *The Times* article had for ever branded GBH as a warmonger in the eyes of the Latin Americans.'

The uncertainty over the visit grew, until eventually a stalemate ensued. Desperate to do something, Worlock decided to invite himself back to Rome, this time in the company of the Archbishop of Glasgow, Thomas Winning. The Pope set up a round-table discussion for them the following day, and at extremely short notice summoned Archbishop Lopez Trujillo, President of the Conference of Latin American Bishops, who had been attending a meeting in Niagara, USA. Over lunch and afterwards, the Pope, Trujillo, Worlock, Winning, Casaroli and one or two others gradually fashioned out a package of proposals, at the heart of which – proposed by himself, Worlock claimed – was the holding of a Mass of Reconciliation in the Vatican, which would be celebrated by the Pope, the two cardinals from Argentina, Aramburu and Primatesta, and the two cardinals from Great Britain, Hume and Gray (Cardinal Archbishop of Edinburgh). Included in the package was an offer by the Pope himself to visit Argentina at the earliest opportunity, and a number of lesser conditions, such as a request to the British Government to stand back and not insist on an official meeting with the Pope[54] (with which it gladly complied). It was also agreed to work out a series of 'limits' – various eventualities which meant that a papal visit was no longer feasible (one such possibility mentioned was the death of Prince Andrew, who was serving with the Fleet as a helicopter pilot, an event which would have triggered a period of official mourning in Britain). The essential problem the package was designed to overcome was the growing resistance throughout Latin America to the idea that the Pope could visit Britain with the war in the South Atlantic still going on. As the Pope himself described it, he was appealing to the four cardinals to help him persuade Catholics in Latin America that visiting Britain was for the good of the Church, and not a display of partiality. Worlock noted, nevertheless, that the Pope always referred to the disputed islands as 'the Falklands', though various Vatican officials insisted on referring to them as 'the Malvinas'.[55]

Meanwhile, knowing this was going on, Cardinal Hume had summoned a meeting of the Bishops' Conference for the same afternoon, and they were standing by to hear the outcome of the Pope's meeting. He might say the visit was definitely off; he might say it was on; or he might impose conditions. Whatever happened, it was the decisive day. Worlock felt triumphant. The package he had helped to assemble seemed to him more than adequate. All he had to do was to relay the good news to those anxiously awaiting his call in London, modestly accept their grateful thanks, and arrange for Cardinal Hume to join him for the Mass of Reconciliation a couple of days later.

Worlock returned to the English College where he had been staying. 'I found myself confronted with an angry telephone message from Westminster', he recalled, 'saying that it was already past their 3 o'clock limit, the bishops were waiting to disperse, would I please phone the Cardinal's secretary at once.'

I suppose I should have taken time to think about my case but when at last I got through I could only sort out in my mind what I regarded as the seven points which had been made at lunch . . . I have to say that far from reflecting the enthusiastic hope I felt at a breakthrough, GBH expressed anger and horror. He had no wish to go to Rome, no wish to meet the Argies, and these conditions would give grave offence in Britain. I tried to explain that these were not conditions but points for consideration if the planning of the visit was to continue. He said his reaction was against what was being proposed but he would put the points to the bishops and someone would phone back . . .

I was desperate when at last George Leonard phoned back after 6 pm. George stood back and GBH came on the phone in what I can only describe as a great fury. He felt cornered, he was being put in a false position, and George Leonard felt that the Foreign Office would regard the package as near treason. GBH had put the package to the bishops, evidently making them into seven conditions.

When GBH had expanded on the seven points, a proposition was put forward that we proceed and that he should join me in Rome as the Pope had suggested. I gather that GBH in the chair abstained. He told me that the vote had gone against him 11 to 8, but then added that one of the bishops (Cormac Murphy-O'Connor) had said afterwards that he had misunderstood the implications for Basil and asked to reverse his vote. Basil pointed out to me that this meant 10 to 9; add his vote from the chair and there was no decision. He was not happy about the whole business. To discuss the 'limits' would mean to pinpoint what would inevitably happen before the visit took place, and then they would all be made to look like traitors or fools. I told him this was a very serious situation and he must take his time. I felt quite shattered.

He went back to the Vatican, where it was reported that the two Argentine cardinals were coming as requested, as was Cardinal Gray. 'They looked at me. I said merely that as a race we were always more cautious . . .' Worlock rang Westminster again shortly before midnight, to see if anything had changed.

It was worse than ever. My notes of that time say that he was in a raging temper. He said again that I had cornered him and put him in an impossible position whereby he was being forced to act publicly against his better judgement and in a way which would be gravely harmful to the Church in England. Moreover he was convinced that my proposals had no real support from the bishops. I told him that if he informed me of that officially, I would return to England the following day, but I would have to tell the Holy Father that the new proposals had no support in England.

It was the Vatican Secretary of State, Cardinal Casaroli, who resolved the *impasse*. Worlock told him what was the problem. Casaroli replied:

Please explain to your dear Cardinal Hume that the Holy Father has summoned the two Argentine cardinals to come to Rome at once. He has already called Archbishop Lopez Trujillo here. Cardinal Gray is already on his way.

Moreover, out of respect for the difficulties, the Holy Father has requested you to invite Cardinal Hume's co-operation. We are not asking him to come here to prove Britain's case nor to negotiate a settlement. We ask his help in explaining to our Latin American brothers why the visit must go ahead, Please help us to help them to understand.

It was a masterpiece of diplomatic tact. Worlock conveyed the message; Hume thought some more; another small problem was removed (whether news of a British landing would automatically abort the papal visit – the answer was no). Eventually he agreed to come. The Pope was informed.

From a conversation with the British minister to the Holy See later the same day, Sir Mark Heath, Worlock gathered that Hume's fears of a negative British reaction were misplaced. The British Government keenly wanted the visit to go ahead, as cancellation would look like papal condemnation of the morality of Britain's position before the forum of world opinion. Meanwhile the Archbishop of Canterbury also chipped in with a telegram, saying that the cancellation of the papal visit would almost invariably be seen in Britain as Vatican endorsement for the illegal Argentine occupation of the Falklands, and would be a tragedy 'at a time when many British Christians are looking afresh at the pastoral role of the Bishop of Rome in the Universal Church'. Worlock related the telegram to Lopez Trujillo, who decided to use it in his conversations with the Argentine cardinals (who would be in no position to see it as the gross overstatement it surely was). And meanwhile the quarrel between Worlock and Hume faded away. When Hume and Leonard reached Rome they seemed elated. 'In spite of the disgraceful phone episodes earlier in the week, there was really no sign of embarrassment.' What did Worlock expect?

The pitch of excitement was not quickly reduced, and the relationship between the two men had to be patched up. The major crisis was behind them, but there were many smaller crises ahead. The Pope was coming after all; there were a million things to see to. To have a successful papal visit in the middle of what was virtually a war was an amazing thing to see, but the Pope knocked the Falklands off the newspaper front pages for nearly a whole week. He did indeed visit Argentina; and though what he said to the bishops in private was never published, it was quite widely reported that he had ticked them off. Patriotism was good, he more or less told them, but it was not permitted to feed one's own patriotism at the expense of another's. So poking Britain in the eye in order to bolster the popularity of an ailing, corrupt and vicious military junta was not acceptable. Whether and to what extent this contributed to the downfall of the Galtieri regime shortly after the capture of the Falklands is impossible to say. It might be an exaggeration to say the Pope helped to undermine the regime's moral authority, as it had no moral authority anyway.

Relations between Hume and Worlock never became easy, but nor did they again become so raw. The papal visit was a success; the two men had to work hard together to make it so, and a great deal of the credit for this lay at Basil Hume's door, as Worlock was on occasion to acknowledge. And after it was over the relationship between the two of them became once more a strength, not a weakness, in the affairs of the Catholic Church of England and Wales. There was in any event a fundamental level of trust between the two. They could have done each other great damage, had they chosen to. They had to close ranks. Instead – and it is tempting to see here the influence of the faith to which they both deeply committed – they did not let personality problems stand in the way of the aims they both shared. It was part and parcel of their faith to do so: they had learnt almost at their mother's knee, so to speak, that anger was a sin, other people's motive had always to be given the most charitable interpretation, spreading ill-will towards another person was wrong, reconciliation was close to the heart of the Gospel message. They would have confessed their sins regularly, renewing their sorrow at their own faults, arising determined to do better in future. In the secular sphere, after the crisis of the papal visit preparations, the prognosis for their relationship would not have been promising. By the grace of God, perhaps, they were able to keep it alive.

From Worlock's point of view, 'managing a difficult Westminster' became a routine problem alongside 'managing a difficult Vatican'. But it was the sort of thing he was good at. One thing that made it easier for him was the advancement of his own protégé Vincent Nichols, to become secretary of the Bishops' Conference of England and Wales in 1984 (the other main contender was Hume's man George Leonard). Nichols was also highly acceptable to the Cardinal too – they developed a very close relationship, and Nichols became an auxiliary bishop of Westminster in 1992. Nichols could handle Hume, so to speak, and also handle Worlock. This left Worlock free to develop his work in Liverpool, and to transfer his emotional energy there. In later years, so close friends have said, he came to accept that Hume was ideal for Westminster in a way he himself could never have been.

The National Pastoral Congress did start one other ball rolling that had the potential to disrupt the relationship between Hume and Worlock once more. It had called for Roman Catholic membership of the British Council of Churches. This was something the other member Churches of the BCC (leaving aside some profound misgivings among the Baptists) had devoutly wished to see. Worlock was for it too. Hume had great misgivings. As secretary of the Bishops' Conference, which he turned into a much higher profile and more proactive role, Nichols became a key member of the Catholic negotiating team, and as such he also became the lubricant in the relationship between Liverpool and Westminster. To get Hume to change his mind was a formidable task, that even involved changing the terms of the proposition itself. Thus it was no longer to be the British Council of Churches of which Catholic membership was sought, but a new set of structures – they became known as 'ecumenical instruments', as if they were to be played by a band of roving musicians – which had to be invented from scratch.

These were designed to make the project as attractive as possible to Hume. But he was not quick to jump. It became quite possible that the BCC would agree to dismantle itself in order to meet Catholic objections to its decision-making structure, and yet the Catholic Church would still refuse to join because of Basil Hume. In holding this show on the road the influence of Nichols, and the respect in which he was increasingly held in the other Churches, became an important factor. Another was the close relationship between Worlock and Sheppard. It provided an alternative channel through which each Church was able to assure the other that it was indeed ecumenically serious.

The process culminated in a conference at Swanwick in Derbyshire in 1987, which all the main players attended, including a substantial Catholic delegation. Most other delegates were aware that the Catholics had a 'Hume problem' – Worlock discussed it at length with Sheppard, day by day – but it is also true they held Hume in great esteem and wanted him on board because of the weight and authority he would bring to the new arrangements. The Hume problem became in many respects a common problem, and the Archbishop of York, Dr John Habgood, who had chaired the overall negotiations, was as keen to find a solution as anyone. After some intense conversations within the Catholic delegation, spread over days (and nights), Hume finally withdrew his opposition. Because the entire conference had become aware how touch and go it had become, the moment at which Hume rose to speak was an electric one. The time had come, he said, for the Catholic Church to move on in its relations with the other Churches of the British Isles from a relationship of co-operation to a relationship of commitment. They were in. It meant all the more because Hume had not been an easy convert; nor was he someone who used the word 'commitment' lightly. It must also be recorded that the leadership of the other Churches had behaved with great patience and magnanimity towards him. Their willingness to pull down the British Council of Churches in order to put in its place an institution that the Catholic Church could join was a decision of extraordinary generosity. Their fathers and grandfathers, after all, would have crossed the road in order to avoid speaking to a Catholic priest.

If the 'Worlock project' after the conclusion of the Second Vatican Council had an agenda to it, the building of a new bond with the other main Churches, not just Anglican but the major Free Churches as well, was its bottom line. Events of 1987 were a moment of realization for him too, therefore. The Liverpool Worlock–Sheppard pattern had become the national pattern. The creation of the new Council of Churches for Britain and Ireland and its subordinate bodies such as Churches Together in England (and similar in Wales and Scotland) can be regarded as a memorial to Worlock as much as to anyone. It was not so much his contribution from 1985 that counted, as his contribution since 1965. He above all had helped to produce the Church that other churches wanted to be alongside.

```
VINTAGE YEAR
=============

In 1899, my boy, in 1899,
The grapes were very fine, my boy,
    a credit to the vine.
But what made it a vintage year
    was not the sparkling wine -
A Cardinal was born, my boy,
    in 1899.......

(Chorus: Drink to him, drink to him.....
                              ad lib).
```

Vintage Year by Derek Worlock. This song refers to Cardinal Griffin (1899–1956). Courtesy of Liverpool Roman Catholic Archdiocesan Archive at St Joseph's, Upholland, Lancashire.

Notes

1 This was Martin Luther's slogan of the Protestant Reformation – 'a reformed Church constantly being reformed'; the equivalent concept preferred by the Second Vatican Council was *semper purificanda*.

2 He must have meant under Church control, as for instance in Catholic universities on the Continent or in the United States.

3 Collins, 1975.

4 Quoted by Adrian Hastings, *A History of English Christianity 1920–1990*, SCM, 1991, p. 577.

5 Hastings, p. 579.

6 Returned to the lay state under the provisions of Canon Law. Laicization freed a priest from the obligation of celibacy and he in turn relinquished all his priestly rights and duties and was free to get a job. He was, nevertheless, still regarded as ordained – were he to return to the active priesthood, he would not have to be ordained again. Priests who left the active ministry without laicization in order to marry were suspended from their priestly functions and assumed to be in a state of sin, rather like Catholics who divorced and remarried without having their first marriage annulled.

7 Numerous instances of this have come to light in the course of the research for this book. Often the recipient of the act of kindness has treasured the memory for twenty years or more. Many more cases no doubt remain hidden.

8 Cocker also left the priesthood eventually.

9 The author attended one ground-breaking Church of England service which was addressed by Bishop Worlock, and was told by the gentle Anglican worshipper in the next pew that he 'never thought he would see the day' when such a thing was possible.

10 Canon Nicholas France, his former private secretary in Portsmouth, recalled that Worlock used to joke that he regularly prayed: 'Lord, I don't mind being a martyr, but don't let me have to die for a condom.'

11 The Pope Paul VI Cafod Memorial Lecture.

12 Portsmouth, Winchester, Guildford, Oxford.

13 Catholic Fund for Overseas Development.

14 It is not the intention of this chapter to duplicate the ground well covered in *Archbishop Derek Worlock, His Personal Journey*, by John Furnival and Ann Knowles, Geoffrey Chapman, 1998.

15 A not unknown symptom of depression, from which Worlock suffered chronically.

16 *The Guardian*, 9 February 1996.

17 *Catholic Herald*, December 1990.

18 A very similar personal relationship existed between Worlock and Pat Jones (see below), who was employed by the archdiocese first as a youth worker, then in developing adult education. She also felt able to confide in him, and found him very sensitive and supportive.

19 A 'nuptial Mass' is one in which the wedding ceremony is incorporated into the celebration of the Catholic Mass, and the high point, after the exchange of vows, is the joint reception of Holy Communion by bride and groom.

20 Furnival and Knowles go no further than to state Worlock 'came with a firm belief' that this was his mandate. There does not appear to be any written message from the Pope to this effect in his files.

21 Conversation with author.

22 Archbishop of Liverpool 1928–53.

23 Archbishop of Liverpool 1953–56.

24 Archbishop of Liverpool 1964–76.

25 Letter to author.

26 Margaret Duggan, *Life of Robert Runcie*, 1983.

27 Worlock was subsequently given 'close police protection' as he was thought to be an obvious target, and his house was guarded by police with dogs.

28 The official version of the origins of the NCP was that it was the brainchild of Heenan, who had also attended the Chur conference and had been embarrassed to find that he could not report to his fellow European bishops what the state of feeling was among the English clergy. The unofficial version puts the initiative down to a group of priests led by Father Michael Buckley.

29 The bishops' regular spring meeting.

30 Despite being in some discomfort because of his as-yet undiagnosed Celiac disease, which gives the sufferer an allergy to gluten.

31 One movement of conservative Catholics in England is actually called 'Faith of Our Fathers', after the title of the well-known hymn.

32 An auxiliary Bishop of Westminster.

33 'Delate' is a technical expression, meaning to report someone for wrongdoing.

34 This sentence is absent from the draft document prepared by Worlock's Easter People team, and must have been added by the bishops themselves.

35 Extract given in Appendix I Document 6.

36 Quentin de la Bedoyere, one of the drafters of the course, says Worlock himself wrote the paragraph the Vatican objected to (letter to author).

37 Bishop of Middlesbrough.

38 Author's note: Worlock once remonstrated with me about something I had written, not because it was wrong but because it would be used by 'various people' to cause trouble. Did I not realize that there were some who took great delight in using every scrap of evidence to write anonymously to the Vatican, who were making his job in Liverpool very difficult? I had to tell him that was not my problem. But the psychopathology of these twentieth-century heresy-hunters is very close to that of seventeenth-century witch-hunters, and the Vatican would be doing the Catholic Church a very great favour if it stopped paying them any attention. It is a cause of great scandal in the Church, as it makes it appear that the Vatican positively encourages and rewards disloyalty.

39 The day before Pope John Paul I died, Cardinal Hume had spoken of his profound conviction that the conclave had made the right choice, under the guidance of the Holy Spirit.

40 Intrinsic evil.

41 The next lines are 'Into the valley of Death/Rode the six hundred'. This ironical nuance would have been completely lost on his non-British hearers. It was a quotation from Tennyson's *Charge of the Light Brigade* which records one of the most disastrous and tragic episodes in British military history, when incompetently commanded British cavalry charged with astonishing gallantry against Russian guns at Balaklava in 1854 during the Crimean War and were cut down in their hundreds. The poem is about the poignant glory – and the supreme folly – of blind obedience. Hume would have known it by heart.

42 'Co-responsibility' had become Catholic jargon for bishops, priests and laity sharing

responsibility for the good of the Church. 'Co-agonizing' was Hume's own invention.

43 This whole passage is a perfect illustration of the contrast between Benedictine spirituality and Counter Reformation spirituality.

44 'Now I see; thank you.'

45 Not previously published.

46 The 'law of gradualness' was proposed by Worlock as the best pastoral approach to people who were not fully complying with Church teaching or discipline in their lives but who were basically in good faith. By teaching, persuasion and example, the Church had to pull them gradually towards greater compliance. It was suggested for inclusion in Worlock's synod interventions by Vincent Nichols; it is also implied in Hume's 'dream' speech. A 'graded' law, on the other hand, simply meant that some people could not be expected ever to comply with Church teaching, but could be allowed to settle for less.

47 One of them began: 'My brothers and sisters in Jesus Christ; thank you for your welcome. Thank you for coming here to greet me. In turn I greet you: peace be with you. Peace be in your homes. Peace be in this great city of Liverpool. I am glad to be here. I am glad to pay my first visit to this region of England and to this city of which you are so proud . . .' It is a brilliant pastiche of the papal style.

48 Peter Nichols, brought from Rome by *The Times* to cover the papal visit to England, noticed immediately that the tone of the papal addresses was quite different from what might have been expected, being more open-minded than the Pope's usual style. Nichols even coined the phrase 'Pope John Paul III' to describe this new and refreshing papal persona.

49 The author's son was a member of the crew of the flagship *Hermes.*

50 After he started to receive treatment for cancer in April 1999, Cardinal Hume agreed to see the author to discuss what happened before the papal visit, thereby allowing an alternative account to be taken into the reckoning in this book. Sadly his health deteriorated so rapidly the interview never took place. It seems Hume was well aware that Worlock had a different version of events from his own. Nevertheless it is not impossible to separate Hume's real attitude and role from Worlock's version of them.

51 Worlock refers to him throughout by these initials, the joke being that they would more commonly be understood as short for 'grievous bodily harm', a serious crime of violence.

52 As an additional health warning, it may be noted that one chapter of these handwritten recollections, relating to the Toxteth riots, was deemed too much at variance with the actual events even to justify inclusion in this project. Worlock sometimes seemed to suffer from a mild version of false memory syndrome.

53 He is saying Leonard had obviously drafted it. Given that he had been praising Leonard's drafting of *The Easter People* and then of papal briefing papers (which later became the substance of papal addresses), this suddenly contemptuous tone is inexplicable. But no more so than his characterization of Hume's cautious and agonized article on the Falklands conflict as the work of an 'imperialist hawk'.

54 The Pope later announced at the meeting with the Argentine cardinals that there was no problem with the proposed meeting between himself and the Queen; although she was British head of state she was also head of the Church of England, and hence the encounter could be construed as an ecclesiastical rather than a political one. As he said this, reported Worlock, the Pope turned his head towards him, and winked.

55 In a curious twist, the only Catholic church on the islands, in Port Stanley, was under

direct papal jurisdiction. The invading Argentines lowered every flag they could find in order to raise their own; but as an act of defiance the (English) Catholic priest insisted they fly the papal flag instead.

10

A Highly Political
Churchman

In matters touching politics and society, Derek Worlock gradually established himself as one of the most thoughtful and outspoken Church leaders of his generation, of any denomination. That is not to acquit him of *naïveté*, nor to say he was right about everything (or even most things). But he was identified with this issue, and glad to be. Given his ministry in Liverpool, this was not inappropriate. If any city did, this one needed some standing up for.

And yet, and yet . . . The more familiar one becomes with the economics of Merseyside, the louder becomes the nagging question – had it contributed to its own misfortune? And if so, did Worlock and his like help it face up to that truth – or to avoid it? To say that the state of Liverpool was purely and simply a tale of social injustice is to shift the onus of responsibility away from the people of Liverpool as a whole, to those – living elsewhere in the country and indeed elsewhere in the world – who are causing the injustice. It is to assert that the problems of Merseyside arise from external factors, 'them' acting unfairly.

Hence things can only get better by making those external factors more favourable. As an analysis this can be fruitful if it points clearly to a single cause or set of causes which follow from a specific choice or set of choices. Those choices can be made differently, and things then turn out differently on the ground. Thus if new industry is being attracted, say, to Newcastle rather than Merseyside by better investment grants or tax regimes relating to Newcastle, then the decision that needs to be changed is the decision to discriminate in favour of Newcastle (or against Merseyside). What this says to the people on the ground, as it were, is that they have a justified grievance against 'those who are doing this to you'. Their proper course of action is to seek to change the behaviour of those who are doing it.

It was in accordance with this analysis that Worlock and Sheppard intervened with employers several times to try to prevent factory closures and consequent redundancies. This demonstration of solidarity with workers whose livelihood was threatened did much to cement bonds of affection and respect between the two episcopal leaders and the people of Merseyside. They made the Churches seem relevant to the real problems in people's lives – and this was a generation of churchmen, at least on the Protestant side, for whom 'becoming relevant' was an imperative.

But there was a cost. This approach can readily generate a state of mind of resentful passivity and helplessness, even self-pity. If that is quickly overcome as conditions ease then it doesn't much matter. If the problems behind the decline of a great industrial and sea-port city like Liverpool are more intractable, however, then the 'victim mentality' becomes part of the problem and not merely a response to it. This is a mind-set which saps morale and energy, and makes it less likely that Liverpool would ever pull itself up by its own bootstraps. And if civic leaders give encouragement to this victim or grievance mentality, for instance by stressing that Liverpool's problems are caused by unfair decisions made by people elsewhere, then they are contributing to the perpetuation of the problem. This is the case even if there is a grain of truth in the allegations of unfairness.

It is not so easy to acquit David Sheppard and Derek Worlock of this charge, though they may well have been aware of the danger. With all due respect to some of the nicest and most interesting people in Britain, Liverpudlians are a little prone to self-pity anyway. Is this merely 'blaming the victim'? Partly. It is, perhaps, blaming the victim at least for behaving like one. The grievance mentality may have been a factor in the reputation for industrial militancy that made many businessmen look askance at the prospect of investing in Merseyside. Sooner or later industry was going to be driven away, and the capitalist-haters would have no capitalists to hate, only the derelict factory buildings they had left behind them. This was indeed what began to happen as local politics in Liverpool became more and more extreme, culminating in the dominance of the Militant Tendency in the local Labour Party which controlled Liverpool City Council. It was political paranoia set to the music of ideology. Militant was a local variant of Trotskyism, itself a variant of Marxist Leninism. Like all such Trotskyist agitation, it believed the structures of capitalist society were inherently unstable and could easily be destabilized. The conflict between class interests were bound to get worse as capitalism became ever more inimical to working-class interests. The approved approach for a Marxist revolutionary of this type was, first, to understand correctly what was happening and likely to happen; secondly to understand that there were only two sides and every individual or institution was on one or the other; thirdly that the judicious cultivation of grievances, even by making things worse for the working classes in the short term, would bring nearer the inevitable day of final conflict and collapse. The revolutionary movement must likely to benefit from that would be one that had most openly identified itself with the struggle. That movement would emerge all-powerful.

Worlock learned a great deal about politics from David Sheppard. He had come to share Sheppard's outlook on the social and political issues of the day, though Sheppard himself – with a touch of ecumenically generous overstatement – would describe it as a convergence. By the time they found themselves alongside each other, in 1976, David Sheppard had already produced *Built as a City* (Hodder and Stoughton, 1974) which was an exhaustive analysis of his inner-city experiences mainly as Bishop of Woolwich in South London.

Worlock had nothing similar, from the Catholic side, to set against it. As Roman Catholic Bishop of Portsmouth he had been managing an area with its own inner-city problems, for his diocese covered Southampton as well as Portsmouth itself. Both towns had a large urban working-class population associated with docks and dockyards (the latter is the RN term for the former). But there is not much evidence that he identified himself with either of those cities in the way he was later to identify with Liverpool. It was still the Catholic style in England for Church leaders to 'look after their own', caused partly by the fact that the Catholic population was largely Irish in origin, partly by a long tradition of Catholic exclusion from mainstream public life.

Although this had something to do with the No-Popery which even in the 1970s could still be described as 'the residual religion of the English', it would be wrong to place all the blame for this institutional myopia on the rest of society. One of the other factors driving the Catholic community inwards on itself was undoubtedly the so-called Modernist Crisis in the final years of the nineteenth century and the opening decade of the twentieth. It painted the secular world as a dangerous place, where the pure Catholic faith was easily contaminated by modern ideas. This attitude was superimposed on existing Catholic distaste for the institutions and habits of 'Protestant Britain' of the eighteenth and nineteenth century, not a friendly place to be a Catholic.

Be that as it may, the shared opinions of the two most articulate spokesmen for Christian involvement in politics during this period meant that what they had to say carried considerable influence in the land, especially in the mainstream Churches such as their own. For a Catholic prelate, Worlock was being brave and adventurous even by associating himself with David Sheppard's ideas. He was not about to subject his new allies to a root-and-branch critique. Nor was he equipped intellectually or by experience to do so. This dislike for ideological analysis meant, of course, that there never was a heavyweight intellectual challenge to the theories which motivated the Militant Tendency in Liverpool, nor any other variety of Marxism current at that time. In the end, the two Liverpool Church leaders dealt with Militant by urging on the Labour Party to take seriously this cuckoo in its nest. It was to be defeated by political activism, not by theoretical debate. On the morning Neil Kinnock launched a bitter attack on Militant at the 1985 Labour Party Conference, Worlock and Sheppard had published a joint article in *The Times*[1] spelling out the ruinous effect Militant was having on the social fabric of Liverpool. 'Militant's intransigence and unwillingness to engage in serious dialogue creates divisiveness and uncertainty in which the most vulnerable elements of the community suffer', they wrote, 'usually school children and elderly people unable to cope with a reduction in services.' Kinnock later told Sheppard it had forced him to make up his mind that the evil had to be rooted out. It became Labour policy to expel members of Militant from the Party, on the basis that they constituted a party-within-a-party that was forbidden by the rules. Gradually Labour politics in Liverpool returned to sanity.

A natural consensus existed among churchmen in the 1960s and 1970s that could be described as post-Beveridge in its welfare policy, Wilsonian in its approach to industrial matters, Macmillanite on issues like housing and foreign affairs. This is well represented in the record written by Trevor Beeson[2] of a project organized by the British Council of Churches, enquiring into the relevance of Christianity to conditions in modern Britain. Characteristically, it did its theology last; and thin gruel it was, too.

In the economic sphere Beeson laments the poor quality of expert input to the project. Then he offers a political analysis of his own, but one which is almost identical to that adopted by Worlock and Sheppard. 'Most noticeably lacking,' he reported,

> was a comprehensive attempt to grapple with the changes to Britain's economic and industrial strategy which are necessary to provide the wealth needed for the ironing out of the most serious inequalities and injustices. It is a sad, but apparently inescapable, fact that the majority of British people are only prepared for the less privileged members of society to have a larger portion of the economic cake at a time when the cake itself is getting larger. In a democracy that means that social reform depends upon economic abundance. Hence the need for the problems of inequality and injustice to be considered in the context of Britain's future prospects. This task has yet to be tackled.

And all this, without any help from experts.

Not surprisingly, a 1970s survey of the political flavour of the member Churches of the British Council of Churches (in which the Roman Catholic Church, the main denomination not yet a full member, had observer status) concluded that their favourite political colour was soft-pink, their favourite remedy for ills in society was government intervention, and they had no great admiration for capitalism (it was at most, like sex, a necessary evil).

This did not necessarily set them much at odds with Conservatives, however, as that party's own politics were at the time still centrist rather than right-wing. There was a general cross-party political ethos in Britain at that time which in an earlier decade had been called Butskellism (a combination of the names of R. A. Butler, the Tory's chief liberal political thinker, and Hugh Gaitskell, the Labour leader before Harold Wilson); in its Tory manifestation it became known as 'One Nation'.

The Great Depression of the early 1930s still cast its shadow over this political generation, on both sides. Many Conservatives of this era came into politics precisely out of a desire to 'do something' for the poor and unemployed. The Conservative Party of the pre-Thatcher era would have been seen as a left-of-centre party had it been in American politics rather than British. This was the consensus which Margaret Thatcher set out to challenge when she relaunched modern Conservatism in the late 1970s. Her arrival at the head of the Conservative Party in 1976 more or less coincided with the beginning of the Worlock–Sheppard partnership.

The Anglican and Protestant Churches were part of the consensus that Thatcher tried to break. One of the reasons the Churches looked increasingly left-wing, and no longer politically non-partisan, was that the Conservative Party (and Government, after 1979) had started to move steadily to the Right. Without changing its outlook, therefore, the Church leadership in Britain, of which Worlock and Sheppard were in the late 1970s representative in their political attitudes, gradually found itself in increasing opposition to the major directions of government policy.

It found itself stranded, so to speak, on a consensus beach, the tide of party politics having withdrawn (in two opposing directions). As Labour moved to the left under Michael Foot, only the Liberals and later briefly the Social Democrats shared the political world-view which the Churches had taken for granted so uncritically up to that time. Thus it was frequently claimed, especially by middle ranking clerics in the Church of England, that only the Church now offered real opposition to government policy, Labour having disqualified itself by its flirtation with the Left and by the internal divisions that resulted. By 'the Church', they really meant the Anglican and Free Church clerical establishments (plus, perhaps, Derek Worlock).

There was a direct link between the Worlock–Sheppard approach to politics and the most famous political intervention of any Church during this period, the Church of England's report *Faith in the City* of 1985. The analysis in that document of 'what was wrong with Britain' was exactly the analysis enunciated by Worlock and Sheppard over the previous decade; indeed, at a popular level they did it 'better together' than *Faith in the City* had done. (It is the analysis they jointly presented in their shared book, *Better Together*.) Bishop Sheppard was vice chairman of the Archbishops' Commission which produced it, and a member of the inner-city group of Anglican bishops who had requested that it be set up.

It was not a Marxist analysis, though labelling it as such was the tactic with which the Conservative Government chose to deal with it. But it did suppose that the major reason why the inner-city areas in Britain were in trouble was because not enough public funds had been spent on them. They were victims, so to speak, of the selfishness of the well-off, who gave lowering their own taxes higher priority than caring for the underprivileged in the decaying heartland of Britain's major cities.

So when Worlock expounded in 1981 on the 'north–south divide' in England and the opening split between the haves and have-nots, this was a note to be heard again and again in the next fifteen years from the lips and pens of both of them – and again and again in church documents and debates of that period, of which *Faith in the City* was the most important. It was a very difficult consensus to challenge; to do so would have seemed like allying oneself with 'selfish' Tory Government policies. Throughout this time, 'Thatcherite' was a term of abuse in British clerical circles so offensive as to be virtually actionable.

Nevertheless this involvement with contemporary political fashion was for Worlock in particular a considerable personal development. His entry into the world of political ideas had come about during the early years of his career, as secretary to Cardinals Griffin and Godfrey. He had made it his business to take under his wing the movement called the Young Christian Workers, essentially a French and Belgian Catholic response to the spread of Marxism among the younger members of the working class in those countries. If the YCW had a political programme, it was that laid out in the 1891 papal encyclical *Rerum Novarum* of Pope Leo XIII and the 1931 sequel of Pope Pius XI, *Quadragesimo Anno*.

David Sheppard offers a brief portrait of a YCW meeting in Rotherhithe, South London, which he had attended while Bishop of Woolwich.

Ten young people around 20 years of age were present (five men and five women). The [Roman Catholic] curate was there, but said nothing unless they referred to him (which they did in discussing a Youth Mass for which they had been responsible). I said nothing until I was asked to comment on the meeting at the end of the evening.

The pattern was the regular YCW programme. First there was a Gospel Enquiry. Most members contributed devotional thoughts about Christ and what He wanted them to be. They stuck closely to the verses from St John which they had read. Next came Facts of the Week, when members spoke about issues at work. In each case they were to do with personal relationships. Then they discussed the youth service and went on to review a dance run particularly for school leavers. They spoke freely of what had gone wrong, of their own responsibility and of the need to encourage the members of the Junior YCW to take more of a lead.

The group was very relaxed. Several were extremely articulate. I felt that most were either already doing non-manual jobs or would want to gain promotion, and that they would probably want to buy a house of their own.

To do so, however, they would have to move away, Sheppard surmised.

He was clearly impressed by what he saw. Much of his book was devoted to lamenting the absence of any significant working-class presence in the Church of England. The pattern of a YCW meeting he described was something that would have been completely familiar to Derek Worlock, who had been in the shoes of that curate – though no doubt less silently – many times. This was one respect in which the partnership between Worlock and Sheppard was destined to thrive.

What is also clear from this passage is that well before he went to Liverpool, Sheppard was aware of the Roman Catholic Church's importance in the inner cities of England, the one denomination still alive and kicking there (notwithstanding that its main priority was to take care of its own members). Catholicism may account for ten per cent of the population in England and Wales, but rather more than ten per cent of the population of the inner cities. The Catholic Church is the largest – in some cases, by far the largest – Church in all of the seven major conurbations in England and Wales; not just Liverpool, but London, Manchester, Newcastle, Cardiff, Leeds and Birmingham. In contrast, it is almost invisible in the county towns and rural areas, which tend to be where the Church of England has its heartland. Both of them are relatively strong in the suburbs, where town meets country.

The emphasis in the YCW, as in other forms of Catholic Action at that time, was on the defence of workers' rights against rapacious employers, and on resistance to Communism. The Church's agents in the world of work were supposed to be specially trained – 'formed' was the fashionable Catholic expression – workers who were consciously fulfilling what was called a 'lay apostolate' in the workplace. But neither of these ideas offered much in the way of social analysis relevant to conditions in Britain in the 1940s and 1950s. The domestic political agenda – nationalization of major industries, establishment of the National Health Service and of National Assistance as a safety net against dire poverty, and the provision of a massive stock of public housing – would have been out of focus to a mind steeped in the social philosophy of Leo XIII or Pius XI. Insofar as these innovations were not even dreamed of in Catholic Social Teaching as it existed in the post-war period, the Catholic reaction to them was likely to be at best lukewarm, more probably hostile.

Ronald Preston writes in his *Confusions in Christian Social Ethics* (SCM, 1994) that it was the senior partner of the YCW, the Catholic Social Guild, which had shown most Catholic interest in post-war social developments in Britain. The Guild promoted Plater College, Oxford, as a centre for studying the social encyclicals of the Popes and as an alternative to Ruskin College as a place where workers could get a university education. Its main concerns were fear of socialism, 'which led it to support the post-1945 Welfare State because it made capitalism benevolent'; a disapproval of strikes; and advocacy of councils of workers and employers to promote the common good. (It is no coincidence that some of these policies resemble those from the Christian Democrat movements of Western Europe, for they too were attempts to build a postwar 'third way' between Marxism and *laissez-faire* Capitalism based on papal teaching.)

But Derek Worlock had no great enthusiasm for Plater College, and appeared to distrust it. He often maintained that he had acquired his passion for social justice sitting at the feet of Cardinal Bernard Griffin, Archbishop of Westminster, whose secretary he was for twelve years. He subsequently painted Griffin, who led the Catholic Church through the momentous years of the post-war Labour Government, as a social reformer of the first rank and a shining apostle of Catholic Social Teaching.

Worlock was not being strictly honest. It is true that as secretary to successive cardinals at Westminster, he had become expert at citing his master as the authority for things he wanted to do, sometimes without the Cardinal's knowledge. 'His Eminence proposes . . .' would always carry more weight than 'I propose . . .' coming from a young priest, albeit one who wrote His Eminence's speeches. It is said clerical wits would amuse themselves over the priestly dinner tables of Westminster archdiocese at that time with such questions as: 'Why is this man Godfrey signing Monsignor Worlock's letters?'

Worlock's own private diaries of the post-war period are indeed filled with the comings and goings of politicians. On more than one occasion an appointment made with the Cardinal for civil servants or politicians was kept by Worlock himself, the Cardinal being ill or away. He would have been responsible for the content of the correspondence the Cardinal sent to political leaders. The dominant concern in all thus, however, was the protection of Catholic interests – especially Catholic schools – rather than the overall good of society.

Griffin's only contribution to the birth of the National Health Service in 1948 was to negotiate the opting out of Catholic hospitals. He did so by threatening to cut off the supply of Irish nurses who were the mainstay of hospital care in Britain at the time. As Michael de la Bedoyere remarked gleefully in his hagiographic biography of Griffin (*Cardinal Bernard Griffin*, Rockliff, 1955): 'Those who knew the whole story were saying that the Cardinal was the first person to get the better of Nye Bevan.' We may well suppose that the primary source for this unattributed remark was Worlock himself, and it was indeed he who was really the first person 'to get the better of Nye'.

Nor was this Catholic self-interest confined to medical matters. It entirely characterized the attitude of the Church to the 1944 Education Act, a far-sighted piece of social legislation which Griffin absurdly condemned as bringing about the death of Catholic education. It characterized the Church's approach to other great reforms. The next paragraph of de la Bedoyere's biography after the quote above goes on: 'The National Assistance Act raised complex questions about the position of priests and nuns within the system.' Nothing here about the extraordinary vision of a land without poverty, which the Act was designed to bring about by guaranteeing a minimum income for every citizen. Only a trivial difficulty concerning priests; and Griffin's extraordinary remark: 'It will be a sad day for England when charity becomes the affair of the State.'

He believed many of the Welfare State reforms threatened the integrity of family life and the value of selfless voluntary work. Any appraisal of the Welfare State after 50 years would have to take account of those fears, and would find them not entirely unfounded. But what is absent from his attitude is any trace of the fierce determination of the nation and its government never again to see barefoot children in the streets with rickets, never again old people dying untended because they could not afford a doctor's bill, never again the General Strike nor the desperate hunger marches of the unemployed.

In contrast, Cardinal Griffin's social agenda in 1945, as summarized by his biographer, was as follows: decent housing 'for fair-sized families' (in order, it seems, to avoid pressure on Catholic families to practise birth control); work for all and family wages; grants to young couples entering marriage; family allowances; recognition of the rights of parents; home-helps for mothers rather than nurseries; medical attention in the home rather than away (whatever that meant); co-operation between parents and teachers; parental control over sex education; opposition to divorce and the use of contraceptives; encouragement of religion in the home. This is a lot less radical even than *Rerum Novarum*, which it claims to be faithful to. It may safely be assumed that in reading thoughts attributed to the Cardinal, we are reading Worlock's actual words. He is singled out for special thanks in the author's Introduction, as the chief among those 'without whom I could never have written it'.

But Griffin, Worlock, and for that matter de la Bedoyere, were not moved by anti-socialism. What was lacking was a sense of responsibility for the whole of society rather than the relatively small part of it that was Catholic. Unconscious and unstated was an image of the British nation as a foreign country, not so much because it wasn't Irish – Griffin was indeed an Englishman – but because, to Catholics of Griffin's generation, it was still distinctly Protestant. Catholics felt excluded from the national discourse. These were not just unecumenical times, but actively anti-ecumenical. It was an 'us-and-them' world. 'They' made the decisions, had the power. 'We' had to defend our interests or have them snatched away.

Since then Worlock's mind had been expanded by his attendance at the Second Vatican Council and his participation in the drafting of its last major document *Gaudium et Spes* (*The Church in the Modern World*). He had become aware that Griffin's indifference or resistance to the reforming programme of the post-war Labour Government was no longer sustainable. He knew that the priorities he had inculcated in his YCW days – and inculcated in others – were scarcely relevant either. Yet the man who arrived in Liverpool to be its new Catholic archbishop in 1976 still tended to see the world in these Catholic 'us' and 'them' terms – except that it was a specific part of his brief to overcome that 'us' and 'them' dichotomy, which in Liverpool offered the dire prospect of sectarian tension in the manner of Belfast. David Sheppard has since remarked , for instance,[3] that when he first got to know him he became aware that almost all Worlock's heroes were Catholics. This quickly changed.

By 1981 they had been together through the gruelling but eye-opening experience of the Toxteth riots, and dealt with many and various other tensions and conflicts in the community. Liverpool was distressed, perhaps the most distressed city in Great Britain. On election two years earlier, the

Conservative Government under Margaret Thatcher had applied the then fashionable 'monetarist' economic policies which had bitten deep into Britain's manufacturing base, nowhere more so than on Merseyside. There was unrest in the streets and factories, and an air of depression, even despair. Partly as a gimmick, partly in order to be seen to be 'doing something', Michael Heseltine was soon to be appointed 'Minister for Merseyside'. He ordered trees to be planted on vacant land in inner-city areas, causing much scouse ribaldry. And there was to be a Flower Festival – greeted similarly, though it was an undoubted success.

In all honesty it would have been difficult to apply Catholic Social Teaching (still at that stage heavily reliant on the encyclicals of 1891 and 1931) to the situation of Liverpool in the late 1970s and early 1980s. Insofar as that specifically Catholic political doctrine was still regarded even by devout Catholics as having anything useful to say, it was thought mainly to apply to relations between rich nations and poor ones. (And what it said about them was that the poor were poor because the rich were rich, an idea which may have been present in Worlock's own emerging analysis of Britain as being divided between 'haves' and 'have-nots'.) *Rerum Novarum* of 1891 was written in the light of the upsurge of urban industrialization across Europe, and particularly reflected German social democratic thinking, but may also have been influenced by Cardinal Manning of Westminster. *Quadragesimo Anno* 40 years later was profoundly influenced by the state of Italian politics, and the desire of the Catholic Church to say something useful for the humanizing of Mussolini's Fascism. Though they both expressed some broad general principles which were of universal validity if somewhat anodyne, anyone trying to apply them to economic conditions in Britain in the mid-1970s, with a view to producing actual policies, would have had a thankless job.[4]

Indeed, it was fashionable among Catholic intellectuals to think that the future probably belonged to some sort of synthesis or fusion of Catholicism and Marxism, as proposed in Liberation Theology then emerging in Latin America. It was orientated towards anti-capitalism. But even that offered no easy short-cuts to remedy Liverpool's many ills. In the back streets full of rented houses, the people to hate were the 'Housing' (the Corporation housing department), who had to be called in for every minor repair to the property. They were, needless to say, slow and inefficient. Indeed, the life of an inner-city resident was almost exclusively ruled by what we now call the public sector – the local authority, the police, the NHS, the Corporation bus service, the schools, and when things went badly wrong, probation officers and social workers. Contact with the private sector was virtually nil. Nobody was trying to make a profit out of these people; nobody cared enough. It is not easy to see in what respect life on a Liverpool housing estate would have differed from life in, say, a city in Communist East Germany or Poland, except there would be less vandalism there. The abiding colour – concrete grey – would have been the same. So would the prevailing mood. Possibly even the sense of humour would have developed along similar lines. But liberation theology required a capitalist oppressor who could be opposed. In Liverpool's case, the 'oppressors' were walking away.

Worlock himself was uninterested in ideologies of any kind, and never flirted with Marxist ideas. But he was only too ready to attach himself to the centre-left political consensus that had grown up in the Anglican and Protestant Churches. This had supported, in many cases with some fervour, most of the reforms of the Attlee Government; and supported the Conservatives' subsequent decision not to unravel these reforms but to go along with them. It seems he had little option. Those were the views a churchman like him was likely to hold. But he committed himself to them, threw himself into battle on their behalf.

*   *   *

It was in 1981 that Worlock made a remarkable speech to the annual seminar of the Society of Local Authority Chief Executives, which had decided to meet in Liverpool. It is a speech which displays both his humour and his considerable – and at times passionate – oratorical powers. It also brings forth his favourite social analysis, one from which he scarcely wavered in the last twenty years of his life. In it he sets out what he sees as the crisis in the social, cultural and economic life of Liverpool, a crisis of poverty, unemployment and alienation.

He made this speech many times, adapting and developing it as each occasion demanded. Hence it repays careful attention, almost on a line-by-line basis. It parades both his strengths and his weaknesses. There is a touchiness about some passages, most of all when he defends himself from public criticism for meddling in affairs about which he knows little (or fears he will be accused of knowing little – Worlock's defensiveness is almost always uncalled-for, for he was almost always on stronger ground than he appeared to think he was).

And there is a rare eloquence, when the matters of which he is speaking start to arouse his indignation. His words become moving, powerful and persuasive. He was acting as, and anxious to be seen to be active as, 'the people's advocate', the spokesman of the powerless. This is not pure politics, though the mass media usually misunderstand it as such. It has deeper religious resonances than that. Throughout Christianity's history, there have been prophetic voices raised on behalf of the poor, sometimes attacking the rich, sometimes the powers-that-be, sometimes even the Church itself, on the grounds that the relief of poverty is an obligation on the faithful, and the failure to do so, therefore, is a grave injustice. This is a thread that pre-dates Christianity, for it is manifested in many passages of the Old Testament. It quickly surfaces again in the New Testament in the passage known as the Magnificat, Luke 1:46–55:

> My soul doth magnify the Lord, and my spirit rejoices in God my Saviour, for he has regarded the low estate of his handmaiden . . . He has shown strength with his arm, he has scattered the proud in the imagination of their hearts, he has put down the mighty from their thrones, and exalted those of low degree; he has filled the hungry with good things, and the rich he has sent empty away.

But as a speech on the relationship of faith to politics his 1981 address to the local authority executives was not particularly Catholic, and certainly departs from the standard model that Catholic churchmen tended to follow on such occasions. Such speakers, if they were invited to speak on such subjects at all, could be expected to employ copious quotations from papal encyclicals, references to the key themes of Catholic Social Teaching such as subsidiarity and solidarity, with an explanation of the natural law and Scriptural basis for such teaching.

In his 1981 speech Worlock sets aside those well-established patterns and speaks in terms which are plainly political, albeit shot through with a profound humanistic morality. It is a speech which any Anglican bishop could have made, though few would have had the talent to do it so well.

The absence of any explicit reference to papal encyclicals or Catholic Social Teaching in the speech is all the more pointed, given that Worlock submitted a copy of it to the Apostolic Delegate in Wimbledon a few days before making it. In September 1981 on behalf of the Holy See the Delegation had sent all the bishops copies of the new social encyclical of Pope John Paul II called *Laborem Exercens*, shortly to be published. Worlock responded by sending in return this text of his, saying that when he had had time to study it he was sure he would find *Laborem Exercens* a helpful contribution.

Others might have recast their remarks in the light of it, but not he. The only purpose of sending such a speech to Wimbledon would be in the hope that it would be passed onwards to the Vatican, possibly even for the Pope's personal attention. Why then did Worlock depart from the normal rules of the game? It may well have been that he had grown to think that

Catholic Social Teaching had nothing to offer places like Liverpool, and he would have to create his own doctrine, as it were, on the hoof.

The danger is that this can lead to what Ronald Preston criticizes in a similar context (the social ethics of the World Council of Churches) as 'the religious consecration of strong feelings'. It 'tends to the moral excommunication of those in the church who disagree'.[5]

The result, however, is that his position can be criticized like any other political contribution, and judged for its political good sense, grasp of economic reality, and position in the Left-Right political spectrum. The reason senior Catholic churchmen usually employ the formula described above is not sheer laziness. It enables them to represent themselves, in reply to critics, as expounding the Church's own doctrine. They can, as it were, hide behind it, and at the same time stand above party politics. Worlock preferred to be in the street, exposed.

In theory at least, all intelligent commentators equipped with the basics of Catholic Social Teaching (whether they personally agreed with it or not) should come to the same conclusion. Is the centralization of power by government compatible with Catholic Social Teaching? No, it is contrary to the principle of subsidiarity. Is the breaking up of trade unions a good thing? No, it is contrary to the principle of solidarity and the right to free association. In this way a Catholic churchman can say controversial things but avoid (or at least diminish) the charge of being personally political or 'political interference' (one of Derek Worlock's favourite expressions). But most political debate is incapable of being reduced to these black-white, Yes-No categories. Catholic Social Teaching cannot say whether the reduction of legal immunity enjoyed by trade unions since 1906 is or is not justified; nor whether the capping of local authority rates by central government is an act of dictatorial centralism or of fiscal prudence. This inability to relate to experience is a problem.

For one who was so active in the political and social field, it is striking that he made so little contribution to the development of Catholic Social Teaching himself. It would certainly have benefited from a dose of good English common sense, or the recognition that theory can only take you so far, before it becomes necessary to listen to what the world has to say. A critique of Catholic Social Teaching – and not just the rather dated generalities of Leo XIII and Pius XI but the much more sophisticated work of Pope John Paul II – was offered by Professor Ian Markham in a lecture in Liverpool not long after Worlock's death (who also quoted Ronald Preston).

While there is much to admire and accept [in this papal doctrinal tradition], there is nevertheless one major defect in the entire position. It seems to me it ignores entirely the revelatory significance of complexity and ambiguity. In other words, for these encyclicals, for this Pope, the ethical task has become very simple: accept the interpretation of the tradition (of which, natural law is a major part) that is proposed by the *magisterium*. The complexities of modern life are not conceded: there is no dialogue with external expertise. Ronald Preston is right to point out that the problem lies in the genre of the encyclical: 'They all lay stress on the continuity of teaching . . . Each contains references to the Bible, to the Church fathers and to previous Popes. Lately there has been an occasional reference to a United Nations document. No other empirical sources are mentioned. No flaws in Church teaching are admitted.' It is the tradition interpreted by the *magisterium* which is in control. As if fuelled by a fear of the whole system unravelling, the ethical task is reduced to simple uncomplicated obedience to those who know better. The experience of all those who think otherwise is simply disregarded.[6]

Maybe it was some such inexpressed intuition on Worlock's part which made him wary of this tradition. But he certainly had things to say. For instance, in his 1981 speech to local authority chief executives, he refers to the phenomenon of alienation which seemed to lie behind the social unrest in Liverpool at the time of the Toxteth riots. But he does not develop it; he hardly seems to be aware that the concept, in this context, would have to be regarded as Marxist at least in its origins and overtones. That does not invalidate it. But he does not take possession of it, as he could have done, as a 'Catholic' concept. What is the relationship between alienation and sin, for instance? Does alienation reduce culpability for personal wrong-doing? Worlock certainly gives this impression. But the theological ice on which he is skating is at times extremely thin. What he has to say differs little from the political opinion of a left-of-centre professor of sociology, such as Professors T. H. Halsey or Stuart Hall. Except, of course, the prose is better.

Worlock and Sheppard had both been asked to take part in the seminar, to explain for the benefit of local authority executives from all over the country what exactly happened in Liverpool at the time of the Toxteth riots that summer, and why; and more importantly still, what was to be done and how should public agencies react. 'What happens if nothing happens?' is the bleak question Worlock was asked to answer.

He begins with some fairly standard pleasantries on the subject of his relationship with Bishop Sheppard, who is also taking part in the seminar. There were very few occasions on which he and Sheppard appeared together, in which one or other of them does not use their companionship to make a humorous point to get the audience to smile and relax. This is how Worlock launches his address on this occasion.

> When the organiser of this conference wrote some days ago to ask whether Bishop Sheppard and I would be wishing to use any audio-visual aids, I replied to the effect that the spectacle of the double-headed hydra customarily proved enough. We are not unused to doing this double act and, perhaps even more remarkable, whereas five or six years ago people in Liverpool would express polite surprise if we were seen together or appeared on the same platform, now we have reached a stage when, if seen alone, we are often asked 'Where's your opposite number?' or even 'Where's your friend?'.

He then explains that the real point to this relationship is joint Christian witness, with a passing suggestion that it was he, Worlock himself, who initiated it.

> Don't be alarmed, I am not about to deliver an address on ecumenism, or even to develop the practical advantages of Christian unity. But I think perhaps I should say that it was a separate approach by the government about four years ago to each religious denomination for its views of its Inner Cities Proposals which led me to say to the others 'If we cannot agree about this, we have no right to talk about Christian Unity. Let's send a joint reply.' And so it has gone on: notably with regard to Bishop David and myself who have known each other longer than Liverpool has known us, but also with the other Church Leaders as well. So much so that now people talk of 'The Mersey Miracle'. Reactions vary according to circumstances and which newspaper you read. Some hail us joyfully as 'The prophetic voice of the Churches in Liverpool': others write somewhat abusive articles about interfering bishops, messing about with politics – described on one occasion as 'Unity in Error'.

There is a risk in all this, Worlock admits – the risk of being seen as politically partisan. It is a risk he is prepared to take. It is not he who speaks of his partnership with Sheppard as a 'miracle' – he merely reports what he has heard, and indeed for fairness he balances it with something disparaging. His listeners would have been in no doubt, of course, which of these two positions they were expected to agree with. And it is characteristic of his style to court the sympathy of his hearers with a slight suggestion of being misjudged and long-suffering, a martyrdom, he would imply, that he is prepared to bear for the sake of the poor and downtrodden.

As a result of the last few months few people are left in doubt about the involvement of the Churches in the life of the community (which usually means its problems). We are not often accused of sitting on the fence. The real lesson seems to be that as long as you talk in generalisations you can be dismissed as guilty of nothing more than harmless generalisations. As soon as you begin to deal with and speak about specific issues, you lay yourself open to the charge of political interference.

He did not choose this role for himself, he insists; it was thrust on him by others, and by events.

But it is a developing process. Three or four years ago now, when British Leyland was threatening to close its Speke factory and we were asked for and gave some advice, the comment was inevitable: 'What does His Holiness know about it?' A year later the Dunlop workers, faced with redundancy, sent their representative to me, almost under cover of darkness, to ask for help. Their employers would not meet them, so we agreed to join their protest march. The meeting between top management and representatives of the men took place (too late as it happened) a few days later. Early this year, when the Tate and Lyle closure was announced, we were asked by the City to join their deputation to the Prime Minister, who declined us the privilege. But when the Toxteth riots took place in July, we were sent for quickly enough. And so it goes on.

What are his credentials for this role? This is one of many points in Worlock's contributions on political and social issues of the day when what he is saying seems at first obvious and incontestable. The more closely and critically it is examined, however, the more it seems open to argument. For instance, in the following passage he treats it as axiomatic that as a Church leader he has a duty to love his neighbour, and to give this a political expression.

But that duty is not peculiar to an archbishop: the scriptural call to 'love one's neighbour as oneself' is addressed to all equally, of whatever condition. It is indeed highly arguable that giving this a political expression is precisely not the duty of an archbishop, who if he does so is trespassing into the proper domain of the layman. The very term 'political expression' implies entering into adversarial debate, and engaging with all the messy compromises of which political life, in reality, must consist. So quite a lot of what he says next must be regarded as subtly tendentious, though an inattentive listener could be excused for regarding a lot of it as pure platitude. (That is what happens when speaker and spoken-to share a consensus.) He goes on:

What is the lesson of all this? I would gladly settle for the word 'reconciliation' which often means being shot at from both sides. In practice the leadership in the Churches must be a voice for the community. It is not so much a call for social and industrial expertise, though we have the duty to try to understand the problems of those we are called to serve. Rather have we the obligation to give practical expression to the Christian injunction to love one's neighbour, and in Merseyside just now that frequently means one's unemployed neighbour. So the problems of unemployment, the need for the industrial regeneration of the area, and the implications of all this on, for example, the family life of our community, these must be on our daily agenda. A positive witness must be given: if it is divided it lacks credibility. But we do not all have to do the same thing all the time. Bishop David is the Chairman for the Area of the Special Programmes for YOP.[7] I serve on a body called the Merseyside Enterprise Forum, made up for the most part of fairly high-powered kings of industry and commerce, called into existence by the County Council to offer advice about the industrial regeneration of Merseyside.

There is no room for debate here – to show more than one Christian point of view would display division and thus 'lack credibility'. It is characteristic of senior churchmen to brook no contradiction when they venture into the field of politics. If party politicians often strike the same note of certainty, at least they admit that they are engaged in an adversarial political process. Certainty, to a politician, is a debating tactic, designed to intimidate one's opponents. Certainty, to a churchman, is a matter of faith; to disagree with them smacks of immorality or heresy. There is the one 'Christian' view; there isn't any other view. It is a tone which irritates many church members and others, even when they happen to agree with much of what is being said.

Where in practice do I fit in? May I give an example? To myself I justified my joining the Enterprise Forum in that I could voice the views of others unlikely to be represented by the other members. When we began to discuss the dissemination of information about microtechnology as a possible way forward for industry in Merseyside, I found myself asking whether enough thought had been given to the implications of advanced technology on the life of the people, especially on family life. Within days I also found myself chairman of a panel of experts to examine the matter and make recommendations. With the help of a senior officer in local government, a trade union official and a high-powered businessman from a multi-national, I laboured away for about eighteen months before we produced our report 'Chips with Everything – or Technology with a Human Face'. It seems that we were almost the first in this particular field. What was most rewarding was that the Forum adopted our recommendations, so did the County Council and gradually they are being given effect. Recently the County and the Churches combined to mount a three-day seminar entitled 'Faith, Hope and Technology'. You can't go much further than that.

He is certainly entitled to the credit that his remarks would have brought him with this audience. Here is a man, they would have said to themselves, who has studied the matter of new technology deeply, and tried at length to tease out its important social implications, not least on family life. *Chips with Everything* was one of the first studies of its kind. Nearly twenty years on it looks somewhat dated, both in its wonder at the approaching miracles of electronics and its dire predictions of what their consequences might be for ordinary people. The real flaws in its argument we will come to later. Essentially they are economic.

Having established who he is, and why he is entitled to be listened to, Worlock now turns to his subject of the day. The pattern of the proceedings for the seminar is that he will stop after completing his stage-setting, to allow Bishop Sheppard to deal with certain specific issues like young people and race. Later he will return to the rostrum to take up the story again.

> It may seem that I am jumping the gun on the first point allotted to me which is 'What happens if nothing happens?'. But the question seems to assume an awful lot of background. I have not known whether I was to speak to you pre-Scarman or post-Scarman: which is how one dates things nowadays.

The Scarman report into the riots in Brixton, South London, was awaited at that time. Worlock was making a relevant point about timing and context, but by using this shorthand he was also signalling that he was fully conversant with the world in which chief executives of local authorities were living.

> But if I am to give a straight answer to the question, it has to be that dread, if already hackneyed word 'alienation', or put more popularly, 'Buy yourself a riot'. I have also learned over the years not to generalise, not to indulge in too many abstract nouns. 'Alienation' really means 'alienated people'. And before leaving Bishop David to do our second bit about young people, school-leavers and the coloured community in particular, I should like to give a final moment to explain what I mean by alienated people: what explanation I could give to Mrs Thatcher as she sat in our Town Hall last July whilst the crowds outside, well covered by the media, brayed for her blood, and she asked 'But why such hatred?'

The question was asked of himself, he implies. He gave another more succinct version of the same encounter in his Pope Paul VI Memorial Lecture in 1995. He said:

In her memoirs *The Downing Street Years*, Margaret Thatcher refers to the advocacy of this city by Bishop Sheppard and myself. At one stage, when feelings were running high, we learned of her intention to fly to Liverpool in order to attend a meeting of the City Council. In the cause of her safety we advised delay, and her intended journey was mercifully stopped at Northolt Airport. Some nights later I was informed by the city's Chief Executive that she was due to arrive unannounced early the following morning, having driven through the night. She would be picked up by the Chief Constable at Burtonwood and driven swiftly to the Town Hall. I should hold myself in readiness.

Bishop David was out of Liverpool that weekend, so when next morning the summons came, I responded with the Bishop of Warrington, his suffragan. By then her presence in the city was known and great chanting crowds had gathered outside the Town Hall. We went in to meet her, with her Secretary, and with her husband reclining in a comfortable chair after the night journey. We treated her to a number of our favourite slogans, such as 'We want reconciliation not recrimination' and 'You cannot impose a solution on this community: it must be worked out with them.' She duly noted these down, and after a while the Bishop of Warrington casually dropped into the discussion the word 'compassion'. This produced an immediate reaction from the Prime Minister, who commented 'Such a patronising word; it's like patting someone on the head.' I ventured to disagree, claiming that my classical education indicated that the word really meant 'suffering with', which was a vital consideration to the Black community in Liverpool 8 at that time. Mrs Thatcher duly added this pearl to the list of gems which she had been noting for possible use in the future. So far as I know, this particular observation never emerged. Perhaps of greater significance was the fact that her husband raised himself in his armchair and remarked 'That's not really one of your words, is it?'

That was the 1995 version. In 1981, with events still warm, the dramatic fiction of an imaginary oration to Mrs Thatcher, if that is what it is, proved more effective. What followed was high Worlock eloquence, rising to a level that shows him deploy his true gift for the language. The effect is hardly spoiled by the doubt that some of those listening may have had whether he really did command the lady's attention, without being seriously interrupted, long enough to deliver his cogent, but hardly brief, analysis of the causes of the Toxteth riots.[8]

I suppose that I could have answered with your first question: 'What happens if nothing happens?' but I have no wish to try to justify the violence and disorder we have seen on our streets this summer. If one says that one as much as understands why they happened, one can be accused of irresponsibility. But merely to attribute them to widespread unemployment is to over-simplify matters. As one Liverpool black put it to me – and, by the way, they have been with us for so many generations, that they hate being called ethnic minorities: they regard themselves as disadvantaged British blacks – as he put it, 'We have been unemployed so long, we have got used to it. Why should that make us riot?' The immediate cause or flash-point was a serious breakdown in police and community relations, but even that must be seen against a background of frustration and this hard-to-identify quality of alienation.

In a situation where national government is Tory, the County Council is Labour-controlled, and the City Council is 'hung' and under Liberal leadership, it is not difficult to think up grounds for frustration. But alienation is more than that. It is a sense of feeling that you have no say in your own destiny, in how you live at home or work, of how your life is controlled. Perhaps the worst quality is that no matter how you may resent such a state of affairs (or, should I say, how you feel?), you have no desire to redress the balance by entering into the ways of the establishment or what the rest of the community accepts as a way of government. How else explain why Liverpool has no black city councillor, or barrister, very few black shop assistants in the big stores, only seven coloured policeman and no black response to efforts at recruitment?

What follows is a moving and indeed frightening analysis of the condition of life on the poor streets of Britain's neglected and dangerous inner cities *circa* 1981, as well said as anyone has ever said it.

All this may seem very negative. The only positive answer I can offer as to how the alienated are to be drawn fully into the life of the community from which they feel themselves separated is to say 'in their own way'. By this I mean a way which has meaning for them, which they can regard as genuine, which may well mean support for something they have already initiated but cannot by themselves bring to fruition. Above all, they seek something which is real rather than symbolic partnership.

They are realistic enough to know that no one hands over assets or help without some strings. But they would reject such assets rather than be unreasonably tied in their own development. Please remember, I am not talking about former colonials awaiting independence, but about many disillusioned and restless people in our inner cities today. Many of the inner cities where these problems are acute are multi-racial, multi-cultural in character. If we are to think of integration rather than absorption, then in the foreseeable future there will have to be more than one way of contributing to our common life.

I am painting a picture which many of you will know, though it would be a great mistake to claim that this analysis is general or that the situation in all inner-city areas is identical. But if nothing happens, if deadlock is reached, if unemployment destroys the sense of dignity in a large part of our community, we shall know alienation in our cities, no-go areas where the vandalism of the past will become violence all too easily.

'No-go areas' are not necessarily territorial. They can be affairs of the spirit. The barrier may be a burned-out bus or a taxi. More often it is an invisible divide which has formed over decades. Prophets may grow hoarse pointing to its danger. Usually it is only recognised when some incident causes an explosion which leaves this unseen barrier shattered in the streets, and with that broken glass, a raw area of cut relationships for which there is no quick healing. That was my answer to Mrs Thatcher's question. I answer your first question the same way: that is what may happen if nothing happens.

This is strong and masterful prose. The phrases are writers' phrases, tailored to the rhythms of English speech. He has unsheathed the language to describe, and by describing to defy, the desolation of urban poverty and the emptiness of unemployment. He told them in his opening he believed 'the leadership in the Churches must be a voice for the community'. In this passage he does indeed become their voice, a true spokesman for the poor of Merseyside.

And yet, and yet, once more. If he can be criticized for not exploring the idea of alienation thoroughly enough, not interrogating it toughly enough from the standpoint of the moral theology and social teaching of his Church, can he also be fairly criticized for that common yet elusive quality, liberal guilt? If he is partly guilty of it, that does not discredit the genuine moral outrage that fires him up in the passages quoted above. But it does suggest that the picture he gives of social disintegration in the inner city of Liverpool is incomplete, and that he ignores some factors that are present out of a decent and compassionate desire not to 'blame the victims'.

Ten years after Toxteth, similar rioting took place in Tyneside, on the Meadow Well housing estate. Poor relations between local youths and the police seemed a factor here too. Two youths had been killed when, being pursued by police, they crashed a car they had stolen for a ram-raiding burglary. In reaction, gangs of black and white young men rampaged round the estate, putting houses and shops to the torch, terrorizing the old and weak.

They were, as the left-wing sociologists Norman Dennis and George Erdos later described it,[9] 'neither immigrants nor the victims of racial prejudice . . . The riot areas were characterised just as much by the statistical deficiency of stable families as they were by a statistical excess of long-term unemployment.' But the breakdown of family life was not a fashionable explanation; unemployment was.

They go on:

Unemployment was indeed the key to the Tyneside riots of 1991. But not unemployment in the sense of the absence of opportunities to work as a paid employee in a drudging job (much less remunerative and exciting than crime). It was unemployment in the sense of the weakening or complete disappearance of the expectation that a young man should prepare himself for the larger employment to which a job is merely instrumental. This is his employment for a lifetime in a partnership of mutual support of a mature man and a mature woman. It is employment in a year-long commitment to maturing and socialising until his child is in turn able to earn its own living and raise its own family.

If there is any connection between the Tyneside riots of the early 1990s and the Merseyside riots of ten years earlier – or for that matter, numerous other instances of violent public disorder, gross criminal damage, and rage against the police – then Dennis and Erdos were pointing the finger of blame in an entirely different direction from that identified by Derek Worlock and David Sheppard. Dennis and Erdos pointed to a collapse of the inner-city working-class culture of family life, primarily focused on the domestic redundancy of males. They were alienated; but the greater alienation was from any systematic sense of values, any understanding of an individual's duty to the community, and any set of responsibilities to themselves and each other beyond that of seeking immediate pleasure and gratification.

Where this stems from is beyond the scope of this book, but Dennis and Erdos see elements of feminism and elements of Marxism at work here, combining to attack and undermine traditional family life. What commands attention to their views is the fact that they both profess to be left-wing socialists themselves, albeit in the tradition known as 'ethical socialism' rather than the more fashionable libertarian socialism.

Worlock also mentions the breakdown of family life, of course. But he sees it as being caused by unemployment, and not, as in the Dennis and Erdos analysis, itself a cause. It may have demanded too much of a leap of the prophetic imagination for a Church leader ten years earlier to have drawn a conclusion like this, so much out of kilter with the liberal intellectual fashion of the time.

No doubt the Dennis–Erdos analysis is itself partial and incomplete. But many clergy with direct experience of the inner city will instinctively recognize it as more than half true.

*   *   *

After David Sheppard had addressed the seminar on 'Young People and the Coloured Community' – a strangely dated title even in 1981 – Derek Worlock returned to his brief to speak about the 'implications of demoralization'.

He offered a description of the condition of the Merseyside economy that was dire and pessimistic. There were parishes in Liverpool, he said, where one-third of the men have been unemployed for several years. In what he called 'the Tate and Lyle parish' in Vauxhall (with one of the highest percentages of Catholics in the city) 46 per cent[10] of those able to work were unemployed even before Tate and Lyle closed down. One woman told him that her husband, her brother and her daughter, all worked in the refinery.

His text is worth considering at length, both because it is a clear and good summary of the problems the city faced at that time and because it illustrates the limitations of a Church leader faced with political and economic causes he understood too little and social consequences he understood only too well. Not least of these was the effect of economic upheaval on marriage – one in ten, he said, were liable to break up under strain. (Two decades later, when the total had reached something more like one in three or four, such figures seem to refer back to a golden age of family stability. Nor, twenty years later, did the explanation quite so obviously lie with economic conditions as he had argued. Changing economic circumstances appeared to have little effect on the inexorable rise in the divorce rate, which has affected the prosperous at least as much as the downtrodden.) He went on:

> In certain areas there is such environmental and cultural deprivation that society itself becomes the enemy. This is the alienation theme to which I spoke earlier. The result can often be violence, vandalism and delinquency. One thing is quite certain. Where a stable supportive family atmosphere is missing or even threatened, there is real danger that the young people of that family fall foul of the society in which their family has failed to find adequate rooting.

What alarmed Derek Worlock most, in fact, was the family tension which resulted when both partners were not working. One aspect of this he foresaw taking on growing importance was the switch to new technologies in manufacturing and services. Often these would provide jobs for which lately redundant male manual or industrial workers were temperamentally, psychologically and educationally ill-fitted.

We have also to face the possible consequences to family life which may arise from the so-called computer revolution. It seems clear that the first effect of the use of technology at its present stage of development will be to create, and to increase already existing, unemployment. (In the enquiry which I led for the Merseyside Enterprise Forum, it was estimated that on Merseyside over the next five years redundancies in the manufacturing sector will be approximately 7,500 of whom slightly less than one-third will be unskilled workers, and in the service sector the figure rises to 19,800 of whom no less than 12,000 will be non-manual office workers from transport and communication, insurance, banking and finance.)

It is not possible to forecast precisely what the chances are of some of these being re-absorbed into new or expanding enterprises on Merseyside. We are always told about the spin-off industries which will come with the 'chip'. All one can say is that on Merseyside, within the next five years, there will almost certainly be 30,000 fewer jobs due to the expanding use of the microprocessor. There is much less certainty about the number of new job opportunities that will be created during that period.

Here I would like to quote the words of a parish priest in Liverpool who is also a sociologist of some distinction. His name is Father John Fitzsimons. 'The psychology of the individual who finds his job disappear is fairly well established', writes Father Fitzsimons. 'At first, for some three months or so, he feels that the situation is transitory and he is kept going by energetic hope. The next six to nine months brings increasing despair, and after a year or so this gives way to lethargy and the feeling of rejection. The effects of the husband's long-term unemployment on the marriage relationship will depend very much on the level of understanding and rapport already reached.'

But it has already been noted on Merseyside that the unemployment of middle-age married men (for the first time in their working lives) is placing a great strain on a number of marriages. The relationship of the couple has been built upon a certain pattern where the man is the main bread-winner. For the greater part of the day he is absent from the home, and is not in for his midday meal. Now he is home nearly all the time, and a new pattern has to be built up and new adjustments made. Unless there is a great deal of understanding and give and take, the strain appears to become intolerable. The man especially may feel that to rejection by society has been added rejection by his wife as well. Where communication has been poor in the past, it is often too late to start to try to build it up. The unease, short temper, dejectedness and frustration overflow into relations with the family. If they are young, they are pushed out onto the streets for longer periods; if they are adolescent, there will be confrontations, verbal and at times even violent. Where there has been no true partnership before, this too will be the occasion of further differences with the wife.

It is also to be noted that a large number of the clerical workers who will be displaced will be women, many of them married and caught in the two-wage economy. The sudden drop in the family income will bring its problems, especially where mortgage payments are involved. To this must be added the realisation that the families affected by this kind of increased unemployment come for the most part from areas which already have the highest rates of long-term unemployment. Thus the polarisation within our society will be accentuated. Very heavy unemployment in one sector of the community and the other possibly living on the profits of the introduction of advanced technology and in theory at least benefiting from the introduction of microprocessor gimmickry in the home.

I am afraid that this is a somewhat depressing picture which I am painting for you. There will be others who will speak of the immense benefit brought to the community by this advanced technology. My fear is that the warnings and the hopes may both be true and we shall merely divide our society more radically between the 'haves' who will have more, and the 'have-nots', who will almost certainly have less. And if this is true within our own communities, the effect can be even more profound in the separation, Brandt-style, of North and South. We may well have a 'two nations' in our own land. The inter-continental divide will be even more profound.

The danger is that when one speaks in this way one is always classed with the Luddites. I have no wish to be a prophet of doom and gloom. But unless firm and constructive action is taken to change the developing scenes, I fear that some of the forecasts of Father Fitzsimons and others may well be true.

It is often argued that the primary task of technology is to lighten the burden of work which man has to carry in order to survive and develop his potential. This may be the sociological principle but to overcome the dangers in the developing situation, it is evident that the power and financial benefits from the widespread introduction of technology must somehow be spread throughout the community. It is recognised that where heavy financial involvement or commitment is concerned, a venture has to pay. But if such benefit can only be derived at cost to the vast majority whose opportunity to work is lost, then the haves must help the have-nots. In other words, the opportunities to use the new technology and benefit from it must in some manner be shared within the community.

This leads some to recommend 'intermediate' technology. In practice it means that its unrestricted use by a few monster-powers, vast multi-nationals or industrial concerns may have to be controlled in some measure for the common good. It was this belief which led Dr Schumacher to advance the thesis 'Small is Beautiful'. He was thinking largely of the problem of the uneven distribution or development of resources to the detriment of the Third World. The same principle may also have significance in the need to develop smaller industries (with technological aids and methods).

In many parts of the country this return to small industrial concerns is already the accepted principle. But it has to be carried out against the problems of areas in which outside industrial concerns are unwilling to invest. Whether we are thinking in terms of inner cities, or regions which are badly placed for dispatching shipments to the continent of Europe, effective encouragement and help will often have to be given to the establishment of small businesses. It is in this as well as in the development of non-conventional als [alternatives? – abbreviation inserted in his own handwriting] to paid employment that the future must lie.

Morale is of great importance in our society. Educational opportunity, housing and employment are all of major consequence where human dignity is concerned. On Monday last I was at Skelmersdale New Town to visit the former Courtaulds factory which is now a centre for Youth Opportunity Programmes for some 500 young people. With the resources and co-operation of the Manpower Services Commission, this Centre, operated by a young priest, with now well-developed supervisory help drawn from the local community, concentrates upon providing its young people with life-skills.

Sadly at the present time only some 40 per cent achieve full employment at the completion of their training period. Yet what they learn both in technique and in the service of the community is doing a great deal to improve the quality of life in the homes from which they come and the community they are learning to serve. It is the most imaginative scheme I have yet come across to prepare today's young people for tomorrow's society where full employment is at least unlikely and where there will have to be a totally new approach to the whole concept of work.

The marvellous thing was to find the young people themselves taking a pride in this project. There was no sign of demoralisation. Some were learning how to operate computers, some were learning home-decoration, some were being trained in the care of the disabled. All appeared to be ready to plough back into their own homes and the local community the benefit of the training and experience they receive. If I have dwelt a little too long on the depressing consequences of unemployment, I am glad to end with that story of hope which I found in that enormous abandoned near-new factory now transformed into a Centre called 'Tomorrow's People Today'. It was a prophetic venture full of meaning.

In the late 1970s and early 1980s this analysis would tend to be regarded as radical and prophetic on the Left, flying in the face of economic reality on the Right. It was for saying such things that Worlock and Sheppard rapidly developed a national reputation as the outspoken 'political' clerics of their generation. It may be taken for granted that neither of them were trying to advance the interests of any one political party, the Labour Party for instance, though there is no doubt on which sets of ears their words would have been heard with the most sympathy. These were exactly the sort of things the TUC was saying too.

Nevertheless to churchmen of this persuasion and generation the analysis stood on its own, regardless of who agreed with it; it would have been regarded as more or less obviously true; as manifestly confirmed by a welter of hard evidence; and as something only the morally disadvantaged would want to deny.

But how much of it stands the test of time? Two of his conclusions have not aged well. First, there is a clear presumption on his part that economic activity is what in American business parlance is known as zero-sum. There may be winners and there may be losers, but broadly they cancel out – add them together, and the result is zero. In those circumstances, the better that life is for some, the worse it is bound to be for others.

That seems to be Worlock's main moral conclusion. The advent of new technology may change the way wealth is distributed and may provide new pockets of winners and a new class of losers, but it too is basically zero-sum. Thus political intervention of some sort will be necessary to protect the losers, share the work, limit the prosperity of the successful for the sake of the whole, and so on.

What is lacking from this picture is any reference to dynamic economic forces creating a constant flow of more wealth – wealth understood not necessarily just as large bank accounts for rich people, but as an overall increase in economic resources in the community, better buildings, better infrastructure, better products, better trained and paid staff, with higher values added at each stage of the economic process. In that light the situation can no longer be described as zero-sum. It is called wealth creation. It is the answer to most of the problems that Worlock is describing in the above passage.

But it requires favourable conditions, and by and large they did not exist. At the time he was speaking the full impact of the Conservative Government's new 'monetarist' theories was being felt especially in long-established heavy industries where profit margins had long been tight.

A House of Commons Select Committee was later to report that the Treasury's monetarist dogma had had far harsher effects at the beginning of the 1980s than had been necessary to control inflation, and it had caused a recession which was much more serious and lasted much longer than would otherwise have been the case. Monetarism was later abandoned and Conservative economic policy-makers became persuaded of the benefits of nineteenth-century *laissez-faire* economics, the so-called free market of deregulation, privatization (which eventually brought about a recession in the early 1990s even more severe than the early 1980s one).

Secondly, the analysis evokes a strong sense of fatalism. There are other factors favourable to wealth creation, of course, one of the most important of which, psychologically, is a willingness to embrace the future rather than to run away from it. The assumption that things can only get worse unless 'the Government does something' – what that something is, is never made clear – is the attitude least likely to encourage risk-taking, enterprise, adventure, vision, or a reversal of Merseyside's economic fortunes. It is the fatalistic attitude most likely to lead to a 'What we have we hold' attitude to jobs, regardless of whether those jobs still made economic sense.

The militancy of Liverpool's factory and dock workers was legendary. They had no more sense of the importance of wealth creation for the well-being of the whole community, and therefore of their families and themselves, than did the clergy. Wealth was something the bosses had, that they wanted. Trade unionism of that time was also wedded to a zero-sum view of business and industry. In the shadow of Marx, there was something inherently evil about employing others in a business whose purpose was to make money. For the employer was deemed to be making himself richer at the price of making his employees poorer.

There is no hint whatever in Worlock's remarks in 1981, nor in anything else he said before or since, that he saw the need for a fundamental change of attitude. His reference to intermediate technology and to the retraining of young people for what sounds like cottage industries appear at best like an admission that mainstream economic forces have deserted Merseyside for good. He saw this economic trend reinforced by the arrival of new technologies, then on the horizon. They did not offer a prospect of deliverance, but only one more threat. In this respect he stands at the head of an entire generation of churchmen who held similar political views.

It has already been noted that Worlock had sent a copy of this text to

Rome, via the Apostolic Delegation in Wimbledon, in response to being sent the Pope's major encyclical on the dignity of work, *Laborem Exercens*. A quick and selective reading of the encyclical may even have assured Worlock that the Pope agreed with his analysis. The truth is quite the contrary. An analysis of the problems of Merseyside he is discussing would have been different, more profound and more constructive, had he incorporated the ideas of *Laborem Exercens*.

Like Worlock, Karol Wojtyla, then Archbishop of Cracow and the future Pope John Paul II, had been involved at the Second Vatican Council and particularly in the preparation of the Council's last important statement, on *The Church in the Modern World* (*Gaudium et Spes*).

He refers to it (as Worlock would surely have noticed with more than passing interest) at the beginning of *Laborem Exercens*. The encyclical was partly written as a result of the Pope's meditation – some of it on his sickbed after the assassination attempt earlier in 1981 – on the industrial situation then developing in Poland. Free trade unions, under the banner Solidarity, were beginning to challenge the Marxist philosophy by which the economy of Poland was then run. It was also a continuation of the tradition of papal teaching on the theme of economics and social justice which began in 1891 by Pope Leo XIII in the encyclical *Rerum Novarum*. One of its effects on Poland was to fortify the resolve of Solidarity members to hold on to the independence of their movement, and to press for a greater sense of dignity in the workplace.

Theoretically Marxism had overcome class conflict and elevated the proletariat to the role of dictator; in practice it had left life at the coal face, dockyard or factory floor just as grim and meaningless – in many ways grimmer and more meaningless – than in the West. It was with that paradox that this masterly encyclical thrust its dagger into the heart of Polish Communism, with incalculable consequences for the history of Eastern Europe by the end of the decade, and indeed for the world.

Laborem Exercens does implicitly contain a doctrine of wealth creation, which becomes explicit in later developments of Catholic Social Teaching such as his 1991 encyclical *Centesimus Annus*. In *Laborem Exercens* he declares the vocation of humanity to work to be part of God's call to 'subdue the earth' and a continuation of God's own creative act in calling the world into existence. But the work must be organized in such a way that each individual worker may feel that he or she is, in some sense, working for themselves (as well as for their employers and for the general benefit). He singles out alienation as a condition undermining the dignity of labour. Instead each worker should have a stake in the success of the enterprise, as well as personal pride in his or her own contribution. And the fruit of human work is cumulative. In no way is the theory of economic activity in *Laborem Exercens* a zero-sum one.

The Pope does not condemn private enterprise, nor does he suggest employers are not entitled to their profits – though not as a result of paying unfair wages to their employees. His reference to the need for workers to have a sense of ownership of their work is not necessarily a call for employee shareholding (though the Pope refers to this favourably). It is more generally a demand for an end to the destructive climate of 'us' and 'them' which results from approaching industrial relations as an expression of Marxist class conflict. His criticisms apply equally to British managers, who were as guilty of regarding their employees as mere units of labour – an attitude *Laborem Exercens* roundly condemns – as the employees themselves were guilty of the attitudes described above.

But if workers have a vocation, they also have a duty. This is as strong in the encyclical as it is absent from Worlock's own thoughts. For him, militant workers in Liverpool are the alienated victims of unjust circumstances. For him, their militancy is excusable and understandable, and not part of the problem.

It would be a mistake, however, to turn Derek Worlock into a politician. He moved smoothly into a late-1970s left-of-centre interpretation of economic forces because that was almost inevitable for a man in his time and place, as inevitable perhaps as the very different position taken by, say, Cardinal Griffin in the late 1940s. Worlock said what was expected of him; and became famous for what he said because he did it repeatedly and well.

It may well be the case that the efforts of Worlock and Sheppard to give a higher profile to the state of Britain's inner cities was one of the factors behind various government initiatives, most famously the appointment of Michael Heseltine as the so-called 'Minister for Merseyside' as the government's direct response to the Toxteth riots.

It could be argued on Worlock's side, therefore, that it was not so necessary that his political and economic analysis be correct (after all, nobody was going to follow it) as that it should be delivered loudly enough to catch the attention of government ministers and other opinion-formers in London.

Similarly for an incoming archbishop to fit himself so neatly into the prevailing political and economic climate of his new diocese was not so different from him smoothly and effortlessly supporting Liverpool football club (or Everton, except when there was a home Derby) when he had previously supported Portsmouth (or Southampton, or West Ham). It was necessary for his 'street cred', especially as he was a middle-class public-school-educated southern Englishman. It signalled that he cared, that at heart he was one of them. He really came to believe this, and so did they.

Had he taken a different tack, his position would have been undermined. At one point he told David Sheppard that there were working-class parishes where only five per cent of the menfolk went to Sunday Mass, because they were disenchanted with the Church's failure to speak up against unemployment. If the cost of seeming to be indifferent was high, the rewards of solidarity were enticing. Thus David Sheppard and Derek Worlock, with support from the leading Methodists and other Free Churchmen in Merseyside, stood by their people at their time of difficulty.

Insofar as it was a flawed approach, this endorsement of the prevailing economic fatalism can only be criticized as an opportunity lost and a mistaken consensus added to. Nobody told the people of Merseyside that they should take control of their own economic destiny. Everybody told them they were helpless victims of a justified grievance, victims of an inevitable conflict of interest between capital and labour, between the selfish rich and the hapless poor. And that 'everybody' included their archbishop. Even though this resignation in the face of economic forces was not the message of the social teaching of Pope John Paul II, it would not have been realistic to expect Worlock to be different. He wasn't in the business of changing the world; he was in the business of being *seen* to be changing the world, which is different.

It has to be said, also, that if his real but unstated goal was to improve the Church's standing among its own people, the better to hold on to their loyalties as Catholics, this was not spectacularly successful either. Urban redevelopment and social mobility have made it difficult to produce reliable statistics to chart what has really happened to the Catholic population of Liverpool, but there is no doubt at all that part of its statistical decline is associated with people falling away from the practice of the faith. This has also been part of a national trend, and is not confined to Catholics. But Liverpool's Catholicism was the most proletarian variety of Christianity in the whole of England: it was a genuine popular working-class 'folk religion'.

But even by 1981 the writing was on the wall. A survey conducted jointly by Gallup and the University of Surrey in 1980 had discovered worrying signs that working-class Catholicism in England was not as deeply rooted as had been supposed. The report which analysed the findings 'cautions against believing that the commitment of the working class to the Catholic Church has ever been strong. Indeed it cites a number of historical studies which suggest the contrary.'[11] To accuse Worlock of having aggravated or even caused the numerical decline in working-class Catholicism in Liverpool in his twenty years there is the opposite of the truth – he did everything in his power, far more than most would have done, to halt the trend.

In March 1985 Derek Worlock delivered an address, 'The Christian in the Post-industrial Era', in Bristol Cathedral to members of the Social and Industry Ministry of the Church of England Diocese of Bristol. Though many of his fears then are identical to those he expressed in 1981, he gave his favourite theme a new twist. Once more his emphasis was on the human cost of redundancy, and the largely malign invasion of the workplace (and indeed the domestic scene too) by what he called the 'chip', i.e. the computer and related technology. Because he was an intelligent man, he was beginning to see that his 1981 absolutism no longer made sense. Perhaps one of the reasons managements had to close down factories when they became unprofitable was because they had not invested enough (out of their profits) in updating machinery, he admitted at one point. That meant 'the chip' was part of the solution, surely. But he did not take the point: it was against his general trend.

What was lacking from his analysis was any appreciation of the urgent need for new enterprises to replace old enterprises when they failed (though he did, in passing, concede that small businesses had a role); the necessity for new technologies to be embraced speedily rather than grudgingly if industry was to survive; and any recognition of the vital importance of training and education. He might have got these ideas from the 1981 papal encyclical *Laborem Exercens*, which discussed in a more profound way than Worlock ever envisaged the relationship between a worker and his work. It is interesting that this address by a man regarded as the Catholic Church's leading authority on the problems of British industry fails to offer any specifically Catholic input to this discussion. It is also relevant to note that this address was given in the interval between two major industrial conflicts, both of which lasted about a year and both of which (for better or for worse) represented a revolution in the nation's industrial life – the 1984 miners' strike, and the 1986 News International dispute. The first was about holding on to jobs in a traditional but declining basic industry, the second about resisting technological changes which rendered the old-fashioned skills of the newspaper print shop obsolete. If recent Catholic history can be divided into 'Before the Encyclical' and 'After the Encyclical', Britain's recent industrial history can certainly be divided between 'Before Wapping' and 'After Wapping.' Worlock was essentially a man of his time, and his time was before Wapping.

Some time ago now I received advance notice from the management of a large tobacco factory that the following day the London headquarters of their firm would have to announce such widespread redundancies in their Liverpool factory that for a major part of the work-force it was tantamount to closure.

The announcement would be made on Friday. On Merseyside we had grown used to a saga of 'black Fridays': minimal press coverage the following day owing to sport and a natural week-end cooling-off period for those involved . . .

I remember this particular case well. It followed reasonably soon after the announcement of the closure of a large biscuit-manufacturing factory, also in Liverpool . . . I should record recollections of visits to both the threatened work-forces, for each was highly significant.

Both factories were staffed largely by local people: I could say 'families' because often we met brothers, sisters, brothers-in-law and sons. At neither factory had there been any recent industrial action and both work-forces had been thanked for their productivity and reliability. At the tobacco factory I was shown two enormous machines, spewing out cigarettes at a rate of knots and under the supervision of one white-coated technician. I was told that each machine had replaced 25 factory hands who had done the job previously at about one-third of the rate of this monster's production. 'Where did the machine come from?' I asked. 'Germany'. 'How much did each cost?' 'Rather more than half a million each.'

At the biscuit factory I was told that our biscuit-eating habits had changed. So had the style of biscuit wrapping. There was now less demand for the old-fashioned round biscuit from Binns Road, Liverpool. In a factory in north London, belonging to the same firm, bigger, more tasty, better-wrapped and more numerous biscuits were being produced by some form of computerised machinery under the supervision of two button-pressing technicians, doubtless also in white coats. The result was that the bell tolled for Binns Road. The firm announced that in addition to redundancy payments, they would make a gift of about £1 million to back any local replacement initiative. This would have been largely covered by grant and tax relief and was an expression of their social responsibility towards the afflicted area – which noted that next year's profits for the company ran close to three figures – in £millions.

The work-force greeted us kindly. Strangely they were for the most part not even bitter. They had seen it coming for some time. They were sad at the final passing of the good old days. This time they did not even blame the government. It was all due to what they called the 'chip'. They looked askance at those who came to talk to them about the mobility of labour and settled down to join their 'brothers and their sisters, their cousins and their aunts' amongst the north-west's long-term unemployed. Some few, very few, made enquiries about grants and aid to set up some small enterprise of their own. Some decided to blow the redundancy money on a last-fling package holiday for the family. After all, what they had known in the past was coming to an end. It would never be the same again.

Bishop Sheppard and I bounced up and down like yo-yos between Liverpool and London, to talk to politicians, kings of industry and commerce and others about what was happening in the north, about mutual responsibility and the danger of two nations, about specific proposals to try to generate new industry or new investment for new forms of employment in Merseyside. The doors remain open, the discussions of particular problems and new strategies continue with sympathetic interest, though often bedevilled by party-political considerations at one end of the line or the other. As adopted Merseysiders, we are far from being dispirited . . . But the political uncertainties of both our city and the metropolitan county council make it difficult to point to specific grounds for hope for those redundant biscuit and 'ciggy' workers and the other victims of constant and dramatic job loss these last ten years or more . . .

Without in any way wishing to play down President Reagan's prophecy that we 'ain't seen nothing yet', technologies of various kinds, especially micro-technology, have already made sufficient inroads into our lives that to speak of the coming technological age is a gross anachronism. Its effects may not yet have been adequately appreciated but insofar as we shall never return to the conditions we knew when 'we never had it so good', it is as well to admit that the new technological era (which some see as a further stage in the industrial revolution) is not just here to stay. It is rolling forward at a quite incredible pace – without most of us realising what it is doing, for better or for worse, to our way of life, way of work, and way of relating to one another.

Certainly there has been a notable increase in awareness of the existence of advanced technology. It has already invaded our homes, either in domestic appliances or via the media. Television programmes on micro-technology and its various challenges are commonplace. But there does not seem to have been comparable concern about its social implications. There are those who think of it in terms of increased and improved productivity, and those who connect it at least indirectly with present levels of unemployment. Reaction to loss of jobs is foreseeable: perhaps the surprising thing is that reaction is still relatively mild. Possibly this is due to the increasing realisation that jobs may be lost by the failure to introduce modern technology (and thereby remain competitive) just as much as by the supplanting of machinery by robots.

It would be a mistake, however, to think of the social implications purely in terms of unemployment. This may have a catastrophic effect on the life of an individual, a family and even a local community which in the past has drawn its well-being from an industry or local factory, suddenly judged unviable. But the direct effect of technology upon life in the home and in the community must not be overlooked. The technological invasion of the home is more insidious than just the wizardry of TV games. All manner of examples have found their way into the domestic scene, such as videos, highly technical washing-machines, perhaps a word-processor and typewriter, and even a computerised weighing-machine in the bathroom. Nor can we disregard the effect on family life of a highly technical missile system, allegedly for our defence, information technologies of the most exotic kind and the biotechnological revolution which has triggered off the ethical problems posed by the Warnock Report.

Even if we think only of what has come into our homes in these last years, it is at least arguable whether these things are to be seen as an extension to the frontiers of culture and education for the masses or an encouragement for laziness and a danger to the community. But we must face up to certain moral consequences of the development of information technology. Positively it makes it relatively unimportant whether the factory or research station is established in the Home Counties or in Merseyside. But if we can stretch our minds a bit, we can see that the scale of technological advance soon lifts such development beyond the control of local authorities. For example, given suitable domestic receivers, television programmes from other countries and commercial satellites will soon be able to be bounced into your sitting-room. If the pornography switch is thought to be impractical for cable-television, the BBC and IBA will soon be hard put to it to exercise their one-time privilege of safeguarding the nation's morals.

Idealists amongst us may conjure up dreams of how the long-term unemployed may be trained by cable television in the skills they need to improve the quality of their lives. Perhaps more realistically we should try to envisage steps whereby the said long-term unemployed may maintain their hope of a better future and their will to work. Not that I am an advocate of the so-called Protestant work ethic, even though it is evident that man does achieve a sense of fulfilment through working to express in some way the creative spirit which is in him. But I have much sympathy with the visionary in a severely deprived area, with massive unemployment, who said how marvellous it would be if men, freed from the drudgery of the grinding work they had always known, might in the future have the freedom to enjoy some of the wonder and beauty of God's creation. But before we can reach such heights, we have to do something to remove the stigma of unemployment and the indignity of the dole.

The very concept of work is of course at the heart of what I am trying to say. If the introduction of technology does not create new jobs on the scale of those they have displaced, nor indeed for the same people, it is vitally important that we recognise that full employment of the conventional kind will not return in the foreseeable future. I stress the words 'of the conventional kind'. The challenge is to see in what manner and in what degree we can find a substitute of the non-conventional kind in which the individual can achieve worthy fulfilment and which may be of some benefit to the community, whether local or at large . . .

I personally would favour the introduction of a vast programme of public works, believing that unemployment figures have reached an unacceptable level in an attempt to keep down taxes and inflation. Quite rightly, emphasis is also placed on the building up of new small businesses. But my point tonight is that we have to give our minds not just to job-sharing and early retirement but to a renewed understanding of what work, seen as a real job, can be.

Even now it is difficult to get a politician or a trade union leader to admit what I am saying about full employment – at least in public. Unemployment has for years been regarded as a temporary phenomenon.[12] Whichever political party is in power the belief is still 'change the government, change the policy and that up-swinging graph of the jobless will come down again, at least until the next time' . . . The truth is that the whole pattern of work is changing.

In 1980 I chaired a committee which was bold enough to try to quantify job-losses in the major industries in Merseyside in the next few years, due to the introduction of technology. It was a fairly detailed estimate which was inevitably attacked as a dangerous exaggeration. It has proved to be a notable under-estimate . . .

I do not have to be a Luddite or a Mrs Grundy to speak of the effect of widespread unemployment upon family life. A recent survey has shown the connection between long-term unemployment and marriage breakdown, and there is a possible connection with alcoholism and even suicide. Men, unemployed for the first time in their lives, accustomed to being bread-winners absent from home all day, find themselves without more than limited interest and domestic occupation and soon feel themselves rejected by wife and family, as well as by the rest of society. This dejectedness rapidly overflows into their relationship with their wives and children: the outlook, hopes and aspirations of the next generation are inevitably affected. But it is interesting to note that whilst children in primary schools are being taught to do their sums on pocket calculators, their parents have in some cases never known what it is to have a real job . . .

Although I speak about the north-west, much of what I am saying is applicable to most of the territory north of a line from the Humber to Bristol. Some would say 'north of Watford', though in afflicted areas this has been adapted to 'north of Finchley'. The truth is that the promise of the best possible redundancy payment does not resolve the future of communities which suddenly find their source of livelihood closed or transferred elsewhere. What is to happen to the local community when a closure is announced and those concerned, whose energies have served the business, industry and nation well in the past, feel that they are entitled to some say in the decision affecting their future? It is the task of management to manage but good redundancy money can seem like 30 pieces of silver to those striving to maintain job opportunities for future generations. This is not of itself a party-political issue. But it is a basic question about relationships and mutual responsibility within the national community as we move into this post-industrial age . . .

Soon after I came to Liverpool, when British Leyland was threatening to close its Speke factory, we were asked for and gave some advice. The immediate comment from the local shop stewards who were unused to such advice was: 'What does His Holiness know about it?' A year later the Dunlop workers, faced with redundancy, sent their representative to see me almost under cover of darkness, to ask for help. Their employers would not meet them, so in the name of the other Church leaders I agreed to join their protest march. We were all there, in some sense in the strangest possible company, when the march took place the following Saturday. The cameras clicked, the microphones appeared and the meeting between top management and representatives of the men followed shortly afterwards. A year later, when the Tate and Lyle closure was announced, we were asked by the City to join their deputation to the Prime Minister, who declined us the privilege. But when the Toxteth riots took place in July, 1981, we were sent for quickly enough. And so it continues and increases.

This involvement in the real problems of people makes great demands upon our time. A few nights ago Bishop Sheppard and I sat down to talk about our joint commitments for the next few weeks. There were eighteen of them, six concerned with major industrial disputes in which our help had been asked.

Generally speaking the leadership in the Churches must be a voice for the community. It is not so much a call for social and industrial expertise, though we do have the duty to listen and try to understand the problems of those we are called to serve. Rather have we the obligation to give practical expression to the Christian injunction to love one's neighbour, and in Merseyside just now that frequently means one's unemployed neighbour. So the problems of unemployment, the need for the industrial regeneration of the area, and the implications of all this on, for example, the family life of the community, these have to be our daily agenda.

I will not weary you with further examples. The Churches have set up their own Unemployment Unit. In spite of the constantly shifting policies of the Department of Employment and the Manpower Services Commission, we encourage our people to initiate all manner of brave projects to train people for life even where no jobs can be found. Bishop Sheppard has just completed seven years as Chairman of the Area Board for Special Programmes. I am actively engaged in the Merseyside Enterprise Forum to help in the industrial regeneration of our part of the country. It is now some time since we were asked whether we had ever actually created any jobs.

But why is it such a bad question? Derek Worlock referred time and again to the north–south divide in Britain, on this occasion taking the dividing line as running 'north of Watford' (or 'north of Finchley', as he wittily amended the usual cliché to make it refer to Margaret Thatcher's parliamentary constituency in north London a few miles from Watford). The division between the 'haves' and the 'have-nots' was thus made geographical. There were times when David Sheppard adopted a similar analysis. Yet both of them must have known from first hand that some of the poorer areas of the whole of Great Britain are south of that line. The Borough of Tower Hamlets in East London, for instance, where Worlock spent his brief 1964–65 interlude as a parish priest, regularly scored worse than any other local authority area in a whole range of measurements of social deprivation. And David Sheppard, before being appointed Bishop of Woolwich, had worked at the Mayflower project in the East End of London: he must have known that too.

So they let the north–south geographical line turn into a victim-oppressor moral line, part of their thesis that the plight of the poorer parts of Britain was caused by the selfishness of the wealthier parts. Unemployment, Worlock implies in this address, could be tackled if those well-to-do people who paid taxes were not too greedy to pay more of them. That may have been the conventional wisdom on the Left in the mid-1980s. It was certainly a view supported by none of the major political parties, or academic economists of Left or Right, by the end of the 1990s. So if this theory was not true, and may even have been perpetuating the very conditions it was complaining about, what was Worlock doing lending it his personal and official moral authority (and strongly implying that there was something deeply immoral about anyone who disagreed with him)?

He visited Ireland often enough, a country whose economy was historically more backwards even than Liverpool's. The economic recovery of Ireland in the 1990s is one of the success stories of modern Europe. It is based, first, on a firm investment in education, especially secondary and tertiary – Ireland's workforce is one of the best educated in Europe. It is based on the encouragement of enterprise and new businesses, bolstered admittedly by large EU funds but wisely used to create growth points in the Irish economy. It is based on the embrace of the very microchip that Worlock saw as the source of all the problems: Ireland's industrial expansion has been into areas of high technology, computers and electronics, of which it has the largest concentration in Europe. Ireland still has unemployment. But it has found how to create a dynamic economy, and in the process how to stop looking for other people to blame. Derek Worlock's contribution to the economic life of Merseyside would have been even more remarkable had he been able to point to a similar way forward.

But this is the dilemma of every Church leader in every generation: whether to sympathize with and console the people in their difficulties, showing to them the compassion which is the hallmark of true religion, or whether to confront them with painful choices, and help them face the demand for change and growth. There is an old prayer – 'Lord, give us the grace to accept the things we cannot change, and change the things we can.' The secret is to distinguish correctly between the two. But to know what can be changed and what cannot requires a sophistication in the understanding of political, social and economic forces that Church leaders are not bred to possess. Even experts can get it wrong. Rather than err in their analysis and raise false hopes, they must, of necessity, choose the path of caution. If they must either blame the system or blame the victim, they will – indeed, they must – blame the system. The other is too cruel. Even if it is sometimes right.[13]

Notes

1 1 October 1985.
2 *Britain Today and Tomorrow*, Collins, 1978. Beeson was a canon of Westminster and later Dean of Winchester.
3 Private letter to author.
4 It was not until 1996, after the death of Derek Worlock, that the Catholic Church in England and Wales produced a coherent and plausible analysis of modern Western industrial and post-industrial society based on Catholic Social Teaching, in its 13,000-word pre-election statement, *The Common Good*. The author was a consultant to that project. By then the Catholic tradition of social doctrine had been greatly extended and deepened by Pope Paul VI and particularly Pope John Paul II. It was said by several bishops during the preparation of the 1996 document that such a project would not have been undertaken in Worlock's day. He would have insisted on taking it over; and knowing that likelihood, the other bishops would not have embarked on it.
5 *Confusions in Christian Social Ethics* by Professor Ronald H. Preston, SCM, 1994.
6 Professor Ian Markham, Liverpool Chair of Theology and Public Life, inaugural lecture at Liverpool Hope University College, 1997, entitled *Shades of Grey: the Pope, Christian Ethics, and the Ambiguity of Human Situations*.
7 Youth Opportunities Programme, a government scheme to give technical training to young people.
8 In a handwritten note to Frank Judd, former Labour MP for Portsmouth North and by then Director of Voluntary Service Overseas, Worlock noted: 'She arrived at crack of dawn today. I had 40 minutes with her to try to get some things straight.'
9 *Families Without Fatherhood*, Norman Dennis and George Erdos, IEA, 1992.
10 I know of two other places in Britain where the rate of male unemployment was said at one time or another to be 46 per cent. A coincidence, perhaps, or is this figure a rough guess, giving an impression of accuracy by its apparent precision? Did the Ministry of

Labour issue official unemployment statistics broken down by Catholic parish? If Derek Worlock meant 'about half' why did he not say so?

11 *Roman Catholic Opinion – a Study of Roman Catholics in England and Wales in the 1970s* by Michael Hornsby-Smith and Raymond Lee, David Wedgewood Ltd, 1980.

12 About a year after Worlock died, an inter-church committee under the chairmanship of David Sheppard produced a report on long-term unemployment which argued that it was in fact curable, though the country would have to spend money before it reaped any benefit. That is not very different from the New Deal welfare-to-work policy of the Labour Government elected in 1997 – though the jury will be out for a while yet on whether it has all the answers.

13 *The Guardian*, 31 August 1999, reported Mike Shields, chief executive of the North-west Development Agency which started work in April 1999, as saying 'Liverpool has escaped from the begging-bowl culture and is now getting on with sorting out its own problems.'

Appendix I

SELECTION OF OFFICIAL ENGLISH CATHOLIC
DOCUMENTS ON CONTRACEPTION[1]

DOCUMENT 1

STATEMENT FOR COUNCIL OF CLERGY

By Archbishop George Andrew Beck, Archbishop of Liverpool, 23
November 1967.

I. Introduction

A letter from one of the deanery conferences draws attention to the acute
pastoral problem caused by the present birth control controversy. It was
appreciated that Pope Paul had said that Catholic practice in this matter
should remain unchanged, but guidance at local level was asked for.

After much thought and advice I have decided that it is my pastoral
responsibility to offer some guidance to the clergy of the archdiocese. I do
this with some reluctance remembering the words of Pope Paul asking the
bishops to refrain from public discussion in this matter, and urging that no
one should for the moment take it upon himself to pronounce in terms differing from the existing norm. What I now say is – at least for the present
– confidential to the clergy and not in any way for publication.

II. The true values of Christian Marriage

1. Marriage is a human institution. It flows naturally from God's creation and is therefore good. It is this ordinary human institution which has been taken up by Christ and made a special vehicle of grace for men. But the fact that Christian Marriage is a Sacrament does not destroy its nature as a human institution. The essential values of this human institution are not vitiated by its new sacramental role. They retain their full significance and importance. The Church in her concern for Christian marriage is necessarily very concerned for the essential values of the natural human institution of marriage.

2. The Church has always understood these essential values as involving the natural goodness of the loving union of husband and wife. She has always stressed that openness to procreation is an essential element in this union. The defence and protection of the natural goodness of marriage and its essential values has been the unchanging core and intention of her teaching on this matter through the ages. At this level there is no question of the Church's teaching being open to CHANGE – in the sense of 'becoming essentially different from what it was formerly'. The Church's teaching is, however, open to DEVELOPMENT. This will occur to the extent that she deepens her understanding of these essential values – how they stand in relation to each other and their implications for parents, for families and for the community as a whole. Any detailed natural guidance that the Church gives with regard to marriage will be based on her understanding of these essential values and will be aimed at guarding and fostering them. Hence, there is a sense in which this detailed guidance can be said to be open to further development (i.e. to the extent that it is dependent on the Church's growing appreciation of the essential values of marriage); but there is another sense in which this detailed guidance can be said to be 'constant' (i.e. insofar as its sole aim must be the protection and furtherance of the essential values of marriage).

3. The Church's persistent concern for the essential natural values of marriage is very much in evidence in our own times. This is clear from the writings of Pius XI and Pius XII and from the teaching of the Second Vatican Council. However, it seems true to say that in recent years the Church's understanding of these essential values has undergone a remarkable development. How this development has come about and a full explanation of all its implications can be found in the reports of the Papal

Birth Control Commission (cf. *Tablet*, 1967, 22 April, 29 April and 6 May). Its essential features were already clear in the Second Vatican Council's Pastoral Constitution on *The Church in the World of Today* (*Gaudium et Spes*). Perhaps its most basic point was that it laid aside the theology of primary and secondary ends and preferred to speak of marriage as a 'community of love'. The essential natural values of marriage which the Church has always defended and promoted were thereby seen to possess an intrinsic unity. They were simply the relational and procreational aspects of this 'community of love'. The deliberate exclusion of either aspect would be contradictory to marriage understood according to its special character as a 'community of love'.

4. This is not a change in the Church's teaching on marriage but simply a development of her understanding. More than 30 years ago Pius XI in *Casti Connubii*, referring to the tradition expressed in the Roman Catechism, wrote: 'This mutual inward moulding of husband and wife, this determined effort to perfect each other, can in a very real sense be said to be the chief reason and purpose of matrimony, provided matrimony be looked at not in the restricted sense as instituted for the procreation and rearing of children, but more widely as a companionship embracing the whole of life so that life is no longer an individual venture but a partnership.' Pius XI is insisting on the relational aspect of the 'community of love'. The Majority Report of the Papal Birth Control Commission which also insists strongly on the essential value of the relational aspect of marriage by no means neglects to stress the other essential value which is the procreational aspect: 'More and more clearly, for a conscience correctly formed, a willingness to raise a family with full acceptance of the various human and Christian responsibilities is altogether distinguished from a mentality and way of married life which in its totality is egoistically and irrationally opposed to fruitfulness. This truly 'contraceptive' mentality and practice has been condemned by the traditional doctrine of the Church and will always be condemned as gravely sinful' (*Tablet*, 22 April 1967, p.4 51, col. 1) There is no doubt that it is the same essential values of marriage which are being taught by Pius XI and the Majority Report.

III. Pastoral considerations

On 29 October 1966 Pope Paul said: ' . . . the mind and norm of the Church have not been changed; they remain as stated in the traditional teaching of the Church. The Ecumenical Council, an exalted witness, has made some judicious contributions, very useful for the integration of the Catholic doctrine on this most important theme, but not such as to change its substantial terms . . . Meanwhile, as we said before in the above-mentioned discourse (23 June 1964), the norm hitherto taught by the Church, integrated with the wise instructions of the Council, demands faithful and generous observance. Nor can it be considered not binding, as if the *magisterium* of the Church were at present in a state of doubt, while it is being subjected to study and reflection on what has been put forward as worthy of attentive consideration.' This statement would seem to demand special attention when it is related to that other passage from *Gaudium et Spes*, para. 51: 'Moral behaviour then, when it is a question of reconciling married love with the responsible transmitting of life, does not depend only on a sincere intention and the evaluating of motives, but must be judged by objective standards. These are drawn from the nature of the human person and of its acts, and have regard for the whole meaning of mutual self-giving and human procreation in the context of true love. This cannot be unless the virtue of married chastity is sincerely cultivated. For children of the Church, taking their stand on these principles, it is not lawful to regulate procreation by embarking on ways which the Church's teaching authority, in expounding the divine law, condemns.'

The pastoral question to be considered is – what is the position of the priest whose advice is sought on this matter? Alternative courses of action have been suggested.

1. Some people argue that whatever the Pope may have said about the need to give faithful and generous observance to the norm hitherto taught by the Church and despite his insistence that this norm cannot be considered as not binding, 'as if the *magisterium* of the Church were at present in a state of doubt', (29 October 1966) nevertheless subsequent silence on the part of the Pope has modified that pronouncement. From this it could be argued that there now exists a *dubium legis*[2] concerning the prohibition of contraceptive practices in marriage. This answer is attractive because it is simple. Nevertheless it does not seem to be a satisfactory interpretation of the facts. The Pope's reiteration of the directive only last year (in fact, scarcely more than twelve months ago) hardly justifies the view that the law is doubtful.

2. Others have suggested that a priest may advise a penitent simply to 'follow his own conscience'. In this matter many people will interpret this as meaning, 'Never mind what the Pope says, follow your own conscience'.

To give this impression could easily undermine the whole authority of the Church's *magisterium*. It is my duty to maintain respect for that *magisterium*. I cannot, therefore, advise any priest to say to a penitent 'Never mind what the Pope says. Follow your own conscience' or anything which most people would interpret as meaning this. To do this would be a pastoral mistake and would give a false sovereignty to conscience. Conscience is not synonymous with private opinion. It is a practical judgement as to what one's obligations are in any given situation. Consequently, the conscience of the Christian will always take account of any directive of Authority – even when its final judgement is that the directive does not bind because its observance constitutes a threat and danger to the very values it is supposed to guard and promote.

3. A priest can follow the strict view proposed in the 'minority report' of the Birth Control Commission. A logical conclusion of this view would seem to be that no contraceptive practice can be allowed and consequently reception of the Sacraments must be refused to any who continue in the practice.

4. The matter can be approached from a different angle which may seem a little more subtle but which could produce a more radical answer. Up to the present the binding force of the Church's teaching on contraception has been seen to emanate from a double source. On the one hand, it has bound the Christian precisely as a Christian because it has been interpreted for him by the Church as a demand of Christ. At this level, it is not essentially different from the other interpretations of the demands of Christ which the Church makes in other areas of life, e.g. the specific demands related to Christian worship, penance, etc.

On the other hand, its binding force has also been seen as emanating from the Natural Law. The important point is that the absolute inviolability of the law on contraception has been drawn from its interpretation as a demand of the Natural Law. The axiom has always been – if a thing is intrinsically evil it cannot be done in any circumstances and for any good reason. The absolute inviolability has been drawn from its Natural Law character, not from its character as a demand of the Church.

The present state of theological thinking seems to be overwhelmingly in favour of rejecting the view that contraception is against the Natural Law, that it is intrinsically evil.

This means that it is legitimate for us to see only one source for the binding force of the Church's teaching on contraception and that is the directive of the Church. Many people think that the Church will alter this directive in the light of contemporary theological thought, but she has not done this yet. The Church's directive still binds; she still says to married Christians – 'For the present I interpret the demands of Christ on you as meaning that you may not practise contraception.' This is similar to her interpreting the demands of Christ for the Christian as requiring participation in the Mass on Sundays. But the Sabbath is made for man, not man for the Sabbath. There are extreme cases when it would be wrong for a Catholic to go to Mass on a Sunday. This is not denying the authority of the Church. It is simply accepting the Church's interpretation of the demands of Christ in the spirit in which Christ intended it to be made. I suggest that the same is true for the Church's interpretation of the demands of Christ in this matter of contraception. No priest should ever say: 'The Church is wrong in forbidding contraception', just as he should never say that the Church is wrong in commanding Sunday Mass. But he can say to an individual 'I do not think you are committing sin by missing Mass in your circumstances'; and likewise it is suggested that he can equally say to an individual 'I do not think you are committing sin by practising contraception in your circumstances.'

IV. Practical conclusions

1. The Church's awareness of the essential values of marriage especially as a 'community of love' has undergone remarkable development in the recent past.

2. If in a given case these values are seriously endangered by following the Church's traditional teaching on contraception an individual couple may judge that they are excused from the observance of the concrete directive which is embodied in this teaching.

3. Judgement on this point in the responsibility of the couple concerned. They must make the decision. Their judgement might be influenced by the following considerations:
(a) Serious danger to the physical or mental health of the mother. (b) Hardship imposed on the family by the birth of another child – whether financially, or from lack of accommodation, or from incapacity of the parents to cope with more children.

(c) The serious probability that future children will not be born alive or will be born suffering from severe mental or physical handicaps.

4. When a couple can achieve the desired result by use of the rhythm method respect for the Church's directive would seem to demand that they should use this method.

5. If the rhythm method is impossible or uncertain, and if the priest is satisfied that the penitent or person consulting him has a proper concern for the essential values of Christian marriage, and a true respect for the authority of the Church, he would be justified in not condemning as sinful a couple's decision to use some means of contraception, for example the contraceptive pill. The human dignity of the two partners requires that there should be respect for each other in the act of total giving, even if that particular act be unproductive of new life.

6. In a very exceptional case a priest might consider that he should not condemn as sinful a couple's decision to resort to permanent sterilisation – for example where there is a grave and certain danger to the life of the mother if another pregnancy were to occur and where both the rhythm method and less drastic measures such as the contraceptive pill were definitely ruled out.

7. There is no question of allowing any form of contraception which works by way of procuring an abortion. Consequently, the plastic coil or loop may not be permitted since it seems very probable that its function is to prevent implantation of the fertilised ovum and it is therefore looked on as a means of producing abortion.

8. Couples who are contemplating marriage should be encouraged to plan their families with a proper sense of 'responsible parenthood' from the very beginning of the marriage. They should all be urged to attend a CMAC[3] course in preparation for marriage in order to get sound Christian guidance in the actual practice of 'responsible parenthood'.

9. A priest would need to counsel prudence to the penitent in talking about this matter to others. He might say, for example 'Not everyone is in the same difficult situation as you are. And not everyone has your respect for the Church's authority and your unselfish attitude to the good of your marriage and the well-being of your children. Because you have judged it is not sinful for you to use the pill in your situation, that does not mean that other

women can do the same without sin. I said that I thought your judgement of conscience is justified. There is so much to consider in this difficult question that I might well say to another that I do not think her judgement of conscience is right. That is why I think it would be wrong of you to go round and tell your friends – Fr. X says you can use the pill. It is just like my telling you that I thought you did right not to go to Mass on Sunday when your husband was ill. If I said that, it would clearly be wrong of you to go round telling people that I said you need not go to Mass on Sunday.'

10. The pastoral duty of the priest is to assist others to make their own judgement of conscience, not to make the judgement for them. His assistance in this matter would involve:
(a) Making sure that the persons concerned are showing due respect for the authority of the Church.
(b) Making sure that the judgement which is made is based on a proper concern for the essential values of Christian marriage.

George Andrew, Archbishop of Liverpool, 23 November 1967

DOCUMENT 2

STATEMENT OF THE CATHOLIC BISHOPS' CONFERENCE OF ENGLAND AND WALES ON '*HUMANAE VITAE*'

September 1968[4]

1. When Pope Paul issued the Encyclical *Humanae Vitae* he asked the Bishops to see that his teaching was presented in its true light 'that is, to show its positive and beneficent aspect'. It is understandable that strong feelings have been aroused. The Encyclical intimately concerns the source of human life. Whatever decision the Holy Father made was bound to be a test of faith. Some Catholics were convinced that a change in the moral teaching and practice of the Church was inevitable. Others were just as strongly convinced that any change would be a betrayal of the Faith. In view of the controversy which the Encyclical has aroused the Bishops of England and Wales earnestly call upon all Catholics to conduct their discussions in a responsible and temperate manner and in a mutually charitable spirit.

Discussion has so far centred mainly on the question of contraception. The impression is given that the Pope set out merely to condemn artificial methods of birth control. This he could have done in a single sentence. The Encyclical speaks at length of the dignity of marriage, the beauty of married love and the obligation of responsible parenthood, although it has not been sufficiently appreciated that the Encyclical was not intended to be a complete treatise on Holy Matrimony. The press has not surprisingly concentrated on the subject of contraception but the faithful and their pastors must study the document as a whole. In it the Pope reaffirms the sublime teaching of the Second Vatican Council's Pastoral Constitution on *The Church in the World Today*. The Encyclical teaches us that marriage 'is not the effect of chance or the product of the evolution of unconscious natural forces. It is the wise institution of the Creator to realise in mankind His design of love. By means of the reciprocal personal gift of self, proper and exclusive to them, husband and wife tend towards the communion of their beings in view of mutual personal perfection, to collaborate with God in the generation and education of new lives. For baptised persons, more-over, marriage invests the dignity of a sacramental sign of grace, inasmuch as it represents the union of Christ and of the Church.' This triple part-nership of husband, wife and God gives marriage its particular sacredness. It is the guarantee that God will never fail to support and guide the married couple by His grace. It is also the reason why the marriage act is not under the sole dominion of husband and wife.

2. Pope Paul wrote his Encyclical only after years of study and prayer. In the heat of controversy some writers appear to have forgotten that the Pope is the Vicar of Christ. It is for him to issue Encyclical letters whenever he thinks it his duty to do so. This right and duty were reaffirmed by the Second Vatican Council. The Dogmatic Constitution on the Church declares: 'This religious submission of will and of mind must be shown in a special way to the authentic teaching authority of the Roman Pontiff, even when he is not speaking *ex cathedra*. That is, it must be shown in such a way that his supreme *magisterium* is acknowledged with reverence, the judgements made by him are sincerely adhered to, according to his mani-fest mind and will. His mind and will in the matter may be known chiefly either from the character of the documents, from his frequent repetition of the same doctrine, or from his manner of speaking'. (25)
It is well known that the Encyclical is the fruit not only of prayer but of years of consultation with bishops, theologians, doctors, scientists and, not least important, married men and women. The Commission set up by Pope John to examine the demographic problem was enlarged by Pope Paul and

entrusted with the study of marriage and the family. No member of the Commission thought that the questions proposed to it could be resolved by a majority vote. Its task was to sift evidence and to present the Pope with its findings. It was always understood that the decision must be made by him alone as Christ's Vicar. The Pope has assured us that he weighed carefully and conscientiously all the evidence submitted to him both by members of his Commission and by hundreds of others.

3. Some have questioned whether in fact Pope Paul rather than a section of his advisers is responsible for the teaching contained in the Encyclical. Those most closely concerned with the Pontifical Commission easily recognise the Pope's own thoughts in this document. From the beginning the Pope regarded this decision as one which he personally must make. He delayed his statement until he was satisfied that he had heard and studied the arguments of every school of thought. Only then did he publish the decision which he had conscientiously made in the sight of God. 'We now intend', he says at the beginning of *Humanae Vitae*, 'by virtue of the mandate entrusted to us by Christ to give our reply to these grave questions'.

4. The Encyclical has provoked serious discussion on the whole exercise of the *magisterium*. It is being argued that in a matter so intimately affecting the lives of millions the burden of responsibility should not rest upon one man even though he is the Vicar of Christ. At the Council it was generally recognised that a question of such delicacy as contraception could not properly be debated in that vast assembly. Collegiality must be the subject of further study, but it cannot be invoked as a reason for refusing assent to the Encyclical.

5. An Encyclical is a statement of principle, not a detailed personal guide. Thus, for example, when speaking of responsible parenthood the Encyclical says: 'The responsible exercise of parenthood implies that husband and wife recognise fully their own duties towards God, towards themselves, towards the family and towards society.'

The Pope does not attempt to tell parents how many children they ought to have. This decision is one to be taken by the parents alone in the light of all the moral considerations laid down in the Encyclical.

One of these considerations is that 'each exercise of the marriage act must remain in itself open to the transmission of life', although, as the Pope points out, in fact 'not every conjugal act is followed by a new life'. Nevertheless it is against the plan of God to take positive steps to destroy the possibility of the transmission of life. The use of marriage during infertile periods, on the other hand, does not destroy the act's 'openness to the transmission of life'.

6. At one time Catholics were at one with most other Christians in holding contraception to be abhorrent. In recent years, however, some Catholics have expressed doubts about the Church's interpretation of the moral law. The very fact that the Pope created a commission to review the question tended to confirm their doubts. It was soon widely believed that a change in the Church's attitude would be announced. Understandably many wives and husbands anticipating the promised statement of the Pope have come to rely on contraception. In this they acted conscientiously and often after seeking pastoral advice. They may now be unable to see that the use of contraception is wrong, at least in their personal circumstances.

A particular difficulty faces those who with proper information and after serious thought and prayer cannot as yet understand or be fully convinced of the doctrines as laid down. This is not surprising in view of the discussions of recent years and the present controversy. For others the problem of putting the doctrine into practice in their lives seems insuperable because of ill-health or other serious obstacles, sometimes because of a conflict of duties. They should bear in mind the great weight which attaches to a pronouncement of this kind by the Holy Father. They should not close their mind but leave it open to the influence of the Holy Spirit, persevere in prayer and be ready to follow His guidance when it is given. They should pray for light to understand the doctrine taught by the Encyclical. It is not unreasonable to ask all to practise the Christian virtue of humility. They must admit that they are fallible and acknowledge the duty of every Catholic to listen with respect to the voice of the Vicar of Christ.

The Belgian Bishops have pointed out that acceptance of the Encyclical: 'Does not depend so much on the arguments proposed in the statement as on the religious motives to which the teaching authority, sacramental instituted in the Church, appeals' (Belgian Hierarchy Statement).

7. The Holy Father realises what difficulties face married people. That is why in the Encyclical he recalls the example of Our Lord who was gentle and patient. He came not to condemn but to save. He was clear and firm in condemning evil but there is no end to his mercy and compassion. In the same spirit the Encyclical makes no sweeping condemnations. There is no threat of damnation. Far from being excluded from the sacraments[5] those in difficulties are invited to receive them more frequently.

8. It cannot be denied that the Encyclical has created a conflict in the minds of many Catholics. Partly by reason of the discussions on contraception since the Council they ask themselves how they can accept the Pope's decision with sincerity. It must be stressed that the primacy of conscience is not in dispute. The Pope, bishops, clergy and faithful must all be true to conscience. But we are also bound to do everything in our power to make sure that our conscience is well informed. Neither this Encyclical nor any other document of the Church takes away from us our right and duty to follow our conscience. But if we were to neglect the guidance of the Church, morality could easily become merely subjective. That would be disastrous. It is well to remember the *Declaration on Religious Freedom* in the Second Vatican Council:

'In the formation of their consciences, the Christian faithful ought carefully to attend to the sacred and certain doctrine of the Church. The Church is, by the will of Christ, the teacher of the truth. It is her duty to give utterance to and authoritatively to teach that truth which is Christ Himself and to declare and confirm by her authority those principles of the moral order which have their origin in human nature itself'.

9. Theologians will seek clarification of the teaching in the Encyclical. Much of the field of human sexuality remains to be explored. We must ourselves continue sponsoring such research with assistance to initiatives already taken and the pooling of experience already gained. The Pope himself exhorts doctors to persevere in their studies in order to benefit the married people who consult them. We need to learn to what extent secular science can contribute to a solution of marriage problems. We must also enquire what are the implications of the Encyclical's reference to the use of therapeutic means. Those competent in these matters will continue their researches but the personal problems have to be faced by faithful couples genuinely wanting to do God's will but facing formidable obstacles. They know that their own living conditions may not quickly be adjusted to accommodate another child.

10. There is a close connection between problems of the family and wider social issues. We therefore take this occasion to remind our priests and people of our Christian obligation to take an active share in social work both at home and in the developing countries. Housing aid and relief of hunger provide a response to the Pope's appeal to all men of good will to work together to raise the standard of life throughout the world.

11. The prospect of pregnancy for some women is a risk to health and

perhaps to life. Such Catholics are concerned not with academic disputes but with stark human decisions. Let them remember that the Church has the charity and understanding of Christ our Lord. An Encyclical cannot consider all pastoral problems in detail but the Church has a care for those of her children with special difficulties. However difficult their circumstances may appear they should never think that they are separated from the love and grace of God.

'Let married couples, then, face up to the efforts needed, supported by the faith and hope which 'do not disappoint . . . because God's love has been poured into our hearts through the Holy Spirit, Who has been given to us' ; let them implore divine assistance by persevering prayer; above all, let them draw from the source of grace and charity in the Eucharist. And if sin should still keep its hold over them, let them not be discouraged, but rather have recourse with humble perseverance to the mercy of God, which is poured forth in the Sacrament of Penance.'

12. During this time of controversy we should all bear in mind that self-discipline and the way of the Cross are part of our Christian calling. The easy way is often not the Christian way. We appeal once more for mutual charity. No one should set himself up as the judge of his neighbour. We are confident that the Holy Spirit will guide the Church to understand the truth of the principles laid down by the Pope in *Humanae Vitae*. In working out these principles bishops, priests and laymen must cooperate in a Christian spirit.

'You are God's chosen people, holy and well beloved; the livery you wear must be tender compassion, kindness, humility, gentleness and patience; you must bear with one another's faults, be generous to each other, where somebody has given grounds for complaint; the Lord's generosity to you must be the model of yours. And, to crown all this, charity; that is the bond which makes us perfect'. (Col. 3:12–14)

DOCUMENTS 3A AND 3B

EARLIER DRAFTS OF THE BISHOPS' STATEMENT

Derek Worlock's files contain two earlier drafts, of which one was written by Bishop Basil Christopher Butler (though whether he took in even earlier material is not clear) and circulated to the bishops by Butler himself. The second version has no single author but incorporates much of Butler's wording, though it alters his general drift to make the overall tone much more supportive of *Humanae Vitae*. Judging from marginal notes in his handwriting, Worlock thought some of Butler's text 'not strong enough'.

The most striking passage of Butler's draft, deleted from the second version and even implicitly contradicted in the final one, refers tentatively to the possibility of the Encyclical being wrong.

DOCUMENT 3A

A Proposed Draft Statement on the Encyclical

1. When the Holy Father sent his recent Encyclical on the regulation of birth to the bishops he expressed the wish that the bishops would strive to present his teaching in its true light, 'that is, to show its positive and beneficient aspect'. The Bishops of England and Wales offer the following response.

2. Public attention has concentrated upon one single aspect of the Encyclical. We therefore urge upon the faithful and their pastors to study the whole document, which presents a noble doctrine of Christian marriage and of the family, reaffirming the great teaching on these subjects to be found in the second Vatican Council's Pastoral Constitution, *Gaudium et Spes*. The Pope tells us that marriage 'is not the effect of chance or the product of the evolution of unconscious natural forces; it is the wise institution of the Creator to realise in mankind His design of love . . . For baptised persons moreover, marriage takes on the dignity of a sacramental sign of grace, inasmuch as it represents the union of Christ and the Church'. Married love is a deliberate commitment of the free will. It is total, faithful and exclusive; and it is 'not exhausted by the communion between husband and wife but is destined to continue, raising up new lives'. It calls not only for parenthood but for 'responsible parenthood', whereby the size of the family is not left to chance but is prudently determined according to the requirement of the family itself and of society at large. We would emphasise the fact that the decision concerning the number of children is one to be taken by the parents alone; and is to be taken by them in the light of all relevant moral considerations.

3. The Pope himself lays down one of these 'norms' of morality, when he teaches that 'each exercise of the marriage act must remain open to the

transmission of life'.[6] The meaning and purpose of the act include this openness, and to take positive steps to destroy this element of meaning is to contradict 'the plan of God and his will'. On the other hand, neither voluntary abstinence from the act nor its use during the infertile period is unlawful, since in neither case does man himself destroy the act's openness to the transmission of life.

4. Such, in brief, is the teaching of the Encyclical on the use of marriage. The Pope shows himself well aware that the ideal he sets before us is a high and difficult one, and he shows his compassion for those who will [find][7] it almost unbearably hard. He encourages them to trust in God and to the constant use of the Church's sacraments, whence they will obtain strength for their Christian endeavours. Nowhere in the Encyclical does he use expressions like 'grave sin' or 'mortal sin'. On the other hand, he nowhere deviates from his teaching that the ideal set forth in the encyclical is the ideal willed by God in the institution of marriage.

5. Catholics do not need to be taught that the Pope is the Visible head of the Church on earth, with authority both to teach doctrinal and moral truth and to guide us in the path of holiness. This teaching and pastoral authority belongs also to the bishops of the Church in union with him, the chief bishop.

6. When the Pope, or the collective body of bishops of which he is the head, issue a definition of an article of faith, or of something absolutely essential to the validity of the faith, we have the right and duty, and are given the grace, to give an unconditional assent to the definition. A statement which does not claim such infallibility – and such a claim is not made in the Encyclical *Humanae Vitae* – our assent to it does not claim to be unconditional.[8] But it does require 'the religious submission of will and mind' which is due especially to 'the authentic teaching authority to the Roman Pontiff even when he is not teaching *ex cathedra*' (*Lumen Gentium*, 6.25).[9]

7. A statement which is not infallible is, at least in principle, reformable. It follows that someone who has competence in the field of truth to which such a statement relates may, after serious consideration and prayer, reach a conclusion which differs in some respect from the teaching contained in the statement. If so, he may adhere to and follow his own convictions. But he must remember that he himself is not infallible and he must remain open to further light on the subject and be ready, if need be, to reconsider

it. He must be loyal to Christ and the Church, and must acknowledge the status of the Church's teaching authority, the bishops and the Pope. It would be wrong for such a man to engage in insubordinate agitation such as would tend to upset the 'communion of charity' which unites us in the Church.

8. Apart from the 'intellectual difficulties' mentioned above, there will be cases where the duty of obedience clashes with other duties; or at least where such a conflict seems to arise. In such cases, the Church asks her children to go on looking for a solution which will do justice to all the requirements of their case, including that of obedience to the Pope. They should by no means suppose that, if they cannot at once find such a solution, they are separated from the love and grace of God.

9. We should all bear in mind: (1) self-discipline and the way of the Cross are of our Christian calling; the easy way is often not the Christian way. (2) We have a duty of charity towards one another which entails respect for each other's conscience – even when our brother's conscience contradicts our own. Prayer and the sacraments are the great 'ordinary means' whereby we may hope to grow in these twin virtues of self-discipline and mutual love.

The text is unsigned, but it came with a complimentary slip from 'Bishop Basil Christopher Butler OSB, Auxiliary Bishop of Westminster'. Archbishop Beck wrote back acknowledging it as 'your memorandum'.

DOCUMENT 3B

The second draft, 'Possible Statement on *Humanae Vitae*, Draft for Discussion' while incorporating some of Butler's text is too close to the final version given above (Document 2) to need quoting in full. Some of the deletions made from this version were obviously thought too argumentative in tone, or struck a defensive note, or even went too far towards the critics. One deletion suggested that disagreeing with the Encyclical was 'legitimate'. Some of the more significant passages missing from the final version were as follows:

'The Encyclical has nevertheless been given a very mixed reception and its positive teaching has been largely ignored.'

'It is well known that the Encyclical is the fruit not only of prayer but of years of consultation with bishops, theologians, doctors, scientists and, most important of all, married men and women. It has been asserted so often as to be regarded as a fact of history that the Papal Commission produced a majority and a minority report, and that Pope Paul rejected the report of the majority. There was, in fact, only one report from the commission.[10] It is widely known that a majority opinion within the commission was in favour of relaxing the Church's opposition to artificial methods of birth control. It should be remembered, however, that members of the commission were merely giving an opinion. It is much easier to make an opinion than to make a binding decision. The Pope has assured us that he weighed all the evidence submitted to him both by members of his commission and by hundreds of others carefully and conscientiously.'

'They may now be unable to see that the use of contraceptives is wrong or may feel unable to break the habit. They should not regard their position as hopeless.'

'It is not enough to dissect the arguments of the Encyclical and debate its binding force and freedom from error. All this is legitimate but we must ask, above all else, who has written the Encyclical and with what authority. This Encyclical contains teaching which if considered with due piety may lead to a higher concept of married love which is a far bigger question than that of contraception.'

'The encyclical is concerned with safeguarding and uplifting Christian marriage. It was not written with the object of imposing fresh burdens upon wives and husbands.'

DOCUMENT 4

FROM THE MINUTES OF THE CATHOLIC BISHOPS' CONFERENCE OF ENGLAND AND WALES, 14–16 OCTOBER 1968

HUMANAE VITAE

It was generally agreed that no new statement should be issued from the Conference and that at present the Hierarchy should not ask the Holy See to issue pastoral directives.

The letter from the Laity Commission was read. A letter from the Social Welfare Commission was discussed, with particular reference to those members of Commissions who publicly opposed the Encyclical. It was considered that greater care may be necessary in choosing members and that Commissions must be kept to their terms of reference.

An essential minimum will have to be asked of those priests who publicly oppose the Encyclical.

After discussion it was agreed:

1. To give bishops the opportunity of speaking personally with the priests concerned, there will be no public statement or press conference after this Bishops' Meeting.

2. Each bishop will interview priests who have publicly opposed the Encyclical and who have not withdrawn opposition.

3. These priests will be required to refrain in preaching, teaching, in the press, on radio and television or on public platforms, from opposing the teaching of the Pope in matters of faith and morals.

4. If a priest is unwilling to give this undertaking it is for the bishop to decide whether, without scandal, he can be allowed to continue to act in the name of the Church. He need not, however, be required to cease celebrating Mass.

5. A priest cannot normally be allowed to hold faculties to hear Confessions unless he undertakes to declare faithfully the objective teaching of *Humanae Vitae* in the confessional and in giving spiritual guidance.

6. In keeping with current canonical practice a priest will be maintained by the diocese until he has been able to find suitable employment.

7. If a Religious has publicly rejected the Encyclical his Superior will be invited by the bishop to take action in line with the policy approved by the Conference of Bishops.

8. In the event of misrepresentation a bishop will be at liberty to publish the above conditions.

Bishops will use these points as a guide when interviewing priests. It was agreed that bishops should try to see these priests at about the same time.

There are priests who are troubled that no action has so far been taken to repair the scandal caused by the public opposition of some priests to the Encyclical. The Cardinal undertook to prepare a model letter *ad clerum* (to be sent to the bishops) to allay this anxiety. At the suggestion of the Archbishop of Cardiff the Cardinal was asked to release this to the Press in order to forestall rumours.

DOCUMENT 5

PASTORAL LETTER OF DEREK WORLOCK
BISHOP OF PORTSMOUTH

TO THE PRIESTS AND PEOPLE OF THE DIOCESE

11th Sunday after Pentecost 1966

My dear brothers in the priesthood and dear brothers and sisters in Jesus Christ:

These last days have seen a storm within the family of the Church. The publication of the Holy Father's Encyclical 'On the Regulation of Birth?' has called forth a spate of comments, official and personal, responsible and some less responsible. On occasion the sincere pursuit of truth has through forceful speech come close to uncharity. We, who love the Church for its Christ-given authority and who have been brought up in a tradition telling us that the surest test of orthodoxy is to think and act with Peter, have read with distress reports of rift.

All this has been about a matter which touches, it is true, the very origin of life and things which intimately concern married people. Clearly other wider and more fundamental issues are also indirectly involved. Yet it is important that we should see this question of the regulation of birth within the whole context of the Christian life, for it is scarcely the acid test of being for Christ or against Him. 'This is my commandment, that you love one another as I have loved you' (John 15:12).

It is praiseworthy that we should be quick off the mark in defence of conscience, though we owe it to others as well as to ourselves to make sure that our conscience is properly informed. The general matter dealt with in the Encyclical has of course been widely discussed in recent years from several different aspects: from the point of view of domestic family life as well as from that of world population. Now the Pope has spoken and his long and carefully-worded statement demands deep study and reflection by the whole Church.

There are however certain points to which I should call your attention. After the long-drawn-out unofficial debate, these latest words of the Holy Father, reaffirming previous Papal teaching on illicit ways of regulating births, have been for many a welcome reassurance. But for others they undoubtedly represent a conscientious difficulty: a fact foreseen by the Pope in reaching what is widely recognised as an agonising decision. It is my duty to point out that the Holy Father's words constitute a definite directive. Some people have been quick to stress that this is not explicitly an infallible pronouncement. But the Pope makes clear the authority he is using, when He[11] says: 'by virtue of the mandate entrusted to us by Christ'. We receive his ruling in that light.

Apart from the authoritative nature of this letter from the Vicar of Christ, its other obvious characteristic is its author's deep pastoral concern for those to whom he is writing. The Pope knows that for many this teaching will be hard. To an increasingly permissive society he holds out a noble concept of marriage and a means of achieving the perfection to which each one of us is called. Where truth is concerned there can be no compromise for the sake of expediency, but there must be deep compassion for those for whom the Christian ideal represents a constant struggle.

The Holy Father urges married persons to approach this question within the framework of the sacramental system. 'Christian married couples' he writes 'must remember that their Christian vocation, which began at baptism, is further specified and reinforced by the sacrament of matrimony. By it husband and wife are strengthened and as it were consecrated for the faithful accomplishment of their proper duties, for the carrying out of their proper vocation even to perfection, and the Christian witness which is proper to them before the whole world.'

Recognising what he calls 'the sometimes serious difficulties inherent in the life of Christian married persons', the Pope recommends that they should draw deeply upon the grace and charity in the Eucharist. He goes further and says that if, even then, their difficulties persist, they should not hesitate to have recourse to the sacrament of Penance, seeking therein forgiveness for their failings and new strength for the future. Doubtless it was in this context that Cardinal Heenan so wisely urged those who found it hard to follow the Pope's ruling not to despair and not to stay away from the sacraments.

Of course, for some there may still remain certain difficulties of conscience. I hope that such persons will discuss these frankly with their priests. We must be humble about the whole matter, without self-righteous arrogance but with absolute honesty to our conscience. There can be no deception in the sacrament of penance for it is to Christ that we confess. Married couples should not hesitate to seek this help and forgiveness in accordance with their culpability. As the Pope Himself says: 'In their difficulties may married couples always find, in the words and in the heart of a priest, the echo of the voice and love of the Redeemer.'

Brothers and sisters in Christ, in these rather anxious days, when the eyes of so many are upon us, we must keep our heads and, more important still, our charity, without which faith and hope are ill-founded. This Pastoral Letter is not so much a plea to you to close the ranks, as an appeal to continue your efforts to live in greater conformity with the precepts of the gospel. There are other immense problems we must face in carrying the message of Christ to the world, and in bringing spiritual truth and material relief to those who hunger after God's justice. We shall do these things better by our efforts now to raise our moral standards and by the exercise of discipline and self-denial.

Please try to study the whole of the Pope's Encyclical, not just the headlines. If you are perplexed, talk it over with your priests. Be sure that I shall also be discussing it with them. In the meantime let us try to be patient and understanding of each others' difficulties. Pray hard for the Church and for our Holy Father Pope Paul. And remember the heartfelt plea of St Paul to the Colossians 'But above all clothe yourselves with love; it holds together and perfects all these things. And in your hearts let stand supreme the peace of Christ, to which you are called as members of one body' (Col. 3:14–15).

Given at Portsmouth on the feast of the Assumption of Our Lady and appointed to be read throughout the diocese at all Masses on the eleventh Sunday after Pentecost 1968.

+ DEREK WORLOCK
Bishop of Portsmouth

Extract from *The Easter People*, the Response of the Catholic Bishops' Conference of England and Wales to the National Pastoral Congress, Liverpool, 1980

14–16 July 1980

100. The family is the basic community in society. In its varied forms it is the universal experience of humanity and is a profound influence on spiritual and emotional growth. For the vast majority of people the most important human relationship they have is marriage. It is a complex relationship which develops from first love, through absorption in young children, concern for jobs and careers, the stresses of the adolescent independence of a growing family, and on perhaps to retirement and the greater isolation of a couple in old age. In marriage a couple grow together. A true understanding of marriage must take account of all these factors. Children should be able to learn within the family how to love and to be loved, how to handle feelings, conflicts, growth and loss. It is in the family that the individual can learn how to be human and how to achieve self-knowledge and an awareness of dependence.

101. We affirm the immense importance and value of marriage and the family as the setting within which most people are called to holiness of life. We recognise also that in a unique way the family carries forward the mission of the Church into the everyday world and, as we have suggested earlier, is in some sense a model of the Church itself in its mission to evangelise society.

102. The Congress showed a sensitive appreciation of the importance and meaning of marriage for Christian life and mission. Delegates urged that the teaching Church should find ways of listening attentively to the experience of married Christians and particularly to their insights into the meaning and consequences of a life-long sexual relationship. It was in reality a plea that committed Catholic laity should be able to contribute to the continuing development of the Church's teaching on marriage. They expressed a need for a renewed positive theology of marriage as covenant, covering all aspects of the marriage relationship. The foundations of such teaching were laid down clearly at the Second Vatican Council in the Pastoral Constitution on the Church in the Modern World (*Gaudium et Spes*, nn.47–52). There has already been a major development throughout this century in the Church's understanding of married love and sexuality,

reflecting advances in the human sciences. It is evidenced in the Church's current teaching on responsible parenthood and in its maturing awareness of the real balance in marriage between fruitfulness and love. It would be unrealistic to claim that the Church has finally achieved a definitive understanding of all that the gospel can reveal to us about Christian marriage. The Council taught that for Christians marriage is 'an image and a sharing in the partnership of love between Christ and the Church' and that the Christian family can show forth to all men 'Christ's living presence in the world and the authentic nature of the Church' (*Gaudium et Spes*, n.48). Marriage partakes of the mystery of the Church and will continually yield up new treasures. An enriched theology of marriage will have to take into account the growth of human relationships, the need for true communication within marriage, and the understanding of sexual intercourse both as a life-giving act and as a communication of love and self to one's partner. It will have to see even more profoundly that sexual love in marriage is a relationship in which a couple affirm each other's identity, by which they heal and sustain each other and through which they make Christ sacramentally present to each other.

103. Within this context of concern for the comprehensive development of the Church's teaching on marriage, the Congress sector on the Family added further reflections on responsible parenthood and on the moral problems which contraception poses for the Catholic conscience. The sector delegates were careful in their formulation in asking for a fundamental re-examination of the Church's teaching on marriage, sexuality and contraception. The mind of this sector of our Congress should be taken in a constructive sense. It is related to the general concern also expressed that the Church's teaching on every aspect of marriage should be developed positively. Development carries with it the idea of organic growth. It involves clearer insight and a deeper understanding of the meaning and implications of truths already possessed and continually meditated upon in the light of fresh knowledge or of changing circumstances. As we have explained, marriage and the family are central to our Christian calling and life, and today both need to be built up, strengthened and better understood and appreciated. Christian marriage – like the mystery of the Church itself with which it is so closely linked – has always to be seen afresh with the eyes of faith nourished by experience and has to be enriched by continuing reflection.

104. The Encyclical *Humanae Vitae* is the authentic teaching of the Church. It has to be read in the light of the Vatican Council's teaching

already referred to. Conjugal love consists in the gift of one person to another, a gift which embraces the human being as a whole, body and soul, and such conjugal love is most completely fulfilled by parenthood. It is in this context of the emphasis to be placed on the value of love that the rejection of the use of artificial contraception is situated. The truth which the Church invites us to reflect upon is that its teaching on responsible parenthood is to be understood within the true meaning of marriage as a total, mutual self-giving, which the Council has expressed in terms of covenant.

105. We must also recognise the unique nature of child-bearing and its place in our human existence. We all need to think more profoundly about the immeasurable value of the individual person. A human being is more than a population statistic. An individual is in a limited and created way an unrepeatable expression of what God himself is. Each person is an image of the infinite God. So human life has an absolute value, each individual a unique worth. Human life is the summit of God's creation. And that is the profoundly Christian insight behind the use of the word 'procreation'. When husband and wife have a child, they share in God's continuing creation. As our Bishops' Conference stated in 1968, there is in procreation 'a triple partnership of husband, wife and God'. We know this insight does not put an end to moral dilemmas, but it is quite definitely a reminder that at this point we touch the mystery of the origin of all life and that we must accordingly develop our thoughts and attitudes with wonder and reverence for life and for God, its author.

106. We are convinced that the Church's mind on the full meaning of marriage and the human relationship within marriage needs continual examination and greater explanation to enable it to be better understood and lived. Any further development on the subject will of course be made in complete fidelity to the Church's *magisterium*. We remind our people that the Synod of Bishops later this autumn will be reflecting on the subject of the family and with the help of our prayers will contribute to a deeper understanding of the subject.

Notes

1 Documents 1, 3a, 3b and 4 have not been published before; Documents 2 and 5 were duplicated as typescripts in 1968 but not subsequently republished and have been out of print ever since. Document 6 was published in 1980 but is now out of print.
2 Legal doubt.
3 Catholic Marriage Advisory Council.

4 It lacks a single date probably because it was the result of various discussions over a period, including an extraordinary meeting of the Hierarchy, which was preceded by working parties and the result tidied up by staff afterwards.

5 There may be a deliberate ambiguity here. The bishops seem to be avoiding the difficult question whether people using contraceptives could receive Holy Communion. 'The Sacraments', because of the plural, must refer also to the Confessional, and Catholics would know that there was a rule that they should not receive Communion in a state of serious sin but should first seek and receive absolution. Whether that was what the bishops meant is unclear – perhaps some of them meant it, and some found the ambiguity useful. The papal encyclical itself said of such people 'if sin should still keep its hold over them' they should persevere with the sacrament of penance.

6 The currently preferred Vatican translation into English of this much quoted phrase from *Humanae Vitae* has less impact: 'each and every marital act must of necessity retain its intrinsic relationship to the procreation of human life' (Vatican Information Service, 1999).

7 Word missing from the original typescript.

8 Not all Butler's syntax was perfect; it has not been tidied up here.

9 Butler was no mean philosopher, but he obviously chose not to address himself to the philosophical problem of someone who, having submitted his mind and will to papal authority, can still reach a conclusion at variance with that authority. To a non-philosopher, it looks like a straight contradiction.

10 Heenan, who undoubtedly had a hand in this wording, knew exactly what had happened because he was there.

11 Capitalization of 'He' here is inconsistent with usage elsewhere in this text; but it has not been edited out because it may be an interesting Freudian slip.

Appendix II

DEREK WORLOCK, HUMORIST

The wartime Worlock was sometime chaplain to the Catholic Scout Guild, London Area, for whose annual show he wrote the following humorous sketch[1] as well as a three-act playlet on the theme of duty and patriotism. (There is no date, but one of the characters in the playlet complains that there were 'no war pictures' in a magazine he has looked at; and food rationing was tight, so it was obviously towards the end of the war.)

THE COMING COOKS OF BRITAIN *by* DEREK WORLOCK

(This may be performed in front of a drop curtain).

The main curtains open to disclose a rather dark stage with lights focussed on the centre. A dixie is hanging from a large tripod and behind on either side are the 1st, 2nd and 3rd Scouts, They wear black cloaks and scout hats with extended crowns. The words throughout are chanted in slow eerie voices, actions to suit the words.

1st Scout[2]   Thrice the SM's voice has called,

2nd S   Thrice; and once the whistle blown.

3rd S   The PLs shout: 'Tis time, 'tis time

1st S   Round about the dixie go.
In, unrationed offal[3] throw;
Thistle that from 'neath my bed

379

Kept awake my weary head,
Made me turn first cold then hot
Boil thou first in charm'ed pot

All   *(passing round the dixie)*
             Double double, what's the trouble?
             Stir the lot and prick the bubble.

2nd S   Damper, buy one, twist and stand.
             Lump of mud and back to land.
             Nettle leaves and chip of log
             Churchyard cat and farmer's dog,
             Dandelion and tuft of grass:
             These should gain us second class![4]

All   *(moving as before)*
             Double double, we'll make trouble
             Fire burn and cauldron bubble.

3rd S   Skipper's hat and scarf and woggles,
             Bosun's motor-cycling goggles,
             Piece of ground sheet, broken guyline
             Keep a look-out on the skyline,
             For they'd surely leave the lot
             If they knew what's in this pot.

All   *(as before)*
             Double double, toil and trouble,
             Stir the lot and prick the bubble.

             (They pause and take a big sniff)

             Ah, Bisto![5]

1st S   When shall we three eat again?
             In peace and quiet or in pain?

2nd S   When the general mob has done,
             When their daily nap's begun.

3rd S   Dinner's due to start at one.

380

1st S	Where the place?
2nd S	Well out of sound.
3rd S	Then to sit upon the ground.
All	Fare is foul and foul our fare, Cooking in the open air.

(Enter the Scout Master, who comes to the dixie, stirs it well, then smells it, rolls up his sleeve to the elbow, plunges his hand into the dixie and extracts a tin of baked beans. They all shake hands.)

SM	Oh, well done! Thanks to this, our gain, Everyone shall share the pain. And now, about the dixie croon Like cherubs of the moon in June And try to make the audience swoon.

(The four link arms and come forward in front of the tripod, to sing 'We are the coming cooks of Britain'. They should each have a tin of baked beans to hold up at the last line of the chorus.)

All	They tell us that the future of the nation Depends on us, and so we must prepare To take diplomas in domestication And learn to make the most of scanty fare. But we should like to hazard a suggestion: For if they want to show a lot of fuss And save themselves from chronic indigestion They'll cut out points,[6] and leave the rest to us.
Chorus	We are the coming cooks of Britain. We're going to see that we at least get fed For we are the greatest crooks in Britain, We never use potatoes when there's bread. All manual labour we are spared. We serve the inner man; To cook a meal we've never dared In dixie pot or pan. We tell the chaps to be prepared

And open up a can
Of baked beans, the staple food of Britain.

(They hold up their tins at this last line.)

All[7]   We'll have to learn the secrets of the larder
If we're to look the problem in the face.
For times are hard and likely to get harder,
And we're to be the saviours of our race.
So come on lads, forget your Mrs Beeton
And learn to peel the dehydrated 'spud';
For though we may not teach such things at Eton,
We'd rather chew potatoes than the cud.

Chorus We are the coming cooks of Britain,
And when we come the devil take the last!
For we are the greatest crooks in Britain –
And pledged to teach all others how to fast.
But though for every hungry scout
The outlook's rather black,
We'll do out best, without a doubt,
To overcome the lack;
And when there's nothing else about
We always can fall back
On baked beans, the staple food of Britain!

(Action as before.)

Notes

1 Worlock had considerable hidden talents as a humorous writer as well as a performer, and later in life sang drily satirical songs he had composed himself at the traditional 'social evening' held on the last night of the annual meeting of the National Conference of Priests each year. But none of them seem to have survived.
2 SM is Scoutmaster; PL is Patrol Leader, a dixie is a metal stewpot.
3 Some of the less appetizing forms of offal were off-ration.
4 A Scout badge.
5 A line from a well-known poster advertising Bisto meat extract for making gravy.
6 British food ration cards during and after the Second World War consisted of 'points', tickets which could be cut or torn off and handed to the shopkeeper to obtain the designated amount of food.
7 Worlock's choice of tune is not given, but is likely to be any well-known song from Gilbert and Sullivan that fits the words.

Bibliography

Giuseppe Alberigo and Joseph A. Komonchak (eds), *History of Vatican II, Volume 1: Announcing and Preparing Vatican Council 11: Toward a New Era in Catholicism* (Orbis/Peeters, 1995).

Giuseppe Alberigo and Joseph A. Komonchak (eds), *History of Vatican II, Volume II: The Formation of the Council's Identity: First Period and Intersession, October 1962–September 1963* (Orbis/Peeters, 1997).

George Andrew Beck (ed.), *The English Catholics 1850–1950* (Burns and Oates, 1950).

Trevor Beeson, *Britain Today and Tomorrow* (Collins, 1978).

Mark Bence-Jones, *The Catholic Families* (Constable, 1995).

John Bossy, *The English Catholic Community, 1570–1850* (Darton, Longman and Todd, 1975).

Humphrey Carpenter, *Robert Runcie, The Reluctant Archbishop* (Sceptre, 1996).

Owen Chadwick, *Britain and the Vatican During the Second World War* (Cambridge University Press, 1986).

Peter Coughlan, *The Hour of the Laity, Their Expanding Role: Exploring 'Christifideles Laici': The Pope's Key Document on the Laity* (E. J. Dwyer, 1989).

Michael de la Bedoyere, *Cardinal Bernard Griffin, Archbishop of Westminster* (Rockliff, 1955).

Norman Dennis and George Erdos, *Families Without Fatherhood* (IEA Health and Welfare Unit, 1992)

Charles Dickens, *Barnaby Rudge*.

Eamon Duffy, *The Stripping of the Altars, Traditional Religion in England 1400–1580* (Yale, 1992).

Margaret Duggan, *Runcie: The Making of an Archbishop* (Hodder and Stoughton, 1983).

David L. Edwards, *Christian England, Volume 3: From the Eighteenth Century to the First World War* (Collins, 1984).

Austin Flannery, OP (ed.), *Vatican Council II, the Conciliar and Post Conciliar Documents* (Costello/William B. Eerdmans, 1992).

Antonia Fraser, *The Gunpowder Plot, Terror and Faith in 1605* (Weidenfeld and Nicolson, 1996).

Bill Frindall (ed.), *The Wisden Book of Cricket Records* (Queen Anne Press, 1981).

John Furnival and Ann Knowles, *Archbishop Derek Worlock, His Personal Journey* (Geoffrey Chapman, 1998).

Graham Greene, *Brighton Rock* (Penguin, 1970).

Peter Harris, Adrian Hastings, John Horgan, Lionel Keane and Robert Nowell, *On Human Life, An Examination of 'Humanae Vitae'* (Burns and Oates, 1968).

Adrian Hastings, *A History of English Christianity 1920–1990* (SCM Press, 1991)

Peter Hebblethwaite, *The Runaway Church* (Collins, 1975).

John C. Heenan, *Cardinal Hinsley* (Burns, Oates and Washbourne, 1944).

John C. Heenan, *Not the Whole Truth: An Autobiography* (Hodder and Stoughton, 1971).

John C. Heenan, *A Crown of Thorns: An Autobiography 1951–1963* (Hodder and Stoughton, 1974).

Michael Hornsby-Smith and Raymond Lee, *Roman Catholic Opinion – a Study of Roman Catholics in England and Wales in the 1970s* (David Wedgewood, 1980).

Hans Küng, *Council and Reunion* (Sheed and Ward, 1961).

David Lodge, *How Far Can You Go?* (Secker and Warburg, 1980).

Thomas Moloney, *Westminster, Whitehall and the Vatican: The Role of Cardinal Hinsley, 1935–1943* (Burns and Oates, 1985).

John Moorman, *The Vatican Observed* (Darton, Longman and Todd, 1967).

Brian Murtough (ed.), *The Pope, the Pill, and the People* (IPC/Daily Mirror, 1968).

Aidan Nichols, OP, *From Newman to Congar: The Idea of Doctrinal Development from the Victorians to the Second Vatican Council* (T. and T. Clark, 1990).

Aidan Nichols, OP, *The Panther and the Hind: A Theological History of Anglicanism* (T. and T. Clark, 1993).

Peter Nichols, *The Pope's Divisions: The Roman Catholic Church Today* (Faber and Faber, 1981).

J. T. Noonan, *Contraception* (Harvard University Press, 1986).

Bernard and Margaret Pawley, *Rome and Canterbury Through Four Centuries* (Mowbrays, 1974).

Ronald H. Preston, *Confusions in Christian Social Ethics: Problems for Geneva and Rome* (SCM Press, 1994).

Leo Pyle (ed.), *The Pill and Birth Regulation* (Darton, Longman and Todd, 1964).

Anthony Rhodes, *The Vatican in the Age of the Dictators 1922–45* (Hodder and Stoughton, 1973).

Thomas D. Roberts (introduced by), *Contraception and Holiness, the Catholic Predicament* (Fontana Books, 1965).

John Rock, *The Time has Come* (Longmans, 1963).

David Sheppard, *Built as a City: God and the Urban World Today* (Hodder and Stoughton, 1974).

Grace Sheppard, *An Aspect of Fear* (Darton, Longman and Todd, 1989).

Michael Walsh, *John Paul II* (HarperCollins, 1994).

Evelyn Waugh, *Brideshead Revisited* (Penguin, 1962).

Derek Worlock, *Take One at Bedtime* (Sheed and Ward, 1962).

Derek Worlock (ed.), *English Bishops at the Council: Third Session* (Burns and Oates, 1965).

Derek Worlock, *Give Me Your Hand* (St Paul Publications, 1977).

Derek Worlock and David Sheppard, *Better Together: Christian Partnership in a Hurt City* (Penguin Books, 1989).

Index

Index

Index